FROMMER'S
EasyGuide

TO

D0040198

Ireland 2017

By
Jack Jewers

Easy Guides are ✦ **Quick To Read** ✦ **Light To Carry**
✦ **For Expert Advice** ✦ **In All Price Ranges**

FrommerMedia LLC

Published by

FROMMER MEDIA LLC

Copyright © 2017 by FrommerMedia LLC. All rights reserved. No part of this publication may be reproduced, stored in a retrieval system, or transmitted in any form or by any means, electronic, mechanical,
photocopying, recording, scanning or otherwise, except as permitted under Sections 107 or 108 of the
1976 United States Copyright Act, without the prior written permission of the Publisher. Requests to the
Publisher for permission should be addressed to customer_service@FrommerMedia.com.

Frommer's is a registered trademark of Arthur Frommer. FrommerMedia LLC is not associated with any
product or vendor mentioned in this book.

ISBN 978-1-62887-268-2 (paper), 978-1-62887-269-9 (ebk)

Editorial Director: Pauline Frommer
Editor: Holly Hughes
Production Editor: Erin Geile
Cartographer: Roberta Stockwell
Cover Design: Howard Grossman

For information on our other products or services, see www.frommers.com.

FrommerMedia LLC also publishes its books in a variety of electronic formats. Some content that appears
in print may not be available in electronic formats.

Manufactured in the United States of America

5 4 3 2 1

FROMMER'S STAR RATINGS SYSTEM

Every hotel, restaurant, and attraction listed in this guide has been ranked for quality and value. Here's
what the stars mean:

★ Recommended
★★ Highly recommended
★★★ A must! Don't miss!

AN IMPORTANT NOTE

The world is a dynamic place. Hotels change ownership, restaurants hike their prices, museums
alter their opening hours, and buses and trains change their routings. And all of this can occur in
the several months after our authors have visited, inspected, and written about these hotels, restaurants, museums, and transportation services. Though we have made valiant efforts to keep all
our information fresh and up-to-date, some few changes can inevitably occur in the periods
before a revised edition of this guidebook is published. So please bear with us if a tiny number
of the details in this book have changed. Please also note that we have no responsibility or liability for any inaccuracy or errors or omissions, or for inconvenience, loss, damage, or expenses suffered by anyone as a result of assertions in this guide.

CONTENTS

ABOUT THE AUTHOR

Jack Jewers has written about Ireland for Frommer's since 2006. Born and raised in England, he loved listening to his great-aunt's tales about life in Dublin during the civil war. Jack proposed to his Irish-American wife at a spa on the Ring of Kerry. It gets a great review in this book.

ABOUT THE FROMMER'S TRAVEL GUIDES

For most of the past 50 years, Frommer's has been the leading series of travel guides in North America, accounting for as many as 24% of all guidebooks sold. I think I know why.

Though we hope our books are entertaining, we nevertheless deal with travel in a serious fashion. Our guidebooks have never looked on such journeys as a mere recreation, but as a far more important human function, a time of learning and introspection, an essential part of a civilized life. We stress the culture, lifestyle, history, and beliefs of the destinations we cover, and urge our readers to seek out people and new ideas as the chief rewards of travel.

We have never shied from controversy. We have, from the beginning, encouraged our authors to be intensely judgmental, critical—both pro and con—in their comments, and wholly independent. Our only clients are our readers, and we have triggered the ire of countless prominent sorts, from a tourist newspaper we called "practically worthless" (it unsuccessfully sued us) to the many rip-offs we've condemned.

And because we believe that travel should be available to everyone regardless of their incomes, we have always been cost-conscious at every level of expenditure. Though we have broadened our recommendations beyond the budget category, we insist that every lodging we include be sensibly priced. We use every form of media to assist our readers, and are particularly proud of our feisty daily website, the award-winning Frommers.com.

I have high hopes for the future of Frommer's. May these guidebooks, in all the years ahead, continue to reflect the joy of travel and the freedom that travel represents. May they always pursue a cost-conscious path, so that people of all incomes can enjoy the rewards of travel. And may they create, for both the traveler and the persons among whom we travel, a community of friends, where all human beings live in harmony and peace.

Arthur Frommer

THE BEST OF IRELAND

Tiny, and with ever-changing scenery, Ireland is an addictive place to explore. Within a few miles you can travel from plunging cliffs and flat pastureland to towering mountains and gloomy peat bogs. You can spend the night in ancient castles or state-of-the-art spa hotels, dine on fine Irish cuisine or snack on crispy fish and chips served in a paper bag. The sheer number of sights, little villages, charming pubs, and adorable restaurants and shops can be overwhelming—that's why we've put together this list of some of our favorite places and things to do in Ireland. We hope that while you're exploring this magical country, you'll find a few of your own.

THE best AUTHENTIC EXPERIENCES

- **Seeing a Traditional Music Session at a Proper Irish Pub:** While there are plenty of shows for the tourist crowd, nothing beats the energy, atmosphere, and authenticity of a genuine small-town traditional music session. Buy a pint, grab a seat (preferably one near a smoldering peat fire), and wait for the action to begin. We've listed some of the best places in this book, including the **Long Valley** in **Cork** (see p. 133) or **Gus O'Connor's** and **McGann's** in little **Doolin, County Clare** (see p. 188).
- **Getting Lost Down the Back Roads of County Kerry:** It's Ireland's most visited county by far, and if you stick to the beaten path, in summer it's thronged with tourists. Instead, veer off onto the winding back roads and allow yourself to get gloriously, hopelessly lost. Forget the clock and embrace a sense of serendipity. There are always new discoveries to be made down its breathtaking byways. See p. 148.
- **Wandering Through Temple Bar** (Dublin, County Dublin): Yes it's touristy; yes it's loud; yes it's the kind of place where people in giant leprechaun costumes hustle for change in return for photos . . . but the energy of Temple Bar is electrifying. Its restaurants and bars buzz with life, its galleries and cultural centers overflow with innovation. See p. 46.

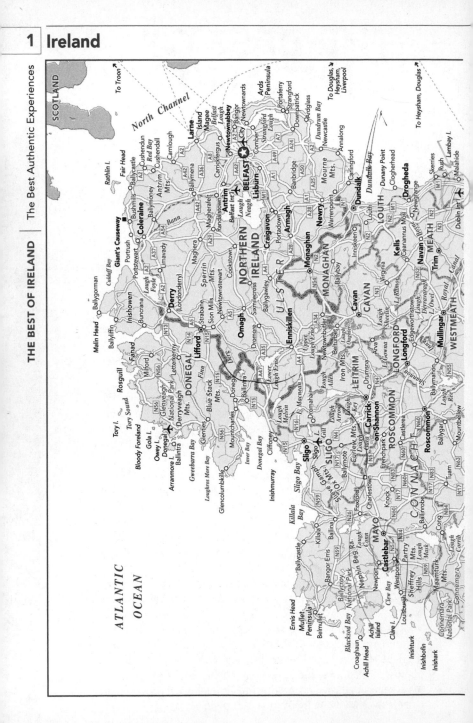

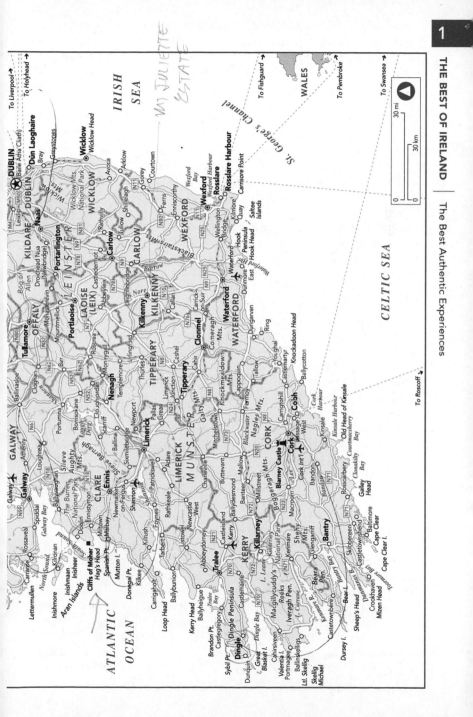

o **Walking Down the Long Stone Passage at Newgrange** (County Meath): Sacred to the ancients, this passage tomb is more than 5,000 years old— that's older than the Egyptian pyramids or Stonehenge. Wander down the long, atmospheric central tunnel and try to visualize just how many generations have passed since it was built—it's a mind-blowing exercise, a real time-warp experience. See p. 104.

o **Browsing the Old English Market in Cork** (County Cork): Cork is a county made for foodies. In addition to Kinsale, a small coastal village that's grown to become something of a hub for top restaurants, the eponymous main city is home to one of the country's finest (and oldest) food markets. A walk through here is a feast for the senses. See p. 139.

o **Driving Through the Burren** (County Clare): Ireland is full of memorable landscapes, but this is the most unique. For miles, this exposed coastal countryside has a haunting, alien feel, although it's strikingly beautiful too. Try to be here as the sun goes down, when the craggy limestone planes turn an evening shade of red. See chapter 9.

o **Photographing the Murals in Belfast and Derry** (County Antrim/County Derry, Northern Ireland): Half a generation has grown up in Northern Ireland without knowing full-on sectarian bloodshed firsthand. Yet in Belfast, the "peace wall" dividing Catholic neighborhoods from near-identical Protestant streets is still covered in political street art, much of it preaching nonviolence. Likewise, "People's Gallery" murals in Derry testify how "the Troubles" affected ordinary citizens. See chapter 12.

o **Stumbling Across a Mysterious Ruin in the Middle of Nowhere** (Almost Anywhere): Ireland is full to bursting with medieval castles, churches, and all manner of impossibly old buildings. We've listed as many as we can in this book—but we don't know it all. And that's the sheer joy of exploring a place like Ireland; you'll be hiking across a hillside, or turn a bend in a country lane, and suddenly come across some craggy ancient ruin that may not appear in any guidebook or on any map. We've made some amazing discoveries this way—keep your eyes open and you will too. (And if you're itching to tell somebody about your find—tell us!)

THE best HOTELS

o **Monart Spa** (Enniscorthy, County Wexford): A sumptuous countryside retreat, this pampering paradise is consistently rated among the top spas in Ireland. It's a serene, adults-only zone in a lovely setting. See p. 112.

o **Temple House** (Ballymote, County Sligo): Proving that not all the best overnight stays are found in luxury hotels, Temple House is a historic countryside B&B that feels like it's in a world of its own. See p. 218.

o **Wicklow Way Lodge** (Oldbridge, County Wicklow): It's hard to fault this lovely B&B with spectacular views of the Wicklow Mountains. So we won't. It's just gorgeous. See p. 98.

o **Aghadoe Heights** (Killarney, County Kerry): Another of Ireland's top spas, this one overlooks the Lakes of Killarney from a high vantage point just north of the town. See p. 150.

o **Ashford Castle** (Cong, County Mayo): Live like royalty for a night at this fairytale castle in County Mayo. The great and the good have been coming here for decades to see what the fuss is about. The fuss, it turns out, is justified. See p. 213.

o **The Bervie** (Keel, County Mayo): Overlooking the Atlantic Ocean on an island off the Mayo coast, the Bervie is a haven of magnificent views and gourmet food. See p. 214.

o **Dolphin Beach House** (Clifden, County Galway): This incredibly special B&B on the Galway coast is a converted early-20th-century homestead with amazing views, gorgeous food, and gregarious hosts. See p. 198.

o **Gregans Castle Hotel** (Ballyvaughn, County Clare): J. R. R. Tolkien took inspiration for *The Lord of the Rings* while staying at this elegant country house amid the lunar landscape of the Burren. See p. 178

THE best RESTAURANTS

o **Fishy Fishy** (Kinsale, County Cork): Kinsale is Ireland's unofficial gourmet capital, and the delightful Fishy Fishy is among its best restaurants. The seafood is so local that the menu tells you who caught it—and we're talking dish by dish, name by name. See p. 135.

o **Brunel** (Newcastle, County Down): Top-quality local seafood presented with photo-worthy flair is the main event at this fantastic little restaurant tucked away in a seaside town in Northern Ireland. See p. 100.

o **Aniar** (Galway, County Galway): Galway City's most sought-after table has a tiny but impeccably judged menu of innovative, modern Irish cuisine. Aniar is one of just a handful of Michelin-starred restaurants in Ireland. See p. 200.

o **Wilde's at the Lodge at Ashford** (Cong, County Mayo): On the grounds of Ashford Castle, Wilde's is a joyous restaurant run by a real star in the making. Diners also get an amazing view of Lough Corrib. See p. 220.

o **Richmond House** (Cappoquin, County Waterford): One of the real destination restaurants of the southeast, the Richmond House—set in a converted 18th-century mansion—serves exquisite seasonal meals, with many ingredients sourced from their own garden. See p. 115.

o **Sabor Brazil** (Dublin, County Dublin): In a rather boring district of Dublin, you'll find this superlative Brazilian-Irish restaurant—proof that the best restaurant experiences are often the most unexpected. See p. 66.

o **Gallagher's Boxty House** (Dublin, County Dublin): Think again if you assume that dining well requires deep pockets. A local man longing to preserve the culinary traditions of his childhood started this hugely popular Temple Bar restaurant. The result is captivating. See p. 58.

THE best PICTURE-POSTCARD TOWNS

o **Adare** (County Limerick): This really is a picture-postcard town, its image having been reproduced alongside a hundred thousand "Wish You Were Heres." Unfortunately the secret is very much out, but if you manage to visit when the roads aren't clogged with tour buses, you'll leave with a memory card full of photos. See p. 191.

o **Dalkey** (County Dublin): The cutest of a string of upscale seaside towns unfurling south from Dublin, Dalkey is both a short drive and a million miles away from the busy city, with a castle, a mountaintop folly, lovely beaches, and some fine restaurants. See p. 93.

o **Kinsale** (County Cork): Kinsale's narrow streets all lead to the sea, dropping steeply from the hills around the harbor. The walk from Kinsale through Scilly to Charles Fort and Frower Point is breathtaking. Kinsale has the added benefit of being a foodie town with no shortage of good restaurants. See p. 126.

o **Kenmare** (County Kerry): It's easy to fall in love with Kenmare, with its stone cottages, colorful gardens, and flowers overflowing from window boxes. It's also home to several elegant hotels, so it makes an enchanting base when exploring the Ring of Kerry. See p. 166.

o **Dingle (An Daingean)** (County Kerry): In this charming medieval town, stone buildings ramble up and down hills, and the small population is relaxed about visitors. It has lots of little diners and picturesque pubs, plus a lovely, historic church. See p. 171.

THE best NATURAL WONDERS

o **Giant's Causeway** (County Antrim): At the foot of a cliff by the sea, this mysterious mass of tightly packed, naturally occurring hexagonal basalt columns is nothing short of astonishing. This volcanic wonder, formed 60 million years ago, looks even better when negotiated (cautiously) on foot. See p. 258.

o **The Burren** (County Clare): We can guarantee this: The Burren is one of the strangest landscapes you're likely to see anywhere in the world. Its stark limestone grassland is spread with a quilt of wildflowers from as far afield as the Alps, and its inhabitants include nearly every species of butterfly found in Ireland. See chapter 9.

o **Mizen Head** (County Cork): While most travelers flock to the overcrowded Cliffs of Moher (p. 186), these spectacular 210m (689-ft) sea cliffs at Ireland's extreme southwest tip are just as stunning. See p. 147.

o **The Twelve Bens** (County Galway): Amid Connemara's central mountains, bogs, and lakes, the rugged Twelve Bens range crowns a spectacular landscape. Some of the peaks are bare and rocky, others clothed in peat. The loftiest, Benbaun in Connemara National Park, reaches a height of 729m (2,392 ft.). See p. 210.

THE best CASTLES & STATELY HOMES

o **Kilkenny Castle** (County Kilkenny): Although parts of this stout towered castle date from the 13th century, the existing structure looks more like a 19th-century palace. Exquisitely restored, it also has vast gardens; former stables now hold art galleries and shops. See p. 125.

o **Powerscourt Estate** (County Wicklow): Restored at last to its former glory (at least on the outside) after decades of misfortune and neglect, the house is surrounded by some of the most exquisite gardens in Ireland. See p. 107.

o **Carrickfergus Castle** (County Antrim): This huge Norman fortress on the bank of Belfast Lough is surprisingly intact and well-preserved, complete with an imposing tower house and a high wall punctuated by corner towers. See p. 249.

o **Castletown House** (County Kildare): Built in the early 18th century, this grand, whitewashed mansion soon became one of Ireland's most imitated buildings. See p. 105.

o **Dunluce Castle** (County Antrim): Set atop a razor-sharp promontory jutting into the sea, these castle ruins are picturesque and evocative. Unlike many other castles, it wasn't demolished by human enemies, but had to be abandoned after a large section collapsed and fell into the breakers below. See p. 258.

THE best PREHISTORIC SITES

o **Hill of Tara** (County Meath): Of ritual significance from the Stone Age to the early Christian period, Tara—the traditional center and seat of Ireland's high kings—has seen it all and kept it a secret. From its top on a clear day you can see all four of Ireland's Celtic provinces. See p. 103.

o **Newgrange** (County Meath): One of the archaeological wonders of Western Europe, Newgrange is the centerpiece of a megalithic cemetery dating back 5,000 years—that's older than the Egyptian pyramids or Stonehenge. Walking down the long, atmospheric central tunnel, trying to visualize just how many generations have passed since it was built, is mind-blowing. But the question remains: What was it all for? See p. 104.

o **Dún Aengus** (County Galway): The eminent archaeologist George Petrie called Dún Aengus "the most magnificent barbaric monument in Europe." No one knows who built this massive stone fort or what year it was constructed. Dún Aengus still stands guard today over the southern coast of Inishmore, the largest of the Aran Islands. See p. 207.

o **Carrowmore and Carrowkeel** (County Sligo): These two megalithic cities of the dead (Europe's largest) may have once contained more than 200 passage tombs. The two together—one in the valley and the other atop a nearby mountain—convey an unequaled sense of the ancient peoples' reverence for the dead. Carrowmore is well presented and interpreted, while Carrowkeel is left to itself for those who seek it out. See p. 226.

THE best EARLY CHRISTIAN RUINS

o **Glendalough** (County Wicklow): Nestled in "the glen of the two lakes," this atmospheric monastic settlement was founded in the 6th century by St. Kevin, who was looking for seclusion and certainly found it here, amid scenic lakes and forests. Although quite remote, Glendalough suffered assaults from the Vikings and English forces and eventually faded away. Today its stone ruins collude with the countryside to create one of the loveliest spots in Ireland. See p. 106.

o **The Rock of Cashel** (County Tipperary): In name and appearance, "the Rock" suggests a citadel, a place designed more for power than prayer. A huge outcropping—or an *up*cropping—of limestone topped with spectacularly beautiful ruins, this was the seat of clerics and kings, a power center to rival Tara. Now the two sites vie only for the attention of tourists. See p. 120.

o **Jerpoint Abbey** (County Kilkenny): Jerpoint is the finest representative of the many Cistercian abbeys whose ruins dot the Irish landscape. Somehow, hundreds of years of rain and wind have failed to completely wipe away medieval carvings, leaving us a rare chance to glimpse how magnificent these abbeys once were. See p. 124.

o **Skellig Michael** (County Kerry): Thirteen kilometers (8 miles) offshore of the Iveragh Peninsula, rising sharply 214m (702 ft.) out of the Atlantic, this remote, rocky crag dedicated to the archangel Michael was chosen by early Irish monks for their austere hermitage. Today the journey to Skellig across choppy seas, and the arduous climb to its summit, makes an unforgettable experience. See p. 168.

THE best FOR LOVERS OF LITERATURE

o **Dublin Writers Museum** (Dublin, County Dublin): Filled with letters, manuscripts, personal possessions, and other eclectic ephemera, this great museum in Dublin is a mecca for lovers of Irish literature. Naturally, it has a great bookshop. See p. 72.

o **Davy Byrnes Pub** (Dublin, County Dublin): This place crops up in *Ulysses* when the hero, Leopold Bloom, famously orders a lunch of burgundy and a Gorgonzola sandwich here. The pub is acutely aware of its heritage, but happily knows better than to ruin the appeal by being too touristy. See p. 90.

o **St. Patrick's Cathedral** (Dublin, County Dublin): In the 18th century, satirist Jonathan Swift (*Gulliver's Travels*) tickled and horrified the world with his vicious wit—all the while maintaining his very respectable day job as dean of St. Patrick's Cathedral. He is buried here alongside his longtime companion, Stella Johnson. See p. 75.

o **An Evening of Food, Folklore, and Fairies** (Dublin, County Dublin): The last few years have seen a resurgence in the age-old art of storytelling, with a new generation embracing this captivatingly simple art form. This is one of the best nights out Dublin has to offer—appropriately held in what might (*might*) be Ireland's oldest pub. See p. 91.

o **County Sligo:** With its many connections to the beloved poet W. B. Yeats, this county is a pilgrimage destination for true fans. The poet's writing was shaped by the landscape, and many of the monuments—Lough Gill, Glencar Lake, Ben Bulben Mountain, and Maeve's tomb—appear in his works. There are also several museums housing first editions, photographs, and other memorabilia, plus Yeats's dark and somber grave in Drumcliffe. See chapter 11.

THE best FAMILY ACTIVITIES

o **Dublin Zoo in the Phoenix Park** (Dublin): Kids love this sympathetically designed zoo featuring wild creatures, animal-petting corners, and a train ride. The surrounding park has room to run, picnic, and explore. See p. 86.

o **Irish National Heritage Park** (County Wexford): Millennia of history are made painlessly educational for children and adults at this engaging "living history" museum. It's a fascinating, informative way to while away a couple of hours or more. See p. 123.

o **Fota Island & Wildlife Park** (County Cork): In this wildlife park, rare and endangered animals roam freely. You'll see everything from giraffes and zebras to kangaroos, flamingos, penguins, and monkeys wandering the grassland. Add in a toddler playground, tour train, picnic area, and gift shop, and you have the makings of a fun family outing. See p. 146.

o **Muckross House & Gardens** (Killarney, County Kerry): This impressive mansion acts as the gateway to Killarney National Park today, but the interior has been preserved in all its Victorian splendor. Nearby, people on the Muckross Historic Farms engage in traditional farm activities while dressed in authentic period clothes. See p. 165.

o **Fungie the Dolphin Tours** (Dingle, County Kerry): Every day, fishing boats ferry visitors out into the nearby waters to see Fungie, the friendliest dolphin you're ever likely to meet, swim right up to the boat. You can even arrange an early-morning dolphin swim. The kid-friendly Dingle Oceanworld Aquarium is right by the harbor as well. See p. 172.

o **Galway Atlantaquaria** (Galway, County Galway): Known more formally as the National Aquarium of Ireland, this is the place that your kids will remember long after their memories of ruined dolmens by the roadside have faded. Highlights include a tank full of small sharks and pools where kids can touch curious rays. See p. 206.

o **Bunratty Castle & Folk Park** (County Clare): Kids love Bunratty, which looks every bit as satisfyingly medieval as an old castle should. The grounds have been turned over to a replica 19th-century village—complete with actors playing Victorian residents going about their daily lives. It's great fun to walk through. See p. 185.

THE best MUSEUMS

- **Chester Beatty Library** (Dublin, County Dublin): Not just a library, this is one of Ireland's best museums, with a wealth of books, illuminated texts, and small art objects. Its collection of rare religious manuscripts is among the most unique in the world. See p. 69.

- **National Museum of Ireland: Archaeology** (Dublin, County Dublin): Ireland's National Museum is split into four separate sites, of which this is far and away the best. The collection dates back to the earliest settlers, but it's the relics from the Viking invasion and the early Christian period that dazzle the most. See p. 74.

- **Irish National Famine Museum** (Strokestown Park, County Roscommon): This reflective museum, part of a grand historic estate, does a brilliant job of making the darkest period in Irish history seem immediate and real, including a collection of heartbreaking letters from destitute tenants to their callous landlords. See p. 227.

- **Ulster Folk & Transport Museum** (Cultra, County Antrim): Ireland has several so-called "living history" museums, where stories of people and times past are told through reconstructions of everyday life. This one, just outside Belfast, is one of the most engaging. See p. 253.

- *Titanic* **Belfast** (Belfast, County Antrim): Belfast is incredibly proud of having built the most famous ocean liner in history, despite its ultimate fate—though, as they're fond of saying, "she was alright when she left here." This gleaming, high-tech museum is the best of several *Titanic*-related attractions in Belfast. See p. 244.

IRELAND IN CONTEXT

These are trying times for Ireland, as it reels from an ongoing economic crisis and struggles to find political equilibrium. But Ireland will bounce back; it has been through worse. The complex history of this small country has conditioned its people to be resilient, and there is something to be said for the Irish spirit, for the ability to find humor in the darkest of places. Every new crisis brings fresh jokes alongside the rage. Every new leader is a target for general hilarity. And while nobody in the country would tell you there is not work to be done, you get the distinct impression that the people—if not the politicians and the bankers who got them into this mess—are ready to do that work.

A BRIEF HISTORY

THE FIRST SETTLERS With some degree of confidence, we can place the date of the first human habitation of the island somewhere after the end of the last ice age, around the late 8000s B.C. Ireland's first colonizers, Mesolithic Homo sapiens, walked, waded, or floated across the narrow strait from what is now Britain in search of flint and, of course, food.

The next momentous prehistoric event was the arrival of Neolithic farmers and herders, sometime around 3500 B.C. Unlike Ireland's Mesolithic hunters, who barely left a trace, this second wave of colonizers began to transform the island at once. They came with stone axes that could fell a good-sized elm in less than an hour, and Ireland's hardwood forests receded to make room for tilled fields and pastureland. Villages sprang up, and more permanent homes, planked with split oak, appeared at this time.

Far more striking, though, was the appearance of massive megalithic monuments, including court cairns, *dolmens* (stone tables), round subterranean passage tombs, and wedge tombs. Thousands of these tombs are scattered around Ireland, and to this day only a small percentage of them have been excavated. These megalithic monuments speak volumes about the early Irish. To visit **Newgrange** (see p. 104) and **Knowth** (see p. 104) in the Boyne Valley and **Carrowmore** (see p. 226) in County Sligo is to marvel at the mystical practices of the early Irish. Even today, little is known about the meaning or purpose of these mysterious stone relics.

Later Celtic inhabitants assumed that the tremendous stones and mounds were raised by giants, a race they called the people of the *sí*—a name which eventually became the *Tuatha Dé Danann,* and, finally, *fairies.* Over many generations, oral tradition downsized the mythical people into "little people," who were believed to have led a magical underground life in thousands of *raths* (earthwork structures) coursing the island like giant mole tunnels. All of these sites were believed to be protected by fairies. Tampering with them was thought to bring bad luck, so nobody ever touched them. Thus, they have lasted to this day—ungraffitied, undamaged, unprotected by fences or wires, but utterly safe.

THE CELTS Of all the successive waves of outsiders who have, over the years, shaped, cajoled, and pockmarked the timeline of Irish history, none have made quite such an impact as the Celts. They came, originally from Central Europe, in waves, the first perhaps as early as the 6th century B.C. and continuing until the end of the first millennium. They fled from the Roman invasion and clung to the edge of Europe—Ireland being, at the time, about as far as you could go to elude a Roman force. In time, they controlled the island and absorbed into their culture everyone they found there.

Despite their cultural potency, however, the Celts developed little in the way of centralized government, existing instead in a near-perpetual state of division and conflict with one another. The island was divided among as many as 150 tribes, grouped under alliances to five provincial kings. The provinces of Munster, Leinster, Ulster, and Connaught date from this period. They fought fiercely among themselves over land, women, and cattle (their "currency" and standard of wealth). No one tribe ever ruled the entire island, though not for lack of trying. One of the most impressive monuments from the time of the warring Celts is the stone fortress of **Dún Aengus,** on the wind-swept hills of the Aran Islands (see p. 207).

THE COMING OF CHRISTIANITY The Celtic chiefs neither welcomed nor resisted the Christians who came ashore beginning in the 5th century A.D. Although threatened, the pagan Celts settled for a bloodless rivalry with this new religion. In retrospect, this may have been a mistake.

Not the first, but eventually the most famous, of these Christian newcomers was a man called Maewyn Succat, a young Roman citizen torn from his Welsh homeland in a Celtic raid and brought to Ireland as a slave, where he was forced to work in a place called the Forest of Foclut (thought to be around modern County Antrim). He escaped on a ship bound for France, where he spent several years as a priest before returning to Ireland as a missionary. He began preaching at sacred Celtic festivals, a tactic that frequently led to confrontations with religious and political leaders, but eventually he became such a popular figure that after his death in 461, a dozen clan chiefs fought over the right to bury him. His lasting legacy was, of course, the establishment in Ireland of one of the strongest Christian orthodoxies in Europe—an achievement for which he was later beatified as St. Patrick.

Ireland's conversion to Christianity was a somewhat negotiated process. The church at the time of St. Patrick was, like the man who brought it, Roman. For Ireland, an island still without a single proper town, the Roman system of dioceses and archdioceses simply didn't make sense. So the Irish adapted the church to their own situation. They built isolated monasteries with extended monastic "families," each more or less autonomous. For several centuries, Ireland flourished in this fashion, becoming a center of monastic learning and culture. Monks and scholars were drawn here in droves, and they were sent out in great numbers as well, to Britain and the Continent, as emissaries for the island's way of thinking and praying. Like their megalithic ancestors, these monks left traces of their lives behind, enduring monuments to their spirituality. Early monastic sites such as gorgeous **Glendalough** in County Wicklow (see p. 106), and isolated **Skellig Michael** off the Kerry coast (see p. 168) give you an idea of how they lived. Striking examples of their work can be seen at Trinity College (which houses the **Book of Kells**—see p. 68) and at the **Chester Beatty Museum** (see p. 69).

THE VIKING INVASIONS Then the Vikings came along and ruined everything.

After centuries of relative peace, the first wave of Viking invaders arrived in Ireland in A.D. 795. The wealthy Irish monasteries were among their first targets. Unprepared and unprotected, the monasteries, which had amassed troves of gold, jewels, and art from followers around the world, were decimated. The round towers to which the monks retreated for safety were neither high enough nor strong enough to protect them and their treasures from the onslaught.

Once word spread of the wealth to be had on the small island, the Scandinavian invaders just kept on coming. Although they were experts in the arts of pillage and plunder, they had no knowledge of or interest in literature. In fact, most didn't know how to read. Therefore, they paid scant attention to the magnificent books they came across, passing them over for more obvious riches. This fortunate quirk of history allowed the monks to preserve their dying culture—and their immeasurably valuable work—for the benefit of future generations.

After the Vikings left, Ireland enjoyed something of a renewal in the 11th and 12th centuries. Its towns grew, its regional kings continued to try (unsuccessfully) to unite the country under a single high kingship, and its church came under increased pressure to conform to the Vatican's rules. All of these factors ripened a prosperous, factionalized Ireland for the next invasion.

It was, tragically, an Irish king who opened the door to the next predator. Diarmait Mac Murchada, king of Leinster, whose ambition was to be king of all of Ireland, decided he could do it, with a little help. So he called on Henry II, the Norman king of England. Diarmait offered Henry a series of incentives in return for military aid: Not only did he bequeath his eldest daughter to whomever led the army, but he also offered them overlordship of the Kingdom of Leinster. To put it bluntly, he made Henry an offer he couldn't refuse. So it was that an English expeditionary force, led by the Earl of Pembroke, Richard de Clare—better known as Strongbow—was sent to Diarmait's aid. After a successful invasion, victorious Strongbow remained in Ireland as governor, and thus gave the English their first foothold in Ireland. What Diarmait did not realize, of course, was that they would never leave.

THE NORMAN INVASION   In successive expeditions from 1167 to 1169, the Normans, who had already conquered England, crossed the Irish Sea with crushing force. During the next century, the Norman-English settled in, consolidating their power in new towns and cities. Indeed, many settlers grew attached to the island and began to integrate with the local culture. Marriages between the native Irish and the invaders became commonplace. As time passed, the Anglo-Normans became more Irish and less English in their loyalties. Meanwhile, independent Gaelic lords in the North and West continued to maintain their territories.

By the late 1400s, English control of the island was effectively limited to the Pale, a walled and fortified cordon around what is now greater Dublin. (The phrase "beyond the pale" comes from this—meaning anything that is uncontrollable or unacceptable.)

ENGLISH POWER & THE FLIGHT OF THE EARLS   During the reign of the Tudor monarchs in England (1485–1603), the brutal reconquest of Ireland was set in motion. Henry VIII was the first to proclaim himself king of all Ireland—something even his warlike ancestors had stopped short of doing—and later that century, the claim was backed up by force. Elizabeth I, Henry's daughter, declared that all Gaelic lords in Ireland must surrender their lands to her, with the dubious promise that she would immediately grant them all back again. Unsurprisingly, the proposition was hardly welcomed in Ireland, and a rebel army was raised by Hugh O'Neill and "Red" Hugh O'Donnell, two Irish chieftains. They scored some significant victories early on in their decade-long campaign, most notably over a force led by the Earl of Essex, whom Elizabeth had personally sent to subdue them. Still, by 1603 O'Neill was left with few allies and no option but to surrender, which he did on March 23rd, the day before Elizabeth died.

In 1607, after failing to win back much of their power and prestige, around 90 of O'Neill's allies fled to mainland Europe, hoping Spain would try to invade again. This never happened. The "Flight of the Earls," as it became known, marked a crucial turning point in Irish history, as the point at which the old Gaelic aristocracy effectively came to an end.

THE COMING OF CROMWELL   By the 1640s, Ireland was effectively an English plantation. Family estates had been seized and foreign (Scottish) labor brought in to work them. A systematic persecution of Catholics, which began with Henry VIII's split from Rome but did not die with him, barred Catholics from practicing their faith. Resentment against the English and their punitive laws led to fierce uprisings in Ulster and Leinster in 1641, and by early 1642 most of Ireland was again under Irish control. Unfortunately for the rebels, any hope of extending the victories was undermined by internal disunion, and then by a fatal decision to support the Royalist side in the Civil War that had just broken out in England. After King Charles I of England was beheaded in 1648, Oliver Cromwell, the commander of the parliamentary forces, was installed as England's ruler. It wasn't long before Cromwell's supporters took on his enemies in Ireland. A year later, the Royalists' stand collapsed in defeat at Rathmines, just south of Dublin.

Defeat of the Royalists did not, however, mean the end of war. Cromwell became paranoid that Ireland would be used to launch a French-backed insurgency; he also detested the country's Catholic beliefs. As the hot, sticky summer of 1649 drew to a close, Cromwell set sail for Dublin with an army of 12,000 men, and a battle plan so ruthless, it is notorious to this day.

In the town of Drogheda, more than 3,552 Irish soldiers were slaughtered in a single night. When a group of men sought sanctuary in the local church, Cromwell ordered the church burned down with them locked inside—an act of such monstrosity that some of his own men risked charges of mutiny to refuse the order. On another day, in Wexford, more than 2,000 were murdered, many of them civilians. The trail of destruction rolled on, devastating counties Galway and Waterford. When asked where the Irish citizens could go to be safe from him, Cromwell famously suggested they could go "to hell or Connaught"—the latter being the most far-flung, rocky, and unfarmable part of Ireland.

After a rampage that lasted 7 months, killing thousands and leaving churches, monasteries, and castles in ruins, Cromwell finally left Ireland in the care of his lieutenants and returned to England. Hundreds of years later, the memory of his infamous violence lingers painfully in Ireland. In certain parts of the country, people still spit at the mention of his name.

THE ANTI-CATHOLIC LAWS   Cromwell died in 1658, and 2 years later the English monarchy was restored. Still, Anti-Catholic oppression continued in Ireland. Then in 1685 something remarkable happened: The new Stuart king, James II, refused to relinquish his Catholic faith after ascending to the throne. It looked for a while as if Catholic Ireland had found a royal ally at last. However, such hopes were dashed 3 years later, when James was ousted from power, and the Protestant William of Orange installed in his place.

James fled to France to raise support for a rebellion, and then sailed to Ireland to launch his attack. He struck first at Derry, laying siege for 15 weeks, before finally being defeated by William's forces at the Battle of the Boyne. The battle effectively ended James's cause, and with it, the hopes of Catholic Ireland for the best part of a century.

After James's defeat, English power was once more consolidated across Ireland. Protestant landowners were granted full political power, while laws were enacted to tamp down the Catholic population. Being a Catholic in late-17th-century Ireland was not exactly illegal per se, but in practice life was all but impossible for non-Protestants. Catholics could not purchase land, and existing landholdings were split up unless the families who owned them became Protestants. Catholic schools were banned, as were priests and all forms of public Catholic worship. Catholics were barred from holding government office, practicing law, or joining the army. Those who refused to relinquish their faith were forced to pay a tax to the Anglican Church. And, since only landowners were allowed to vote, Catholics whose land had been taken away also lost the right to vote.

The new British landlords settled in, planted crops, made laws, and sowed their own seeds. Inevitably, over time, the "Anglos" became the Anglo-Irish. Hyphenated or not, they were Irish, and their loyalties were increasingly unpredictable. After all, an immigrant is only an immigrant for a generation; whatever the birthright of the colonists, their children would be Irish-born and -bred. And so a sort of stability set in for a generation or three, albeit of a kind that was very much separate and unequal. There were the haves, the wealthy Protestants, and the have-nots, the deprived and disenfranchised Catholics.

This unhappy peace held for some time. But by the end of the 18th century, the appetite for rebellion was whetted again—in the coffee shops and lecture halls of Europe's newest boomtown: Dublin.

THE UNITED IRISHMEN & THE 1798 REBELLION By the 1770s, Dublin was thriving as never before. As a center for culture and learning, it was rivaled only by Paris and London; thanks to the work of such architects as Henry Gratton (who designed the **Custom House,** p. 82, and the **Four Courts,** p. 83), its very streets were being remodeled in a grand, neoclassical style that was more akin to the great cities of Italy than of southern Ireland.

While the urban classes reveled in their newfound wealth, the stringent Penal Laws that had effectively cut off Catholic workers from their own countryside drove many of them to pour into the city, looking for work. Alongside Dublin's buzzing intellectual scene, political dissent soon brewed. Even after a campaign by Irish politicians succeeded in getting many of the Penal Laws repealed in 1783, Dublin was a breeding ground for radicals and political activists. The results were explosive.

When war broke out between Britain and France in the 1790s, the United Irishmen—a nonviolent society formed to lobby for admission of Catholic Irishmen to the Irish Parliament—sent a secret delegation to persuade the French to intervene on Ireland's behalf against the British. Their emissary in this venture was a Dublin lawyer named Wolfe Tone. In 1796 Tone sailed with a French force bound for Ireland, determined to defeat forces loyal to the English crown, but they were turned back by storms.

In 1798, full-scale insurrection led by the United Irishmen spread across much of Ireland, particularly the southwestern counties of Kilkenny and Wexford, where a tiny republic was briefly declared in June. But it was soon crushed by Loyalist forces, which then went on a murderous spree, killing tens of thousands of men, women, and children, and burning towns to the ground. The nadir of the rebellion came when Wolfe Tone, having raised another French invasion force, sailed into Lough Swilly in Donegal and was promptly captured by the British. At his trial, Tone wore the uniform of a French soldier; he slit his own throat while in prison waiting to be hung.

The rebellion was over. In the space of 3 weeks, more than 30,000 Irish had been killed. As a final indignity in what became known as "The Year of the French," the British tricked the Irish Parliament into dissolving itself, and Ireland reverted to strict British rule.

A CONFLICT OF CONFLICTS   In 1828, a Catholic lawyer named Daniel O'Connell—who had earlier formed the Catholic Association to represent the interests of tenant farmers—was elected to the British Parliament as Member of Parliament for Dublin. Public opinion was so solidly behind him, he was able to persuade the British prime minister that the only way to avoid civil war in Ireland was to force a Catholic Emancipation Act through Parliament. O'Connell remained an MP until 1841, when he was elected Lord Mayor of Dublin, a platform he used to push for repeal of the direct rule imposed from London after the 1798 rebellion. O'Connell organized enormous rallies (nicknamed "monster meetings") and provoked the conservative government to such an extent that it eventually arrested him on charges of seditious conspiracy. The charges were dropped, but the incident—coupled with growing impatience toward his nonviolent approach—eroded his power base. "The Liberator," as he had been known, faded, his health failed, and he died on a trip to Rome.

THE GREAT FAMINE   Even after anti-Catholic legislation began to recede, the vast majority of farmland available to Ireland's poor, mostly Catholic, rural population was meager and hard to cultivate. One of the few crops that could be grown reliably was the potato, which therefore became the staple diet of the rural poor. So when, in 1845, a fungus destroyed much of the potato crop of Ireland, widespread devastation followed.

To label the Great Irish Famine of the 1840s and '50s as merely a "tragedy" would be inadequate. It was, of course, tragic—but even worse was that it was not random, not unavoidable. The fact is that what started out as crop failure was turned into a disaster by the callous response of the British establishment.

As the potato blight worsened, it became apparent to many landlords that their farm tenants would be unable to pay rent. Instead of helping to feed their now-starving tenants, these landlords shipped their grain overseas, determined to recoup what they were losing in rent. The British Parliament, meanwhile, was reluctant to send aid, putting the reports of a crisis down to, in the words of Prime Minister Robert Peel, "the Irish tendency to exaggerate."

People started to die by the thousands.

Eventually it became clear to the government that something had to be done. Emergency relief was sent to Ireland in the form of cheap, imported Indian cornmeal, which contained virtually no nutrients. Malnutrition led to the spread of diseases such as typhus and cholera, in the end claiming more victims than starvation itself. To make matters worse, the cornmeal was not simply given to those in need of it. Fearful that handouts would encourage laziness among the "shiftless poor," the British government forced people to work for their food. Pointless make-work projects were initiated, just to give the starving men something to do for their cornmeal; roads were built that led nowhere, and elaborate follies constructed that served no discernible purpose. Some of these still litter the countryside, memorials to cruelty and ignorance.

One of the most difficult things to comprehend, more than a century and a half later, is the sheer futility of it all. For behind the statistics, the memorials, and the endless personal anguish, lies perhaps the most painful truth of all: that the Famine was easily preventable. Enormous cargoes of imported corn sat in Irish ports for months, until the British government felt that releasing them to the people would not adversely affect market rates. Meanwhile, huge quantities of meat and grain were exported from Ireland. (Indeed, in 1847, cattle exports went up 33% from the previous year.)

Given the circumstances, it is easy to understand why so many chose to leave Ireland. More than a million emigrated over the next decade, about three-quarters of them to America, the rest to Britain or Europe. They drained the country. In 1841, Ireland's population was 8 million; by 1851 it was 6.5 million.

THE STRUGGLE FOR HOME RULE As the Famine waned and life returned to something like normality, the Irish independence movement gained new momentum. New fronts, both violent and nonviolent, opened up in the struggle for what was now called Home Rule. Significantly, the Republicans now drew considerable support from overseas—particularly from America. There, groups such as the Fenians fundraised and published newspapers in support of the Irish cause, while bold schemes—such as an 1866 "invasion" of Canada with fewer than 100 men—generated awareness, if little else.

Back home in Ireland, partial concessions were won in Parliament. By the 1880s, nationalists such as Charles Stewart Parnell, the MP for Meath, were able to unite various factions of Irish nationalists (including the Fenian Brotherhood in America) to fight for Home Rule. In a tumultuous decade of legislation, Parnell came close to winning Home Rule—until revelations about his long affair with Kitty O'Shea, the wife of a supporter, brought about his downfall as a politician.

By 1912, a bill to give Ireland Home Rule was passed through the British House of Commons, but was defeated in the House of Lords. Many felt that the political process was all but unstoppable, that it was only a matter of time before the bill passed fully into law. Then World War I broke out in 1914, forcing the issue onto the back burner once again. Many in the Home Rule movement began to grow tired of pursuing their goal through legal political channels.

THE EASTER REBELLION On Easter Monday 1916, a group of nationalists occupied the **General Post Office** (p. 84) in the heart of Dublin, from which they proclaimed the foundation of an Irish Republic. Inside were 1,500 fighters, led by schoolteacher and Gaelic League member Patrick Pearse and Socialist leader James Connolly.

The British government, panicking over an armed uprising on its doorstep while it fought a massive war in Europe, responded with overwhelming force. Soldiers were sent in, and a battle raged in the streets of Dublin for 6 days before the leaders of the rebellion were captured and imprisoned. (The walls of the post office and other buildings and statues up and down O'Connell Street still have bullet holes.) Pearse, Connolly, and 12 other leaders were imprisoned, secretly tried, and speedily executed.

Ultimately, though, the harsh British reaction was counterproductive. The ruthlessness with which the rebellion's ringleaders were pursued and dispatched acted as a lightning rod for many who were still on the fence about how best to gain Home Rule. It's a fact that has become forgotten in the ensuing hundred or so years: On that cold Monday morning when Patrick Pearse stood on the post office steps to read a treatise on Irish independence, a great many Irish didn't support the rebellion. Many believed that the best course of action was to lay low until the war had ended, when, they felt, concessions would finally be won. Others felt that the uprising was simply the wrong thing to do, as long as sons of Ireland were sacrificing their lives in the trenches of Europe.

The aftermath of 1916 all but guaranteed, for better or for worse, that Ireland's future would be decided by the gun.

REBELLION & COMPROMISE   A power vacuum was left at the heart of the nationalist movement after the Easter Rising, and it was filled by two men: Michael Collins and Eamon de Valera. Collins was a Cork man who had returned from Britain in order to join the Irish Volunteers (later to become the Irish Republican Army, or IRA), while de Valera was an Irish-American math teacher who came back to Ireland to set up a new political party, *Sinn Féin.*

When de Valera's party won a landslide victory in the general election of 1918, its MPs took the provocative step of refusing to take their seats in London. Instead, they proclaimed the first *Dáil,* or independent parliament, in Dublin. De Valera went to rally support for the cause in America, while Collins stayed in Ireland to concentrate on his work as head of the Irish Volunteers. Tensions escalated into violence, and for the next 2 years, Irish nationalists fought a tit-for-tat military campaign against the British in Ireland. The low point of the struggle came in 1920, when Collins ordered 14 British operatives to be murdered in their beds. In response, British troops opened fire on the audience at a football game at Croke Park in Dublin, randomly killing 12 innocent people.

A truce was eventually declared on July 9, 1921. Six months later, the Anglo-Irish treaty was signed in London, granting legislative independence to 26 Irish counties (known together as the Irish Free State). The compromise through which that freedom was won, though, was that six counties in the north would remain part of the United Kingdom. Sent to negotiate the treaty, Collins knew that that compromise—which he felt was the best he could get at the time— would not be accepted by the more strident members of his rebel group. He also knew they would blame him for agreeing to it in the first place. When he signed the treaty he told the people present, "I am signing my own death warrant."

As Collins feared, nationalists were split between those who accepted the treaty as a platform on which to build, and those, led by the nationalist de Valera, who saw it as a betrayal. The latter group would accept nothing less than immediate and full independence at any cost. Even the withdrawal of British troops from Dublin for the first time in nearly 800 years did not quell their anger. The result was an inexorable slide into civil war. The flashpoint came in April 1922, when violence erupted around the streets of the capital, raging on for 8 days until de Valera's supporters were forced to surrender. The government of the fledgling free state ordered that Republicans be shot on sight, leading to the deaths of 77 people. And Collins had been right about his own fate: Four months later, he was assassinated while on a visit to his childhood home.

A REPUBLIC AT LAST The fallout from the civil war dominated Irish politics for the next decade. De Valera split from the Republicans to form another party, *Fianna Fáil* ("the Warriors of Ireland"), which won the election of 1932 and governed for 17 years. Despite his continuing dedication to the Republican ideal, however, de Valera was not to be the one who finally declared Ireland a republic, in 1948. Ironically, that distinction went to a coalition led by de Valera's opponent, Douglas Hyde. Hyde's victory in the 1947 election was attributed to the fact that de Valera had become too obsessed with abstract Republican ideals to govern effectively.

STUCK IN NEUTRAL One of the more controversial decisions that Eamon de Valera made while in office was to stay neutral during World War II. His reasons for this decision included Ireland's relatively small size and economic weakness, as well as a protest against the British presence in Northern Ireland. While that may have made sense to some extent, it left Ireland in the peculiar position of tacitly favoring one side in the war, but refusing to help it. After the death of Adolf Hitler in April 1945, de Valera alienated the Allies further by sending his personal sympathies to the German ambassador.

His stance didn't find much favor among the Irish population, either. During the war, as many as 300,000 Irish men found ways to enlist in the British or U.S. armies. In the end, more than 50,000 Irish soldiers perished in a war their country had refused to join.

TROUBLE ON THE WAY After the war, 2 decades passed without violence in Ireland. Then, in the late 1960s, sectarian conflict erupted in the North. What started out as a civil rights movement, demanding greater equality for Catholics within Northern Ireland, soon escalated into a cycle of violence that lasted for 30 years.

It would be a terrible oversimplification to say that the Troubles were a clear-cut struggle between those who wanted complete Irish unification and those who wanted to remain part of the United Kingdom. That was, of course, the crux of the conflict. However, many other factors, such as organized crime and terrorism, together with centuries-old conflicts over religious, land, and social issues, make the conflict even harder for outsiders to understand.

The worst of the Troubles came in the 1970s. In 1972, British troops inexplicably opened fire on a peaceful demonstration in Derry, killing 12 people—many of them shot while tending to the wounds of the first people injured. The IRA took advantage of the public outrage to begin a civilian bombing campaign on the British mainland. The cycle of violence continued inexorably for 20 years. All the while, none of the myriad sides in the conflict would talk to each other. Finally, in the early 1990s, secret talks were opened between the British and the IRA, leading to an IRA cease-fire in 1994 (although the cease-fire held only shakily—an IRA bomb in Omagh 4 years later killed 29, the most to die in any single incident of the Troubles).

The peace process continued throughout the 1990s, helped significantly by the mediation efforts of U.S. President Bill Clinton, who arguably became more involved in Irish affairs than any president before him. Eventually, on Good Friday 1998, a peace accord was finally signed in Belfast. The agreement committed all sides to a peaceful resolution of the conflict in Northern Ireland, and reinstated self-government for the region in a power-sharing administration. However, it stopped short of resolving the territorial issue once and for all. In other words, Northern Ireland is still part of the U.K., and will be for the foreseeable future.

To some extent, the conflicts rage more bitterly and more divisively than ever before. The difference is that, with notable exceptions, nowadays they are fought through the ballot box, rather than the barrel of a gun. In 2005, the IRA fully decommissioned its weapons, and officially dissolved itself as a paramilitary unit. Since then, there have been wobbles—including the occasional act of violence by splinter groups who don't want to accept peace—but these have been very few and far between.

THE CELTIC TIGER While Northern Ireland struggled to find peace, the Republic of Ireland flourished. The 1990s brought unprecedented wealth and prosperity to the country, thanks in part to European Union subsidies, and partly to a thriving economy, which acquired the nickname "the Celtic Tiger" for its new global strength. Ireland became a rich country, widely seen as one of the best places in the world to live and work.

However, that boom came crashing down after the banking crisis of 2008. The Irish government was forced to seek financial aid from the European Union, a package worth more than 50% of the whole economy, to save the country from bankruptcy. The op-ed pages of Irish newspaper expressed real feelings of betrayal and a sense of opportunity lost. Things have improved a lot since then, but the crash changed Ireland for good, as much in terms of its character than mere economics.

The past decade has been one in which Ireland has addressed serious questions about its own identity. Certain things that once seemed indelible to Irish society are now evolving, and the country is becoming more socially liberal. The influence of the church, while still profound, is less keenly felt than it once was. One of the most powerful emblems of this change came in 2015, when a referendum to allow same-sex marriage passed by a landslide—making this the first country in the world to pass such a law through a popular vote.

IRELAND IN CULTURE

LITERATURE Ireland holds a place in literature disproportionate to its small size and modest population. Four writers from this tiny country have won the Nobel Prize for literature. Inspired by the country's unique beauty, the inequities of its political system, and its cruel legacy of poverty and struggle, Ireland's authors, poets, and playwrights wrote about the Irish for the Irish, and to raise awareness in the rest of the world. No matter where you live, you've probably been reading about Ireland all your life.

One of the country's best-known early writers was satirist **Jonathan Swift,** who was born in Dublin in 1667. Educated at Trinity College, he left Ireland for England in 1688 to avoid the Glorious Revolution. Though he spent much of his adult life in London, he returned to Ireland when he was over 50 years old, at which point he began to write his most famous works. Greatly moved by the suffering of the poor in Ireland, he translated his anger into dark, vicious humor. His tract *A Modest Proposal* is widely credited with inventing satire as we now know it. His best-known works have political undertones—even *Gulliver's Travels* is a political allegory.

Best known for his novel *Dracula,* the novelist and theater promoter **Bram Stoker** was born in Clontarf, a coastal suburb of Dublin, in 1847. As a young man fresh out of Trinity College, he began reviewing theater productions for local newspapers, which is how he met the actor Henry Irving. He spent much of his time promoting and working for Irving, writing novels on the side for extra money. He spent most of his life in England, which largely inspired his work, although it is said that **St. Michan's Church** in Dublin (see p. 81), with its ghostly crypt, and **St. Mary's** in Killarney (see p. 166) helped to contribute to *Dracula*'s creepy feel.

Born in Dublin in 1854, **Oscar Wilde** was a popular and successful student at Trinity College, winning a scholarship to continue his studies in England at Oxford. After a flamboyant time there, he graduated with top honors and returned to Ireland, only to lose his girlfriend to Bram Stoker in 1878, after which he left Ireland forever. His writing—including the novel *The Picture of Dorian Gray,* plays including *The Importance of Being Earnest,* and books of poetry—was often overshadowed by his scandalous personal life. While a statue of him stands in Dublin in **St. Stephen's Green** (p. 87), his works were largely inspired by British and French writers, and he spent most of his life abroad.

George Bernard Shaw was born in Dublin in 1856 and attended school in the city, but never went to college, as he came to loathe the organized education system. His literary style was, therefore, self-taught, and he spent his life studying and writing. He moved to England as a young man and lived much of his life in a village in Hertfordshire in England. As a result, many of his works have a distinctly English feel. His plays are known both for their sharp wit and for their sense of outrage over unfairness in society and the absurdity of the British class system. He is the only person ever to have won both the Nobel Prize and an Oscar (for *Pygmalion*).

William Butler Yeats was born in Sandy Mount outside Dublin in 1865, and attended the Metropolitan School of Art in Dublin, but his poetry and prose were heavily inspired by County Sligo, where he spent much of his time (and where he is buried, in **Drumcliffe** churchyard, p. 227). One of the leading figures of the Irish literary revival in the early 20th century, he won the Nobel Prize in 1923.

James Joyce was born in the Dublin suburb of Rathgar in 1882 and educated at Jesuit boarding schools, and later at Trinity College. He wrote vividly—and sometimes impenetrably—about Dublin, despite spending much of his life as an expat living nomadically in Europe. His controversial and hugely complex novels *Ulysses* and *Finnegan's Wake* are his most celebrated (and least understood) works. They and his collection of short stories, *Dubliners,* touch deeply on the character of the people of Dublin.

The poet and playwright **Samuel Beckett** was born in 1906 in the Dublin suburb of Foxrock and educated at Trinity College. His work, however, was heavily influenced by German and French postmodernists, and he spent much of his life abroad, even serving with the Resistance in France during World War II. Best known for his complex absurdist play *Waiting for Godot,* he won the Nobel Prize in 1969.

The controversial writer, erstwhile terrorist, and all-round bon vivant **Brendan Behan** was born in Dublin in 1923. Behan came by his revolutionary fervor honestly: His father fought in the Easter Rising and his mother was a close friend of Michael Collins. When he was 14, Behan joined Fianna Éireann, the youth organization of the IRA. An incompetent terrorist, he was arrested on his first solo mission to blow up England's Liverpool Docks when he was 16 years old. His autobiographical book, *Borstal Boy,* describes this period in his life in exquisite detail. His play *The Quare Fellow* made him an international literary star, and he would spend the rest of his life as a jolly, hopeless alcoholic, drinking his way through London, Dublin, and New York, better known for his quick wit and bons mots than for his plays.

Among modern Irish writers, the best known is arguably the poet **Seamus Heaney.** Born in 1939 near a small town called Castledawson in Northern Ireland, he won scholarships to boarding school in Derry and later to Queen's University in Belfast. His years studying ancient Greek and Latin literature and Anglo-Saxon writing heavily influenced his poetry, but all of his writing is marked by his life in the troubled region where he grew up. His works, including *The Cure at Troy* (based on the works of Sophocles), *The Haw Lantern, The Government of the Tongue,* and a modern translation of *Beowulf,* ultimately earned him the Nobel Prize in 1995. Heaney's death in the summer of 2013 brought an outpouring of affection from fans across the world.

reading LIST

If you want to know about Ireland and the Irish, plenty of talented writers in and out of the country are willing to tell you.

Jonathan Bardon's *A History of Ireland in 250 Episodes* is a good general introduction to Irish history. The book is broken up into 250 short chapters—learned without being too dense, and a very useful primer.

To understand more about the Famine, try the British author **Cecil Woodham-Smith's** *The Great Hunger*. Written in 1962, it's still viewed as the definitive, dispassionate examination of this dark period in Irish history.

The author **Tim Pat Coogan,** son of an IRA volunteer, has written two excellent books, *The Irish Civil War* (2001) and *The Troubles: Ireland's Ordeal 1966–1996* (1997), both of which are essential reading for anyone wanting to understand the complexities of 21st-century Ireland. He

also wrote a controversial biography, *Eamon de Valera,* criticizing the former Irish president's actions and legacy.

For a look at Ireland in recent history, try **John Ardagh's** *Ireland and the Irish* (1995) or **F. S. Lyons's** *Ireland Since the Famine* (1973).

The late Dublin-born journalist **Nuala O'Faolain** wrote two top-selling memoirs, *Are You Somebody?* (1996) and *Almost There* (2003), which give the reader an insider's view of living and growing up in modern Ireland.

The late Irish-born American writer **Frank McCourt** earned acclaim and won the Pulitzer Prize for *Angela's Ashes* (1996), his grim memoir of a childhood spent partly in Limerick and partly in Brooklyn. The book is very controversial in Ireland, however; many in Limerick claim it is not an accurate representation of the city during that time.

Other contemporary Irish writers include **Marian Keyes** (whose hugely popular novels include *Lucy Sullivan is Getting Married* and *This Charming Man*); **Roddy Doyle** (*The Commitments, Paddy Clarke Ha Ha Ha*), the late **Maeve Binchy** (*A Week in Winter, Circle of Friends*), and **Colm Tóibín** (*Brooklyn, Nora Webster*).

FILM Many controversial, complex, and difficult Irish subjects have been tackled by an international array of directors and actors.

The Commitments (directed by Alan Parker, 1991) may be the most famous Irish musical ever made. With its cast of young, largely inexperienced Irish actors playing musicians dedicated to American soul music, it's a delightful piece of filmmaking.

Michael Collins (directed by Neil Jordan, 1996) is a fine biopic about the Irish rebel, filmed largely on location and starring the Irish actor Liam Neeson.

Veronica Guerin (directed by Joel Schumacher, 2003) is a dark, fact-based film (with the Australian actress Cate Blanchett doing an excellent Irish accent) about a troubled Irish investigative reporter on the trail of a drug boss.

Intermission (directed by Jim Crowley, 2003) is a lively urban romance filmed on location in Dublin, featuring the Irish actor Colin Farrell (talking in his real accent for a change). A great look at Dublin in the middle of its economic boom.

The Wind that Shakes the Barley (directed by Ken Loach, 2006), with a mostly Irish cast and English director, won the Palme d'Or at Cannes for its depiction of Ireland's early-20th-century fight for independence.

Once (directed by John Carney, 2007) is a touching, Oscar-nominated portrait of two struggling young musicians—an Irish singer (played by the Irish actor/musician Glen Hansard) and a Czech piano player trying to make it big in Dublin. The film was subsequently turned into a hit stage musical.

The controversial drama ***Calvary*** (directed by John Michael McDonagh, 2014) is about a small-town priest who receives a death threat from one of his parishioners, leading him to discover dark truths about his community.

Brooklyn (directed by John Crowley, 2015) is an incredibly touching drama about a young Irish woman who emigrates to New York in the 1950s. The film, adapted from Colm Tóibín's novel, was nominated for a Best Picture Oscar.

MUSIC   Music is inescapable in Ireland, and if you hear a band play in a bar and you like them, we strongly advise you to buy a CD from them.

In the days of Internet radio, the best way to discover new sounds is to tune in to Irish radio stations online. Links to stations that stream live can be found at **www.radiofeeds.co.uk/irish.asp**. Good places to start are stations run by **RTÉ,** the national broadcaster, particularly the music and entertainment-oriented **2FM** (www.rte.ie/2fm); **Today FM** (www.todayfm.com), a national station that's extremely popular with a young demographic; and **TXFM** (www.txfm.ie), a Dublin-based station that specializes in the latest indie and alternative sounds.

Some cool, quintessentially Irish names to check out: **Damien Rice,** who has risen to huge chart success over the past decade; **Lisa Hannigan,** a singer-songwriter with a line in infectiously romantic indie-pop; **Hozier,** a singer-songwriter from County Wicklow who began to make waves globally in 2014; Cork-based electro-pop duo **Young Wonder,** who mix brash big beats with beautiful vocals; and **Soak,** an absurdly talented young Derry native who has wowed the music world with her simple but enchantingly beautiful ballads.

Traditional music is still alive and well in Ireland, particularly in close association with Irish step dancing. The folk culture is primarily found outside of Dublin, although some pubs in the city do still showcase traditional music. The coastal village of **Doolin,** in County Clare (see p. 188), is well known for its concentration of pubs featuring traditional Irish music, but the city of **Cork** also has a number of lively music pubs (see p. 133), as does the town of Ballyshannon in County Donegal. Local pubs in small towns almost always can be counted on to host Irish music and sometimes dancing, too.

EATING & DRINKING IN IRELAND

Restaurants

Restaurants in Ireland have become surprisingly expensive in recent years, and even with the economic crash, the cost of eating out here is still well above the European average. On the plus side, Ireland's restaurants are varied and interesting—settings range from old-world hotel dining rooms, country mansions, and castles to sky-lit terraces, shop-front bistros, riverside cottages, thatched-roof pubs, and converted houses. Lately, appreciation has grown for creative cooking here, with an emphasis on locally grown produce and meat.

Before you book a table, here are a few things you should know.

RESERVATIONS   Except for self-service eateries, informal cafes, and some popular seafood spots, most restaurants encourage reservations; most expensive restaurants require them. In the most popular places, Friday and Saturday nights are often booked up a week or more in advance, so have a few options in mind if you're booking at the last minute.

PRICES   Meal prices at restaurants include national sales taxes (universally referred to as "VAT," which stands for Value Added Tax), at the rate of 13.5% in the Republic of Ireland and 20% in Northern Ireland.

TIPPING   Many restaurants include the tip as a 10% to 15% service charge added automatically to the bill (it's usually listed at the bottom, just before the bill's total). When no service charge is added, tip around 12% or so, depending on the quality of the service. But do check your bill, as some unscrupulous restaurants do not make the service charge obvious, hoping you'll tip twice.

Pubs

The pub continues to be a mainstay of Irish social life. Every city, town, and hamlet has a pub. Most people have a "local"—a favorite pub near home—where they go for a drink and some conversation with neighbors, family, and friends. Pubs are more about socializing than drinking; many people you see in the pub are just having a soft drink.

PUB FOOD   Pub food is usually a lot better than its name suggests; the menu likely will include a mix of sandwiches and traditional Irish food, including stews and meat pies. In recent years, many pubs have converted or expanded into restaurants, serving excellent, unpretentious meals at (somewhat) reasonable prices. Check the menu before you sit down at a table (most places post them by their doors).

PUB HOURS   Pubs in the Republic set their own hours, although closing times are bound by the type of alcohol license they have. Those with a regular license must shut by 11:30pm, or 12:30am on Saturday; those with late licenses can stay open until 2:30am, or 2am on Sunday. Northern Ireland is governed by different laws: On Friday and Saturday nights, many pubs stay open until midnight or 1am, a few even later, particularly in large towns and cities.

"Closing time" is actually the time when the barmen must stop serving alcohol, so expect to hear a shout for "Last orders!" or, occasionally, the marvelous if antiquated "Time, gentlemen, please!" Anyone who wants to order his or her last drink does so at that point. The pubs don't actually shut their doors for another 20 to 30 minutes. When the time comes to really close, bartenders shout "Time to leave!" lights are turned up, and people make their way to the doors.

SUGGESTED ITINERARIES

I reland is such a small island that you can cover a lot of ground in a week and feel quite at home within two. Even with the best of intentions and all the energy in the world, you'll never see it all on a short visit. However, with a few long days and a savvy attitude, it is possible to see a sizable chunk of the island in just a week. The suggested itineraries over the next few pages will help you get the most out of this extraordinary and varied country—no matter how long you have to see it.

HOW TO SEE IRELAND

Let's get one thing straight: You don't *have* to rent a car to see Ireland. If you want to see some of the major towns and cities, and those parts of the countryside that can easily be reached on tours or public transport, then don't bother renting a car. However, if your ideal Ireland involves wandering through the countryside, visiting small villages, climbing castle walls, hailing history from a ruined abbey, or finding yourself alone on a rocky beach—you effectively cannot do those things independently without a car. Out of the main towns, public transportation exists, but it's slow and limiting. Every major town has car-rental agencies, if you decide to explore by car.

Just remember: They drive on the *left*.

The next step is deciding **where to start.** If you're flying into Shannon Airport, then it makes sense to start out on the west coast. If you're flying into Dublin, you might as well explore that city first, then either head up to the North and the ruggedly beautiful Antrim Coast, or south down to the Wicklow Mountains, Kilkenny, and the rolling green hills of Wexford and Waterford. Still, if you fly into Dublin but your heart is in Galway, no worries: You can easily traverse the width of the country in a few hours (once you get out of Dublin's stultifying sprawl).

So taking all of these factors into consideration, the question remains: **What do you most want to see?** We can't answer that question for you, but we can give you some themed itineraries that we have used ourselves. All of these tours (bar one) assume you have a week to see the country. Where there's potential for a longer trip, we've given suggestions for extending your stay. Pick and choose what appeals to you, add in your own favorite shopping or scenic drives, and turn it all into a custom-made holiday.

THE REGIONS IN BRIEF

The island of Ireland is divided into two political units: the **Republic of Ireland,** which makes up the vast majority of the country, and **Northern Ireland,** which along with England, Scotland, and Wales is part of the United Kingdom. Of Ireland's 32 counties, all but 6 are in the Republic.

The ancient Gaelic regions that once divided Ireland are still used in conversation and directions: Ulster is north; Munster is south; Leinster is east; and Connaught is west. Each region is divided into counties:

> **In Ulster** (to the north)   Cavan, Donegal, and Monaghan in the Republic; Antrim, Armagh, Derry, Down, Fermanagh, and Tyrone in Northern Ireland
>
> **In Munster** (to the south)   Clare, Cork, Kerry, Limerick, Tipperary, and Waterford
>
> **In Leinster** (to the east)   Dublin, Carlow, Kildare, Kilkenny, Laois, Longford, Louth, Meath, Offaly, Westmeath, Wexford, and Wicklow
>
> **In Connaught** (to the west)   Sligo, Mayo, Galway, Roscommon, and Leitrim

DUBLIN & ENVIRONS   With 40% of the Republic's population living within 97km (60 miles) of Dublin, the capital is the center of the profound, high-speed changes that have transformed Ireland into a prosperous and increasingly European country. Within an hour's drive of Dublin are Dalkey, Dún Laoghaire, and many more engaging coastal towns, as well as the rural beauty of the Wicklow Mountains and the prehistoric ruins in County Meath.

THE SOUTHEAST   The southeast offers sandy beaches, Wexford's lush and mountainous countryside, Waterford's famous crystal factory, Kilkenny and Cahir's ancient castles, the Rock of Cashel, and the Irish National Heritage Park at Ferrycarrig.

CORK & ENVIRONS   Cork, Ireland's second-largest city, is a buzzy university town and a congenial gateway to the south and west of the island. Within arm's reach are Blarney Castle (and its famous stone), the culinary and scenic delights of Kinsale, the Drombeg Stone Circle, Cape Clear Island, and Mizen Head.

THE SOUTHWEST   The once remote splendor of County Kerry has long ceased to be a secret, so at least during the high season, be prepared to share the view. The Ring of Kerry encircling the Iveragh Peninsula is the most visited attraction in Ireland after the Book of Kells. (That's both a recommendation and a warning.) Other highlights include the rugged Dingle Peninsula and two sets of islands with intriguing histories: the Skelligs and the Blaskets.

THE WEST   The west of Ireland offers a first taste of Ireland's wild beauty and striking diversity. County Clare has an array of impressive castles— Knappogue, Bunratty, and (just over the county line in Galway) Dunguaire— and unforgettable natural offerings, particularly the unique landscapes of the Burren.

GALWAY & ENVIRONS   Galway Town is busy, colorful, and funky—a youthful, prospering port and university city and the self-proclaimed arts capital of Ireland with theater, music, dance, and an exciting street life. County Galway is the gateway to Connemara's moody, magical landscapes, while offshore lie the mysterious, desolate Aran Islands, Inishmore, Inishmaan, and Inisheer.

THE NORTHWEST   Farther up the west coast to the north, County Mayo is the home of the sweet town of Westport on Clew Bay. Achill Island (accessible by car) has beaches and stunning cliff views. County Sligo inspired the poetry of W. B. Yeats with its many megalithic sites such as the stone circles, passage tombs, dolmens, and cairns at Carrowmore, Knocknarea, and Carrowkeel.

NORTHERN IRELAND   Across the border, Northern Ireland's six counties are still one of the less touristed parts of the island. Here you'll find the stunning Antrim Coast, the extraordinary basalt columns of the Giant's Causeway, and the Glens of Antrim. The old city walls of Derry and Belfast's elaborate political murals make a trip across the border well worthwhile.

THE BEST OF IRELAND IN 1 WEEK

There's something terribly romantic about flying into Dublin. The compact, laid-back city awaits a few miles down the road, packed with old-fashioned pubs, modern restaurants, and absorbing sights all laid out for walking. If you've never been here, a couple of days in Dublin make for a quick primer on Ireland. It's just enough time to do some shopping on **Grafton Street,** head up O'Connell Street to the **General Post Office,** and discover the Georgian beauty of **St. Stephen's Green** and **Merrion Square.** You can give the surface of the city a good brush in a couple of days, and then head south to **Kilkenny** and **Wicklow,** on to **Waterford, Cork,** and **Kerry,** and up to **Clare** for a quick glance before the clock runs out. It is only hitting the high points but, as high points go, they're hard to beat.

Days 1 & 2: Arrive in Dublin

If you're arriving from North America, you start with an advantage: Most flights arrive early in the morning, which effectively gives you an extra day's sightseeing. Check into your hotel, say yes to any tea and scones offered, take a minute to relax, and then head out on foot. Get a map from your concierge and just start walking.

Stay south of the River Liffey and head down Dame Street to **Dublin Castle** (p. 82), home of the magical **Chester Beatty Library** (p. 59) with its vast collection of gorgeous illuminated manuscripts. Later, take in **St. Patrick's Cathedral** (p. 75) and the vibrant green quadrangles of **Trinity College** (p. 75), before heading down to Merrion Square, with its handsome granite architecture and two of the main sites of Ireland's **National Museum** (a third is on the city's west side). The **Archaeology** museum has an extraordinary hoard of ancient gold, while the recently refurbished **Natural History** building contains an array of objects from the ancient past. It's a short stroll from here down to **St. Stephen's Green,** where you can rest your feet and enjoy the floral view. Then stroll up **Grafton Street** for some shopping before collapsing in your hotel.

On **Day 2,** have a hearty breakfast in your hotel before striking out for the trendy cultural hub of **Temple Bar.** Stroll north to the river, then take a right and walk along the noisy, vibrant waterfront to the landmark arc of the **Ha'penny Bridge.** Walk across and head east on **O'Connell Street,** where you can walk past its many statues to the bullet-ridden columns of the **General Post Office** (p. 84), site of the 1916 Easter Rising. After exploring its displays, head farther up O'Connell Street to the **Dublin Writers Museum** (p. 72), which bookish types love for its extensive display of memorabilia. Let someone else do the work in the evening, either on a walking tour—such as the **Irish Music Pub Crawl** (p. 83), perhaps—or some good-natured scares aboard the **Dublin Ghost Bus** (p. 85) or **Castle Dracula** (p. 93). Those in search of less organized fun may prefer the atmospheric **Evening of Food, Folklore & Fairies** (p. 91)

Day 3: South to Wicklow & Kilkenny

It takes less than 2 hours to drive from the hustle and traffic of Dublin to the peace and quiet of the **Wicklow Mountains** (p. 109). Drive through the town of Enniskerry to the great estate of **Powerscourt** (p. 107) on the south end of the village. After lunching in its Avoca Café, head on to **Glendalough** (p. 106) and feel your soul relax in the pastoral mountain setting of this ancient monastic retreat. From there, drive on to the colorful village of **Kilkenny** where you can spend the rest of the day shopping in its pottery and crafts shops and exploring noble **Kilkenny Castle** (p. 125). This is a good place to spend your first night outside of Dublin.

Day 4: West to Waterford & Cork

Waterford, Ireland's oldest city, is less than an hour south of Kilkenny, so you'll be able to get there with plenty of time to fit in a half day's sightseeing. Have a quick look around some or all of the **Waterford Treasures** museums (p. 118), before dropping in for a tour of the **House of Waterford Crystal.** After lunch, you have a choice—either head to **Cork** (p. 137), Ireland's busy second city, or **Kinsale** (p. 140), a smaller, quieter harbor town. Both have plenty to keep you busy for the rest of the day and make a good base for the night. But they're very different places, so it depends if you want a bustling or peaceful experience.

Days 5 & 6: The Ring of Kerry

If you're not allergic to touristy things, you could stop at **Blarney Castle** (p. 137) on your way out of Cork in the morning; otherwise, on to County Kerry at the southwest tip of the island. Here, the most popular place to explore—and one of the busiest tourist spots in Ireland—is the **Ring of Kerry** (see "The Ring of Kerry" in chapter 8). It is a beautiful drive, but crowded with tourist buses. If you brave the masses, you'll see extraordinary countryside filled with historic sites and tiny villages.

If it's quiet you're after, head for the short section of the Ring that runs from lovely **Kenmare** (p. 166) to the bucolic peace of **Killarney National Park** (p. 162). Here you can indulge in a buggy ride around the lake.

Day 7: County Clare

Time is short now, so you'll only get a taste of County Clare. (Make yourself a promise to return.) Head for the perilously tall (and way too popular) **Cliffs of Moher** (p. 186), where the view seems to stretch all the way to America. Then you've a choice: Spend the rest of the day exploring **Bunratty Castle** (p. 185)—where medieval fortress meets historical theme park—or marveling at the otherworldly landscape of the **Burren** (see chapter 9), with the R480 road winding its way through the extraordinary limestone landscape. What a way to end your trip!

THE BEST OF IRELAND IN 2 WEEKS

With 2 weeks, your visit to Ireland will be much more relaxed. You can stretch out a bit more in your travels, heading to less crowded counties with more time to meet the locals. In your second week, head up to Galway, Mayo, and Donegal, taking time to smell the heather along the way.

Days 1–7

Follow "The Best of Ireland in 1 Week" itinerary, as outlined above.

Day 8: The Burren

After spending **Day 7** exploring Clare, you'll discover that you need more time to really get the most out of this big, varied place. If you didn't make it to the Burren, spend most of your day here. Otherwise, you could visit another of the county's great medieval buildings such as **Knappogue Castle** (p. 189) or the exquisite ruins of **Corcomroe Abbey** (p. 187). In a different vein, lovers of live music will want to spend the evening in **Doolin** (p. 188). It's one of the very best places in the country to catch proper traditional music.

Days 9 & 10: County Galway

Start the day with a drive up from Clare to Galway City (it will take around an hour). You could spend a relaxing day walking the delightful streets of this artsy, vibrant town, take a cruise out to the misty **Aran Islands** (see "The Aran Islands," p. 207), or, if you've got kids to keep amused, take them to the fabulous **Galway Atlantaquaria** (p. 206). Use the following day to explore **Connemara National Park** (p. 210). If it's time to get out from behind the wheel, you can see this lovely park by horseback (see p. 211). You could either head back to Galway City for a second night or pick a B&B in the countryside.

Day 11: County Mayo

Drive up from Galway through the spectacular scenery of Mayo, where the rocky shoreline plunges into the cobalt sea. Head to the south Mayo town of **Westport,** a delightful, peaceful place to wander. Depending on whether or not you have a family to entertain, you could either spend a couple of hours at **Westport House and Pirate Adventure Park** (p. 224) or visit the **National Museum of Ireland: Country Life** (p. 224) near Castlebar. Ancient history buffs may want to press ahead to County Sligo at this point (see below), but if it's a quiet retreat you're after, drive across the strangely empty flatlands to **Achill Island** (p. 225). The route along the coast and across the bridge to the island is slow and windy, but the views are fantastic. If you do make it out to Achill, consider an overnight stay at the **Bervie** (p. 214), where the sea is right outside the door.

Day 12: County Sligo

Depending on where you based yourself for the night, you may be in for a long drive, so start early. **Sligo Town** (p. 226) has a few worthwhile attractions, but mostly it will be useful as a stop for lunch. The real reason to come this far lies in the surrounding countryside. There is an astonishing concentration of ancient burial sites here, including **Carrowkeel** and **Carrowmore,** which contains the world's oldest piece of freestanding architecture. Our favorite place to stay the night in these parts is the extraordinary **Temple House** (p. 218).

Day 13: Belfast

The day begins with a long drive across country, but your reward is Ireland's second-largest city—Belfast, the vibrant capital of Northern Ireland. Recover from the drive with a hearty lunch at one of the city's many fine pubs, before taking a whistle-stop tour of what this energetic town has to offer: the gleaming new *Titanic* **Belfast** (p. 244) and the other attractions around the marvelously regenerated docklands; the **Ulster Museum** (p. 245), or maybe just a no-pressure browse around **St. George's Market** (p. 249). In the evening, be sure to drop in for a pint at what may very well be Ireland's most handsome pub—the beautiful **Crown Liquor Saloon** (p. 243).

Day 14: Heading Home

If you've managed to book yourself a flight home from Belfast, well done! Your day just got a whole lot easier. Rise early and spend the morning hearing about the city's fascinating recent past on one of the excellent **Black Taxi Tours** (p. 243). If you need to head back to Dublin for an evening flight, the drive should only take a couple of hours—so you might just be able to squeeze in some last-minute sightseeing on the way. Some of Ireland's finest ancient sites, such as **Newgrange** (p. 104) and **Knowth** (p. 104), lie just north of the capital—virtually en route to the airport!

IRELAND FOR FREE OR DIRT CHEAP

Ireland is no longer a cheap country to visit—and hasn't been for some time. The economic crash of the late 2000s and early 2010s drove prices down a bit, but hotels and restaurants are still pricey. Still, here's the good news: You can visit a lot of great sites for free in Ireland, including some of the country's biggest tourist attractions. You can also save a lot of money by sticking mainly to places that can be reached by public transport, thus eliminating the need to rent a car (every place we list is easily accessible by train or bus). You'd be surprised how much of Ireland you can see without blowing the budget. We're starting this tour in Northern Ireland (maybe you got a great deal on a flight to Belfast!), because it's one of the more budget-friendly regions. For more information on train and bus timetables, see **www.irishrail.ie** and **www. buseireann.ie**.

Day 1: Belfast

Belfast is rich with free attractions—here are just a few. The excellent **Ulster Museum** (p. 245) displays artifacts from across 9,000 years of Irish history. Right next door is the **Belfast Botanic Gardens & Palm House** (p. 242), and it's only a short walk from the campus of **Queen's University** (p. 248). **Belfast City Hall** (p. 247) runs free guided tours. Another exceptional Victorian landmark, **Belfast Cathedral** (p. 246), is also free, as is **Cave Hill Country Park** (p. 247), a tranquil place with good walking trails and incredible views of the city. Last but not least, because Belfast is still most famous for the sectarian strife of the mid- to late-20th century, a highlight of your visit may be to view the political murals remaining in the epicenter of the conflict, the Falls and Shankill roads areas (p. 242). These neighborhoods are now safe for visitors to explore, and the street art is all free. To get the most out of them, however, you may want to spend some of that cash you've saved so far on a **Black Taxi Tour** (p. 243).

Catch a train from Belfast to Dublin (Connolly Station). Time: 2 hr. 10 min. Fares start at about €22 for adults.

Days 2 & 3: Dublin

Ireland's capital is also the number one destination in the country for free sites. The **Chester Beatty Library** (p. 69) is, for our money, one of the best museums in Europe. The collection of illuminated gospels and early copies of the Bible, Torah, and Koran would justify a steep entrance fee, but it won't cost you a cent. Three of the four separate museums constituting the **National Museum of Ireland** are in Dublin—**Archaeology, Natural History,** and **Decorative Arts and History**—and all are free. Each contains some incredible treasures, and collectively they have enough to keep you occupied for a day or more. All of Dublin's best major art galleries are free, including the **National Gallery of Ireland** (p. 73), the **Irish Museum of Modern Art** (p. 78), the **Temple Bar Gallery** (p. 80), and the excellent **Hugh Lane Gallery** (p. 72). Many of Dublin's most historic public buildings don't charge admission. **Áras an Uachtaráin** (the Irish President's House, p. 72) is free, though accessible only by tour on a first-come, first-served basis; the queue forms at the visitor center in Phoenix Park. The **Bank of Ireland/Parliament House** (p. 86) and the **Four Courts** (p. 83) are also free. The **General Post Office** on O'Connell Street (p. 84) is still a working post office but has a small number of exhibits devoted to the Easter Rising, including the original Declaration of Independence. Add to this the great public spaces such as **Phoenix Park** (p. 87), **St. Stephen's Green** (p. 87), and **Trinity College** (p. 76), and you'll see it's possible to spend a full 2 days here without spending a penny on sightseeing.

Catch a train from Dublin (Heuston Station) to Galway. Time: 2 hr. 40 min. Fares start at about €33 for adults.

Day 4: Galway

Ireland's artsy, seductive west coast city offers plenty of free pursuits. The **Galway Arts Centre** (p. 205) usually has good exhibitions, and you can often score cheap tickets for performances. The **Galway City Museum** (p. 206) makes for a stellar introduction to the region, with its fine collection of artifacts from the medieval period onward. **St. Nicholas' Collegiate Church** (p. 209), the oldest church in the city, contains a 12th-century crusader's tomb and other extraordinary historic pieces. Make sure you devote some time to just wandering the streets of this eminently walkable town; its central medieval district is a tiny, tangled area featuring plenty of photogenic corners.

Catch a bus from Galway Bus Station to Cork (Parnell Place Bus Station). Time: 3½ hr. with one change, or 4 hr. 20 min. direct. Fares start at about €27 for adults.

Day 5: Galway to Cork

Busy, youthful Cork City doesn't have a great deal of free historic attractions, but if you're up for a large dose of culture, you'll find plenty to do

SAVING MONEY ON trains & buses

The cost of rail travel can quickly mount up, but there are ways to save money. Whenever you can, *book in advance*. The example fares listed in this itinerary are all pre-booked; walk-up fares can be higher. The downside for booking that way is that you have to specify times of travel—but Irish Rail has a handy policy of letting you upgrade a pre-booked ticket into something more flexible for just €10.

If you're going to be spending a lot of time on public transportation, you should also strongly consider buying a money-saving pass. **Eurail Pass** is good for travel on Irish Rail trains, Expressway coaches, and the Irish Continental Lines ferries between France and Ireland. They cost around €129 for a 3-day pass and €177 for a 5-day pass. (Days can be non-consecutive, so long as they're all used within a month.) Youth passes (ages 16–25), family, and first-class passes are also available. The passes are valid throughout Ireland (including Northern Ireland). For further details, or for purchase, visit www.eurail.com.

This can add up to significant savings, but there are a couple bits of small print to note. First, it's still advisable to make seat reservations to guarantee a space—this may cost a few extra euros each time in booking fees. Also, not everybody can buy a pass. E.U. citizens aren't allowed to buy Eurail passes.

Eurail passes can also be purchased from **Railpass** (www.railpass.com), **STA Travel** (www.sta.com; *℃* **800/781-4040** in the U.S.), and other travel agents.

without paying a cent. Start with a trip to the **Old English Market** (p. 139) for a browse and a cheap lunch. Afterward, head to the **Crawford Art Gallery** (p. 139)—it's one of the very best in Ireland and completely free. More excellent free art is to be found at the **Lewis Glucksman Gallery** (p. 140) on the campus of **University College Cork.** In the evening, check out a few of Cork's exceptional pubs, which are among the best in the country for traditional music (see "A Tuneful Pint" on p. 133).

Catch a train from Cork to Killarney. Most change at Mallow. Time: 1 hr. 20 min. direct, or 2 hr. with change. Fares start at about €29 for adults.

Day 6: Cork to Killarney

It's not exactly difficult to reach **Killarney National Park** (p. 162) from Killarney town; you just walk toward the cathedral and turn left. This 65-sq.-km (25-sq.-mile) expanse of forest, lakes, and mountains is crisscrossed with several well-conceived nature trails, plus more challenging routes for serious hikers. Formerly the grounds of a great mansion, the **Knockreer Estate** (p. 164) still has lovely gardens and beautiful views. Free sites in Killarney Town itself include the rather grand neo-Gothic **St. Mary's Cathedral.**

Catch a train from Killarney to Dublin—again, nearly all change at Mallow. Time: 3½ hr. Fares start at about €44 for adults.

Day 7: Homeward Bound . . .

Assuming your airline will let you fly out of Dublin, an early-ish train back to the capital should allow you some time to pick up any of the free sites you didn't manage to cover earlier in the tour. Otherwise, you'll have to catch a train straight from Killarney to Belfast for your flight home (about 7½ hr. with up to three changes; fares from Killarney start at about €38 adults). And that's it! You've done a fair bit of Ireland without breaking the bank. Pick your accommodations early and wisely to save the most. There are plenty of inexpensive B&Bs listed in this book for all of these cities. Your other main expense will be rail fares, but there are ways to save money on those too (see "Saving Money on Trains & Buses" on p. 35).

IRELAND FOR FAMILIES

Traveling with children is always a bit of an adventure, and you'll want all the help you can get. Luckily, Ireland—with its vast open countryside, farm hotels, and castles—is a fairy-tale playground for kids. You may have trouble finding babysitters outside major towns, so just take the kids with you. Most restaurants, sights, and even pubs (during the day) welcome children. The best part of the country for those traveling with kids is arguably Cork and Kerry, where everything seems to be set up for families. Here's a sample itinerary to give you some ideas.

Days 1 & 2: Dublin

The sprawling greens of **Phoenix Park** (p. 87) are a great place for little ones to let off steam (it's the best place in the city for a picnic too, if the weather's good). Within the park, **Dublin Zoo** (p. 86) is designed to cater to the younger ones (you can take a train ride around the zoo, for instance). Inquisitive young minds will be inspired by the cabinets of curiosity at the **National Museum of Ireland: Natural History** (p. 75), and have their interest piqued by **Number Twenty-Nine: Georgian House Museum** (p. 79), a house which has been kept exactly as it would have been at the turn of the 19th century. The guides at another museum, the **Little Museum of Dublin** (p. 78), do a great job of putting the ordinary lives of Dubliners in the last hundred years into context for younger visitors—or if that's a bit too much like real learning, there's the nearby **National Wax Museum Plus** (p. 79). If your kids want something a little flashier, try a **Viking Splash Tour** (p. 85), a historical whirl around the city in a World War II amphibious vehicle, complete with headlong splash into the River Liffey. Kids with a high threshold for the ghoulish may get a kick out of the creepy crypts at **St. Michan's Church** (p. 81); if that's too scary, even younger kids are all but guaranteed to love an evening aboard the **Dublin Ghost Bus** (p. 85).

Day 2: County Cork

Okay, so it's not exactly untouched by the tourism fairy, but kids find plenty to love about **Blarney Castle** (p. 137), just outside Cork City. They can kiss the famous stone if they don't mind an attendant holding them upside down. A few miles away, the **Fota Island & Wildlife Park** is a well-designed zoo where the docile animals (those that don't bite, kick, or stomp) roam among the visitors.

Days 3 & 4: County Kerry

Kerry is probably Ireland's most kid-friendly county, so there's enough to keep you busy here for at least a couple of days. On the Dingle Peninsula, Fungie, star of the **Dingle Dolphin Boat Tours** (p. 172), has been entertaining kids and grown-ups alike for the last 30 years. On the Iveragh Peninsula, Kenmare's **Seafari** cruises and seal-watching trips (p. 167) teach kids about conservation issues by putting them in touch with the underwater residents of Kenmare Bay. **Blueberry Hill Farm** (p. 169), in Sneem, is a working, old-fashioned farmstead where kids can help milk cows, make butter, and take part in a treasure hunt. Meanwhile, an underground tour of the atmospheric **Crag Cave** (p. 175) is a surefire winner, with the added bonus of its Crazy Cave adventure playground. And don't overlook what **Killarney National Park** (p. 162) has to offer little ones— what could be better than a ride around the mountains and lakes in an old-fashioned horse-drawn "jarvey"?

Day 6: Bunratty Folk Park

You could spend most of the day at **Bunratty Castle & Folk Park** (p. 185), an attraction that combines one of Ireland's best medieval castles with a living history museum. It's a brilliant recreation of a 19th-century village, complete with costumed actors strolling down the street, chatting to passers-by, and even working in the shops. Bunratty is also the setting for a hugely popular **Medieval Banquet.** It's raucous, but surprisingly good fun; book an early evening sitting to suit young bedtimes.

Day 7: Heading Home

If you have time before the drive back to the airport, head into the **Burren** (see chapter 9). Young imaginations will be fired up by the dolmens and other ancient sites that litter the otherworldly landscape. It's also where you'll find the **Burren Birds of Prey Centre** at Aillwee Cave (p. 184), a working aviary with buzzards, falcons, eagles, and owls in flight.

Beyond a Week . . .

If your trip extends beyond a week, there are plenty of standout attractions for kids to be found farther north.

The Atlantaquaria (p. 206), just outside **Galway City,** is a new, state-of-the-art aquarium, while pony trekking across Connemara National Park (p. 211) is a unique way to see this beautiful, windswept landscape. In **Mayo,** Westport

House and Pirate Adventure Park (p. 224) has all the components necessary for high-activity fun; young girls in particular will enjoy learning all about the region's real-life pirate hero, Grace O'Malley (see p. 223).

If you're going as far as **Belfast,** the attractions around the new Titanic Quarter hold plenty of youthful appeal. Try the hands-on science center, **W5** (p. 248), and the state-of-the-art *Titanic* **Belfast** museum (p. 244). And the nearby **Antrim Coast Drive** (see p. 256) has two highlights that children will adore: the perilous (but fun) Carrick-a-Rede Rope Bridge (p. 257) and the awe-inspiring alien shapes of the Giant's Causeway (p. 258).

3 | IRELAND OFF THE BEATEN PATH

We start this tour in Belfast, a city in the middle of an immense transformation since the 1998 Good Friday Agreement that finally established a detente in Northern Ireland. Tourism has steadily increased in this region over the last decade, but the crowds still have yet to arrive en masse. If the best sites of the Antrim Coast were in County Cork or Kerry, they'd be overrun with tourists; as it is, one can still visit a spectacular setting such as the Giant's Causeway and find oneself alone with nature. This tour then heads west to take in a couple of Sligo's prehistoric sites and continues south for a visit to Achill Island, a peaceful retreat off the coast of County Mayo.

Days 1 & 2: Belfast

Northern Ireland's capital—and the Irish island's second largest city—is a historic, vibrant town. Start with a visit to the **Ulster Museum** (p. 245) and experience some of the city's more recent past firsthand with a **Black Taxi Tour** (p. 243). The new museums in the Titanic Quarter, such as the immense *Titanic* **Belfast** (p. 244), provide a more high-tech dose of history; alternatively, you could immerse yourself in the city's present by exploring its busy shopping districts. The **Belfast Botanic Gardens & Palm's House** (p. 242) and **Queen's University** (p. 248) are also worth a look. Round off the day with a pint at one of Belfast's extraordinarily pretty pubs like the **Crown Liquor Saloon** (p. 243) and a meal at one of the small but growing number of world-class restaurants.

Day 3: County Antrim

One of the North's loveliest counties, Antrim is home to two gorgeous parks: the **Castlewellan Forest Park** (p. 250) with formal gardens and gorgeous woodland walks, and the **Tollymore Forest Park** (p. 252) with beautiful walks and even more incredible views.

Alternatively, the Antrim coast road is one of Ireland's great coastal drives—and one of the least spoiled. Fewer tourists venture this far north; those who do will reap spectacular rewards. Start in **Carrickfergus,** with a brief stop to look around its medieval castle (p. 249), before heading north along the coast road. For the best views, take the **Torr Head Scenic Road** (p. 259) located just after the village of **Cushendun** (p. 257). From up here on a clear day, you can see all the way to the Mull of Kintyre in Scotland. The Antrim coast's most remarkable asset is the **Giant's Causeway** (p. 258), an uncanny natural rock formation comprised of thousands of tightly packed basalt columns. You could do the drive in about 2 hours, but you'll want to allow considerably longer than that to give yourself time to stop along the way. There are places along the coast to spend the night, or you could go straight on into **Derry.** It's about another hour on from the Giant's Causeway.

Day 4: Derry to Sligo

Straddling the border between Northern Ireland and the Republic, this vibrant town was synonymous with political strife. Although it's peaceful these days, it's still a divided place—the residents can't even agree on what to call it. Road signs from the Republic point to Derry; those in the North point to Londonderry. How can a place like that not be full of character and history? Check out the award-winning **Tower Museum** (p. 264) and the Gothic, 17th-century **Cathedral of St. Columb** (p. 264) before recharging for a long drive to County Sligo in the afternoon.

Day 5: County Sligo

Nestled within the gentle, verdant hills of this underrated county are some dramatic archaeological sites. Within a short drive from Sligo Town are two of the most incredible: **Carrowkeel Passage Tomb Cemetery** (p. 226) packed with 14 cairns, dolmens, and stone circles, and the impossibly ancient **Carrowmore Megalithic Cemetery** (p. 226). Here's a thought to ponder while clambering around the latter: The innocuously named tomb 52A is thought to be 7,400 years old, making it the earliest known piece of freestanding stone architecture in the world.

Day 6: Sligo to Achill Island

This is a wild and beautiful place of unspoiled beaches and spectacular scenery. But you'll also find a handful of excellent little hotels and B&Bs, mostly in the vicinity of **Keel,** the island's most attractive village. This is also major outdoor sports territory, as the constant wind off the Atlantic Ocean is ideal for windsurfing, hang gliding, and any other sport that depends on a breeze. One of the best (and least known) discoveries on Achill Island is a deserted village on the slopes of **Mount Slievemore** (p. 225). Not too many people venture up there, making it an even more extraordinary and moving place to visit.

Day 7: Achill Island to Shannon

It's a long drive to whichever airport you're flying home from, but a flight out of Shannon will give you the most spectacular route. If you can extend your trip a little, **Clare Island** (p. 224) is a lovely place to spend a day. Even more peaceful and isolated than its near neighbor, Achill, Clare's permanent population amounts to just 150 people, and you can go a long way without bumping into any of them.

DUBLIN

For such an ancient town, Dublin is doing a pretty good job of not showing its age. Despite its stony gray appearance, the Irish capital is actually one of Europe's most youthful cities, with the average age of its population somewhere around 36 years old. It's growing rapidly, too—a full 50% more people now call Dublin home than did in the year 2000, and almost a third of Ireland's entire population now lives in the greater Dublin area. This is by far Ireland's most cosmopolitan city, and its most diverse; at times it feels more like a modern European city than it does the Irish capital. Edgy bars and cafes buzz alongside pubs that have stood for centuries, and chic boutiques are snuggled into the medieval precincts of the old city. It's yours to discover afresh—and even if you think you know what to expect, you're almost certain to be surprised by what you find.

4

ESSENTIALS

Arriving

BY PLANE   Aer Lingus (www.aerlingus.com; ℂ **081/836-5000**), Ireland's national airline, operates regular, direct, scheduled flights between Dublin International Airport and numerous cities worldwide. Direct routes from the United States include Boston, Chicago (O'Hare), New York (JFK), Orlando, and San Francisco. **American Airlines** (www.aa.com; ℂ **1800/433-7300**), **Delta** (www.delta.com; ℂ **800/241-4141**), and **United** (www.united.com; ℂ **1800/864-8331**) all fly direct to Dublin from at least one of those same cities. From Canada, direct flights are operated by **Air Canada** (www.aircanada.com; ℂ **1888/247-2262**). From Australia, **Qantas** (www.qantas.com; ℂ **13-13-13** from within Australia) flies to Dublin with a change in London or Dubai. **Air New Zealand** (www.airnewzealand.co.nz; ℂ **080/0737-000**) flies to Dublin, changing in San Francisco or Los Angeles and then London. Most major European airlines have direct flights to Dublin.

   Dublin International Airport (www.dublinairport.com; ℂ **01/814-1111**) is 11km (6¾ miles) north of the city center. A travel information desk in the arrivals concourse provides information on public bus and rail services throughout the country.

An excellent airport-to-city shuttle bus service called **AirCoach** (www. aircoach.ie; ☎ **01/844-7118**) operates 24 hours a day, making runs every 15 minutes. Its buses go directly from the airport to Dublin's city center and south side. Not all the major stops are covered on every service, so do check that you've got the right one before you board. City center fares are €6 to €7 one-way, depending on where you are going; fares to Ballsbridge, Dún Laoghaire, or Dalkey run around €10. Children aged 5 to 12 are €2 to €5.50; children 13 and over are counted as adults. You buy your ticket from the driver. Although AirCoach is slightly more expensive than the Dublin Bus (see below), it is faster—the journey to the city center takes about 25 minutes and it goes to the main hotel districts.

If you need to connect with the Irish bus or rail service, Dublin Bus's route 747, otherwise known as the **Airlink** (www.dublinbus.ie; ☎ **01/844-4265**), provides express coach services from the airport into central Dublin and beyond. Buses go to the city's central bus station, **Busáras,** on Store Street and on to **Connolly** and **Heuston** railway stations. Service runs daily from 5am until 11:30pm (Sun 7am–11:20pm), with departures every 15 to 20 minutes; it takes about 40 minutes to travel from the airport to Busáras. One-way fare is €7 for adults, €3.50 for children 11 and under.

Finally, **Dublin Bus** (www.dublinbus.ie; ☎ **01/873-4222**) has regular daily connections between the airport and the city center from 6am to 11:30pm. The one-way trip takes around 55 minutes in reasonable traffic. Fares start at around €3.50 adults, €3.30 children. Consult the travel information desk in the arrivals concourse to figure out which bus stops closest to your hotel.

For speed and ease—especially if you have a lot of luggage—a **taxi** is the best way to get directly to your hotel or guesthouse. Depending on your destination, fares average between €20 and €35, plus €1 for each additional passenger (but they shouldn't charge you extra for luggage). A tip of a couple of euro is standard. Taxis are lined up at a first-come, first-served taxi stand directly outside the arrivals terminal (turn right out of the entrance and you'll see it in front of you). It may be a good idea to check with the driver to see whether the Dublin tunnel is closed; taking the circuitous alternative through north Dublin often ends up saving a lot of time and money, if so.

BY FERRY Passenger and car ferries from Britain arrive at the Dublin ferry port, on the eastern end of the North Docks. (In 2015, the regular ferry service between Dún Laoghaire and Holyhead in the U.K. ended after 204 years, so this is now the only option.) Contact **Irish Ferries** (www.irishferries.ie; ☎ **0818/300-400**); **P&O Irish Sea** (www.poirishsea.com; ☎ **0871/66-6464** from the U.K.); or **Stena Line** (www.stenaline.com; ☎ **01/204-7777**) for bookings and information. Irish Ferries also sails to Dublin from Cherbourg in northern France. Buses and taxis serve both ports.

BY TRAIN Called Iarnród Éireann in Gaelic, **Irish Rail** (www.irishrail.ie; ☎ **1890/77-88-99** for timetables, ☎ **1850/366-222** to prebook tickets) operates daily train service to Dublin from Belfast, Northern Ireland, and all major cities in the Irish Republic, including Cork, Galway, Limerick, Killarney, Sligo, Wexford, and Waterford. Trains from the south, west, and southwest arrive at **Heuston Station,** Kingsbridge, off St. John's Road; from the north and northwest at **Connolly Station,** Amiens Street; and from the southeast at **Pearse Station,** Westland Row, Tara Street.

BY BUS   Bus Éireann (www.buseireann.ie; ✆ **01/836-6111**) operates daily express coach and local bus service from all major cities and towns in Ireland into Dublin's central bus station, **Busáras,** on Store Street.

BY CAR   If you are arriving by car from other parts of Ireland or on a car ferry from Britain, all main roads lead into the heart of Dublin and are well signposted to **An Lar** (City Centre). The quickest way into Dublin from the airport is to take the **Dublin Tunnel.** The toll for cars is €3, or €10 between the hours of 6am and 10am, Monday to Friday. To bypass the city center, the **East Link** (toll bridge, €2) and **West Link** are signposted, and **M50** circuits the city on three sides. From Wexford Town, Galway, or Belfast, the drive takes around 2 hours; from Cork, 2½ hours.

Getting Around

If your stay in Dublin is short, geography is on your side. The vast majority of the capital's best sites are concentrated in the city center, an area of no more than a few square kilometers. This leads to your first, most important (and quite frankly, easiest) decision: If you have a car, leave it behind at your hotel (or as close as you can get—parking is notoriously difficult). Dublin's streets are crowded and confusing, with baffling one-way streets, bad signage, and terrible traffic.

However, cars aside, Dublin is a very easy and convenient city to get around. Public transportation is good and getting better, taxis are plentiful and reasonably priced, and your own two feet can easily carry you from one end of town to the other. In fact, with its perennial traffic and parking problems, it's a city where the foot is mightier than the wheel.

BY BUS   After walking, buses are the most convenient and practical way to get between the city center sights. Dublin Bus operates a fleet of double-deckers, single-deckers, and minibuses (the latter charmingly called "imps"). Most originate on or near O'Connell Street, Abbey Street, and Eden Quay on the Northside, and at Aston Quay, College Street, and Fleet Street on the south side. Look for bus stop markers resembling big blue or green lollipops— they're every few blocks on main thoroughfares. To tell where a bus is going, look at the destination street and bus number displayed above its front window; those heading for the city center indicate that with an odd mix of Latin and Gaelic: VIA AN LAR.

Bus service runs daily throughout the city, starting at 6am (10am on Sun), with the last bus at about 11:30pm. On Friday and Saturday nights, **Nitelink** service runs from the city center to the suburbs from midnight to 4am. Buses operate every 30 minutes for most runs; schedules are posted on revolving notice boards at bus stops.

leap CARDS

If you're likely to use public transport a lot while in Dublin (which we highly recommend), do as the locals do: Get a **Leap Card,** a pre-paid card for reduced-cost travel on all Dublin buses (including Airlink and Nitelink), DART, Luas, and commuter trains. You can buy them at around 400 shops in and around the city—look for the distinctive green logo depicting a somewhat over-excited frog in mid-leap. (In Dublin Airport, you can pick one up at the small **Easons, Kiosk,** and **Spa** shops.) Ticket machines in some city center DART and railway stations also dispense Leap Cards, or you can order them online at **www.leapcard.ie**. They're free, but you have to pay a refundable deposit of €5 adults, €3 children, and buy at least €5 worth of credit up-front.

Inner-city fares are based on distances traveled. Daytime journeys that take place entirely within the designated "City Centre Zone" cost €0.70. This stretches from Parnell Square in the north, to Connolly Station and Merrion Square in the east, St. Stephen's Green in the south, and Ormond Quay in the west. Longer journeys cost anything from €1.75 all the way up to around €5 if you're going as far as the outer suburbs.

You pay on board the bus, using an automatic fare machine located in front of the driver. **No Dublin bus accepts notes or gives change.** If you don't have the exact money in coins, the driver will issue you with a "change receipt." You must then take this to the Dublin Bus headquarters on O'Connell Street to collect your change (a process not designed to encourage refunds). The sole exception to this rule is route 747 ("Airlink"), which runs between the airport and the city center. It accepts notes and gives change normally.

BY DART An acronym for Dublin Area Rapid Transit, the electric DART trains travel aboveground, linking the city center stations at **Connolly Station, Tara Street,** and **Pearse Street** with suburbs and seaside communities as far as Malahide to the north and Greystones to the south. Service operates roughly every 10 to 20 minutes Monday to Saturday from around 6am to midnight and Sunday from 9:30am to 11pm. For further information, contact DART, Dublin Pearse Station (www.dart.ie; ✆ **1850/366-222**).

BY TRAM The sleek, modern (and wheelchair accessible) light rail tram system known as **Luas** runs from around 5:30am to 12:30am Monday to Friday, 6:30am to 12:30am Saturday, and 7am to 11:30pm on Sunday. (The last trams to certain stations are earlier—be sure to check the timetable.) There are two lines, Red and Green: The Green Line runs southeast from St. Stephen's Green to Sandyford in the south; the Red Line runs west from the Point, near the 3Arena in Dublin Docklands, to Connolly Railway Station, and then swings down to the southwestern suburbs of Saggart and Tallaght. For more information, contact Luas (www.luas.ie; ✆ **1850/300-604**). The Luas network is currently undergoing long-term expansion work, which will extend the lines farther into the suburbs, with a projected completion date at the end of 2017. Until then, construction and roadworks are making Dublin's already chronic traffic problems worse—so, as the long-suffering locals will tell you, disruption is to be expected.

ON FOOT   Marvelously compact, Dublin is ideal for walking. Just remember to look right and then left (and in the direction opposite your instincts if you're from North America) before crossing the street. Pedestrians have the right of way at specially marked, zebra-striped crossings (these intersections usually have two flashing lights).

BY TAXI   It can be quite difficult to hail a taxi on the street; instead, they line up at taxi stands (called "ranks") outside major hotels, at bus and train stations, and on prime thoroughfares such as Upper O'Connell Street, College Green, and the north side of St. Stephen's Green. You can also phone for a taxi; see the numbers listed in the "Fast Facts" section on p. 45.

Visitor Information

Dublin Tourism operates several walk-in visitor centers in greater Dublin that are open every day except Christmas. The principal center is on Suffolk Street, Dublin 2, open from Monday to Saturday from 9am to 5:30pm, Sunday and bank holidays 10:30am to 3pm. (It's easy to spot—just look for the rather racy statue of Molly Malone pushing her cart past the front door.) The Suffolk Street office has a currency exchange counter, a car-rental counter, an accommodation reservations service, bus and rail information desks, a gift shop, and a cafe. For accommodation reservations throughout Ireland by credit card (including some good last-minute deals on Dublin hotels), contact Dublin Tourism at **www.visitdublin.com** or ✆ **1890/324-583.** A tourism center is also in the arrivals concourse of both terminals at Dublin Airport and the ferry terminal at Dún Laoghaire Harbor.

[Fast FACTS] DUBLIN

ATMs/Banks   Nearly all banks are open Monday to Friday 10am to 4pm (to 5pm Thurs). Convenient locations include the **Bank of Ireland,** at 2 College Green, Dublin 2, 88 Camden St. Lower, Dublin 1, and at Trinity College; and the **Allied Irish Bank (AIB),** at 100 Grafton St., Dublin 2, and 37 O'Connell St., Dublin 1.

Currency Exchange   Currency-exchange services, signposted as **Bureau de Change,** are in most Dublin banks and at many branches of the Irish post office system, known as **An Post.** A bureau de change operates daily during flight arrival and departure times at Dublin Airport. Some hotels and travel agencies offer bureau de change services. *Tip:* The best rate of exchange is almost always when you use your bank card at an ATM.

Dentists   For dental emergencies, your hotel will usually contact a dentist for you; otherwise, try **Smiles Dental Spa,** 28 O'Connell St. (✆ **1850/323-323**); or

Molesworth Dental Surgery, 2 Molesworth Place (✆ **01/661-5544**).

Doctors & Hospitals   For emergencies, dial ✆ **999.** If you need a doctor, your hotel should be able to contact one for you. Otherwise you could try **Dame Street Medical Center,** 16 Dame St. (✆ **01/679-0754**), or the **Suffolk Street Surgery,** 107 Grafton St. (✆ **01/679-8181**).

Emergencies   For police, fire, or other emergencies, dial ✆ **999.**

Luggage Storage If you arrive at your hotel too early to check in, or if check-out is in the morning and your flight isn't until the evening, many hotels will look after your baggage. Alternatively, the **tourism office** (☎ **01/410-0700**) at 37 College Green, opposite Trinity College, can store bags securely for €5 per 24 hours. There's also a "Left Luggage" facility at the Terminal 1 parking lot at Dublin Airport.

Mail & Postage **General Post Office,** O'Connell St. (☎ **01/705-8833**) is open Monday through Saturday, 8:30am to 6pm. Postage for a letter or postcard costs €0.68 within Ireland and Northern Ireland, €1 to the rest of the world.

Newspapers & Magazines Look for *Totally Dublin* (www.totally dublin.ie), a free monthly entertainment guide, at tourism offices. One of the best online magazines is *In Dublin* (www.indublin.ie), which has comprehensive event listings. The main Irish daily broadsheet newspapers are the *Irish Times* and the *Irish Independent.* Tabloid papers include the *Irish Sun,* the *Irish Daily Mirror,* and the *Herald.*

Pharmacies Dublin does not have 24-hour pharmacies. **City Pharmacy,** 14 Dame St. (☎ **01/670-4523**) stays open until 9pm weekdays, 7pm Saturdays; **Boots the Chemist,** 20 Henry St. (☎ **01/873-0209**) stays open until 9pm on Thursday, 8pm on Friday, 6pm Sunday, and 7pm all other days. There are also branches of Boots at 12 Grafton St. (☎ **01/677-3000**) and in the **St. Stephen's Green Centre** (☎ **01/478-4368**), but not all branches keep the same hours.

Taxis Taxi ranks are outside major hotels, at bus and train stations, and on Upper O'Connell St., College Green, and the north side of St. Stephen's Green. To call a cab, try **NRC Cabs** (☎ **01/677-2222**), **Trinity** (☎ **01/708-2222**), or **VIP/ACE Taxis** (☎ **01/478-3333**).

City Layout

Dublin is divided down the middle by the curves of the River Liffey, which empties into the sea at the city's farthest edge. To the north and south, canals encircle the city center: The Royal Canal arcs across the north and the Grand Canal through the south. Traditionally, the area south of the river has been Dublin's buzzing, prosperous hub. It still holds most of the best hotels, restaurants, shops, and sights, but the Northside is on the upswing, and hip new bars and hotels give it a trendy edge. Dublin is compact and easily walked in an hour. In fact, a 45-minute walk from peaceful St. Stephen's Green, up bustling Grafton Street, and across the Liffey to the top of O'Connell Street offers a good overview of the city's prosperous present and troubled past.

MAIN STREETS & SQUARES In the town center just south of the river, the main east-west artery is **Dame Street,** which changes its name to College Green, Westmoreland Street, and Lord Edward Street at various points as it connects **Trinity College** with **Dublin Castle** and **Christ Church Cathedral.** On one side of Dame Street are the winding medieval lanes of **Temple Bar,** Dublin's party central thanks to plenty of pubs. On the other side of Dame Street are tributary streets lined with shops and cafes. Where Dame Street becomes College Green, the sturdy gray-stone walls of Trinity College make an excellent landmark to get your bearings. At the southwest corner of the campus you'll find the top of **Grafton Street,** a lively pedestrianized shopping lane crowded with tourists, musicians, and artists, which leads to the bucolic park of **St. Stephen's Green.** From there, heading back up via

MURKY origins

For most visitors, the very word "Dublin" may conjure up a heady mix of history and romance, but it actually has a more prosaic origin. The name comes from the ancient Celtic words *dubh linn*, meaning "the black pool." Specifically, it refers to a natural inlet where the River Liffey met the River Poddle, and the waters were dark and murky. Long since buried, the inlet is thought to be somewhere around Dublin Castle.

However, an allusion to these watery origins still survives in the city's Gaelic name, *Baile Átha Cliath*, which means "the town of the hurdled ford"—a *ford* being a point where a stream or river crosses a road. When fords were "hurdled" in medieval times, it meant that they were covered at low tide with woven sheets of willow, making them easier to cross.

Kildare Street will take you past **Leinster House,** where the Irish Parliament meets, and a turn to the right brings you to **Merrion Square,** another of Dublin's extraordinarily well-preserved Georgian squares.

To cross the River Liffey and get to the Northside, most visitors choose to walk across the photogenic arch of the **Ha'penny Bridge** (see p. 84), while locals take the less attractive **O'Connell Bridge** nearby. You can be different and cross via the Ha'penny's sleekly modern neighbor, the **Millennium Bridge,** which is beautifully illuminated after dark. The O'Connell Bridge leads directly onto **O'Connell Street,** a wide, statue-lined boulevard that is the north's main thoroughfare. O'Connell Street runs north to **Parnell Square,** which holds a couple of marvelous museums and marks the top edge of central Dublin. From the bottom to the top, O'Connell Street is lined with statues, starting with an absurdly ornate representation of its namesake politician Daniel O'Connell surrounded by angels (still pocked with bullet holes left from the Easter Rising). The street running along the Liffey's embankment is called by everyone the **North Quays,** though its name changes on virtually every block, reflecting the long-gone docks that once lined it.

In the older section of the city, **High Street** is the gateway to medieval and Viking Dublin, from the city's two medieval cathedrals to the old city walls and nearby Dublin Castle.

Dublin Neighborhoods in Brief

Trinity College Area On the south side of the River Liffey, Trinity College stands at virtually the dead center of the city. Its shady quadrangles and atmospheric stone buildings are surrounded by bookstores, shops, and noisy traffic.

Temple Bar There are really two Temple Bars, depending on when you visit. During the day, Temple Bar is an artsy, cultured district full of trendy shops and modern art

galleries. But such refinement gives way to an altogether more raucous atmosphere at night. With its myriad selection of pubs, bars, and hip clubs, this is definitely where it's at in Dublin after dark.

Old City Dating from Viking and medieval times, the cobblestone enclave of the historic Old City includes Dublin Castle, the remnants of the city's original walls, and Christ Church and St. Patrick's cathedrals.

Liberties Adjacent to Old City, the Liberties district takes its name from the fact that it was once just outside the city walls, and therefore exempt from Dublin's jurisdiction. Although it prospered in its early days, Liberties fell on hard times in the 17th and 18th centuries and has only felt the touch of urban renewal in the last decade or so. Its main claim to fame is the Guinness Brewery.

St. Stephen's Green/Grafton Street Area The biggest tourist draw in town, this district is home to Dublin's finest hotels, restaurants, and shops. The neighborhood is filled with impressive Georgian architecture and is primarily a business and shopping zone.

Fitzwilliam & Merrion Squares These two leafy squares between Trinity College and St. Stephen's Green are surrounded by grand Georgian town houses. Some of Dublin's most famous citizens once lived here; today, many of the houses are offices for doctors, lawyers, and government agencies.

O'Connell Street (North of the Liffey) The epicenter of Dublin's stormy political struggles, the north was once a fashionable area, but it lost much of its charm as it declined in the 20th century. It has experienced something of a resurgence in recent years, and now is home to some high-profile hotels, shops, and restaurants. But it still feels a little more down-at-heel than the Southside. With four theaters within walking distance of O'Connell Street, this is also Dublin's theater district.

North Quays (Liffey Boardwalk) Once the center of Dublin's shipping industry, the quays are a series of streets named after the wharves that once stood at water's edge. A modern pedestrian boardwalk now runs along the quays from the O'Connell Bridge to Grattan Bridge.

Smithfield Urban renewal in the 21st century has transformed this formerly seedy market area into a trendy district east of Phoenix Park, with such attractions as the Old Jameson Distillery.

Ballsbridge/Embassy Row Immediately south of the Grand Canal, this upscale suburb is just barely within walking distance of the city center. Primarily a prestigious residential area, it is also home to hotels, restaurants, and embassies.

WHERE TO STAY IN DUBLIN

With a healthy mix of plush hotels and grand old guesthouses, Dublin excels in providing a place to rest your head at the end of a day. Unfortunately, finding a really great, *affordable* place to stay is a tougher prospect. In this book we have tried to list as many of these "finds" as we can. However, if you're prepared to stay slightly outside of the city center, your options open up quite a bit (remember that public transportation, including taxis, is relatively cheap). This is particularly true in the leafy suburb of Ballsbridge (just south of the city center), which is fast becoming a center for affordable accommodations.

Wherever you're staying, try to book as far in advance as possible. The most sought-after places fill up fast. Always try to book online. Many hotels offer Web-only specials—sometimes through such third-party sites as Booking.com or Trivago.com—deals that can amount to massive savings on the rack rate. Remember, the fact that times are tough in the global economy right now cuts both ways: Hotels are eager to secure your business. There are some truly amazing deals out there, if you know where to look. Don't be shy about asking about any available discounts or special offers.

Dublin Hotels

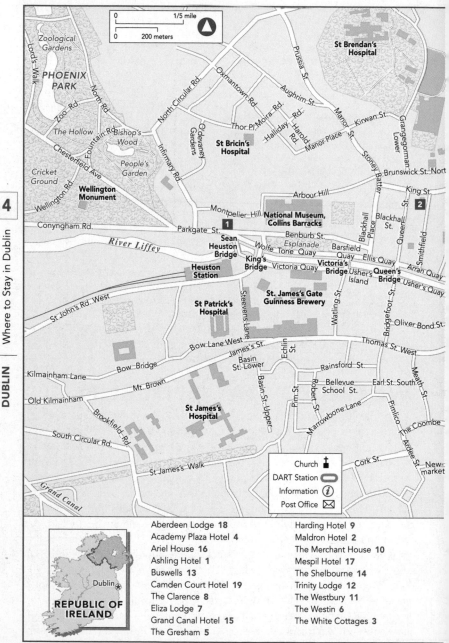

Aberdeen Lodge **18**
Academy Plaza Hotel **4**
Ariel House **16**
Ashling Hotel **1**
Buswells **13**
Camden Court Hotel **19**
The Clarence **8**
Eliza Lodge **7**
Grand Canal Hotel **15**
The Gresham **5**

Harding Hotel **9**
Maldron Hotel **2**
The Merchant House **10**
Mespil Hotel **17**
The Shelbourne **14**
Trinity Lodge **12**
The Westbury **11**
The Westin **6**
The White Cottages **3**

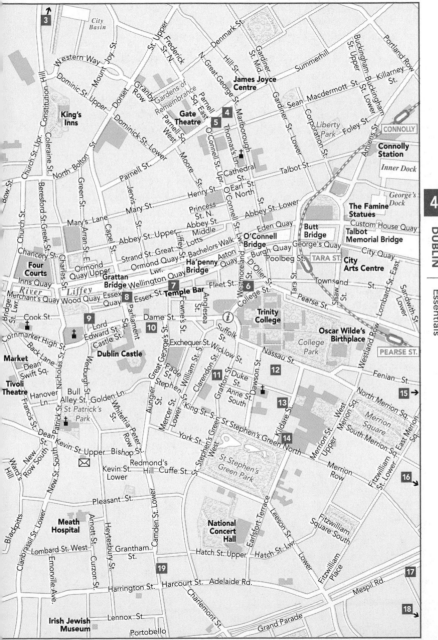

3

City Basin

Western Way

Mount Joy St.

Dominic St. Upper

King's Inns

Dorset

Granby Row

Gardens of Remembrance

Constitution Hill

Coleraine St.

North Bolton

Parnell St.

Green St.

Mary's Lane

Mary's St.

Arran St.

Capel St.

St. Upper Frederick St. N.

Denmark St.

Hill St.

Gardiner St. Mid.

Summerhill

Buckingham St. Upper

Portland Row

Killarney St.

Parnell Sq. East

Parnell St.

Moore St.

James Joyce Centre

Marlborough

Gardiner St. Lower

Sean Macdermott St.

Buckingham St. Lower

Corporation St.

Foley St.

Amiens St.

Liberty Park

CONNOLLY

Connolly Station

Inner Dock

Gate Theatre

4

5

Thomas's Ln.

Cathedral St.

O'Earl St. North

Henry St.

Princess St. N.

Abbey St. Middle

Talbot St.

Abbey St. Lower

Eden Quay

Butt Bridge

The Famine Statues

George's Dock

Custom House Quay

Talbot Memorial Bridge

Bow St.

Beresford St. Greek St.

Chancery St.

Church St. Upr.

North King St.

Four Courts

Inns Quay

Liffey

Charles St.

Jervis St.

Strand St. Great

Ormond Quay Upper

Grattan Bridge

Wellington Quay

Liffey St. Lwr.

Bachelors Walk

Ha'penny Bridge

O'Connell Bridge

Aston Quay

Burgh Quay

Poolbeg St.

George's Quay

D'Olier St.

TARA ST.

City Quay

City Arts Centre

River

Merchant's Quay

Bridge St.

Cook St.

9

Lord Edward St.

8

Wood Quay

Essex Quay

Parliament St.

Essex St.

7 **Temple Bar**

Fownes St.

Anglesea

Fleet St.

College St.

Westmoreland St.

Pearse St.

Shaw St.

Townsend St.

Lombard St. Lower

Sandwith St. Lower

Cornmarket High St.

Back Lane

Market

10

Dame St.

Great George's St. S.

Exchequer St.

Wicklow St.

Suffolk St.

Trinity College

Oscar Wilde's Birthplace

PEARSE ST.

Westland Row

Nassau St.

College Park

Fenian St.

Dean Swift Sq.

Tivoli Theatre

Hanover Ln.

Nicholas St.

Werburgh St.

Dublin Castle

Castle St.

Fade St.

William St.

Clarendon St.

Grafton St.

Dawson St.

St Duke St.

Anne St. South

Kildare St.

11

12

13

15

Francis St.

Bull Alley St.

Golden Ln.

Whitefriar St.

Peter St.

Mercer St. Lower

King St. S.

Stephen St.

York St.

St Stephen's Green West

Merrion St. Upper

Merrion St. Lower

Merrion Sq. South

Merrion Sq. West

Merrion Square

North Merrion Sq.

East Merrion Sq.

St Patrick's Park

Dean Kevin St. Upper

Bishop St.

Redmond's Hill

Cuffe St.

St Stephen's Green North

14

Merrion Row

Fitzwilliam St. Lower

16

Ward's Hill

New Row South

Kevin St. Lower

Pleasant St.

Meath Hospital

Clanbrassil St. Lower

Emorville Ave.

Lombard St. West

Heytesbury St.

Arnott St.

Camden St. Lower

Curzon St.

Grantham St.

National Concert Hall

Earlsfort Terrace

Leeson St. Lower

Fitzwilliam Square South

Fitzwilliam Place

17

Mespil Rd.

Blackpitts

19

Harrington St.

Harcourt St.

Adelaide Rd.

Hatch St. Upper

Hatch St. Lower

Charlemont St.

18

Irish Jewish Museum

Lennox St.

Portobello

Grand Parade

Irish immigration authorities require visitors to have already arranged a place to stay at least for the first night. If you arrive in Dublin without a reservation, however, don't despair. One of the best sources of last-minute rooms (often at a discount) is **www.visitdublin.com**. The website lets you view hotels and guesthouses with immediate availability.

Historic Old City & Temple Bar/Trinity College Area

Temple Bar is the youngest, most vibrant niche in a young, vibrant town. Stay here and you'll be on the doorstep of practically anywhere you'd want to go. That said, it can get *very* noisy at night, so request a room on a top floor or at the rear of the establishment if you want some shut-eye.

EXPENSIVE

The Clarence ★★   Back in the 1990s, when the Celtic Tiger was starting to roar, the Clarence became something of a symbol of the "new" Dublin. Chic, fashionable, and with megastar owners to boot (Bono and the Edge from U2, who can still occasionally be spotted here), it spoke of Dublin's revival as a modern and cultured capital city. These days, with the economy slowing down, the Clarence has lost some of its original luster—U2 have sold their share, and a refurbishment is overdue in places. The surrounding profusion of trendy bars and restaurants also means that street noise is a problem (despite what they all tell you, no hotel smack-dab in the middle of the capital's party district can ever *really* guarantee a quiet night's sleep.) However, the friendly and professional staff goes a long way toward making up for the disappointing edges. Pleasant, well-sized guest rooms are done in contemporary tones (chocolate and cream or white with accents of scarlet and black). Most of the furniture is the work of Irish designers, and beds are luxuriously comfortable. And a definite plus is the price tag—rooms here are relative bargains, considering that this still qualifies as a big-name hotel in the city. The trendy (and pricey) new **Cleaver East** restaurant serves ultra-contemporary Irish cuisine, and stopping by the **Octagon Bar** for a pint of Guinness is an absolute must. The basement **Liquor Rooms** nightclub, which has a nice retro speakeasy vibe, is one of the best places in Temple Bar for late night cocktails (see p. 46).

6-8 Wellington Quay, Dublin 2. www.theclarence.ie. ℗ **01/407-0800.** 49 units. €179–€260. Breakfast €18–€25. Dinner, bed and breakfast packages available. Valet parking €5 per hour. **Amenities:** Bar; restaurant; A/C; gym; room service; spa; free Wi-Fi. Bus: 26, 66, 66A, 66B, 66D, 67, 67A.

The Westin ★★   With its grand, imposing facade (due to its former incarnation as a bank), this hotel boasts some handsome original 19th-century features in its interior, and even those parts that feel more modern have an impeccably well-maintained elegance to them. Guest rooms are large and with a refined modern decor, with subtly distressed wood furniture and wide leather headboards on outrageously comfortable beds. The Mint Bar remains a fashionable hangout for the Dublin glitterati, and the basement **Exchange**

restaurant serves excellent, modern European food. The only thing missing is a spa, but you can book pampering treatments in your room.

Westmoreland St., Dublin 2. www.thewestindublin.com. ⓒ **01/645-1000.** 163 units. €310–€400. Rates include breakfast. Dinner, bed and breakfast packages available. Valet parking €28 per day. **Amenities:** Bar; restaurant; gym; room service; free Wi-Fi. Bus: 1, 7B, 7D, 9, 11, 13, 16, 16C, 25N, 26, 33N, 39N, 40, 41N, 44, 100, 133.

MODERATE

Buswells ★★   The traditional air of a gentleman's club prevails at this midprice hotel in central Dublin. Original features of the Georgian building are maintained, from the intricate cornices of the 19th-century plasterwork to the polished marble fireplaces and heavy curtains. Therefore it can come as a surprise to find the small but decently furnished guest rooms are modern in style (rather bland, even, after the lovely, traditional spaces one walks through to get to them). Visitors with mobility problems should be certain to ask for a room on a lower floor, because the old building (actually three town houses merged together) is full of stairs to climb. Pleasant though it is, Buswells' real selling point is the location—just a few minutes' walk to Trinity College in one direction and St. Stephen's Green in the other. You're in the very heart of the action here.

23–25 Molesworth St., Dublin 2. www.buswells.ie. ⓒ **01/614-6500.** 69 units. €141–€209. Hotel covers cost of parking at nearby lot (overnight only). Cheaper rates do not include breakfast. **Amenities:** Restaurant; bar; room service; free Wi-Fi. DART: Pearse. Bus: 7B, 7D, 10, 10A, 11, 11A, 11B, 13, 14, 14A, 15, 15A, 15B, 15C, 15X, 20B, 25X, 32X, 27C, 33X, 39B, 40A, 40C, 41X, 46A, 46B, 46C, 51D, 51X, 58X, 67X, 84X, 92.

Eliza Lodge ★   Right in the middle of Temple Bar, above a popular Italian restaurant and overlooking the River Liffey, this smart hotel could hardly feel more in the thick of the action. Guest rooms are simple and compact, with large windows letting in plenty of natural light, although the modern bathrooms can verge on shoebox size. Like so many other hotels in this neighborhood, however, its biggest drawback is the flipside of its greatest asset: the location. Temple Bar is the liveliest part of a busy capital city, and the fact that Eliza Lodge is also on a major traffic intersection hardly acts as an aid to restful sleep. That's good enough reason to fork over extra for an upper floor room, which also gets you a better view of the river.

23-24 Wellington Quay (on the corner of Eustace St.), Dublin 2. www.elizalodge.com. ⓒ **01/671-8044.** 18 units. €179–€329. Discount parking at nearby lot (€7 overnight, €14 for 24 hr.). Rates include breakfast. Dinner, bed and breakfast packages available. **Amenities:** Restaurant, A/C; free Wi-Fi. Bus: 26, 39B, 51, 51B, 51C, 51D, 51X, 66, 66A, 66B, 66D, 67, 67A, 68, 69, 69X, 78, 78A, 79, 79A, 90, 92, 206, 748.

Harding Hotel ★★   Just central enough not to feel like a trek to the main tourist sites, but just far enough to escape the inevitable nighttime crowds that descend on nearby Temple Bar, this is an excellent, low-cost option on the western edge of the city center. The polished wood and bright, floor-to-ceiling windows of the cheerful lobby give off a pleasantly old-fashioned vibe, even

learning the lingo: **"BANK HOLIDAYS"**

No, they don't give banks extra vacation time in Ireland. North Americans may be baffled by this phrase, which you'll see a lot on lists of opening times. It simply means a public holiday, often on a Monday—something like a "3-day weekend." Many shops are either closed or run on reduced hours on Bank Holidays.

There are currently nine regular Bank Holidays in Ireland: New Year's Day (Jan 1); St. Patrick's Day (Mar 17); Easter Monday; the first Monday in every month from May to August, except July; the final Monday in October; Christmas Day (Dec 25); and St. Stephen's Day (Dec 26).

though most of the hotel is quite modern. The comfortable guest rooms are a terrific value. Even in high season, you can occasionally find a double room for less than €125, and triple rooms typically cost just a little bit more than standard doubles. This makes the Harding a particularly standout option for families. It's not overly fancy, but it's pleasant, clean, and has everything you need.

Copper Alley, Fishamble St., Dublin 2. www.hardinghotel.ie. © **01/679-6500.** 52 units. € 80–€170 double. No parking. Breakfast not included in lower rates. **Amenities:** Wi-Fi (free), restaurant, bar, accessible rooms. Bus: 37, 39, 39A, 39B, 39C, 39X, 49, 49A, 49X, 50, 50X, 56A, 70, 70A, 70X.

The Merchant House ★   Mainly geared toward business travelers and couples, the accommodations here are different from a conventional guest-house. The Merchant House is a series of swanky guest suites, with various services attached but no dedicated reception area. The upside to this is a greater degree of privacy and freedom. The downside is that, while the entrance is secure and private, the building isn't staffed all the time. (Travelers who prefer their local color not too, well, colorful, should also be warned that it's next door to a fetish store—albeit a fairly discreet one.) The suites themselves are extremely well designed; features of the original 18th-century building were beautifully retained when the place was renovated in 2006. Nicely modern touches include flatscreen TVs and elegant contemporary furnishings, and fancy optional extras include a dedicated chauffeur. The bed-and-breakfast rate includes daily housekeeping service and breakfast at a nearby cafe.

8 Eustace St., Dublin 2. www.themerchanthouse.eu. © **01/633-4447.** 4 units. €120–€145. No children. No parking. Breakfast not included in lower rates. **Amenities:** Wi-Fi (free), A/C. Bus: 39B, 49X, 50X, 65X, 77X.

O'Connell Street Area/North of the Liffey

The Northside has some good offerings in the way of hotels. Though in some respects a less sought-after area, it's still very central and within walking distance of all the major sights and shops. Hotel rates tend to be lower than they are just across the bridge.

MODERATE

The Gresham ★★   One of Dublin's most historic hotels, the Gresham is also one of the oldest—it opened in 1817, though it was almost destroyed during the Easter Rising of 1916. Most of the current building dates from the 1920s; the public areas retain a glamorous Art Deco feel, preserved during a big modernization of the hotel in the mid-2000s. Although the suites are nothing short of opulent, the cheaper guest rooms are really quite basic—but they're comfortable, quiet, and most importantly, surprisingly affordable for a hotel with this kind of pedigree. The **Writer's Lounge,** a beautiful remnant of its Jazz Age heyday, is a popular spot for afternoon tea. Overlooking both the hotel lobby and busy O'Connell Street, it's a good perch for people watching. The main O'Connell Street taxi rank is directly outside, or it's about a 15-minute walk to Temple Bar.

23 Upper O'Connell St., Dublin 1. www.gresham-hotels.com. ℭ **01/874-6881.** 298 units. €90–€265. No children under 3. Discount parking at nearby lot (€15 overnight). Breakfast not included in lower rates. Dinner, bed and breakfast packages available. **Amenities:** Wi-Fi (free), 2 restaurants, 2 bars, room service, discounted use of nearby gym and swimming pool (€10). Luas: Abbey St. Bus: 2, 3, 4, 5, 7, 7A, 7B, 7D, 8, 10, 10A, 11, 11A, 11B, 13.

INEXPENSIVE

Academy Plaza Hotel ★★   Owned by the Best Western chain, this is a large, modern, low-frills option popular with business travelers but well located for travelers exploring central Dublin. The lobby is small but pleasant, with wood paneling and leather furniture; rooms are compact and simple, with cream walls, rust-and-brown-colored carpet, and well-insulated windows to shield you from street noise. Some rooms are bigger than others, so if size matters, request a deluxe room. Bathrooms are decent and modern, with showers above the baths. Breakfasts are sizeable, if not terribly varied, and can be ordered in your room (for a charge). The staff is pleasant, and the location, for the money, is very good.

10-14 Findlater Place, off O'Connell Street, Dublin 1. www.academyplazahotel.com. ℭ **01/878-0666.** 304 units. €87–€149. Parking €12 per day. Rates include breakfast. **Amenities:** Free Wi-Fi. Luas: Abbey St. Bus: 2, 3, 4, 5, 7, 7A, 7B, 7D, 8, 10, 10A, 11, 11A, 11B, 13.

St. Stephen's Green/Grafton Street Area

St. Stephen's Green may be only a 10-minute walk from the hustle and bustle of Temple Bar and Trinity College, but it's infinitely calmer and less harried. This is a good area if you're looking for a little peace and quiet.

EXPENSIVE

The Shelbourne ★★★   Dublin hotels simply don't come with a better historic pedigree than this—the Irish Constitution was written in this very building (room 112, to be precise). The Shelbourne was acquired by the Marriott group a few years ago, but traditionalists need not fear: The hotel is still its grand old self. A feeling of *fin de siècle* elegance pervades throughout the public areas, with high plaster ceilings, crystal chandeliers, and a winding iron staircase. Guest rooms have a much more discreet, contemporary elegance, with extremely luxurious beds and a host of modern extras. There's also an excellent spa, and you can even book a session with a Genealogy Butler if you need a little expert help in tracing your Irish roots. Afternoon tea at the Shelbourne is a true Dublin institution; consider splurging on a booking, even if you can't spring for a night here.

27 St. Stephen's Green, Dublin 2. www.marriott.com. (C) **01/663-4500.** 190 units. €332–€540. Valet parking €25 per day. Breakfast €21–€29. Dinner, bed and breakfast packages available. **Amenities:** Wi-Fi (free), restaurants (3), bars (3), afternoon tea, gym, spa, A/C; accessible rooms. Luas: St. Stephen's Green. Bus: 7B, 7D, 10, 10A, 11, 11A, 11B, 14, 14A, 15, 15A, 15B, 15C, 15X, 20B, 25X, 32X, 39X, 40A, 40C, 41X, 51X, 70B, 84X.

The Westbury ★★★ Virtually made for well-heeled shopaholics, this top-end hotel on Grafton Street is a luxurious and stylish retreat. Bedrooms are huge and modern, with subtle floral wallpaper, handmade furniture, and soothing beige and cream tones. Beds are comfortable (although with so much space to spare, they could be bigger) and a few are modern-style four-posters. Wilde, the excellent modern Irish restaurant, is a beautiful space overlooking Grafton Street; it also serves one of the city's finest afternoon teas. There's also a more relaxed bar and bistro. Check the website for package deals, including dinner-bed-and-breakfast and theater options.

Grafton St., Dublin 2. www.doylecollection.com. (C) **01/602-8900.** 205 units. €249–€374. Parking €20 per day. Rates include breakfast. **Amenities:** Bar; 2 restaurants; room service; gym; free Wi-Fi. Bus: 11, 11a, 11b, 14, 14a, 15a, 15c, 15x, 20b, 27c, 33x, 39b, 41x, 46b, 46c.

MODERATE

Camden Court Hotel ★ Although not quite "budget," this large hotel just south of St. Stephen's Green is still a great value for what you get. A "practical base" kind of hotel, rather than one overflowing with character and charm, the Camden Court is nonetheless well equipped, with good-size and modern guest rooms (especially the family rooms), a pool, and a massage salon to soothe away those sightseeing aches and pains. You'd probably pay significantly more if this place was just a few blocks farther to the north; as it is, the only real drawback is that you're a 10- to 20-minute walk away from the center.

Camden St. Lower (near jct. with Charlotte Way), Dublin 2. www.camdencourthotel. com. (C) **01/475-9666.** 246 units. €165–€220. Parking (free). Breakfast not included in lower rates. **Amenities:** Wi-Fi (free); bar; restaurant; gym; swimming pool; beauty salon; room service; accessible rooms. Luas: Harcourt St. Bus: 15X, 16, 16A, 19, 19A, 65, 65B, 65X, 83, 122.

Trinity Lodge ★ This small hotel is full of quirks—not all of them convenient (there's no elevator and plenty of stairs, for instance), but the bedrooms are comfortable, contemporary, and surprisingly large for a place in this price range. A converted town house, the hotel was built in 1785, and some of the bedrooms retain a historic feel in their design. Quadruple rooms offer outstanding value for families. South Frederick Street is little more than a stone's throw from Trinity College, and it's also a comparative rarity in the city center—it's generally quite peaceful at night. Breakfast is basic, but there are plenty of other options in the neighborhood.

12 South Frederick St., Dublin 2. www.trinitylodge.com. © **01/617-0900.** 16 units. €180–€285. Two-night minimum on some summer weekends. Rates include continental breakfast; 10% discount on cooked breakfasts at nearby cafes. Discounted parking at nearby lot (€3 overnight, €13 for 24 hr.). **Amenities:** Wi-Fi (free); restaurant; A/C; room service (7am–11pm). Rail: Connolly. Luas: St. Stephen's Green. DART: Pearse. Bus: 7B, 7D, 10, 10A, 11, 11A, 11B, 14, 14A, 15, 15A, 15B, 15C, 15X, 20B, 25X, 27C, 32X, 33X, 39B, 41X, 46B, 46C, 51D, 51X, 58X, 67X, 84X, 92.

Smithfield

Although the official boundaries of Smithfield are rather vague, this North-side district, to the east of the city center, encompasses a few famous landmarks, such as the **Guinness Storehouse** ★ (see p. 80) and **St. Michan's Church** ★★ (p. 81). There are some good, midprice hotels here that can offer greater value than their central counterparts.

MODERATE

Ashling Hotel ★★   Close to Heuston Station and Phoenix Park on the western end of the city center, the Ashling is a modern six-story hotel. Guest rooms have generic corporate-style decor but are fairly spacious; it's worth paying extra for a deluxe room to get better views of the city. There's a good restaurant offering classic Irish dishes, and a daily lunchtime "carvery" (roast meat, served buffet style). Central Dublin is a 10-minute tram ride, or a 25-minute walk; handily, this is also the last stop before the airport on the Airlink coach (see p. 41). *Tip:* Stroll through Coppies Memorial Park, opposite the hotel, to see the semi-nude bronze statue of Anna Livia, a character in James Joyce's *Finnegans Wake.* She appears to float above a pool of water—thus earning her the nickname "the Floozie in the Jacuzzi." For more on Dublin statues' nicknames, see p. 73.

Parkgate St., Dublin 8. www.ashlinghotel.ie. © **01/677-2324.** 225 units. €134–€210. Rates include breakfast. Parking (€10 for 24 hr.). Dinner, bed and breakfast packages available. **Amenities:** Restaurant; bar; free Wi-Fi. Luas: Museum. Bus: 25, 26, 66, 66A, 66B, 67, 69.

Maldron Hotel ★   Part of a small Irish hotel chain, the Maldron Smithfield is a good midprice option, located a 5-minute walk from the Old Jameson Distillery or St. Michan's Church. The guest rooms have recently been refurbished in a streamlined, modern style; they won't win any design awards, but they're quiet and spotlessly clean. A few have balconies. There's a restaurant and bar, although there's plenty of nightlife in the nearby area—including the **Cobblestones** ★★★ (see p. 90), one of the best places in the city for live traditional music. Check for discounts for longer stays.

Smithfield Plaza, Dublin 7. www.maldronhotelsmithfield.com. © **01/485-0900.** 92 units. €103–€210. Parking (€10 for 24 hr.). Rates include breakfast. **Amenities:** Restaurant; bar; Wi-Fi (free). Luas: Smithfield. Bus: 37, 39, 39A, 70, 83, 83A, 74.

Ballsbridge & the Southern Suburbs

South of the canal, this prestigious Dublin residential neighborhood is coveted for its leafy streets and historic buildings. Half the foreign embassies in Dublin are located in this district. It's also growing as a hotel quarter—the distance from the city center means that you'll get so much more for your money by staying here.

MODERATE

Aberdeen Lodge ★★ Drive up to this elegant Regency building in the springtime, and its front can be so covered in ivy, it looks like a vertical lawn with spaces cut for the windows. Inside, the decor is rather endearingly old-fashioned; neat-as-a-pin public spaces have heavy, antique-style furnishings and embroidered pillows scattered hither and thither. Guest rooms are comfortable and quiet, if a little plain, but modern bathrooms are a big plus. Some have views of the large garden, where guests can take tea—often in the company of the hotel's friendly cat. Aberdeen Lodge is a short walk to the nearest DART station, and from there it's a short hop to the city center. Alternatively, a 5-minute stroll takes you to a pleasant walking path through a park beside the coast. If you do come this way, look out for the gray-stone tower, now stuck rather ignominiously between a public toilet and a pay phone—it's an example of a Martello Tower, a small defensive fortification that was built by the British to ward off a feared invasion from France in the early 19th century.

55 Park Avenue, Ballsbridge, Dublin 4. www.aberdeen-lodge.com. ℂ**01/283-8155.** 11 units. €162–€185. Parking (free). Rates include breakfast. **Amenities:** Wi-Fi (free); restaurant; bar; use of nearby spa. DART: Sydney Parade, Sandymount. Bus: 2, 3, 18, 84N.

Ariel House ★★★ This charming guesthouse in Ballsbridge has won several plaudits over the last few years. And rightly so—it's a smoothly run, great-value-for-the-money operation, situated on a quiet Victorian street. The most obvious landmark you can see is, depending on your point of view, either a hideous blot or a great day out—the Aviva Stadium, one of Ireland's major sports grounds, literally a block away. Inside the hotel, the vibe is decidedly old-school, with a subtle contemporary flourish. The small, simple guest rooms are tastefully decorated in earthy oatmeal or cream with brocade-pattern bedspreads. The lounge is a pleasant space with an honesty bar; musically inclined guests are even free to tickle the ivories of the piano. The breakfast menu doesn't veer too far from the traditional Irish staples, but it's exceptionally well done. As long as you're not staying on a match day, the neighborhood is quiet enough to make you feel tucked away from the crowds, but with good transport links to central Dublin.

50-54 Lansdowne Rd., Ballsbridge, Dublin 4. www.ariel-house.net. ℂ**01/668-5512.** 37 units. €130–€180. Parking (free). Breakfast not included in lower rates. **Amenities:** Wi-Fi (free); honesty bar; afternoon tea; room service. DART: Lansdowne Road. Bus: 4, 7, 8, 84.

Grand Canal Hotel ★   Overlooking the 18th-century Grand Canal—a major part of Dublin's industrial heritage, long since abandoned as anything but a picturesque waterway—this large hotel is a strikingly modern place. As at many hotels in this neighborhood, you can't escape the looming carbuncle of the Aviva Stadium, and this modern hotel is a particular favorite of sports fans in town for a game. But it's also a haven for business travelers and tourists looking for a pleasant but no-frills place to stay. It wins no awards for style, but it's cheerful, spotlessly clean, and the bedrooms are huge by Dublin standards. The city center is a just short journey by public transport. You could even walk if you wanted to work off one of the hearty hotel breakfasts—Trinity College is about 25 minutes on foot.

Grand Canal St. Upper, Ballsbridge, Dublin 4. www.grandcanalhotel.ie. ℂ **01/646-1000.** 142 units. €95–€162. Theatre and O2 Arena packages available. Parking (free). Breakfast not included in lower rates. **Amenities:** Wi-Fi (free); restaurant; bar; room service; accessible rooms. DART: Grand Canal Dock. Bus: 4, 5, 7, 7A, 8, 45, 63, 84.

Mespil Hotel ★   Another reasonable option in Ballsbridge, the Mespil is about a 15-minute walk from St. Stephen's Green. Accommodations here are certainly of a higher standard than what you're likely to find uptown for the same price. (Stays of more than 1 night usually qualify for discounts if you book online.) The guest rooms are spacious and feature modern decor and comfortable beds. In common with most hotels of this type, breakfast is served buffet style—tasty and excellent fuel, although all that fried meat and eggs certainly gets wearing after a couple of days. One nice little bonus: An excellent gourmet food market is held just outside by the canal, every Thursday from 11am to 2pm. See **www.irishvillagemarkets.com** for more details.

50-60 Mespil Rd., Dublin 4. www.mespilhotel.com. ℂ **01/448-4600.** 255 units. €159–€189. Parking (limited). Breakfast €12. **Amenities:** Wi-Fi (free); restaurant; bar; gym; room service; accessible rooms. Bus: 10, 10A, 15X, 49X, 50X, 66D, 92.

North of Dublin

Skerries is a pleasant seaside commuter town, north of Dublin. It's most definitely outside of the city—about 30km (18½ miles) from Temple Bar—but transport links are reasonably good. Of course, those seeking peace and quiet at the end of the day will see this as a selling point.

INEXPENSIVE

The White Cottages ★★★   The sea is an ever-present feature at this pleasant, whitewashed little B&B in Skerries, a pretty commuter town just north of Dublin. The coastline is literally feet away from the wooden terrace at the back, and the sound of the waves can help soothe you to a restful sleep at night. Guest rooms are decorated in summery white and blue colors, with jaunty, candy-striped accents. The owners are welcoming and extremely helpful—Joe, the co-owner, is a mine of information about the local area, and his wife Jackie displays some of her art around the house. Breakfasts are good, and in summer you can get afternoon tea (€20) or a "romantic picnic" lunch

(€25), although you have to fend for yourself at dinnertime (Joe can provide an exhaustive list of places to eat nearby). The only major snag is that Skerries is far outside of the city; the train journey to the center takes about 40 minutes, and the bus over an hour. Still, it's nothing more than local commuters do every day, and you'll be hard-pressed to find a more tranquil and welcoming retreat after a long day's sightseeing.

Balbriggan Rd., Skerries, Co. Dublin. www.thewhitecottages.com. © **01/849-2231.** 4 units. €90. Parking (free). Rates include breakfast. **Amenities:** Wi-Fi (free); picnic lunches. Rail: Skerries. Bus: 33.

WHERE TO EAT IN DUBLIN

The economic boom years of the early 2000s in Dublin brought with it a new generation of international, sophisticated restaurants. Ireland embraced a foodie culture in a way that it never really had before. However, as the economy crashed, so too came a minor resurgence in the popularity of traditional Irish fare, even in expensive restaurants. That's not to say that the food in Dublin is on the downswing—far from it—it's just become easier to find traditional-style Irish food in the city than it was a decade ago. In other words, Ireland is both re-embracing and re-inventing its national food heritage.

All that being said, Dublin is still a notoriously expensive city in which to eat out. Prices have certainly come down in recent years, but you're still likely to pay much more for a meal here than in a comparable U.S. city; maybe about the same as you'd expect in Paris or London. But when the food here is good, it's very good, so if you can afford to splurge once or twice while you're in town, do so—you're in for a treat.

Temple Bar Area

Gallagher's Boxty House ★★★ IRISH   There's a great story behind this captivating and hugely popular restaurant in Temple Bar. While living in Venezuela as a young man, the owner was struck by the pride his fellow workers took in simple, traditional home cooking. He came home and founded a restaurant to preserve and update some of the Irish traditions in his own style. Boxty is a distinctive kind of potato pancake (see box below). It's the house signature dish, served with a variety of delicious meat and fish fillings. Also on the menu are steaks, seafood, and Irish stews. Their tasty Irish variant on the hamburger is made with cumin-and-garlic-spiced lamb and caramelized onion. Reservations are recommended on weekends, but even on busy nights they can usually squeeze you in (*squeeze* being the operative word if you're seated in the very cozy basement).

20-21 Temple Bar, Dublin 2. www.boxtyhouse.ie. © **01/677-2762.** Main courses €15–€25. Daily noon–10:30pm. Luas: Jervis. Bus: 22, 39B, 49X, 50X, 65X, 66, 66A, 66B, 66D, 67, 67A, 69X, 77X.

Gourmet Burger Kitchen ★★ BURGERS   This upscale British-New Zealand chain has recently started springing up in Ireland, and a welcome import it is, too—they make some of the most reliably good burgers in town.

boxty

"Boxty on the griddle, boxty on the pan. If you can't bake boxty, sure you'll never get a man." –Traditional Irish rhyme.

A decade or so ago you'd have been hard pressed to find much in the way of traditional Irish food in Dublin, save for the odd bowl of Irish stew. These days, however, there's a real revival of interest in the old foodie ways—albeit in an updated form. Some of Dublin's trendiest restaurants embrace Ireland's culinary heritage, often with a sophisticated, contemporary twist.

Boxty—which comes from an old Gaelic term meaning "poor bread"—is one such dish that you're likely to encounter on fashionable menus. It's basically a potato pancake, made with buttermilk and, sometimes, eggs. Each region has its own distinctive spin. Usually boxty is fried, although it can also be baked or served as a dumpling (similar to the Polish *pierogi*). More often than not, modern chefs will accompany their boxty with meat or fish, in various creative (and delicious) ways.

Portions aren't huge but there's something for everyone—get yours classic and simple, or opt for one of the more imaginative creations (such as the Kiwiburger, served with beetroot and pineapple, or the spicy Habanero, with a fruity chile-tomato salsa). There are even some good veggie choices, such as the delicious Kumara burger, made with fluffy sweet potato. There's a second Dublin branch at 5 South Anne St. (© **01/672-8559**).

Temple Bar Sq., Dublin 1. www.gbk.ie. © **01/670-8343.** Main courses €8–€13. Thurs–Sat noon–11pm; Sun–Wed noon–10pm. Luas: Jervis. Bus: 22, 39B, 49X, 50X, 65X, 66, 66A, 66B, 66D, 67, 67A, 69X, 77X.

The Old Storehouse ★★ IRISH/PUB   There isn't much innovation on the menu of hearty Irish classics at this popular pub in Temple Bar—and that's precisely why it's so popular. What you get is delicious, traditional pub food: fat, juicy burgers served with vine tomatoes and cocktail sauce; bangers and mash (sausages and mashed potato) with ale gravy; or perhaps some steamed mussels with garlic bread. There's a small wine list, but the beer selection is better. As much of a draw as the food is the nightly live music; all traditional and all free, with up to 20 acts a week in the summer. The Old Storehouse doesn't accept reservations, so be prepared to wait for a table when it's busy.

Crown Alley, off Cope St., Dublin 2. www.theoldstorehouse.ie. © **01/607-4003.** Main courses €13–€20. Daily noon–10pm. Bus: 39B, 49X, 50X, 65X, 77X.

Queen of Tarts ★★ CAFE   This cheerful little tearoom in the heart of Temple Bar is a delightful pit stop for a pot of tea and some form of sweet, diet-busting snack. Cakes and tarts are the specialty; it's all good, but try the lemon meringue pie or the old-fashioned Victoria sponge (white cake with a jam filling and a dusting of sugar on top). They also serve delicious, generously proportioned breakfast until noon during the week, 1pm on Saturday, and a decadent 2pm on Sunday. At lunchtime you can order soups or sandwiches, but it's the cakes that keep us coming back. There's a second branch

Dublin Restaurants

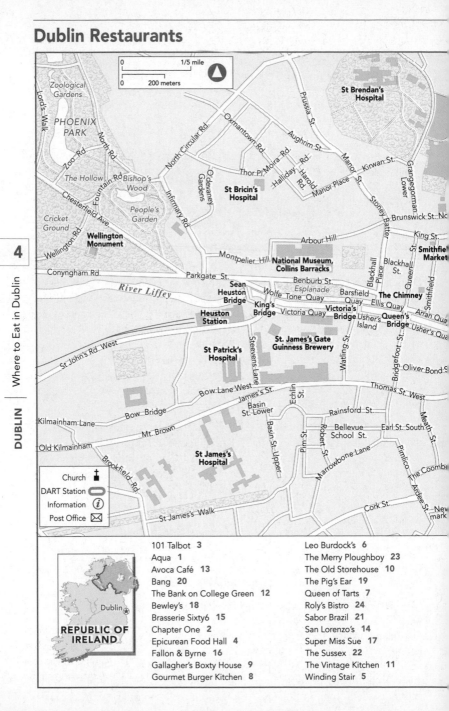

101 Talbot **3**
Aqua **1**
Avoca Café **13**
Bang **20**
The Bank on College Green **12**
Bewley's **18**
Brasserie Sixty6 **15**
Chapter One **2**
Epicurean Food Hall **4**
Fallon & Byrne **16**
Gallagher's Boxty House **9**
Gourmet Burger Kitchen **8**

Leo Burdock's **6**
The Merry Ploughboy **23**
The Old Storehouse **10**
The Pig's Ear **19**
Queen of Tarts **7**
Roly's Bistro **24**
Sabor Brazil **21**
San Lorenzo's **14**
Super Miss Sue **17**
The Sussex **22**
The Vintage Kitchen **11**
Winding Stair **5**

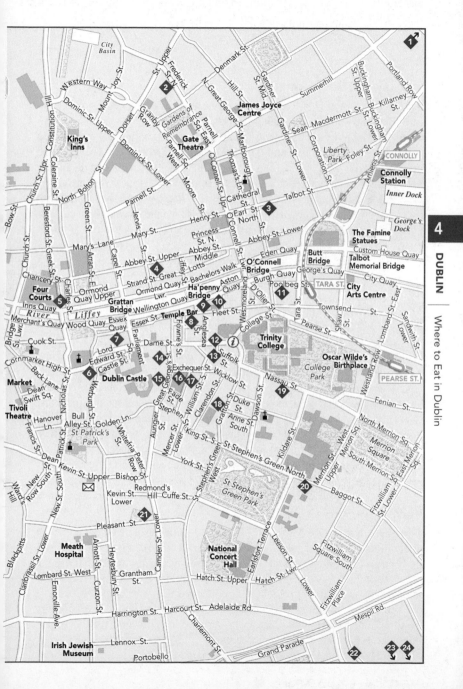

just around the corner on Lord Edward St., directly opposite the junction with Cork Hill (with City Hall on the corner).

Cows Lane, Dame St., Dublin 2. www.queenofarts.ie. ℰ **01/633-4681.** Breakfast €5–€10. Lunch €8–€12. Mon–Fri 8am–7pm; Sat–Sun 9am–6pm. Bus: 37, 39, 39A, 39C, 70, 70A.

Trinity College Area

Avoca Café ★★ CAFE So much better than just another department store cafe, this is a great place for breakfast, lunch, or a mid-shopping snack. The morning menu is more varied and interesting than at most hotels; free-range scrambled eggs with arugula salad, several types of pancakes, French toast, and even the ubiquitous "full Irish" with (rarely found in Ireland) American-style bacon. Lunches are healthy and delicious—think crab salad with home-baked bread or a plate of Middle Eastern–style mezze made with Wicklow lamb and served with baba ganoush and hummus. The delicious soups are famous with the locals. Or you could just drop in for a tempting slice of cake and a restorative cup of tea.

11-13 Suffolk St., Dublin 2. www.avoca.ie. ℰ **01/677-4215.** Breakfast €3–€12. Lunch €13–€20. Mon–Fri 9:30am–5:30pm (serving coffee and scones only 4:30–5:30pm); Sat 9:30am–5:30pm (coffee and scones only 5–5:30pm); Sun 11am–5pm. Bus: 15X, 32X, 33X, 39X, 41X, 51D, 51X, 58X, 70X, 84X.

The Bank on College Green ★★ PUB Undoubtedly one of Dublin's most jaw-droppingly handsome interiors, this place would be worth visiting even if it didn't serve great pub food. Built as a bank in 1892, at the height of Victorian opulence, it retained several remnants of the original when it was converted into a pub (including the wonderful old-style safes that you can still see downstairs). A small and fairly traditional lunch menu of burgers, fish and chips, sandwiches, and salads gives way to a more extensive selection in the evening, including steaks, pasta, and a handy sharing plate. In the hour after local offices close, you'd be lucky to walk in and snag a table right away, but waiting for a table at least gives you an opportunity to admire the beautiful architecture. Come on Sunday for a leisurely brunch (11am–5pm) or a traditional roast at lunchtime.

20 College Green, Dublin 2. www.bankoncollegegreen.com. ℰ **01/677-0677.** Main courses €13–€25. Weekdays noon–4pm and 6–10pm; Sat and Sun noon–5pm and 6–10pm. Bus: 15X, 32X, 33X, 39B, 39X, 41X, 49X, 50X, 51X, 58X, 65X, 70X, 77X, 84X.

The Pig's Ear ★★★ MODERN IRISH A deliciously inventive approach to traditional Irish tastes pervades this super-cool restaurant overlooking Trinity College. However, this isn't one of those trendy eateries in which the menu is too concerned with being clever to be satisfying. Classic ingredients are offered with modern flair: smoked salmon cured with Earl Grey tea, or roast chicken served with hay-smoked butter, hazelnuts, and kale. You certainly won't be able to miss this place from the outside—just look for the shocking-pink door with a candy-striped awning.

4 Nassau St., Dublin 2. www.thepigsear.ie. ℰ **01/670-3865.** Main courses €19–€28. Mon–Sat noon–2:45pm and 5:30–10pm. Closed Sun. DART: Pearse St. Bus: 25X, 32X, 33X, 41X, 51D, 51X, 58X, 67X, 84X, 92.

The Vintage Kitchen ★★★ IRISH   An antidote to over-fussy fine dining, the Vintage Kitchen is a stripped-down, funky little restaurant. Vintage artworks line the dining room—everything's for sale, but there are no fixed prices, so just make an offer if you like something. There aren't many tables, and they don't even have an alcohol license; you're encouraged to bring your own bottle if you want wine. However, the classic Irish cooking is truly excellent, artfully presented in a contemporary style, and generously proportioned too. Start with Donegal smoked haddock chowder, before tackling an enormous chicken supreme with burnt honey and bacon, or a flavorsome dish of cod with Roaring Bay mussels and lumpfish caviar. If dinner here is a bit steep for you, come for lunch—main courses are just €12, and small plates half that. Make reservations for dinner.

7 Poolbed St., Dublin 2. www.thevintagekitchen.ie. ℰ **01/679-8705.** Fixed-price menus €28 two courses, €34 three courses. Tues–Fri noon–2:30pm and 5:30–10pm; Sat 5:30–10pm. Closed Sun and Mon. DART: Tara St. Bus: 65, 65B.

Near Dublin Castle

Brasserie Sixty6 ★★ IRISH/INTERNATIONAL   This cheerful, well-run bistro is a popular choice with locals for special occasions. Roast meats cooked rotisserie-style are a specialty. Try the garlic-and-lemon chicken served with herb stuffing and a bunch of sides, or dig into citrus-glazed duck with potatoes roasted in duck fat. The rest of the menu is made up of modern bistro fare like roast monkfish with artichokes or a simple, juicy steak with fondant potatoes and peppercorn sauce. Vegetarians are catered to as well, with choices such as vegetable tagine and haloumi Caesar salad, and pretty much all of their food is celiac-friendly. It's not cheap, although the pre-theater menu is an excellent value (€25 for 3 courses, served all night Sun–Wed, and until 6:30pm Thurs–Sat). There's also a popular brunch served until 4pm on Sundays, accompanied by a live jazz band.

66 South Great Georges St., Dublin 2. www.brasseriesixty6.com. ℰ **01/400-5878.** Main courses €12–€33. Mon–Fri noon–10; Sat–Sun 10am–10pm. Bus: 15E, 15F, 16, 16A, 19, 19A, 65, 65B, 65X, 83, 122.

Fallon & Byrne ★★ MODERN EUROPEAN   A top-floor adjunct to the wonderful food and wine store, Fallon & Byrne, this food hall serves delicious, seasonal Irish fare sourced from artisan producers. Nothing seems to have come very far—crab from the tiny port of Castletownbere, County Cork; lamb from Lough Erne; or oysters from Carlingford. The menu strikes a nice balance between ambitious dishes and more down-to-earth options, so while you may find turbot served with pink grapefruit and crushed new potatoes, you could just as easily opt for a simple burger topped with Cashel blue cheese and smoked bacon. They also have vegetarian and vegan menus. If you prefer to fend for yourself, the enormous selection of deli items downstairs is available to go.

11-17 Exchequer St., Dublin 2. www.fallonandbyrne.com. ℰ **01/472-1010.** Main courses €12–€33. Wed–Thurs noon–3pm, 6–10pm; Fri–Sat noon–3pm, 6–11pm; Sun noon–4pm, 6–9pm; Mon–Tues 12–3pm, 6–9pm. Bus: 15E, 15F, 16, 16A, 19, 19A, 65, 65B, 65X, 83, 122.

Leo Burdock's ★ FISH & CHIPS   Proof that not all great food experiences come with a hefty price tag, Leo Burdock's is probably the most famous fish-and-chip shop in Ireland. In fact, it's virtually de rigueur for passing celebrities to pop in; the photographic "wall of fame" includes Sandra Bullock, Russell Crowe, and Tom Cruise. But don't come expecting cutting-edge cuisine; Leo Burdock's still trades on the same simple, winning formula that it has since 1913: battered fresh fish (cod, sole, ray, or scampi) and thick chips (like very fat fries), all cooked the old-fashioned way, in beef drippings. There are other options on the menu, including hamburgers, but frankly, why come to a place like this if you don't order the one thing for which it's world-famous?

2 Werburgh St., Dublin 8. www.leoburdock.com. © **01/454-0306.** Main courses €3–€8. Daily noon–midnight. Bus: 49X, 50X, 54A, 50X, 56A, 77, 77A, 77X, 78A, 150, 151.

San Lorenzo's ★★ BREAKFAST/ ITALIAN   This funky Italian restaurant serves good, all-round Italian specials in the evening, but that's not what it's famous for in Dublin. San Lorenzo's is one of the most popular spots in town for brunch at weekends. Abandon your hotel "full Irish" and come here for the heavenly French toast, made with caramelized bananas and topped with a cocoa-pop square (a kind of breakfast cereal made with chocolate-flavored puffed rice), whipped cream, and thick chocolate sauce; or opt for the Belgian waffles with salted caramel ice cream. There's a Latin edge to many of the savory options—huevos rancheros, brunch tacos, or even a pulled pork hash. Just be prepared to wait for a table.

South Great Georges St., Dublin 2. www.sanlorenzos.ie. © **01/478-9383.** Brunch: €9–€19. Lunch main courses: €7–€16. Dinner main courses €8–€38. Mon 5–9:30pm; Tues–Wed 12:30pm–3pm, 5–9:30pm; Thurs–Fri 12:30–3pm, 5–10pm; Sat 10:30am–3pm, 5–10pm; Sun 10:30am–4pm, 5:30–9pm. Bus: 15E, 15F, 16, 16A, 19, 19A, 65, 65B, 65X, 83, 122.

O'Connell Street Area/North of the Liffey

101 Talbot ★★ IRISH/ INTERNATIONAL   This cheery and informal spot, a 3-minute walk from the G.P.O. on O'Connell Street, is strong on delicious Irish cuisine with global influences and a healthy twist. The bright, airy dining room is lined with modern art. Specials may include seasonal vegetables with Taleggio cheese gratin, or roast Lough Erne lamb with herb-encrusted potato rosti. The early bird menu (two courses for €20, 5–7:15pm) is a particularly good deal, and popular with pre-theater diners attending the Abbey Theatre just around the corner.

101-102 Talbot St., Dublin 1. www.101talbot.ie. © **01/874-5011.** Main courses €16–€24. Tues–Sat noon–3pm and 5–11pm. Closed Sun and Mon. Luas: Abbey St. Bus: 20B, 32X, 33X, 41, 41A, 41B, 41C, 42, 42A, 42B, 43, 51A, 130, 142.

Chapter One ★★★ MODERN IRISH   The vaulted basement of the excellent **Dublin Writers Museum** ★★ (see p. 72) houses one of the city's most feted restaurants, with a fixed-price menu that makes excellent use of local flavors and organic ingredients. Feast on gourmet dishes such as seabass, cockles, and mussels with smoked cod roe cream, or duck breast with baked celeriac. The separate set menu for vegetarians has dishes such as aged cauliflower prepared with pine nut and walnut milk. Adventurous diners will relish the chef's table: Seated in a little booth right inside the kitchen, guests are served a special six-course menu (€100 per person) while the culinary theater happens before your eyes. The wine list is excellent; consider splurging on a Meerlust Rubicon 2008, an outstanding and little-seen South African vintage with a sublime, smoky flavor. *Tip:* The lunch menu is only half the price of dinner.

19 Parnell Sq. North, Dublin 1. www.chapteronerestaurant.com. © **01/873-2266.** 4-course fixed-price menu €70. Tues–Fri 12:30–2pm and 5:30–10:30pm; Sat 7:30–10:30pm. No lunch Sat. Luas: Abbey St. DART: Connolly St. Bus: 1, 2, 14, 14A, 16, 16A, 19, 19A, 33X, 39X, 41X, 48A, 58X, 70B, 70X.

Epicurean Food Hall ★ MEDITERRANEAN An energetic coming-to-gether of flavors from disparate corners of the global village, this delightful food hall is a voyage of discovery for the epi-curious. The selection of lunch options changes quite regularly, but long-standing kitchens include **Istanbul,** specializing in Mediterranean dishes and Turkish kebabs; **Saburritos,** which serves a combination of authentic and California-style Mexican street food; **Rafa's Temaki,** which claims to be the first place in Ireland to sell *temaki* (a healthful, fast-food-style combination of Japanese sushi and sashimi); and **La Corte,** an Italian deli. The various stalls share a common seating area, or you can order it to go.

1 Liffey St. Lower, Dublin 1. www.epicureanfoodhall.com. © **01/283-6077.** Main courses €4–€13. Mon–Sat 9am–8pm; Sun 11am–8pm. Luas: Jervis. Bus: 39B, 69X.

Winding Stair ★★ MODERN IRISH A sweet old bookstore downstairs and a chic restaurant upstairs, the Winding Stair is situated a stone's throw from the Ha'penny Bridge. The views of the Liffey are romantic, but of course it's the inventive modern Irish cooking that pulls in the crowds. After a starter of Dingle Bay crab or spiced beef carpaccio with goat's cheese, you could opt for steamed cockles and mussels with brown shrimp mayo or the beef rib-eye with sticky onions. The enormous wine list, which is helpfully arranged by character rather than region, features several decently priced options. The fixed-price lunch (€21–€26) comes with a glass of house wine, and the pre-theater menus (€26–€30) are a great value—but you must be out by 8:15pm.

40 Lower Ormond Quay, Dublin 1. www.winding-stair.com. © **01/872-7320.** Main courses €22–€28. Daily noon–5pm, 5:30–10:30pm. Luas: Jervis. Bus: 39B, 51, 51B, 51C, 51D, 51X, 68, 69, 69X, 78, 78A, 79, 79A, 90, 92, 206.

St. Stephen's Green/Grafton Street Area

Bang ★ MODERN IRISH The presence of so many place names on the menu indicates how much this place has embraced the slow food ethos. The vast majority of ingredients are regionally sourced from specialist Irish producers. You may find Clare Island salmon served with local radishes and pickled cucumber; John Dory from Kilkeel; or perhaps a rib-eye steak from County Fermanagh. If it all seems too hard to choose from, you could opt for one of the tasting menu (€69). The wine list is expertly chosen, and there's also a delightfully put together, seasonal cocktail menu—try the beehive julep, with spiced whisky, manuka honey, and black walnut bitters. Pre-theater set menus cost €25 for two courses.

11 Merrion Row, Dublin 2. www.bangrestaurant.com. © **01/400-4229.** Main courses €22–€33. Mon–Tues 5:30–10pm; Wed 12:30–10pm; Thurs–Sat 12:30–11pm. Closed Sun. Luas: St. Stephen's Green. Bus: 25X, 51D, 51X, 65X, 66X, 67X, 77X.

Bewley's ★ CAFE   A Dublin landmark since 1927, Bewley's has a literary pedigree as well as a historic one. James Joyce was a regular (it makes an appearance in his book *Dubliners*), and a host of subsequent literary greats made this their regular stop-off for a cup of joe and a slice of cake. It's still hugely popular, but not just for coffee; you can get a pretty good pizza, salad, or burger here, in addition to a modest menu of light snacks. Fun fact: The distinctive, ornate faux-Egyptian facade owes its existence to the fact that, when the place opened, Europe was in the grip of a craze for all things Ancient Egyptian, following the discovery of Tutankhamen's tomb just 5 years before.

78-79 Grafton St., Dublin 2. www.bewleys.com. © **01/672-7720.** Breakfast €3–€12. Lunch and dinner €9–€16. Mon–Wed 8am–10pm; Thurs–Sat 8am–11pm; Sun 9am–10pm. Bus: 11, 11A, 11B, 14, 14A, 15A, 15C, 15X, 20B, 27C, 33X, 39B, 41X, 46B, 46C.

Sabor Brazil ★★★ BRAZILIAN   A good Brazilian restaurant isn't high on the list of things one expects to find in Dublin—even less so, an innovative and wildly fashionable spot in a slightly dicey neighborhood south of the center. And yet Sabor Brazil not only serves outstanding food, it also delivers a fun and memorable experience. The tiny dining room is decorated in a wry combination of rococo and Latinate flourishes. The menu (€100 per person for seven courses, no a la carte) fuses contemporary Brazilian flavors with an Irish inflection: grilled prawns with chile and *vatapá* (a Brazilian dish made with coconut, cilantro, and coconut milk), or *pastel* (kind of like South American dim sum) filled with whatever the chef decides is best that day. A vegetarian alternative is always available. Reservations are essential, preferably a while in advance (with a €25 booking deposit, credited to your bill on the night), and the restaurant caters to couples only.

50 Pleasants St., Off Camden St., Dublin 8. www.saborbrazil.ie. © **01/475-0304.** Tasting menu only €100. Tues–Sun 6–11pm (last reservation 8:30pm). Bus: 65, 65X.

Super Miss Sue ★★ SEAFOOD   There are actually three restaurants here under the Super Miss Sue umbrella, each serving up excellent seafood to a trendy crowd. **Luna** is the most formal of the three, but the quirky **Café** has the best atmosphere. Cod, tuna, salmon, prawns, and oysters are served several ways, or you could go for one of the enormous house special platters. There are also steaks if the fruits of the sea don't tempt you. They also do a popular brunch at weekends. Dubliners may tell you that the best of the SMS treats are to be had at the third option—**Cervi,** the excellent "chipper." On Friday nights, Cervi does delicious fish, chips, and a soda to-go for just €10.

2-3 Drury St., Dublin 2. www.supermisssue.com. © **01/679-9009.** Main courses €12–€26. Platters €45-€60. Mon–Wed, Sun noon–10pm; Thurs–Sat noon–11pm. Bus: 65, 65X.

Fitzwilliam Square Area

The Sussex ★★ IRISH   One of the best proponents of gastropub cuisine—the reinvention of traditional Irish cooking into something chic and fashionable—is this refined pub (above another popular bar) 10 minutes' walk south of St. Stephen's Green. The menu takes classic pub fare and prepares it beautifully—fish and chips with pea and mint puree; linguine served with tiger prawns, clams, garlic, and chile; or a delicious house burger served with Cork cheddar. For dessert, try the *posset* (a syllabub-like concoction containing cream and lemon) served with spiced shortbread. As you'd expect, all the ingredients are sourced as locally as possible, with plenty of attention to what's in season. The wine list is well judged, with plenty of reasonably priced options. *Tip:* The lunch menu is an edited version of what's for dinner—but significantly cheaper.

9 Sussex Terrace (at jcn. of Sussex Road, Dublin 4 (above M. O'Briens Pub). www.the sussex.ie. © **01/676-2851.** Main courses €15–€31. Mon noon–3pm; Tues noon–3pm, 5–11pm; Sun 5–11pm. No dinner Mon. Bus: 7B, 7D, 11, 11A, 11B, 27C, 39B, 39X, 46B, 46C, 46D, 46E, 58C, 58X, 70B, 70X, 116.

Ballsbridge & the Southern Suburbs

Roly's Bistro ★★ BISTRO   This lovely, easygoing bistro, just down the street from the United States Embassy, is one of the best places to eat south of the city center. Local meats and fish predominate; start with some Thai-style Castletownbere crab, or perhaps a traditional leek-and-potato soup (great comfort food if it's a cold evening). For the main event, try the roast chicken with colcannon potato, or, if you want to splurge a bit, the specialty beef rib-eye, aged for 30 days in 12 feet of Himalayan rock salt. There's also an adjacent cafe, with a slightly more stripped-down fixed price menu (€22 for two courses, or €25 for three). Reservations are recommended.

7 Ballsbridge Terrace, Dublin 4. www.rolysbistro.ie. © **01/832-0690.** Main courses €20–€34. Daily noon–3pm and 5:45–10pm. Bus: 4, 7, 8, 18.

North of Dublin

Aqua ★★★ SEAFOOD   With a jaw-dropping view of Dublin Bay, this has to be one of the most romantic dining spots in the region, and definitely worth a splurge. Service is excellent—attentive without being overbearing—and the seafood is delicious and fresh as can be. You can start with a half dozen oysters from Carlingford Lough, before moving on to roast cod with a tomato and chorizo sauce, or some roast monkfish with a curry infusion. There's also a small range of tasty meat options for those who aren't wowed by the bounty of the sea. The only drawback is the cost—this place isn't cheap—but substantially cheaper early bird menus are available until 7:30pm (6:30pm on

Sat). Howth is a small commuter suburb of Dublin, about 16km (10 miles) northeast of the city center. The restaurant is about a 10-minute walk from the Howth DART station; a cab out here from the city should run you about €30.

1 West Pier, Howth, Co. Dublin. www.aqua.ie. ℂ **01/832-0690.** Main courses €17–€42. Tues–Sat 12:30–3:30pm, 5:30–10pm; Sun noon–5pm, 5:30–8:30pm. DART: Howth. Bus: 31.

South of Dublin

The Merry Ploughboy ★ IRISH/PUB   An exuberant live show of traditional music and dancing accompanies dinner at this hugely popular pub in Rathfarnham, one of Dublin's farther-flung southern suburbs. Admittedly it's all very touristy, but you certainly get your money's worth—the show runs for 2 hours, and the food, while limited, is actually pretty good. Expect plates along the lines of Guinness-braised beef served with root vegetables and rosemary jus or trout in a dill-and-lemon crust. The only real drawback is the time it takes to get here (Rathfarnham is about 6km/3¾ miles) from the center), although a dedicated minibus will pick you up and take you back at the end of the night for the bargain price of €7.50 round-trip.

Edmondstown Rd., Rockbrook, Rathfarnham, Dublin 16. www.mpbpub.com. ℂ**01/493-1495.** Dinner and show €50. Bar menu €9–€24. Daily dinner arrive 6:30–7pm; show 8–10pm. Bar food: Mon–Sat 12:30–9:30pm; Sun 12:30–8pm. Special bus leaves from and returns to six locations in central Dublin (€7.50 per person; must be pre-booked).

EXPLORING DUBLIN

Wandering Dublin—just walking down its Georgian streets with a map only in case you get *really* lost—is one of the great pleasures of a visit here. The city center, where the vast majority of the sights are located, is small enough to traverse on foot (or via short bus or taxi rides). One minute, you're walking along a quiet leafy street and suddenly the Irish Parliament appears before you. A few minutes later, it's gorgeous Merrion Square. Then, you're facing the granite buildings of Trinity College—and on and on. So pack a sturdy pair of shoes, have your umbrella at the ready, and head out to discover how rewarding this wonderful old town can be.

Top Attractions

Book of Kells and Old Library ★★ LIBRARY   It's definitely one of Ireland's national treasures, this magnificent hand-drawn manuscript of the four gospels, dating to the year 800, with elaborate calligraphy and colorful illumination drawn by Irish monks. It's an astonishing work of art—but whether it really warrants the fuss involved in seeing it is debatable. In high season you may face a lengthy queue, only to find it hard to peer past the hordes of onlookers into the dim glass box where the book is kept—and you're handsomely charged for the privilege. (Another way to secure a more comfortable viewing experience is by taking a Trinity College Tour—see p. 76—or you can book fast-track tickets online for an extra €3.) If you do come, however, take a little extra time to check out the Library's handsome

Long Room. The grand, chained library holds many rare works on Irish history and presents frequently changing displays of classic works. The Book of Kells is located in the Old Library building, on the south side of Library Square, inside the main campus.

The Library Building, Trinity College, College Green, Dublin 2. www.tcd.ie/visitors/book-of-kells. ℂ **01/896-2320.** Admission €10 adults; €9 seniors, students, and children; €20 families; admission plus campus tour, €13 adults, €12 seniors and students, €26 families. June–Sept Mon–Sat 9am–6pm; Sun 9:30am–6pm; Oct–May Mon–Sat 9:30am–5pm; Sun noon–4:30pm. Last admission 30 min. before closing. DART: Pearse St., Connolly St. Luas: Lower Abbey St., St. Stephen's Green. Bus: Nassau St. entrance (for Old Library/Book of Kells): 25X, 32X, 33X, 41X, 51D, 51X, 58X, 67X, 84X, 92. College Green entrance: 7N, 15N, 15X, 44N, 46N, 48N, 49N, 51D, 51X, 54N, 56A, 70B, 70X, 77A, 77N, 92.

Chester Beatty Library ★★★ LIBRARY This dazzling collection of early religious texts and other priceless artifacts is named in honor of Sir Alfred Chester Beatty, an Anglo-American industrialist who donated his unique private collection to the Irish nation when he died in 1968. And what a collection it is! Highlights of the bequest include breathtaking illuminated gospels and early Bibles (including the oldest known fragment in existence, from 150 A.D.); impeccable 15th-century Qurans; Quranic scrolls from the 8th and 9th centuries; and sacred Buddhist texts from Burma and Tibet. Recent acquisitions include an epic 17th-century Japanese scroll running nearly twice the length of a gallery, and a collection of extremely steamy Egyptian love letters dating from 1800 B.C. (The translations are apparently too explicit to be displayed publicly.) If there's a better museum of this size in Ireland, we have yet to find it. Why queue and pay a tenner to see two pages from the Book of Kells when you can lose yourself in this wonderful place for free?

On the grounds of Dublin Castle, Dame St., Dublin 2. www.cbl.ie. ℂ **01/407-0750.** Free admission. Mar–Oct Mon–Fri 10am–5pm; Sat 11am–5pm; Sun 1pm–5pm; Nov–Feb Tues–Fri 10am–5pm; Sat 11am–5:30pm; Sun 1pm–5pm. Luas: Jervis. Bus: 37, 39, 39A, 39B, 39C, 49, 49A, 49X, 50, 50X, 56A, 65X, 70, 70A, 70X, 77, 77A, 77X, 123.

Christ Church Cathedral ★★ CATHEDRAL This magnificent cathedral was designed to be seen from the river, so walk to it from the riverside in order to truly appreciate its size. It dates from 1038, when Sitric, Danish king of Dublin, built the first wooden Christ Church here. In 1171, the original foundation was extended into a cruciform layout and rebuilt in stone by the Norman warrior Strongbow. The present structure dates mainly from 1871 to 1878, when a huge restoration took place—the work done then remains controversial to this day, as much of the building's old detail was destroyed in the process. Still, magnificent stonework and graceful pointed arches survive. (There's also a statue of Strongbow inside, and some believe his tomb is here as well, although historians are not convinced.) The best way to get a glimpse of what the original building must have been like is to visit the 12th-century crypt, which has been kept untouched. An intriguing side note: Christ Church once displayed what was believed to be the preserved heart of St. Laurence

Dublin Attractions

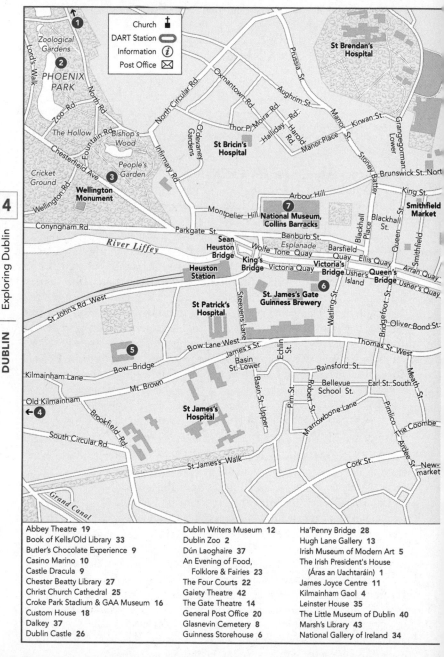

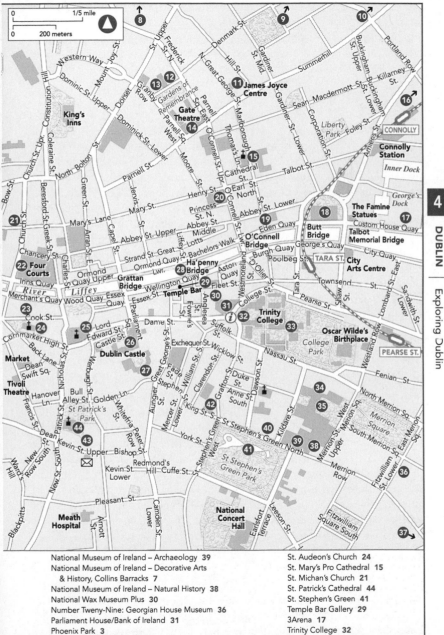

National Museum of Ireland – Archaeology **39**
National Museum of Ireland – Decorative Arts
  & History, Collins Barracks **7**
National Museum of Ireland – Natural History **38**
National Wax Museum Plus **30**
Number Twenty-Nine: Georgian House Museum **36**
Parliament House/Bank of Ireland **31**
Phoenix Park **3**

St. Audoen's Church **24**
St. Mary's Pro Cathedral **15**
St. Michan's Church **21**
St. Patrick's Cathedral **44**
St. Stephen's Green **41**
Temple Bar Gallery **29**
3Arena **17**
Trinity College **32**

O'Toole (1128–80). However, in 2012, the holy relic was stolen in an audacious nighttime raid. Nothing else was taken, including items of much higher value, leading police to surmise that it was stolen to order for a collector. The heart is still missing.

Christchurch Place, Dublin 8. www.christchurchcathedral.ie. © **01/677-8099.** Admission €6 adults; €4.50 seniors and students; €2 children € (15 and under); €15 families. Free entry for prayer or services. Apr–Sept Mon–Sat 9am–7pm; Sun 12:30–2:30pm, 4:30–6pm; Mar and Oct Mon–Sat 9am–6pm; Sun 12:30–2:30pm, 4:30–6pm; Nov—Feb Mon–Sat 9am–5pm; Sun 12:30–2:30pm. Bus: 37, 39, 39A, 39B, 39C, 39X, 49, 49A, 49X, 50X, 54A, 56A, 70, 70A, 70X, 78A.

Dublin Writers Museum ★★ MUSEUM   Manuscripts, early editions, personal possessions, and other pieces of ephemera relating to Ireland's most famous writers are on display at this great museum in Parnell Square. The exhibits are laid out across two rooms, tracing the development of Irish literature up to the present day. Lovers of Behan, Joyce, Shaw, Stoker, Wilde, Yeats, and the other greats of the canon will find plenty to love here—from the trivial (Brendan Behan's postcard from Los Angeles extolling its virtues as a place to get drunk) to the profound (a first edition of Patrick Kavanagh's *The Great Hunger*, complete with a handwritten extra section that his publisher refused to publish, fearing it too controversial). You can take a self-guided audio tour, and there's an excellent bookshop, of course. Talks, readings, and other special events are occasionally held here; check the website for details.

18 Parnell Sq., Dublin 1. www.writersmuseum.com. © **01/872-2077.** Admission €7.50 adults; €6.50 seniors and students; €5 children; €18 families. Mon–Sat 10am–5pm; Sun 11am–5pm. Last admission 45 min. before closing. Bus: 1, 2, 8, 14, 14A, 16, 16A, 19, 19A, 33X, 39X, 40, 40A, 40B, 40C, 41X, 48A, 58X, 70B, 70X, 116, 120, 123, 145.

Hugh Lane Gallery ★★ ART MUSEUM   This small art gallery punches above its weight with a strong collection of Impressionist works. Highlights of the collection include Degas's *Sur la Plage* and Manet's *La Musique aux Tuileries*. There are also sculptures by Rodin, a stunning collection of Arts and Crafts stained glass by Dublin-born artist Harry Clarke (don't miss his masterpiece, *The Eve of St. Agnes*); and numerous works by modern Irish artists. One room holds the maddeningly cluttered studio of the Irish painter Francis Bacon that the gallery purchased from London and moved to Dublin, where it has been reconstructed behind glass. They moved everything—right down to the dust. It's an excellent, compact art museum, and a great place to spend an afternoon.

Parnell Sq. North, Dublin 1. www.hughlane.ie. © **01/222-5550.** Free admission. Tues–Thurs 10am–6pm; Fri–Sat 10am–5pm; Sun 11am–5pm. Closed Mon. Bus: 1, 2, 8, 10A, 14, 14A, 16, 16A, 19, 19A, 33X, 39X, 40, 41X, 46A, 46B, 46X, 48A, 58C, 58X, 70B, 70X, 116, 145.

The Irish President's House (Áras an Uachtaráin) ★★ HISTORIC HOUSE   Set in Phoenix Park, Áras an Uachtaráin was once the Viceregal Lodge, the summer retreat of the British viceroy, whose main digs were in Dublin Castle. From what were never humble beginnings, the original 1751 country house was expanded several times, gradually becoming the splendid

monumental WIT

Few cities have such a love-hate relationship with their statues as Dublin. Locals have an acerbic nickname for each one, many of them unprintable. The very buxom statue of Molly Malone (heroine of the titular Irish folk song, who sold "cockles and mussels, alive, alive, oh . . ."), which stands in front of the Tourism office on Suffolk Street, is variously known as, "the Tart with the Cart," "the Trollope with the Scallop," or "the Flirt in the Skirt." The James Joyce statue on O'Connell Street is "the Prick with a Stick"; the statue of Anna Livia (a character in *Finnegans Wake* who symbolized the Liffey), rising from an ornamental pond in Croppies Park, is "the Floozie in the Jacuzzi"; and, depending on who you talk to, the Spire of Dublin on O'Connell Street is either "the Stiletto in the Ghetto," "the Skewer in the Sewer," "the Stiffy by the Liffey," or "the Nail in the Pale."

neoclassical white mansion you see today, which now serves as the official residence of Ireland's President. Guided tours leave from the Phoenix Park Visitors Centre every Saturday. After an introductory historical film, a bus brings visitors to and from the house for a 1-hour tour of the state reception rooms (tours run a little longer in summer, when the gardens are included on the itinerary, weather permitting). As the building is still the official home of the Irish president, a strictly limited number of tickets are given out, on a first-come, first-served basis. The house may occasionally be closed for state events, so it's wise to call ahead. *Note:* For security reasons, no backpacks, travel bags, strollers, cameras, or mobile phones are allowed on the tour.

Tour departs from Phoenix Park Visitor Centre, Dublin 8. www.president.ie. © **01/677-0095** (Phoenix Park visitor center). Free admission. Sat tours hourly, 10:30am–3:30pm. Bus: 37.

Kilmainham Gaol ★★★ HISTORIC SITE

Equal parts memorial and exhibition, this is an extremely powerful place to visit for anyone interested in the Irish struggle for independence from British rule. Many prominent revolutionaries were imprisoned here in the 19th and early 20th centuries. Many were also executed, including the leaders of the 1916 Easter Rising (one of them, James Connolly, broke his foot during the fighting, and so was shot while sitting down). It wasn't just political prisoners who suffered here; leaders of the suffragette movement also found themselves doing time in the grim cells, not to mention a roll call of notorious murderers and criminals.

Inchicore Rd., Kilmainham, Dublin 8. www.heritageireland.ie/en/dublin/kilmainham gaol/. © **01/453-5984.** Admission €6 adults; €4 seniors; €2 students and children; €14 families. Apr–Sept daily 9:30am–6pm; Oct–Mar Mon–Sat 9:30am–5:30pm; Sun 10am–6pm. Last admission 1 hr. before closing. Luas: Suir Road. Bus: 13, 40, 51B, 51C, 63, 69, 78A, 79, 123, 206.

National Gallery of Ireland ★★ ART MUSEUM

George Bernard Shaw loved this place so much that he left it one-third of his royalties in perpetuity after he died. He saw it as paying a debt, so important was the gallery to his education. It is still a place to wander, wonder, and just be in thrall to so much beautiful art. Highlights of the permanent collection include paintings by Caravaggio, Gainsborough, Rubens, Goya, Rembrandt, Monet, and Picasso. The Irish national portrait collection is housed in one wing, while another area is devoted to the career of Jack B. Yeats (brother of W. B. Yeats), an Irish painter of some note. Major exhibitions change regularly, and the subjects are often more imaginative than just the usual run of retrospectives and national landscapes (although those appear too); recent shows have included an intriguing exhibition of mixed media sculpture, recreating images of Irish migration in the 18th and 19th century. In keeping with the "art for all" ethos that so enamored Shaw, entry to the permanent collection and many of the temporary shows is free.

Merrion Sq. West, Dublin 2. www.nationalgallery.ie. ℂ **01/661-5133.** Free admission. Mon–Wed, Fri–Sat 9:30am–5:30pm; Thurs 9:30am–8:30pm; Sun 11am–5:30pm; public holidays 10am–5:30pm. DART: Pearse. Luas: St. Stephen's Green, Grafton St. Bus: 4, 5, 7, 7A, 8, 13, 13A, 39, 39A, 44, 45, 46A, 48A.

National Museum of Ireland: Archaeology ★★★ MUSEUM   The most impressive of the four sites that collectively make up the National Museum of Ireland, this excellent museum is devoted to the ancient history of Ireland and beyond—from the Stone Age up to the early modern period. Highlights include a stunning collection of Viking artifacts from the archaeological digs that took place in Dublin from the 1960s to the early 1980s—a haul so important that in one fell swoop the history of Viking settlement in Ireland was rewritten. There is also an enormous range of Bronze Age gold and metalwork, as well as iconic Christian treasures from the Dark Ages, including the Ardagh Chalice, the Moylough Belt Shrine and the Tara Brooch. Other notable artifacts include "Ralaghan Man," a carved wooden Bronze Age statue from County Cavan; a collection of 2nd-century Roman figurines and homewares; and an extraordinary granite table made in Egypt circa 1870 B.C. The other sites of the NMI are the Natural History Museum on nearby Kildare Street; the Decorative Arts and History branch at Collins Barracks in Benburb, just west of the city center; and the Country Life branch in Castlebar, County Mayo (see p. 224).

Kildare St., Dublin 2. www.museum.ie. ℂ **01/677-7444.** Free admission. Tues–Sat 10am–5pm; Sun 2–5pm. Bus: 7B, 7D, 10, 10A, 11, 11A, 11B, 14, 14A, 15, 15A, 15B, 15C, 20B, 25X, 32X.

National Museum of Ireland: Decorative Arts & History, Collins Barracks ★★ MUSEUM   As the name of this branch of the National Museum of Ireland suggests, the collection tells the story of Irish (and world) history through fashion, jewelry, furniture, and other decorative arts, with the bulk of the collection spanning the 1760s to the 1960s. One gallery is devoted to the work of Eileen Gray (1878–1976), an Irish architect and furniture designer who became one of the most important figures of the modernist movement; another showcases the extraordinary collection of Asian art bequeathed to the Irish nation in the 1930s by Irish-American philanthropist Albert Bender. Set in a converted 18th-century army building, this branch of the National Museum isn't entirely devoted to the arts; eight galleries cover Irish military history from the 16th century to the present day, including a fascinating section about the Easter Rising of 1916.

Collins Barracks, Benburb St., Dublin 7. www.museum.ie. ℗ **01/677-7444.** Free admission. Tues–Sat 10am–5pm; Sun 2–5pm. Luas: Museum. Rail: Heuston. Bus: 39B, 70N.

National Museum of Ireland: Natural History ★★ MUSEUM

Before a huge renovation completed in 2010, this vast museum was a venerable but rather moth-eaten institution. Today, the building has never looked better, right down to the grand Victorian staircase, closed for years, that takes visitors to the upper floors. The core collection itself has changed little since the museum was founded in the mid-19th century, ranging from small stuffed native Irish animals and primates to the skeletons of enormous sea creatures. While there are recent additions—including the Discovery Zone, in which visitors can open a series of drawers to discover unusual specimens within—it still feels quaintly old-fashioned. Sadly, as of 2016, safety problems have required closing the balcony levels (the number of emergency exits doesn't meet modern building codes). These contain some of the most unique parts of the collection, such as the avian galleries and the "crystal jellies" collection—beautiful oversize glass models of microscopic sea creatures, made in the 19th century by the eccentric and brilliant Blaschka brothers of Dresden. Hopefully those galleries will have re-opened by the time you visit.

Merrion St., Dublin 2. www.museum.ie. ℗ **01/677-7444.** Free admission. Tues–Sat 10am–5pm; Sun 2–5pm. Bus: 4, 5, 7A, 8, 15X, 44, 44B, 44C, 48A, 49X, 50X, 51X, 63, 65X, 77X, 84.

St. Patrick's Cathedral ★★ CATHEDRAL

The largest church in Ireland, and one of the most beloved places of worship in the world, St. Patrick's is one of two Anglican Cathedrals in Dublin. Most of what you can see dates from the 14th century, but religious buildings stood here nearly a thousand years before that. It is mainly early English in style, with a square medieval tower that houses the largest ringing peal bells in Ireland, as well as an 18th-century spire. A moving collection of war memorials is tucked away at the very back of the cavernous nave, including a very low-key tribute to the Irish dead of World War II. (Ireland was neutral in that war, but around 300,000 men volunteered to fight with the Allies.) Admission includes an irregular program of lunchtime classical music recitals at the Cathedral—call or check the website for details. *Tip:* You can download an MP3 audio tour from the Cathedral's website for €2.50; click "Visit" then "Facilities."

St. Patrick's Close, Dublin 8. www.stpatrickscathedral.ie. ℗ **01/453-9472.** Admission €6 adults; €5 seniors and students; €3 children; €15 families. Mar–Oct Mon–Fri 9:30am–5pm; Sat 9am–6pm; Sun 9–10:30am, 12:30–2:30pm, 4:30–6pm. Nov–Feb Mon–Fri 9:30am–5pm; Sat 9am–5pm; Sun 9am–10:30am, 12:30–2:30pm. Guided tours Mon—Sat 10:30am and 2:30pm. Last admission 30 min. before closing. Bus: 49, 49A, 49X, 50X, 54A, 56A, 77, 77A, 77X, 150, 151.

Trinity College ★★ UNIVERSITY The oldest university in Ireland, Trinity was founded in 1592 by Queen Elizabeth I to offer an education to the children of the upper classes and protect them from the "malign" Catholic influences elsewhere in Europe. Now it is simply the most respected university in Ireland. Among its alumni are Bram Stoker, Jonathan Swift, Oscar Wilde, and Samuel Beckett, as well as an array of rebels and revolutionaries who helped create the Republic of Ireland. The campus spreads across central Dublin just south of the River Liffey, with cobbled squares, gardens, a picturesque quadrangle, and buildings dating from the 17th to the 20th centuries. You can wander the campus for free; alternatively, between May and September, **Trinity College Tours** take in all of the main sights, including a ticket for the Old Library and the Book of Kells (see p. 68).

College Green, Dublin 2. www.tcd.ie.© **01/896-1000.** Campus tours €5; including Old Library €12 (half-price for students, Oct–Mar) Library and Book of Kells only €9. Campus tours €6; including Old Library €13 adults, €12 seniors and students, €26 families. Library and Book of Kells only €10 adults, €9 seniors and students. Call or go online for times. DART: Pearse St., Connolly St. Luas: Lower Abbey St., St. Stephen's Green. Bus: College Green entrance (for tours): 7N, 15N, 15X, 44N, 46N, 48N, 49N, 51D, 51X, 54N, 56A, 70B, 70X, 77A, 77N, 92. Nassau St. entrance (for Old Library/Book of Kells): 25X, 32X, 33X, 41X, 51D, 51X, 58X, 67X, 84X, 92.

Other Museums & Libraries

Croke Park Stadium & GAA Museum ★ SPORTS MUSEUM Croke
Park is the headquarters, and main sports ground, of the Gaelic Athletic Association (GAA), which oversees most of the traditional Irish sports—including hurling, rounders (similar to baseball), and Gaelic football. This museum does a good job of setting out the history of these games and putting them into the wider historical context of the importance of sport to the Irish way of life. The interactive exhibits include a large video archive, and you can take a tour of the stadium too. But the most excitement is, of course, to be had on match days—check the website if you want to come and hear the roar of the crowd for real.

Jones Rd., Dublin 3. www.crokepark.ie.© **01/819-2300.** Tour and museum: €13 adults; €9.50 seniors and students; €8.50 children under 12; €34–€38 families. Museum only: €6 adults; €5 seniors and students; €4 children under 12; €16 families. **Museum** open Mon–Sat 9:30am–5pm; Sun 10:30am–5pm (June–Aug open until 6pm Mon–Sat); on match days, call to confirm hours. **Tour times:** July–Aug hourly 10am–4pm (10am–3pm Sun). Sept–June Mon–Fri 11am, 1, 3pm (also 4pm in June); Sat 10, 11am, noon, 1, 2, 3pm; Sun 11am, noon, 1, 2, 3pm (also 10am in June). On match days, call to confirm hours. Bus: 1, 11, 13, 16, 33, 41, 41B, 41C, 44.

Glasnevin Cemetery & Museum ★ CEMETERY North of the city
center, the Irish national cemetery was founded in 1832 and covers more than 50 hectares (124 acres). Most people buried here were ordinary citizens, but there are also many famous names on the headstones, ranging from former Irish Taoiseach (prime minister) Eamon de Valera to other political heroes and rebels including Michael Collins, Daniel O'Connell, Countess Constance

A TOUR OF trinity college

A beautiful, grand, romantic place to wander around, the Trinity campus is open free of charge to the public year-round, although there might be some access restrictions during exam periods.

Trinity's most striking and famous monument, the white **Campanile** (bell tower), grabs your attention as soon as you enter through the main archway. Dating from the mid-19th century, it stands on the site of the college's original foundations, from 300 years earlier.

Built in the 18th century to a design by Thomas Burgh, the neoclassical **Old Library Building** is the only section of the campus that you have to pay to see. It's where you'll find the **Book of Kells,** although the library's magnificent **Long Room** is worth seeing in its own right (see p. 69).

Home to the geography and geology departments, the **Museum Building** is one of Trinity's hidden gems. It was built in the mid-19th century with a combination of Byzantine and Moorish influences. Walk through and look up to the domed ceiling and the green marbled banisters.

Set between these two architectural masterpieces, the stark 1967 **Berkeley Library building** sharply divides opinion. Designer Paul Koralek's library honors Bishop George Berkeley, famed for his philosophical theory of "immaterialism" (things that can't be proved cannot exist), which went against the theories of both Isaac Newton and the Catholic Church. The gleaming sculpture outside the library is **Sphere Within Sphere** by Arnaldo Pomodoro (1983).

Also facing the Old Library across Fellows Square, the 1970s **Arts Building** includes the **Douglas Hyde Gallery,** which displays modern art. Exhibitions switch out about every 3 months and admission is always free.

Tucked away in the far northeastern corner of the campus, the excellent **Science Gallery** is a combination art space, science museum, and debating forum, with fun and thought-provoking exhibitions, workshops, public lectures, and even shows. Entry is free, except to certain special events. See **www.dublin. sciencegallery.com** for more details.

One of the more benign remnants of English rule, the **College Park Cricket Pitch** is a small park where you'll often find a cricket match in progress on summer weekends. If you don't know the rules of cricket, it may be hard to follow—the sport is notoriously arcane for the uninitiated—but you can still enjoy the picturesque sight of the players in their white uniforms.

Markievicz, and Charles Stewart Parnell. Literary figures also have their place here—you can find writers Christy Brown (immortalized in the film *My Left Foot*) and Brendan Behan. There's a small museum devoted to the cemetery and its famous occupants. Guided tours run daily, or you can download a self-guided tour app for your smartphone for €10 via the cemetery's website. Maps showing who is buried where are also for sale in the flower shop at the entrance.

Finglas Rd., Glasnevin, Dublin 11. www.glasnevintrust.ie. ℘ **01/882-6550.** Museum and tour €12 adults and seniors, €8 students and children, €25 families; museum only €6 adults, €4 seniors, students, and children, €15 families. Museum: Mon–Fri 10am–5pm; Sat–Sun and public holidays 11am–5pm. Tours: Mon—Fri 11:30am and 2:30pm; Sat—Sun 10:30 and 11:30am, 12:30, 1:30, and 2:30pm. Bus: 4, 9, 40, 83, 140, 58X, 66X, 67X, 70X, 84X, 92.

Irish Museum of Modern Art ★ ART MUSEUM This small but handsome museum, located in a beautiful 17th-century former hospital building, has a strong collection of modern art dating from the 1940s to the present day. Highlights include a striking series of mid-1970s photographs by Serbian conceptual artist Marina Abramovic; etchings and lithographs by Alice Maher, Louis le Brocquy, and Marcel Duchamp; and the Madden Arnholz Collection, made up of around 2,000 old master prints, including works by Hogarth and Rembrandt. The beautifully restored grounds are also used as an exhibition space, with a number of changing pieces set among the formal lawns and clipped box hedges.

Royal Hospital, Military Rd., Kilmainham, Dublin 8. www.imma.ie. ✆ **01/612-9900.** Free admission. Tues–Fri 11:30am–5:30pm; Sat 10am–5:30pm; Sun and public holidays noon–5:30pm. Last admission 45 min. before closing. Closed Mon. Luas: Heuston. Bus: 26, 51, 51B, 78A, 79, 90, 123.

The James Joyce Centre ★ MUSEUM This idiosyncratic museum is set in a handsome Georgian house that once belonged to the Earl of Kenmare. Joyce himself never lived here; however, he was rather taken with a former owner of the house named Denis Maginni—an eccentric Irishman, who added an "i" to his name to give himself an air of Italian sophistication. (Maginni appears as a character in Joyce's masterpiece *Ulysses.*) Today, the center functions as both a small museum and a cultural center devoted to Joyce and his work. Actual exhibits are a little sparse, but they hold interesting (at least for Joyce fans) lectures and special events, and also organize a Joyce-themed walking tour of Dublin. Unsurprisingly, this place becomes an explosion of activity around Bloomsday (June 16th), the date upon which *Ulysses*'s fictional events take place. Unlike the rest of Dublin, which spends a single day celebrating its most famous 20th-century literary hero, the James Joyce Centre turns it into a week-long festival.

35 North Great George's St., Dublin 1. www.jamesjoyce.ie. ✆ **01/878-8547.** Admission €5 adults; €4 seniors, students and children. Apr–Sept Mon–Sat 10am–5pm, Sun noon–5pm; Oct–Mar Tues–Sat noon–5pm, Sun noon–5pm. Last admission 30 min. before closing. Bus: 1, 4, 7, 7b, 7d, 8, 9, 11, 13, 16, 38, 38a, 38b, 40, 44, 122, 123, 140, 747.

The Little Museum of Dublin ★★ MUSEUM Stuffed full of ephemera relating to the lives of ordinary Dubliners—art, toys, photographs, newspapers, prints, and other artifacts of the everyday—this delightful little museum chronicles what it was like to live in the city throughout the 20th century. Thoughtfully laid out inside a beautifully preserved Georgian town house, the vast majority of the items on display were donated by the people of Dublin, and the collection is being added to all the time. In among the curios are genuine documents of social history, including items relating to the First World War, the struggle for independence, and the suffrage movement. Several objects have charming anecdotes connected—such as the music stand that, in June 1963, was hurriedly borrowed from the home of a local antique dealer by visiting U.S. President John F. Kennedy, when he realized he had nowhere to put his papers during a speech. While it probably packs more of an emotional punch for native Dubliners, the exhibits tell an engaging story for outsiders as well. Tours (on the hour) are lively and informative, and the guides are great with children.

15 St. Stephen's Green, Dublin 2. www.littlemuseum.ie. ✆ **01/661-1000.** Admission €7 adults; €5 seniors; €4.50 students and children; €14 families. Deluxe ticket (includes private guided tour) €12. Sun–Wed 9:30am–5pm; Thurs 9:30am–8pm. Luas: St. Stephen's Green. Bus: 15X, 32X, 39X, 41X, 46X, 51X,

Marsh's Library ★★ LIBRARY   Unlike Trinity College's Long Room, which is largely for show these days, Marsh's Library is still a functioning library. Founded by Narcissus Marsh, the Archbishop of Dublin, in 1701, its interior is a magnificent example of a 17th-century scholar's library that has remained much the same for 3 centuries. Its walls are lined with scholarly volumes, chiefly focused on theology, medicine, ancient history, and maps, along with Hebrew, Greek, Latin, and French literature. You can still see the wire cages in which readers would be locked in with the more valuable tomes. There's a particularly excellent collection of books by and about the great satiric writer Jonathan Swift, which includes volumes with his editing comments in the margins—ironically, perhaps, given that Swift himself said of Archbishop Marsh, "He is the first of human race, that with great advantages of learning, piety, and station ever escaped being a great man."

St Patrick's Close, Dublin 8. www.marshlibrary.ie. ✆ **01/454-3511.** Admission €3 adults; €2 seniors and students; children 15 and under free. Mon, Wed–Fri 9:30am–5pm; Sat 10am–5pm Closed public holidays and last week in Dec. Bus: 49, 49A, 50X, 54A, 56A, 77A, 77X, 150, 151.

National Wax Museum Plus ★ MUSEUM   Ireland's answer to Madame Tussaud's, this small museum occupies the former armory of the Parliament House (see p. 86). It's mostly aimed at kids, with more hands-on, interactive attractions beyond the usual wax tableaux (hence the "Plus"). At the "Wax Factor" studio, you can sing along to a variety of pop hits and have yourself superimposed into the videos (take away a DVD for €7), and in the Wax Hands room you can have a wax model of your hand made, because now who wouldn't want that? The waxwork galleries themselves include displays on Irish history and mythology; great Irish writers; and, perhaps most successfully, the Chamber of Horrors, which sometimes features live actors waiting to administer additional scares (over-16s only).

4 Foster Pl., Dublin 2. www.waxmuseumplus.ie. ✆ **01/645-8813.** Admission €12 adults; €10 seniors, students, and children 13—17; €8 children 5—12 (children 4 and under free); €35 families. Daily 10—7; last admission 45 min. before closing. Bus: 9, 13, 16, 27, 40, 54a, 65, 65b, 68, 77a, 83, 150.

Number Twenty-Nine: Georgian House Museum ★★ MUSEUM A little time capsule of family life in Georgian Dublin, Number 29 is a fascinating curiosity. Rooms are kept as close as possible to how they would have looked in the period from 1790 to about 1820. The differences between family living spaces and the basement servants' quarters are, unsurprisingly, stark. Two elegant drawing rooms, with rich carpets and expensive blue wallpaper and crystal chandeliers, stand in sharp relief to the spare housekeeper's bedroom or the simple, homely kitchen. At the same time, however, the industriousness of the kitchen is quite a revelation—medicines and cosmetics were made here from scratch by the servants, in addition to all the family's meals. The self-guided audio tour is informative, or if you can't bear to be in a place like this without being able to ask questions, there's a full tour daily at 3pm.

Corner of Fitzwilliam St. Lower and Mount St. Upper, Dublin 2. www.numbertwenty nine.ie. ℂ **01/702-6165.** Admission €6 adults; €3 seniors and students; children 15 and under free. Tues–Sat 10am–5pm. Last admission 30 min. before closing. Tours: 3pm. DART: Pearse. Bus: 15X, 49X, 50X, 65X, 77X.

Temple Bar Gallery ★★ ART GALLERY/STUDIOS   This big, rambling art gallery sums up all that is good about Temple Bar. Founded in 1983 in the heart of Dublin's "Left Bank," this is one of the largest studio and gallery complexes of its kind in Europe. It's filled with innovative work by contemporary Irish artists—more than 30 of them, in a variety of disciplines, including sculpture, painting, printing, and photography. The colors and creativity are dazzling, and it's run by helpful, friendly people. Only the gallery section is open to the public, but you can make an appointment in advance to view individual artists at work. The Studios host free talks and discussion panels, featuring the great and the good of the Irish arts scene. Call or go online for details.

5–9 Temple Bar, Dublin 2. www.templebargallery.com. ℂ **01/671-0073.** Free admission. Tues–Sat 11am–6pm. Bus: 26, 37, 39, 39A, 39B, 39C, 49X, 50X, 65X, 66, 66A, 66B, 66D, 67, 67A, 69X, 70, 70A, 77X.

Brewery

Guinness Storehouse ★ FACTORY TOUR   Opened in 1759, the Guinness Storehouse is one of the world's most famous breweries, producing the distinctive dark stout, known and loved the world over. You can explore the Guinness Hopstore, tour a converted 19th-century building housing the World of Guinness Exhibition, and view a film showing how the stout is made; then move on to the Gilroy Gallery that's dedicated to the graphic design work of John Gilroy (whose work you will inevitably have seen if you've ever been in an Irish pub); and last but not least, stop in at the breathtaking Gravity Bar. Here you can sample a glass of the famous brew in the glass-enclosed bar 61m (200 ft.) above the ground, complete with 360-degree views of the city.

St. James's Gate, off Robert St., Dublin 8. www.guinness-storehouse.com. ℂ **01/408-4800.** Admission €20 adults; €16 seniors and students over 18; €14 student under 18; €6.50 children 6–12 (children 5 and under free); €47 families. Sept–May daily 9:30am–5pm (last admission); July–Aug daily 9:30am–6pm (last admission). Luas: St. James's Hospital. Bus: 123.

Churches & Cathedrals

St. Audeon's Church ★ CHURCH   Near the only remaining gate of the Old City walls (dating from 1214), this is said to be the only surviving medieval parish church in Dublin. Although it is partly in ruins, significant parts have survived, including the west doorway, which dates from 1190, and the

13th-century nave. (*Note:* While this St. Audeon's is Church of Ireland, nearby is another St. Audeon's Church, that one Catholic and dating from 1846. It was in the latter church that Father "Flash" Kavanagh used to say the world's fastest Mass so that his congregation was out in time for the football matches.) Entrance to the ancient church is through a visitor center. The center's exhibition, relating the history of St. Audeon's, is self-guided; visits to the church itself are by guided tour, and it is only open in high season.

14 High St., Dublin 8. www.heritageireland.ie. ⓒ **01/677-0088.** Free admission. Apr–Oct daily 9:30am–5:30pm. Bus: 49X, 50X, 51B, 51C, 51N, 54A, 78A, 206.

St. Mary's Pro Cathedral ★ CATHEDRAL   No, there isn't a pro and amateur league for Cathedrals in Ireland—"pro" simply means "temporary." And therein lies a fascinating piece of historical trivia. Contrary to popular belief, Dublin has no Roman Catholic Cathedral (St. Patrick's and Christ Church have been part of the Anglican Church of Ireland since the 16th century). But the Vatican views Christ Church as Dublin's "true" Catholic Cathedral. Therefore, St. Mary's has been designated the "temporary" official Catholic cathedral in Dublin . . . since 1820. Tucked away on a rather unimpressive back street, it's nonetheless the heart of the city's Northside. It was built between 1815 and 1825 in Greek Revival Doric style, with an exterior portico modeled on the Temple of Theseus in Athens, with six Doric columns. The Renaissance-style interior is patterned after the Church of Saint-Philippe du Roule of Paris. The church is noted for its awe-inspiring Palestrina Choir, which sings a Latin Mass every Sunday at 11am (during term times).

83 Marlborough St., Dublin 1. www.procathedral.ie. ⓒ **01/874-5441.** Free admission. Mon–Fri 7:30am–6:30pm; Sat 7:30am–7pm; Sun 9am–1:30pm, 5:30–7:30pm; public holidays 10am–1:30pm. DART: Connolly, Tara St. Luas: Abbey St. Bus: 2, 3, 4, 5, 7, 7A, 7B, 7D, 8, 10, 10A, 11, 11A, 11B, 13, 20B, 27, 32X, 33X, 39X, 40A, 40C, 41, 41A, 41B, 41C, 41X, 42, 42A, 42B, 43, 51A, 116, 123, 130, 142, 747.

St. Michan's Church ★★ CHURCH   Built on the site of an early Danish chapel (1095), this 17th-century edifice has fine interior woodwork and an organ (dated 1724) on which Handel is said to have played his *Messiah.* But the church is more famous for its two underground crypts—one of which is filled with mummified bodies that have lain for centuries in an extraordinary state of preservation. A few still have their hair and fingernails; on others you can see desiccated internal organs under the skin. The tallest mummy is known as "the Crusader"; his legs were broken in order to fit him into the coffin. Others in residence include "the Nun" and "the Thief"—although their true identities were lost when the church records were destroyed during the civil war in 1922. It's a macabre place, but a fascinating one. Word is that Bram Stoker was inspired to write *Dracula* in part by having visited as a child. *Note:* The church is wheelchair accessible, but the vaults are not.

Church St., Dublin 7. www.stmichans.com. ⓒ **01/872-4154.** Admission €5 adults; €4 seniors and students; €3.50 children; €15 families. Crypt: Mid-Mar to Oct Mon–Fri 10am–12:45pm, 2–4:45pm; Sat 10am–12:45pm. Nov to mid-Mar Mon–Fri 12:30–3:30pm; Sat 10am–12:45pm. No crypt tours Sun. Luas: Four Courts, Smithfield. Bus: 51D, 51X.

DUBLIN walking tours

Small and compact, Dublin was made for walking, and some of the best experiences the city has to offer involve taking it at your own pace, map in hand. If you'd like more guidance, however, consider one of the following tour services.

You could hardly be in better or more learned hands for the **Historical Walking Tours of Dublin** (www.historicaltours.ie; **℡ 087/688-9412**), whose guides are all post-grad students at Trinity College, Dublin. Established for nearly 30 years, these engaging tours offer peerless historical insight. Tours leave from the front gates of Trinity College on College Green, daily at 11am and 3pm from May to September; daily at 11am in April and October; and Friday to Sunday at 11am from November to March. Tickets cost €12 adults, €10 students and seniors (accompanied kids are free), and you can just pay the guide on the day. An intriguing variety of private tours are also available—subjects include Medieval Dublin; Irish Food; and even a Running Tour for those who could take their history with a workout. These need to be booked in advance and cost €160.

If you prefer to take in the sights at a more leisurely pace, with a bit of liquid refreshment to keep things lively, try the **Literary Pub Crawl** (www.dublinpub crawl.com; **℡ 01/670-5602**). Walking in the footsteps of Joyce, Behan, Beckett, Shaw, and other Irish literary greats, this tour visits Dublin's most famous pubs and explores their deep literary connections. Actors provide humorous performances and commentary between stops. Tours start at the **Duke Pub,** 8 Duke St. (**℡ 01/679-9553**), daily at 7:30pm from April to October; and Thursday to

Historic Architecture & Buildings

Custom House ★ ARCHITECTURAL SITE   Completed in 1791, this beautifully proportioned Georgian building has a long classical facade of graceful pavilions, arcades, and a central dome topped by a statue of Commerce. Although it burned to a shell in 1921, the building has been masterfully restored. The exterior is the main attraction here, and most of the interior is closed to the public; however, those with a real interest in finding out more about the building and its history can drop by the small visitor center, which has exhibitions and an audiovisual presentation telling the story of its reconstructions.

Custom House Quay, Dublin 1. ℡ **01/888-2000.** Admission €1.50 adults; €4 families; students free. Visitor center: mid-Mar to Nov Mon–Fri 10am–12:30pm, 2–5pm; Sat–Sun and public holidays 2–5pm. Dec to mid-Mar Wed–Fri 10am–12:30pm, 2–5pm; Sun 2–5pm. Luas: Busáras. Bus: 27C, 41X, 53A, 90, 90A, 92, 151, 747, 748.

Dublin Castle ★ CASTLE   The center of British power in Ireland for more than 700 years, this 13th-century castle was finally taken over by the new Irish government in 1922. You can wander the grounds for free, but they're somewhat plain; the official tour takes in the much more impressive State Apartments, the early18th-century Treasury, and the Gothic-style Chapel Royal chapel building that boasts fine plaster decoration and a carved-oak gallery. The castle's only extant tower—a 13th-century structure once

Sunday at 7:30pm from November to March. Tickets cost €12 adults, €10 students. A limited number of tickets are sold at the Duke on the night, but it's best to book online. No children are allowed, for obvious reasons.

More excellent sightseeing for the thirsty can be enjoyed on the **Traditional Irish Music Pub Crawl** (www.discover dublin.ie/musical-pub-crawl; ✆ **01/475-3313**). Tours are led by two professional musicians, who sing as you make your way from one famous musical pub to another in Temple Bar. The evening is touristy, but the music is good. Tours meet upstairs at **Oliver St. John Gogarty's** pub, Fleet Street and Anglesea Street (✆ **01/671-1822**). Tours run daily at 7:30pm from April to October; and Thursday to Saturday at 7:30pm from November to March. The cost is €12

adults, €10 students. You can book in advance or buy on the night. Again, no children.

In 2016, Ireland celebrated the 100th anniversary of a rebellion that would profoundly change Irish history—the failed Easter Rising. The **1916 Rebellion Walking Tour** (www.1916rising.com; ✆ **086/858-3847**) takes you into the heat of the action at the General Post Office, explaining how the anger rose until the rebellion exploded on Easter Sunday in 1916. The 2-hour tour is well thought out and run by local historians who wrote a book on the events of that year. Tours run March to October, 11:30am from Monday to Saturday, and 1pm on Sunday. Tickets cost €12. Booking is advisable. Meet at the International Bar, 23 Wicklow St. (✆ **01/677-9250**).

used to imprison suspected traitors—now holds a small museum dedicated to the Garda (Irish police). The castle's Upper Yard was, in 1583, the scene of Ireland's last trial by mortal combat; today it is dominated by an impressive Georgian structure called the Bedford Tower. The Irish crown jewels used to be kept in the Bedford Tower—until they were stolen in 1907 (they have still never been found). If it's open, check out the Medieval Undercroft, an excavated site on the grounds where an early Viking fortress once stood. *Note:* This is a government building, so areas are may be closed for state events.

Dame St., Dublin 2. www.heritageireland.ie. ✆ **01/645-8813.** €6.70 adults; €5.70 seniors; €3.20 students and children (11 and under). Guided tour €8.50 adults; €7.50 seniors; €4 students and children. Mon–Sat 9:45am–4:45pm; Sun and public holidays noon–4:45pm. Luas: Jervis. Bus: 13, 37, 37, 39, 39A, 39B, 39C, 49, 49A, 49X, 50, 50X, 54A, 56A, 65X, 70, 70A, 70X, 77, 77A, 77X, 123, 150, 747.

The Four Courts ★ ARCHITECTURAL SITE   Home to the Irish legal courts since 1796, this fine 18th-century building was designed by James Gandon (who also designed the Custom House; see above). It is distinguished by its graceful Corinthian columns, massive dome, and exterior statues of Justice, Mercy, Wisdom, and Moses. Badly damaged by the fighting during the civil war of 1922, this building was later artfully restored, although some details, such as the statues of famous Irish lawyers that used to adorn the niches of the Round Hall, were lost. Tours are available, but frustratingly only for law students (who must book as part of a group). The only way to see the interior is usually to watch a trial in progress.

Inns Quay, Dublin 8. www.courts.ie. ✆ **01/888-6000.** Luas: Four Courts. Bus: 25, 25A, 51D, 51X, 68, 69, 78, 79, 79A, 83, 151, 172.

General Post Office ★ HISTORIC SITE   Don't be fooled by the nondescript name: With a facade of Ionic columns and Greco-Roman pilasters 60m long (197 ft.) and 17m high (56 ft.), this is more than a post office—it is the symbol of Irish freedom. Built between 1815 and 1818, it was the main stronghold of the Irish Volunteers during the Easter Rising. On Easter Sunday, 1916, Patrick Pearse stood on its steps and read a proclamation declaring a free Irish Republic. It began, "In every generation the Irish people have asserted their right to national freedom and sovereignty." Then he and an army of supporters barricaded themselves inside. A siege ensued that ultimately involved much of the north of the city, and before it was over, the building was all but destroyed. It had barely been restored before the civil war broke out in 1922, and it was heavily damaged again. It's still a working post office today, although the small **Letters, Lives and Liberty Museum** does house a few diverting exhibits, including the original Declaration of Independence. That's all very much a secondary attraction, though; touching the bullet holes in the walls out front is a far more powerful way to experience a sense of this building's history.

O'Connell St., Dublin 1. www.anpost.ie. ✆ **01/705-8833.** Free admission (museum €2). Post Office building: Mon–Sat 8:30am–6:00pm. Closed public holidays. Museum: Mon–Sat 10am–5pm. Luas: Abbey St. Bus: 10, 10A, 32X, 33X, 39X, 40A, 40C, 41X, 46A, 46B, 46C, 46D, 46E, 116, 123, 145, 747.

Ha'penny Bridge ★ LOCAL LANDMARK   Built in 1816, and one of the earliest cast-iron bridges in Europe, the graceful, pedestrian-only Ha'penny Bridge (pronounced Hay-penny) is the still the most attractive of Dublin's bridges. Officially named the Liffey Bridge, it's universally known by the toll it once charged to cross it: half a penny. The turnstiles were removed in 1919 when passage was made free. The bridge is at its prettiest after sundown, when the old lamps atop its three filigreed arches are lit, and the underside at each end is illuminated in green. In recent years it became traditional for couples to leave padlocks latched onto the bridge, with their names inscribed, before throwing the keys into the water. Dublin's city government now forbids the practice, seeing them more as an eyesore than a symbol of eternal love.

Connects Wellington Quay and Lower Ormond Quay, Dublin 2. Luas: Jervis. Bus: 39B, 51, 51B, 51C, 51D, 51X, 68, 69, 69X, 78, 78A, 79, 79A, 90, 92, 206.

Leinster House ★ ARCHITECTURAL SITE   The home of the Dáil (Irish House of Representatives) and Seanad (Irish Senate), this is the modern center of Irish government. Dating from 1745, it was originally known as Kildare House and was the seat of the Dukes of Leinster. Like the Parliament

DUBLIN bus tours

Convenient, comfortable, and—remember this when the heavens open in June—relatively immune to inclement weather, bus tours are a great way to pack a lot of sightseeing into a little time. And while Dublin has more than its fair share of standard tourist buses, some are more original.

For a lively tour of Dublin's Viking history, the **Viking Splash Tour** (www.vikingsplash.ie; ✆ **01/707-6000**) in a reconditioned World War II amphibious "duck" vehicle starts on land and eventually splashes into the Grand Canal. Viking helmets, though supplied, are optional. Tickets are €22 adults, €20 seniors and students, €17 children ages 13 to 17, €12 children ages 2 to 12, and €70 families. Children ages 2 and under aren't allowed for safety reasons.

Of the many "hop on, hop off" style bus tours of the city, one of the best is the **Dublin Sightseeing** tour, run by **Dublin Bus** (www.dublinsightseeing.ie; ✆ **01/703-3028**). The 24-stop tour takes you all around the city center and out as far as Kilmainham Gaol (see p. 73). You can leave and rejoin the tour as many times as you like in a day. Buses run all day, every 10 minutes from 9am to 3:30pm, every 15 minutes until 5:30pm, and every 30 minutes until the last bus at around 6:30pm. Tickets cost €22 adults, €20 seniors and students, €10 children ages 5 to 14. Large discounts are sometimes offered for families if you book online.

The **North Coast and Castle Tour** and the **South Coast and Gardens Tour,** also run by Dublin Bus, take you on all-day excursions to the picturesque coastal regions on the far fringes of Dublin. Tickets for both tours include entry to a separate attraction; the medieval Malahide Castle and its landscaped park to the north, and **Powerscourt House and Gardens** (see p. 107) to the south. The cost is €25 adults, €12 children.

A spooky evening tour in a bus decked out in, um . . . spooky wallpaper, **Dublin Ghost Bus** (www.dublinsightseeing.ie/ghostbus; ✆ **01/703-3028**) addresses Dublin's history of felons, fiends, and phantoms. You'll see haunted houses, learn of Dracula's Dublin origins, and even get a crash course in body snatching. It's all ghoulish fun but actually quite scary in places, so it's not recommended for kids who don't have "teen" in their age. Tickets cost €28.

Likewise, the entertaining **Gravediggers Tour** (www.thegravedigger.ie; ✆ **085/102-3646**) takes you in pursuit of a few ghoulish and well-intentioned scares. Just when it all seems like too much for the faint-hearted, the bus stops at the Gravediggers Pub by Glasnevin Cemetery (see p. 76) for a fortifying drink—included in the ticket price of €25. Live actors and 4-D technology help bring the whole experience to life. Or should that be . . .

House building (see below), it is said to have been a major influence on the architects of Washington, D.C.; the resemblance to Irish-born James Hoban's design for the White House, built 78 years later, is certainly clear enough. When the Dáil is not in session, tickets are available for guided tours, three times a day, on Mondays and Fridays. You don't have to book, but numbers are strictly limited. To reserve tickets, the events desk prefers an email (event.desk@oireachtas.ie; include your full name, address, and telephone number), or you can call ✆ **1890/252-4551**. *Note:* You need to bring photo ID (such as a driver's license or passport) to gain admission, and you shouldn't bring large or bulky bags.

Kildare St. and Merrion Sq., Dublin 2. www.oireachtas.ie. ⓒ **01/618-3186** or 3781. Free admission. Entry by tour only, Mon and Fri 10:30am, 2:30, 3:30pm. (Additional tours when Dáil and Seanad in session, Tues and Wed 7 and 8pm). Bus: 4, 5, 7A, 8, 7B, 7D, 10, 10A, 11, 11A, 11B, 14, 14A, 15, 15A, 15B, 15C, 15X, 20B, 25X, 32X, 44, 44B, 44C, 48A, 49X, 50X, 51X, 63, 65X, 77X, 84.

Parliament House ★ ARCHITECTURAL SITE The grand colonnaded facade of this building, which dates to the 1730s, was allegedly the model for the Capitol building in Washington, D.C. The Irish Parliament met here until 1801, when, by an extraordinary quirk of history, it voted for its own abolition. William Pitt the Younger, then Prime Minister of Britain, had promised sweeping reform of the anti-Catholic laws if Ireland agreed to a formal union with Britain. They did so, but Pitt was deposed by King George III, the reforms never happened, and the Irish lost what little self-government they had. Today the building is owned by the Bank of Ireland, but you can see parts of the magnificent interior featuring oak woodwork, 18th-century tapestries, and a sparkling crystal chandelier. Friendly porters are on hand to fill you in on the history. In our experience, they may also give informal tours of rooms you can't normally see, if you ask nicely.

2 College Green, Dublin 2. ⓒ **01/671-1488.** Free admission. Mon–Wed, Fri 10am–4pm; Thurs 10am–5pm. DART: Tara Street. LUAS: St. Stephen's Green, Jervis St. Bus: 9, 13, 16, 27, 40, 54a, 65, 65b, 68, 77a, 83, 150.

Parks & Gardens

Dublin Zoo ★★ ZOO If you've got kids and they're in need of a change from castles, churches, and history, here's the antidote. This modern, humane zoo in Phoenix Park provides a home for more than 235 species of wild animals and tropical birds. The animals live inside a series of realistically created habitats such as "African Savanna," home to giraffes, rhinos, and ostriches; "Gorilla Rainforest," a 12,000 square meter (7½ sq. mile) enclosure that houses five lowland gorillas; "Asian Forest," home to Sumatran tigers and lions; "the South American House" with an eclectic range of almost unbearably cute species, including tiny pygmy marmosets and two-toed sloths; and the new "Pacific Coast," opened in 2015, home to sea lions (you can watch them swim underwater), and a flamingo aviary big enough for the gracious birds to take flight. There are playgrounds and gift shops scattered throughout. Feeding times and scheduled talks are posted on the zoo's website (several times daily from Mar–Sept, weekends only from Oct–Feb). A restaurant is on site, as well as plenty of smaller cafes and picnic areas for those who prefer to bring their own meals.

Phoenix Park, Dublin 8. www.dublinzoo.ie. ⓒ **01/474-8900.** Admission €18 adults; €14 seniors and students; €13 children 3–15; €5.80 special needs child; €9.20 special needs adult; €48–€58 families. Mar–Sept daily 9:30am–6pm; Oct 9:30am–5:30pm; Nov–Dec 9:30am–4pm; Jan 9:30am–4:30pm; Feb 9:30am–5pm. Last admission to zoo 1 hr. before closing; last admission to African Savanna 30 min. before closing. Luas: Heuston (15-min. walk). Bus: 25, 26, 46A, 66, 66A, 66B, 67, 69.

Phoenix Park ★ PARK The vast green expanses of Phoenix Park are Dublin's playground, and it's easy to see why. This is a well-designed, user-friendly park crisscrossed by a network of roads and quiet pedestrian walkways that make its 704 hectares (1,739 acres) easily accessible. Avenues of oaks, beech trees, pines, and chestnut trees are shady hideaways, or you can sun yourself in broad expanses of grassland; livestock graze peacefully on pasturelands, deer roam the forested areas, and horses romp on polo fields. It's a relaxing place to spend a restful afternoon, but there's also plenty to do here should you feel active. The home of the Irish president (see p. 72) is in the park, as is the Dublin Zoo (see above). The visitor center is partly located inside **Ashtown Castle,** a towerhouse built in the 1430s that—hard to believe, but true—was only discovered in 1978, when a later building that had completely incorporated it was being demolished. Free parking is adjacent to the center. Also next to the center is the **Victorian Tea Kiosk,** which serves snacks and light lunches, and has toilets. It's open from 10am to 4:30pm daily. The park is 3km (2 miles) west of the city center on the north bank of the River Liffey.

Phoenix Park, Dublin 8. www.phoenixpark.ie. ℂ **01/677-0095.** Free admission. Park open 24 hours; visitor center open Apr–Dec daily 10am–6pm; Jan–Mar Wed–Sun 9:30am–5:30pm. Last admission 45 min. before closing. Bus: 37 (Castleknock Road entrance); 37, 38, 39, 70 (Navan Road entrance); or 46A (North Circular Road entrance).

St. Stephen's Green ★ PARK This lovely city center park is filled with public art, and there always seems to be something new and imaginative hidden amid its leafy walkways. Among them is a beautiful statue commemorating the Irish rebel Wolfe Tone (beside an affecting monument to the Great Famine) and a garden of scented plants for blind visitors. This is a great place for a summer picnic. If the weather's fine, you can take a buggy ride through the park; rides leave from the Grafton Street side and cost around €30 to €50 for up to four passengers.

Dublin 2. Luas: St. Stephen's Green. Bus: 20B, 32X, 33X, 39X, 40A, 40C, 41X, 46B, 46N, 46X, 51X, 58X, 70B, 70X, 84X, 92.

Shopping

The hub of mainstream shopping south of the Liffey is indisputably **Grafton Street,** a combination of big chains, chichi department stores, and little shops. It's also a popular site for street performers, where you're almost guaranteed an impromptu show on a sunny day.

Avoca ★★ CLOTHING/HOUSEWARES A Dublin institution, Avoca is wonderland of vivid colors, intricately woven fabrics, soft blankets, light woolen sweaters, children's clothes, and toys, all set in a delightful store spread over three floors near Trinity College. All the fabrics are woven in the Vale of Avoca in the Wicklow Mountains. The shop also sells pottery, jewelry, vintage and antique clothing, food, and adorable little things you really don't need, but can't live without. Hands down, this is one of the best stores in Dublin. The top-floor **cafe** is a great place for lunch (see p. 62). 11-13 Suffolk St., Dublin 2. www.avoca.ie. ℂ **01/677-4215.** Mon–Wed and Sat 9:30am–6pm; Thurs–Fri 9:30am–7pm; Sun 11am–6pm. Bus: 15X, 32X, 33X, 39X, 41X, 51D, 51X, 58X, 70X, 84X.

TEMPLE BAR street markets

Not all the best shopping in Temple Bar is to be found indoors: It's also home to three of Dublin's finest street markets.

The **Designer Mart** is a great showcase for fashion designers and craftspeople from all over Ireland. It takes place in uber-trendy Cow's Lane every Saturday from 10am until 5pm.

The **Book Market** takes over Temple Bar Square all weekend, from 10am to 6pm. It's relatively small, but there's always some piece of printed treasure or other to be unearthed among its secondhand book stalls.

A must for foodies, the **Food Market** makes its presence felt through the tempting aromas that waft around Meeting House Square from 10am to 4:30pm on Saturday. Should the weather take a turn for the worse, there's even a retractable roof to keep you dry while you deliberate over which Irish farmhouse cheese to take away, before waiting in line for a freshly cooked snack.

Brown Thomas ★★ DEPARTMENT STORE   The top-hatted doorman out front sets a deceptively formal tone for this great old Dublin institution; we've always found it a relaxed and friendly place, even if the credit card seems to take a bit of a beating. Stop by for most of the major fashion labels before getting your nails done, having a one-to-one at the cosmetics counters, and indulging yourself at the bar and cafe or the elegant new restaurant. 88-95 Grafton St., Dublin 2. www.brownthomas.com. ✆ **01/605-6666.** Mon–Wed, Fri–Sat 9am–9pm; Thurs 9am–10pm; Sun 10am–8pm. Luas: St. Stephen's Green. Bus: 11, 11A, 11B, 14, 14A, 15A, 15C, 15X, 20B, 27C, 32X, 33X, 39B, 39X, 41X, 46B, 46C, 51X, 58X, 70X, 84X.

Claddagh Records ★★★ MUSIC   Renowned among insiders in traditional Irish music circles, this is where to find "the genuine article" in traditional music and perhaps discover a new favorite. Not only is the staff knowledgeable and enthusiastic about new artists, but they're able to tell you which venues and pubs are hosting the best music sessions that week. They have a second branch at 2 Cecilia St., Temple Bar (✆ **01/677-0262**). 5 Westmoreland St., Dublin 2. www.claddaghrecords.com. ✆ **01/888-3600.** Mon–Fri 10am–5:30pm; Sat noon–5:30pm. Luas: Jervis. Bus: 1, 7B, 7D, 9, 11, 13, 16, 16C, 25N, 26, 33N, 39N, 40, 41N, 47, 49, 68, 68A, 69, 69X, 100X, 101X, 133, 150, 700, 704X.

The Design Tower ★★ MARKET/GIFTS   A cutting-edge convocation of hot designers and craftspeople work at this former sugar refinery at the Grand Canal Quay on the eastern side of the city. Occupants include Seamus Gill, who makes extraordinary, almost organic-seeming silverware; conceptual artist and fashion designer Roisin Gartland; and jewelry designer Brenda Haugh, whose work includes interesting modern interpretations of Celtic motifs. Some designers here have walk-in shops, but most prefer appointments, so call ahead if you want to see someone specific. The Design Tower is near Grand Canal Dock DART station, or about a 20-minute walk from Grafton Street. Trinity Centre, Grand Canal Quay, Dublin 2. www.thedesigntower.com. ✆ **01/677-0107.** Mon–Fri 10am–5pm; individual studio opening times vary. DART: Grand Canal Dock. Bus: 1, 2, 3, 50, 56A, 77A.

House of Ireland ★ IRISH GIFTS   An excellent "one-stop shop" for quality Irish souvenirs, this is the place to come for Waterford and Galway crystal, Belleek china, jewelry, linens, and clothing by big-name Irish designers such as Eugene and Anke McKernan, John Rocha, and Louise Kennedy. Just one trip here and nobody back home needs to know that you didn't really scour the country for that perfect knickknack or gift. Left your souvenir shopping until the last minute? There are two smaller outlet branches at Dublin Airport. 37-38 Nassau St., Dublin 2. www.houseofireland.com. © **01/671-1111.** Mon–Wed 9am–6pm; Thurs 9am–8pm; Fri–Sat 9am–6pm; Sun 12:30–5:30pm. Bus: 15X, 25X, 32X, 33X, 39X, 41X, 51D, 51X, 58X, 67X, 70X, 84X, 92.

Mayfly ★★ CRAFTS/ GIFTS   You know you're visiting somewhere that's quintessentially Temple Bar when the directions on the website tell you to look out for the cow in the buggy out front. This is a treasure trove for deliciously creative, artsy gifts, jewelry, clothing, and other doodads that are impossible to resist. Artists whose work is for sale include Courtney Tyler, who turns old watch faces into interesting jewelry, and embroiderer Victoria White, who makes misfit toys by hand. 11 Fownes St., Dublin 2. www.mayfly.ie. © **086/376-4189.** Sun–Wed 11am–6:30pm; Thurs–Fri 11am–7pm; Sat 10am–7pm. Bus: 39B, 49X, 50X, 65X, 77X.

Powerscourt Centre ★★ MARKETPLACE   In a restored 1774 town house, this four-story complex consists of a central sky-lit courtyard and more than 60 boutiques, craft shops, art galleries, snack bars, wine bars, and restaurants. The wares include all kinds of crafts, antiques, paintings, prints, ceramics, leatherwork, jewelry, clothing, chocolates, and farmhouse cheeses. You can also book a behind-the-scenes tour to learn more about the history of the house. You can see the old kitchen and cellars, the former lord and lady's bedrooms and dressing rooms, the music room, ballroom, and dining room. For details and booking, contact Shireen Gail at shireengail@gmail.com or © **086/806-5505.** 59 South William St., Dublin 2. www.powerscourtcentre.com. © **01/679-4144.** Mon–Wed, Fri 10am–6pm; Thurs 10am–8pm; Sat 9am–6pm; Sun noon–6pm. Luas: St. Stephen's Green. Bus: 11, 11A, 11B, 14, 14A, 15A, 15C, 15X, 20B, 27C, 32X, 33X, 39B, 39X, 41X, 46B, 46C, 46N, 46X, 51X, 58X, 65X, 70X, 84X.

Weir & Sons ★ JEWELRY   Established in 1869, the granddaddy of Dublin's fine jewelry shops sells new and antique jewelry, as well as silver, china, and crystal. The ground floor of the main branch, on the corner of Grafton and Wicklow streets, also has a section devoted to 17th-, 18th-, and 19th-century antique silver from Ireland and Britain. A second branch is in Dundrum, about 7km (4⅓ miles) south of the city center. 96-99 Grafton and 1-3 Wicklow sts., Dublin 2. www.weirandsons.ie. © **01/677-9678.** Mon–Wed, Fri–Sat 9:30am–6pm; Thurs 9:30am–8pm. Closed Sun. Bus: 15X, 32X, 33X, 39X, 41X, 51X, 58X, 70X, 84X.

Nightlife

3Arena ★ CONCERT HALL   This enormous indoor arena (known as **the O2** until recently) is the biggest venue in Dublin, and the fifth-best attended in the world at this writing. It's the go-to place for major international acts, standup comedy, and other big-ticket entertainment events—all top-of-the-bill stuff. North Wall Quay, Dublin 1. www.3arena.ie. Box Office: ✆ **081/871-9300;** Enquiries: 01/819-8888. Luas: The Point. Bus: 151.

Abbey Theatre ★ THEATER   Since 1903, the Abbey has been the national theater of Ireland, and it remains one of the most respected and prestigious in the country. The original theater, destroyed by fire in 1951, was replaced in 1966 by the current functional, although uninspired, 492-seat house. In addition to its main stage, the theater has a 127-seat basement studio, the **Peacock,** where it presents newer and more experimental work. 26 Lower Abbey St., Dublin 1. www.abbeytheatre.ie. ✆ **01/878-7222.** Ticket prices vary; generally between €13 and €40. Event times vary; call ahead. Rail: Tara St., Connolly. Luas: Abbey St. Bus: 2, 3, 4, 5, 7, 7A, 7B, 7D, 8, 10, 10A, 15, 15A, 15B, 15C, 15E, 15F, 20B, 27B, 27C, 29A, 31, 31B, 32, 32A, 32B, 32X, 33, 33X, 38, 38A, 38C, 41, 41A, 41B, 41C, 41X, 42, 42A, 42B, 43, 45, 46A, 46B, 46C, 46E, 51A, 70B, 70X, 121, 122, 130, 142, 145.

The Brazen Head ★★★ PUB   This is a serious contender for the coveted title of "oldest pub in Ireland," having served the locals continually since at least 1661 (although an alehouse was reputedly on the same spot for hundreds of years before that—they claim 1198 as the foundation date, and who's to argue?). It was once a hangout for Irish revolutionaries, and Joyce mentioned the place in *Ulysses;* today it's more famous for lively traditional music sessions. Every night features a different act; worthies who've played here over the years include Van Morrison, Tom Jones, and Garth Brooks. It's also the venue for the fantastic **Evening of Food, Folklore & Fairies** ★★★ (below). 20 Lower Bridge St., Dublin 8. www.brazenhead.com. ✆ **01/677-9549.** Mon–Thurs 10am–midnight; Fri–Sat 10am–12:30am; Sun 11am–midnight. Luas: Smithfield. Bus: 25, 25A, 25B, 25X, 26, 37, 39, 39A, 51D, 51X, 66, 66A, 66B, 66X, 67.

Cobblestones ★★★ PUB   We recently asked a Dublin taxi driver to recommend the best place for live music in Temple Bar. Answer: "Now why would you bother, when the Cobblestones is so close?" This is a real authentic musician's place, as much a traditional music venue as a pub, such is the standard of the music. Free sessions are in the front bar nightly, with ticketed acts in the Backroom, a dedicated performance space. 77 North King St., Smithfield, Dublin 7. www.cobblestonepub.ie. ✆ **01/872-1799.** Mon–Thurs 4–11:30pm; Fri–Sat 4pm–12:30am; Sun 1–11pm. Luas: 37, 39, 39A, 70, 70N.

Davy Byrnes ★★ PUB   "He entered Davy Byrnes," wrote James Joyce of Leopold Bloom, the hero of *Ulysses.* "Moral pub. He doesn't chat. Stands a drink now and then. But in a leap year once in four. Cashed a cheque for me once." For a place with such impeccable literary connections as this, it's no surprise that so many writers make this a pilgrimage spot when they're in town. Joyce himself was a regular, although the food has certainly improved since his day—the menu of pub classics and sandwiches is actually pretty good, and fairly priced. *Ulysses* fans will be delighted to hear that you can still order a gorgonzola sandwich, Bloom's snack of choice. 21 Duke St., off Grafton St., Dublin 2. www.davybyrnes.com. ✆ **01/677-5217.** Mon–Wed 11am–11:30pm;

Thurs–Fri 11am–12:30am; Sat 10:30am–12:30am; Sun 12:30–11pm. Bus: 11, 11A, 11B, 14A, 15A, 15C, 15X, 20B, 27C, 33X, 39B, 41X, 46B, 46C.

Doheny & Nesbitt ★ PUB   From the outside, this pub brings to mind a Victorian medicine cabinet, all polished wood with a rich blue-and-gold sign. Its proximity to the political and economic heart of the capital makes it a perennial hangout for politicos, lawyers, economists, and those who write about them—which can make for some spectacularly good eavesdropping. (Its name inspired a catchphrase, "the Doheny & Nesbitt School of Economics," to describe the movers and shakers who used to shoot the breeze here during Ireland's boom years of the 1990s and 2000s.) To admire its cozy interior, a midweek daytime visit is best—this place gets packed in the evenings (especially on summer weekends) and even more so when a big sports match is on. 5 Baggot St. Lower, Dublin 2. www.dohenyandnesbitts.ie. ℂ **01/676-2945.** Wed–Thurs 10am–12:30am; Fri–Sat 10am–2am; Sun noon–11pm; Mon 10am–11:30pm; Tues 10am–midnight. Bus: 10, 10A, 25X, 51D, 51X, 65X, 66D, 66X, 67X, 77X.

An Evening of Food, Folklore & Fairies ★★★ DINNER THEATER The concept of this wonderful evening is timeless, yet brilliant in its simplicity. No high-tech smoke and mirrors; just compelling tales from Irish folklore, passionately told by masters of the storytelling craft. The whole thing takes place in an atmospherically lit room inside the Brazen Head, one of the oldest pubs in Dublin. During dinner, the storytellers spin their yarns—not all of them fantastical in nature, but each one hugely absorbing. The meal, included in the price, is suitably traditional: beef-and-Guinness stew or bacon and cabbage with mashed potatoes. If you haven't had your fill of tradition by the end of it all, you can go downstairs and hear some live music in the bar. The Brazen Head Pub, 20 Bridge St. Lower, Dublin 8. www.irishfolktours.com. ℂ **01/218-8555.** Tickets including dinner €46 adults, €42 seniors and students, €29 children (minimum age 6). Mar–Dec nightly 7pm. Jan–Feb Thurs and Sat 7pm. Bus: 25, 25A, 37, 51C, 51D, 51X, 66, 66D, 69X, 70, 70A, 78A, 79, 79A, 90, 92.

Gaiety Theatre ★ PERFORMING ARTS   The elegant little Gaiety, opened in 1871, hosts a varied array of performances, including everything from opera to classical Irish plays and Broadway-style musicals. (The Gaiety's annual pantomime, or Christmas show, is a big event in the city's theatrical calendar.) And when the thespians leave, the partygoers arrive. On Friday and Saturday from midnight on, the place turns into a nightclub, with four bars hosting live bands and DJs, spinning R&B, indie, blues, or hip-hop. There are even occasional cult movie showings. Don't forget to check out the ornate decor before you get too tipsy. The Gaiety Theatre, South King St., Dublin 2. www.gaietytheatre.ie. ℂ **081/871-9388.** Ticket prices vary; generally between €15 and €50. Event times vary; call ahead. Luas: St. Stephen's Green. Bus: 11, 11A, 11B, 14, 14A, 15A, 15C, 15X, 20B, 27C, 33X, 39B, 40A, 40C, 41X, 46B, 46C, 46N, 46X, 51X, 58X, 67X, 70X, 84X.

The Gate Theatre ★ THEATER   Just north of O'Connell Street off Parnell Square, this recently restored 370-seat theater was founded in 1928 by Irish actors Hilton Edwards and Michael MacLiammoir to provide a venue for a broad range of plays. Its program today still includes a blend of modern works and the classics. Although less known by visitors, the Gate is easily as distinguished as the Abbey. Cavendish Row, Parnell Sq., Dublin 1. www.gatetheatre. ie. © **01/874-4045.** Ticket prices vary; generally between €20 and €30. Event times vary; call ahead. Bus: 1, 2, 14, 14A, 16, 16A, 19, 19A, 33X, 39X, 40, 40A, 40B, 40C, 41X, 48A, 58X, 70B, 70X, 120. 123.

Grogan's Castle Lounge ★★ PUB   There's a friendly, chatty vibe at this satisfyingly old-fashioned place, considered one of Dublin's "quintessential" pubs. There's nothing modern or polished about the dimly lit, atmospheric interior, save for the slightly incongruous art collection on the walls (most of it is for sale). Grogan's reputation rests mostly on its eclectic clientele, ranging from grizzled old folks who have been coming here for years to hipster-ish, artsy types in search of a low-fi hangout. 15 South William St., Dublin 2. www.groganspub.ie. © **01/677-9320.** Mon–Thurs 10:30am–11:30pm; Fri–Sat 10:30am–12:30am; Sun 12:30pm–11pm. Bus: 15, 32X, 33X, 39X, 41X, 51X, 58X, 70X, 84X.

The Long Hall ★★ PUB   The polished walnut-and-brass interior of this Victorian pub elicits purrs of delight from thirsty patrons as soon as they walk in the door. One of Dublin's most gorgeously, seductively . . . well, *Irish* of pubs, the Long Hall is named for the bar that runs the entire length of the interior. Regulars have to fight for space alongside the tourist crowd, but it's more than worth squeezing in for a look at the interior. 51 South Great George's St., Dublin 2. © **01/475-1590.** Mon–Wed 4–11:30pm; Thurs 1–11:30pm; Fri–Sat 1pm–12:30am; Sun 1–11pm. Bus: 11E, 15F, 16, 16A, 19, 19A, 39X, 65, 65B, 65X, 83, 122.

Outlying Attractions

Butler's Chocolate Experience ★ FACTORY TOUR   Ireland is awash with brewery tours, but rare is the chance to look around a real-life chocolate factory. The world-famous chocolatiers, whose cafes are scattered throughout Dublin, have been based in the city since the 1930s. The delectable confections are now produced at a completely unlovable-looking industrial park on the road to Malahide, but like all the best soft-centered chocolates, the sweet part is on the inside. The tour takes you around the factory to see the luxury chocolate makers in action. (Don't worry, there are plenty of tastings.) You have to book tours in advance, and space is quite limited. No chocolates are made on Saturday, so the weekday tours are definitely the most fun.

Clonshagh Business and Technology Park, Oscar Traynor Rd., Dublin 17. www.butlers chocolates.com/chocolateexperience. © **01/851-2151.** Admission €13 adults; €47.50 families. Mon–Sat 10am, noon and 3:30pm. Booking essential. Bus: 130. From Dublin take R105 to R107 toward Malahide; after about 3.5km (2½ miles), turn left onto Oscar Traynor Rd., take fifth right turn, and look for sign on the left.

Casino Marino ★★ ARCHITECTURAL SITE   Stand down, gamblers— this "casino" simply means "little house." Built around 1770, this unique and unexpected little architectural gem sits in the middle of a suburban park. The tiny neoclassical exterior is exquisitely proportioned, with Corinthian columns and elaborate detail around the white stone cornices. Inside, unlikely though it seems from the compact exterior, a full 16 rooms are decorated with rich 18th-century architectural details. Entry is by tour only, but the cheerful guides help put it all into context. Tours start on the hour, every hour.

Casino Park (signposted from R107, Malahide Road), Dublin. www.heritageireland.ie. © **01/833-1618.** Admission €4 adults; €3 seniors; €2 families €10 children and students. Mid-Mar to May and Oct daily 10am–5pm; June–Sept 10am–6pm. Last admission 45 min. before closing. Closed Nov to mid-Mar. Bus: 14, 20B, 27, 27A, 27B, 27C, 42, 43, 127, 128, 129.

Castle Dracula ★ INTERACTIVE ENTERTAINMENT Well, this is certainly a novel way to spend a Friday night. Part live theater, part museum, this homage to Dublin-born author Bram Stoker is set up as a tour of "Castle Dracula," through a series of elaborately constructed sets and tunnels. Costumed actors try to scare you and make you laugh in almost equal measure, while you learn more about Bram Stoker and the Dracula phenomenon along the way. (They even have a real lock of Stoker's hair, allegedly taken from his corpse by his wife.) The tour ends in an underground auditorium made to look like a spooky graveyard, where you watch a live show that includes comedy and two magicians. The emphasis is on laughs rather than scares (although, as there are a few, no kids under 14 are allowed—nor are pregnant women, supposedly, although who are they kidding?) Tickets must be booked in advance. Clontarf DART station is literally next door, or it's about a 15-minute cab ride from the center of Dublin.

Meet at Westwood Gym, Clontarf Rd. (next to Clontarf DART), Dublin. www.castledracula.ie. © **01/851-2151.** Admission €25 adults; €20 seniors, students and children 15–18. Late Feb to Aug Sat only 7pm (arrive 6:45pm). May not run every week—check website for schedule. DART: Clontarf. Bus: 130.

Dalkey Castle & Heritage Centre ★ HERITAGE SITE Housed in a 15th-century tower house, this center tells the history of venerable Dalkey town in a few sweet, if unsophisticated, displays. Tours run by costumed guides tell the tale of the building (complete with live performance), or you can duck out of the tour and take in the view from the battlements instead. Adjoining the center is a medieval graveyard and the Church of St. Begnet (Dalkey's patron saint), whose foundations date back to Ireland's early Christian period. Dalkey itself is worth a wander; a heritage town with plenty of historic buildings, it also has lots of charming pubs, restaurants, and boutiques.

Castle St., Dalkey (16km/10 miles southeast of Dublin on R119). www.dalkeycastle.com. © **01/285-8366.** Admission €8.50 adults; €7 seniors and students; €6.50 children 5–12; €25 families. Mon, Wed–Fri 10am–5pm; Sat–Sun 11am–5pm. DART: Dalkey. Bus: 7D, 59.

Dún Laoghaire ★ TOWN The bustling harbor town of Dún Laoghaire (pronounced Dun *Lear*-y) is one of a string of Dublin commuter towns that, in the 2000s, became known as "Bel Eire" for their beauty and for the density of Irish celebrity residents. It boasts plenty of interesting shops, a bucolic park, and a lovely promenade along the harbor.

13km (8 mi) southeast of Dublin on R118. Rail: Dún Laoghaire. DART: Sandycove & Glasthule. Bus: 7, 7N, 46A, 46N, 59, 63, 75, 111.

DAY TRIPS FROM DUBLIN

Driving in or out of Dublin along the big, bland motorway, it's easy to dismiss the region immediately surrounding the city's urban sprawl. However, you'll find plenty to do within a half-hour drive north, south, or west of Dublin. Rural landscapes, ancient ruins, stately homes—some of Ireland's most iconic sights are surprisingly close to the city. And while it's possible to see any of them on a quick day trip, some fine hotels and restaurants in the area reward visitors who opt to stay overnight instead.

North of Dublin, you'll find the remnants of ancient civilizations at prehistoric sites Newgrange and Knowth, while the nearby green hills of the Boyne Valley hold the long-lost home of early Irish kings. **To the west,** Kildare is Ireland's horse country, with a couple of handsome stately homes and interesting historical sites that also make this area worth checking out. **South of Dublin,** the Wicklow Mountains rise from the low, green countryside, dark and brooding. A beautiful region, dotted with early religious sites and peaceful river valleys, the hills also make a good starting point if you're heading on to the south of Ireland (see chapters 6 and 7).

ESSENTIALS

Arriving

BY BUS   Bus Éireann (www.buseireann.ie; ℗ **01/836-6111**) operates services from the central bus station (Busáras) out to each of the regions listed in this chapter, although there aren't always connections to remote sites. If you have specific attractions in mind, check if they're included in a bus tour—see the box on p. 101.

BY TRAIN   Irish Rail (www.irishrail.ie; ℗ **1850/366-222**) trains leave Dublin's Heuston station for Kildare at least once an hour. The journey takes between 25 and 45 minutes. Several direct trains depart daily from Dublin's Connolly station to Wicklow; the journey takes an hour.

BY CAR   Most of the attractions listed in this chapter are easily accessible by car in about an hour from Dublin. The roads are good in the regions around the city, although traffic can be a problem—particularly during rush hour, when all roads around Dublin slow to a crawl. In reasonable traffic, Newgrange and Knowth are about an hour north of the city; Kildare Town and its nearby attractions are just under an hour to the southwest; and Glendalough is about an hour's drive south. The Dublin Tourist Office has excellent road maps.

WHERE TO STAY
Where to Stay North of Dublin

Bellinter House ★   On the banks of the River Boyne outside Navan, this imposing greystone Palladian country house was designed by the same man who built Russborough House (p. 108) and Powerscourt (p. 107). The hotel has been restored to resemble a 19th-century country getaway, with an atmosphere of relaxed elegance. The lounges are gorgeous, with oak-paneled walls, fires crackling at the hearth, and deep leather chairs to sink into with a good book. Most guest rooms are less glamorous than the public areas; the more expensive rooms are, inevitably, the most beautiful. But all have large, modern bathrooms and comfortable beds. The restaurant is highly rated for its butter-rich, French-influenced Irish cuisine, and locally sourced meat and produce. Breakfasts are huge—even the tea selection is enormous There's a tiny spa, with a hot tub and steam room, and guests are free to explore the sprawling grounds and to fish on the river. Excursions to nearby sites can be arranged. Get directions from the hotel before setting out—on a tiny farm road, this place can be hard to find.

Bellinter, Navan, Co. Meath. www.bellinterhouse.com. ✆ **046/903-0900.** 34 units. €200–€370. Free parking. Breakfast included. **Amenities:** Wi-Fi (free); restaurant; bar; spa.

Ghan House ★★   Overlooking Carlingford Lough, Ghan House is a sweet, old-fashioned hotel. Guest rooms are good-sized and traditionally furnished, with antiques and sofas. Most are in the main 17th-century building, though there is also a modern extension, and many have views of the lake or mountains. "Superior" rooms have half-tester beds and deep Victorian bathtubs. The award-winning restaurant serves excellent modern Irish menus—roasted boar or fresh local beef—and the owners hold cooking and wine tasting classes on site. Check the website for special offers, including midweek packages that include dinner, bed and breakfast packages.

2 Ghan Rd., Carlingford, Co. Louth. www.ghanhouse.com. ✆ **042/937-3682.** 12 units. €75–€125. Free parking. Breakfast included. **Amenities:** Wi-Fi (free); restaurant; bar.

Trim Castle Hotel ★   This modern hotel is a stone's throw from Trim castle (you really could hit it with a rock quite easily, not that we're encouraging you). Lounges and restaurants are bright and cheerful. Guest rooms are not huge but are well-appointed, with modern bathrooms. Some rooms have direct views of the evocative ruins. The good, bistro-style restaurant offers reasonably priced classic Irish fare (€25 for three courses), and a lovely rooftop patio overlooking the castle is a fine place to take a coffee and soak up the view. Book early for the best rates. There are lots of half-price deals in the spring, in particular.

Castle St., Trim, Co. Meath. www.trimcastlehotel.com. ℂ **046/948-3000.** 68 units. €85–€185. Free parking. Breakfast included. **Amenities:** Restaurant; bar; room service; Wi-Fi (free)

Where to Stay West of Dublin

Barberstown Castle ★★ Although parts of this hotel were built as recently as the early 2000s, enough genuine old castle is still on view as you approach for it to look and feel satisfyingly, well, *castle*-like. The oldest section dates from the 12th century, and even the modern guest rooms manage to feel pleasantly antique; some have four-poster beds. Family rooms are available too. The formal **Barton Rooms** restaurant serves classic Irish bistro fare (although it's very pricey), and there's also a tearoom. One spot of trivia: For what it's worth, Barberstown Castle was the home of guitarist Eric Clapton in the 1970s.

On R403, Straffan, Co. Kildare. www.barberstowncastle.ie. ℂ **01/628-8157.** 55 units. €144–€240. Free parking. Breakfast included. **Amenities:** Restaurant; room service.

Griesmount ★★ The ancestors of the great British polar explorer Ernest Shackleton built this charming country manor set amid acres of gently rolling green hills. There must be something in the water here, as current owners Carolyn and Robert have a rather adventurous past of their own, having traveled and lived in Africa for many years before settling down to run Griesmount as a B&B. Guest rooms are traditionally furnished, with famously comfortable beds—the guestbook is full of praise for the heavenly four-poster—and two rooms have views of the River Griese. Carolyn's delicious, hearty breakfasts are served in a room overlooking an old ruined mill. Dinners can also be arranged with notice. Griesmount has a 2-night minimum stay on weekends.

Fullers Court Rd., Ballitore, Co. Kildare. www.griesemounthouse.com. ℂ **059/862-3158.** 3 units. €80–€140. Free parking. Breakfast included. **Amenities:** Wi-Fi (free).

Martinstown House ★★ An elegant country house getaway near the famous Curragh racecourse (see p. 106), Martinstown dates mostly from the 1830s. Bedrooms are decorated with more than a few nods to its early Victorian origins, with heritage color schemes and antique-style furniture. Excellent four-course dinners (€49) are served around a single, long, candlelit table, which gives the appealing sense of an upper-class house party from a bygone age. Expect seasonal fare such as roast duck with crispy roast potatoes, or grilled sole with lemon and caper butter. *Note:* Although the Curragh is just 8km (5 miles) away, a frustrating road layout means driving between Martinstown and the racecourse takes up to a half-hour each way.

Off L6078 (follow signs for Martinstown), Ballysaxhills, Curragh, Co. Kildare. www.martinstownhouse.com. ℂ **045/441269.** 6 units. €175–€295. Free parking. Breakfast included. **Amenities:** Restaurant; Wi-Fi (free).

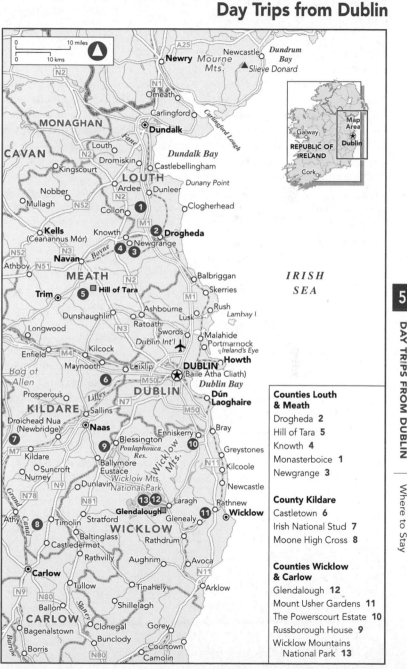

Counties Louth & Meath

Drogheda **2**
Hill of Tara **5**
Knowth **4**
Monasterboice **1**
Newgrange **3**

County Kildare

Castletown **6**
Irish National Stud **7**
Moone High Cross **8**

Counties Wicklow & Carlow

Glendalough **12**
Mount Usher Gardens **11**
The Powerscourt Estate **10**
Russborough House **9**
Wicklow Mountains
    National Park **13**

Where to Stay South of Dublin

BrookLodge & Macreddin Village ★★ A winning combination of top-end hotel, spa, and holiday village, BrookLodge is a luxurious hideaway. Guest rooms are understated and contemporary in design, while suites—which come with a stylish mezzanine level—offer plenty of extra room for not much greater cost. The hotel is surrounded by an entire village of activities, from golf, hiking, and horseback riding, to an artisan baker, deli, and crafts store. The award-winning spa, **Wells,** is worth trying out—most 1-hour treatments cost around €75. The main restaurant, the excellent **Strawberry Tree** ★★★ (see p. 101), was the first in Ireland to gain full organic certification—many of the ingredients are so local that there's a good chance your dinner was at least partly foraged by the kitchen staff.

Macreddin Village (btw. Aughrim & Aghavannagh), Co. Wicklow. www.brooklodge. com. ✆ **040/236-444.** 86 units. €175–€285. Free parking. Breakfast included. **Amenities:** 2 restaurants; bars; 2 pubs; room service; spa; gym; pool; golf course; Wi-Fi (free).

Powerscourt Hotel ★★★ The grand, sweeping Palladian frontage of this gorgeous hotel is almost as impressive as its namesake, Powerscourt House (see p. 107). Guest rooms are large and elegantly furnished; some have balconies with views of the Wicklow Mountains. Everything here is above par. The lounges are gorgeous, with soaring ceilings, beautiful furniture, and exquisite views. The sleek in-house spa, **Espa,** is positively sci-fi in its high-tech design (the pool is lit by illuminated Swarovski crystals) with a menu of treatments including a 90-minute "warming peat ritual," and a "shillelagh massage," in which you are, we kid you not, rubbed with a lucky stick (both treatments are €145). The hotel has three eateries: The **Sika** restaurant serves outstanding modern European cuisine (truffled goats' cheese, duck breast with blood-orange puree) at sky-high prices; the **Sugar Loaf** lounge, marginally less formal, offers a gorgeous afternoon tea; and **McGill's Pub** is more casual. Needless to say, service throughout the hotel is impeccable.

Powerscourt Estate, Enniskerry, Co. Wicklow. www.powerscourthotel.com. ✆ **01/274-8888.** 200 units. €180–€295. Free parking. Breakfast €22–€28. **Amenities:** Wi-Fi (free); 2 restaurants; bar; pub; room service; gym; pool; spa.

Wicklow Way Lodge ★★★ Though the outside of the building looks plain, it's hard to fault this modern B&B, just 6km (4 miles) from Glendalough (see p. 106). Guest rooms are simple but tastefully furnished, with lots of polished wood and toasty underfloor heating. They also have—how could they not?—enormous windows to take advantage of the picture-perfect surroundings. There's one family room (children are charged 50% of the adult rate), although because of the split-level design of the house, very young kids aren't allowed. Hosts Marilyn and Seamus are a joy; genuinely kind and helpful, they're full of tips for the best walking paths. There's homemade bread at breakfast, with fresh local eggs—and you should try the porridge too! A haven of tranquility and charm.

Oldbridge, Roundwood, Co. Wicklow. www.wicklowwaylodge.com. ✆ **01/281-8489.** 5 units. €100. Free parking. Breakfast included. **Amenities:** Wi-Fi (free in lounge only).

WHERE TO EAT

Where to Eat North of Dublin

The Bay Tree ★★ IRISH   This restaurant isn't much to look at from the outside, but inside it's a cozy, romantic option. Endorsed by Michelin since 2014 (not starred, but recommended), the cooking is top-notch, allowing the freshest, local ingredients plenty of space to shine without overloading the palate. Start with seared scallops served with capers and golden raisins, before moving on to a plate of spiced duck breast with roasted beetroot, or perhaps some beef sirloin with chunky chips (super thick French fries). Follow it up with some crème caramel made with local honey. The Bay Tree has an attached B&B, where pleasant, modern bedrooms cost €80 to €90.

Newry St., Carlingford, Co. Louth. ℂ **042/938-3848.** Main courses €18–€30. Mon–Thurs 6–9pm; Fri–Sat 6–9:30pm; Sun 1–4:30pm and 6–8pm (closed Mon–Tues in winter).

Burke's Restaurant ★ INTERNATIONAL   The Burke family has run this friendly, unpretentious little diner in Drogheda for over 25 years, making it a local institution. The enormous, overflowing full Irish breakfasts are a staple (and pretty reasonable at €8, given that it provides carbs enough to keep you going for a week). The lunch menu focuses on unpretentious comfort food—fried chicken, burgers, and local fish. Drop by in the afternoon for tea and sample the delicious house-recipe pancakes. The restaurant is just around the corner from St. Peter's Church on West Street.

6 Peter St., Drogheda, Co. Louth. ℂ **086/830-4479.** Main courses €7–€12. Mon–Sat 9:30am–6pm.

Vanilla Pod ★★ MODERN EUROPEAN   Imaginative Irish cooking with international influences is the focus of this great little restaurant in Kells. The menu is seasonal and features regional ingredients in dishes such as local lamb with apricot and walnut stuffing; lemon sole filet served with crab, prawns and lemon; or a simple potato-and-pear tart with blue cheese from the Boyne Valley. Vanilla Pod is in the popular Headfort Arms Hotel.

At the Headfort Arms Hotel, John St., Kells, Co. Meath. ℂ **046/924-0084.** Main courses €16–€24. Mon–Thurs 5–10pm; Fri–Sat 5–11pm; Sun 12:30–9:30pm.

Where to Eat West of Dublin

Cunningham's ★ THAI/PUB FOOD   Inside and out, Cunningham's is a fairly traditional, run-of-the-mill Irish pub—which makes it all the more unlikely that it also serves some of the best Thai food in the area. Delicious, authentic-style meals are prepared by the Thai chef, Chock, and served in the bar nightly. You could go for a spicy red, green, or panang curry, made with coconut and chili, or a classic pad Thai served with crispy wontons. The menu also has a few traditional pub options, such as burgers and steaks, but it's the Thai food that packs in the crowds. Some nights include live music.

Main St., Kildare, Co. Kildare. www.cunninghamskildare.com. ℂ **045/521-780.** Main courses €11–€21. Mon–Sat noon–10pm.

Silken Thomas ★ INTERNATIONAL   Named for a local 16th-century knight who was a dashing rebel, this atmospheric pub offers simple, tasty, unfussy meals in a jovial atmosphere. The menu is something of a global tour, with Mexican fajitas, Chinese stir-fries, and Indian curries happily served alongside burgers, steaks, fish and chips, and other familiar Irish fare. They do a popular "carvery" (buffet-style lunch) from noon daily, and if you're here on a Friday and Saturday night and just not ready to go home, stick around after 11:30pm, when it becomes a nightclub.

The Square, Kildare, Co. Kildare. www.silkenthomas.com. ℂ **045/522-232.** Main courses €13–€26. Food served Mon–Sat 8am to around 10pm.

Trax Brasserie ★★ IRISH   This laid-back but elegant brasserie in tiny Naas, about 22km (13½ miles) northeast of Kildare, is a real find. The 1880s building was originally a railway shed, hence the subtle hints of the industrial in the dining room, such as exposed stone walls and "slabs of slate" serving plates. The fixed-price two- and three-course menus focus on classic Irish flavors with an international flair. You might start with some deep-fried brie with apple-and-ginger chutney, before moving on to a main course of buttered seabass, or duck leg confit with an orange glaze.

Friary Rd., Naas, Co. Kildare. www.traxbrasserie.ie. ℂ **045/889-333.** Fixed-price menus €26–€29. Wed–Sat 5–10pm; Sun 12:30–2:45pm, 5–8:30pm.

Where to Eat South of Dublin

Brunel ★★ MODERN IRISH   This place has won plenty of accolades over the years, and still deserves its reputation for excellent modern Irish cuisine. All meats and produces are sourced regionally. The menu changes regularly, but you can expect to find such dishes as citrus-cured salmon with saffron, or beef filet with asparagus and mashed potato. Vegetarians are well served, with a full menu of non-meat choices. The only flaw is the service, which can be hit or miss.

At the Tinakilly Country House Hotel, Rathnew, Co. Wicklow (on R750, off the N11). www.tinakilly.ie. ℂ **040/469-274.** Reservations recommended. Main courses €18–€32. Mon–Sat 6–10pm; Sun noon–4pm.

Chakra by Jaipur ★★ INDIAN   If you need a break from Irish food, or just fancy something a little more adventurous, this outstanding Indian restaurant is a great choice. It's not the most idyllic location, in a concrete-and-glass shopping mall down a rather nondescript street in Greystones, but inside the decor is bright and cheerful. And the food is truly excellent. You might start with a *murgh malai* kebab, made with free-range chicken, saffron mascarpone, and beetroot; before following on to the *lahsooni machhi,* a curry made with local monkfish, turmeric, cilantro, and rock salt; or the succulent *tawa jhinga kadai*—griddled tiger prawns in a sauce made with caramelized onions.

1st Floor, Meridian Point, Church Rd., Greystones, Co. Wicklow. www.jaipur.ie. ℂ **01/201-7222.** Main courses €15–€25. Mon–Sat 5:30–11pm; Sun 1–5pm.

bus trips FROM DUBLIN

Although you'll need a car to fully explore what the regions around Dublin have to offer, it's possible to see virtually all of the big attractions by taking guided bus tours. Most leave from central Dublin, quite early in the day, and deposit you back around 5 or 6pm. Book tours directly with the operator; Dublin tourist offices can also help. Here are a few of the most popular ones.

Newgrange Tours by Mary Gibbons (www.newgrangetours.com; ✆ 086/355-1355) are among the most respected of the guided tours that visit the ancient burial site. Mary is an excellent guide, and her tours have an allocated entry slot at Newgrange, meaning you don't have to wait. They run daily from several pickup points in Dublin, starting at 9:30am Monday to Friday and 7:50am Saturday and Sunday. The cost is €35, or €30 for students.

Bus Éireann (www.buseireann.ie; ✆ 01/836-6111) runs day trips from the main bus station in Dublin. The **Boyne Valley and Newgrange Tour,** which also stops at the **Hill of Tara,** includes admission to Newgrange. It runs from about April to September, on Thursday and Saturday. The **Glendalough, Powerscourt Garden and Wicklow Panorama** trip stops at Glendalough, Powerscourt, and the Wicklow Gap. The price includes a guided tour of Glendalough. It also runs from about April to September,

from Thursday to Saturday. Both tours cost €35.

Glendalough Bus (www.glendaloughbus. com; ✆ 01/281-8119) runs day trips from the top of Dawson Street, Dublin 2 (opposite the Mansion House), to Glendalough every day at 11:30am. Tickets cost €20 and you buy them from the driver.

Coach Tours of Ireland (www.coach toursofireland.ie; ✆ 01/898-0700 or 087/996-6660) runs a popular **Day Tour of Wicklow,** including the scenic **Sally Gap** mountain pass and **Glendalough.** Tours cost €28 adults, €18 children.

The **Wild Wicklow Tour** (www.wild wicklow.ie; ✆ 01/280-1899) takes in Dún Laoghaire Harbour and Dalkey, before heading to Glendalough and the Sally Gap. They even take you to a pub for lunch (not included in the price). The tours—which are perhaps skewed toward youthful travelers—leave from several points in Dublin, starting at 8:50am. Tickets cost €28 adults, €25 seniors, students, and children.

Paddy Wagon Tours (www.paddywagon tours.com; ✆ 01/823-0822) run a number of rather touristy trips from Dublin as far as Kilkenny, including ones that cover **Kildare, Trim Castle,** and the **Browne's Hill Dolmen.** Tickets start at €25 and rise to €60 for longer day trips (to, for example, the **Giant's Causeway**—see p. 258).

The Strawberry Tree ★★★ MODERN IRISH   The main restaurant of the excellent **BrookLodge** ★★ complex (see p. 98) is rightly regarded as one of the best places to dine in the region. The beautiful, blue-tinged dining room makes a wonderful setting for any gathering. This was the first restaurant in Ireland to receive full organic certification, and that ethos guides the outstanding modern Irish menu, which takes localism seriously. Depending on the season, you might find wild mackerel with shaved fennel, or wood pigeon with crispy coppa ham and white tomato foam. If you're feeling gregarious, book a place on the "big table"—a communal table that seats up to 40, on which you're served a set menu in the style of a feast.

At the BrookLodge, Macreddin Village (btw. Aughrim and Aghavannagh), Co. Wicklow. www.brooklodge.com.© **040/236-444.** Fixed-price menus €65. Tues–Sun 7–9pm (also Mon in Aug only).

EXPLORING NORTH OF DUBLIN: COUNTIES MEATH & LOUTH

North of Dublin's conurbation, the River Boyne rolls through the rich, fertile countryside of counties Meath and Louth. The Boyne is more than a river—it's an essential part of Irish lore, linking Ireland's ancient past (the prehistoric passage tombs of Newgrange, the storied Hill of Tara) with more modern history (the infamous 1690 Battle of the Boyne, when the Protestant King William III defeated the deposed and exiled Catholic King James II for the crown of England). Today the Boyne Valley is a much more peaceful place, but it offers visitors a wealth of historic treasures tucked away among miles of farmland and smooth, rolling hills.

VISITOR INFORMATION The **Dundalk Tourist Office** is on Market Square, Dundalk (© **042/935-2111**). It's open Monday to Saturday from 9:30am to 1pm and 2pm to 5pm. The **Drogheda Tourist Office** (West St., Drogheda, Co. Louth; © **041/987-2843**), is open Monday to Saturday from 9:30am to 5:30pm (closed Saturdays from Dec–Apr). The **Bru na Boinne Center,** the center for Newgrange and Knowth, is at Newgrange, Donore, Co. Meath (© **041/988-0300**). It's open the same hours as those two sites.

Top Attractions North of Dublin

Drogheda ★ TOWN A modest, industrial commuter town of 30,000 people, 56km (35 miles) north of Dublin, Drogheda (pronounced "Draada" in the local accent) has two historic churches—both, confusingly, with the same name. The bigger of the two, **St. Peter's Roman Catholic Church,** in the town center, is remarkably impressive, with its French Gothic rose window and imposing 68-meter (222 ft.) spire. But its main claim to fame is more grisly; St. Peter's contains the shrine of St. Oliver Plunkett (1625–1681), the Archbishop of Armagh, who was beheaded for his part in an alleged Catholic plot to assassinate Charles II. His severed head can still be seen, shriveled and wizened inside a glass case, as the centerpiece to his shrine. The other St. Peter's, **St. Peter's Church of Ireland,** a simple greystone church at the northern end of the town, has its own notorious back story, dating back to 1649, during Oliver Cromwell's bloody conquest of Ireland. On September 11th, after an 8-day siege, around 2,000 Irish soldiers loyal to the deposed monarch, Charles I, were massacred. Fleeing the carnage, 140 took refuge in St. Peter's steeple. Refusing to heed their surrender, Cromwell ordered them to be burned alive using wood from the pews—an act so heinous that some of his own men refused, risking a charge of mutiny. St. Peter's has been rebuilt

HIGH CROSSES: icons of ireland

You see them all over Ireland, often in the most picturesque rural surroundings, standing alone like sentries; high Celtic crosses with faded stories carved into every inch of space. They are extraordinary, mournful, and unforgettable, but when they were created, they served a useful purpose: They were books, of sorts, in the days when the written word was rare and precious. Think of the carvings as illustrations acting like cartoons, explaining the Bible to the uneducated population. When they were created, the crosses were probably brightly painted as well, but the color has long been lost to the wind and rain.

One fine example of a high cross is at **Moone Abbey** ★ in County Kildare. The 9th-century cross features finely crafted Celtic designs as well as biblical scenes: the temptation of Adam and Eve, the sacrifice of Isaac, and Daniel in the lions' den. One of the most famous high crosses, however, can be found at **Monasterboice** ★, a group of early Christian ruins near Drogheda, about 53km (33 miles) north of Dublin. The **Muiredach Cross,** as it's known, has carvings telling the stories of Adam and Eve, Cain and Abel, David and Goliath, and Moses, as well as the wise men bringing gifts to the baby Jesus. At the center of the old cross, the carving is thought to be of Revelation, while, at the top, St. Paul stands alone in the desert. The western side of the cross tells the stories of the New Testament, with, from the top down, a figure praying, the Crucifixion, St. Peter, Doubting Thomas, and, below that, Jesus's arrest. On the base of the cross is an inscription found often carved on stones in ancient Irish monasteries. It reads in Gaelic, "A prayer for Muiredach for whom the cross was made." Muiredach was the abbot at Monasterboice until 922, so the cross was probably made as a memorial shortly after his death.

Monasterboice is on the M1 motorway, about 8km (5⅓ miles) north of Drogheda, County Louth. Admission is free.

twice since the terrible event. (Check out the spooky carved skeletons on one tomb in the nave.) The small **Drogheda Museum** is located in the 17th-century **Millmount Fort,** overlooking the town, where the walls were finally breached at the end of the siege. Tours cost €3, but they're a little long, so stick with the self-guided version.

Off M1, half way between Drogheda and Dundalk, Co. Louth. **St. Peter's R.C. Church:** West St. www.saintoliverplunkett.com. ⓒ **041/983-8536.** Free admission. Daily 10am–5pm (or later). **St. Peter's Church of Ireland:** Peter St. and William St. www. stpetersdrogheda.ie. No phone. Free admission. Daily 10am–3pm (or later). **Millmount Fort:** Millmount, off John St. www.millmount.net. ⓒ **041/983-3097.** Admission €3.50 adults; €3 students; €2.50 seniors and children; €8 families. Mon–Sat 10am–5:30pm, Sun and holiday Mon 2–5pm. Last tours 1 hr. before closing.

Hill of Tara ★ ANCIENT SITE   Legends and folklore place this hill at the center of early Irish history. Ancient tombs have been discovered that date back to the Stone Age; pagans believed that the goddess Queen Maeve reigned from here. By the 3rd century, a ceremonial residence had been built here for the most powerful men in Ireland—the high kings, who ruled as much by myth as by military strength. Every 3 years, they would hold a weeklong *feis* (a kind of giant party-cum-government session), at which more than 1,000 princes, poets, athletes, priests, druids, musicians, and jesters celebrated. Laws were passed, disputes settled, and matters of defense decided. But the last *feis* was held in A.D. 560, and thereafter Tara went into a decline as power shifted. Today, all that's left of the hill's great heritage are grassy mounds and some ancient pillar stones; all that survives of the Iron Age forts are depressions in the soil. That said, it's still a magnificent spot with views that extend for miles. You can learn the hill's history at a visitor center in the old church beside the entrance. Guided tours are available for those who want to know what lies beneath the smooth, green surface.

Signposted on N3, about 12km (7½ mi) south of Navan, Co. Meath. www.hilloftara.org. ℂ **046/902-5903** (visitor center); **041/988-0300** (out of season). Admission €4 adults; €3 seniors; €2 students and children; €10 families. Hill open all year round. Visitor Centre: Mid-May to mid-Sept daily 10am–6pm.

Knowth ★★★ ANCIENT SITE   This extraordinary prehistoric burial site was only discovered in 1968, and much of it is yet to be excavated. It is mainly composed of two massively long underground burial chambers, the longer of which stretches for 40m (131 ft.). In the mound, scientists found the largest collection of passage tomb art uncovered thus far in Europe, as well as a number of underground chambers and 300 carved slabs. Surrounding the mound, 17 satellite graves are laid out in a mysterious complex pattern. And still, nobody can give a definitive answer to the biggest riddle of all: What was it all for? Even now, many of Knowth's secrets have not been uncovered—excavation work is ongoing (you may even get a chance to see the archaeologists digging). All tickets for here and Newgrange (see below) are issued at the **Brú na Bóinne Visitor Centre** near Donore. There is no direct access to the monument; a shuttle bus takes visitors over.

Brú na Bóinne Visitor Centre, on N51, 2km (1¼ miles) west of Donore, Co. Meath. www.knowth.com. ℂ **041/988-0300.** Visitor center and Knowth: €5 adults; €3 seniors; €3 students and children; €13 families. Combined ticket with Newgrange: €11 adults; €8 seniors; €6 students and children; €28 families. Open daily: June to mid-Sept 9–7pm; May and late Sept 9am–6:30pm; Feb–Apr, Oct 9:30am–5:30pm; Nov–Jan 9am–5pm.

Newgrange ★★★ ANCIENT SITE   Ireland's best-known prehistoric monument is one of the archaeological wonders of Western Europe. Built as a burial mound more than 5,000 years ago—long before the Egyptian pyramids or Stonehenge—it sits atop a hill near the Boyne, massive and mysterious. The mound is 11m (36 ft.) tall and approximately 78m (256 ft.) in diameter. It consists of 200,000 tons of stone, a 6-ton capstone, and other stones weighing up to 16 tons each, many of which were hauled from as far away as County Wicklow and the Mountains of Mourne. Each stone fits perfectly in the overall pattern, and the result is a watertight structure, an amazing feat of engineering. The question remains, though: Why? Archeologists are still trying to figure out whether it was built for kings, political leaders, or long-forgotten rituals. Inside, a passage 18m (59 ft.) long leads to a central burial chamber that sits in pitch darkness all year—except in December, when, during the winter solstice (Dec19–23), a shaft of sunlight travels down the arrow-straight passageway for 17 minutes and hits the back wall of the burial chamber. You can register for a lottery to be in the tomb for this extraordinary event, although competition is fierce. As part of the daily tour, you'll walk down the passage, past elaborately carved stones and into the chamber, which has three sections, each with a basin stone that once held cremated human remains. *Tip:* There's no direct access to the site; you have to come via the **Brú na Bóinne Visitor Centre** near Donore, where you park and take a shuttle bus the rest of the way.

Brú na Bóinne Visitor Centre: on N51, 2km (1¼ mi) west of Donore, Co. Meath. www.newgrange.com. ℂ **041/988-0300.** Visitor center and Newgrange: €6 adults; €5 seniors; €3 students and children; €15 families. Combined ticket with Knowth: €11 adults; €8 seniors; €6 students and children; €28 families. Open daily: June to mid-Sept 9–7pm; May and late Sept 9am–6:30pm; Feb–Apr, Oct 9:30am–5:30pm; Nov–Jan 9am–5pm.

EXPLORING WEST OF DUBLIN: COUNTY KILDARE

The smooth, rolling hills of Kildare are rich in more ways than one. The fertile soil produces miles of lush green pastures perfect for raising horses, and the population is one of the most affluent in the country, with plenty of cash for buying horses. This is the home of the Curragh, the racetrack where the Irish Derby is held, and of smaller tracks at Naas and Punchestown.

VISITOR INFORMATION The Kildare Heritage Centre, in Market Square, Kildare Town (ℂ **045/530-672**) is open Monday to Saturday from 9:30am to 1pm and 2 to 5pm.

Top Attractions West of Dublin

Castletown ★★ HISTORIC HOUSE The fine, symmetrical architecture of this spectacular Palladian-style mansion has been imitated many times across Ireland over the centuries. Made of clean, white stone, with elegant rows of tall windows, Castletown was built between 1722 and 1729, designed by Italian architect Alessandro Galilei for then-speaker of the Irish House of Commons, William Connolly. Today, it's beautifully maintained, and the fully restored interior is worth the price of admission. Visitors are free to wander around the surrounding parkland; a cafe offers tea and cakes, should you need a rest. Two glorious follies on the estate were built as make-work for the starving population during the Famine: One is a graceful obelisk, the other an extraordinarily playful barn, created as a slightly crooked inverted funnel, around which winds a stone staircase. Its name, appropriately enough, is the "Wonderful Barn."

Signposted from R403, off main Dublin-Galway rd. (N4), Celbridge, Co. Kildare. www.castletownhouse.ie. ℂ **01/628-8252.** Admission €7 adults; €5 seniors; students and children; €17 families. Tours mid-Mar to Oct Tues–Sun 10am–4:45pm. Call ahead to confirm times, as they change frequently.

Irish National Stud with Japanese Gardens & St. Fiachra's Garden ★ FARM/GARDENS   Some of Ireland's fastest horses have been bred on the grounds of this government-sponsored stud farm, located handily close to Ireland's best-known racetrack, **The Curragh** (on the N7 in Curragh; www.curragh.ie; ⓒ **045/441-205**). Horse lovers and racing fans will be in heaven walking around the expansive grounds watching the well-groomed horses being trained. A converted groom's house has exhibits on racing, steeplechase, hunting, and show jumping, plus a rather macabre display featuring the skeleton of Arkle, one of Ireland's most famous horses. The peaceful **Japanese Garden,** dating from 1906, has pagodas, ponds, and trickling streams, and the beautifully designed visitor center has a restaurant and shop. A garden dedicated to St. Fiachra—the patron saint of gardeners—is in a beautiful natural setting of woods and wetlands, and the reconstructed hermitage has a Waterford crystal garden of rocks and delicate glass orchids.

Off the Dublin-Limerick rd. (N7), Tully, Kildare, Co. Kildare. www.irish-national-stud.ie. ⓒ **045/522-963.** Admission €13 adults; €9.50 seniors and students; €7 children 5–15; €30 families. Daily 9am–6pm; last admission 1 hr. before closing. Tours daily 10:30am, noon, 2:30pm; also 4pm (may be fewer tours outside of summer season; call to check).

5 EXPLORING SOUTH OF DUBLIN: COUNTY WICKLOW

Wicklow's northernmost border is just a dozen or so miles south of Dublin, making it one of the easiest day trips from the city. The centerpiece of the region is the beautiful **Wicklow Mountains,** traversed by the well-marked **Wicklow Way** walking path, which wanders for miles past mountain tarns and secluded glens. Tucked into the mountains, you'll find the isolated monastery of **Glendalough** and picturesque villages such as **Roundwood, Laragh,** and **Aughrim.**

VISITOR INFORMATION   The **Wicklow Tourist Office,** Fitzwilliam Square, Wicklow Town (www.visitwicklow.ie; ⓒ **040/469-117**), is open Monday to Friday year-round from 9:20am to 5:15pm.

Top Attractions South of Dublin

Glendalough ★★★ RELIGIOUS SITE   Tucked away amid deep forests and surrounded by rolling hills, this evocative, misty glen is a truly magical place. First established by a monk known as St. Kevin in the 6th century, Glendalough was originally devoted to Christian worship and scholarly learning. Sacked first by the Vikings and later by the English, it was eventually abandoned by the monks who once sought refuge here. Those beautiful round towers were actually hideouts with retractable ladders that the monks would pull up after them when the raiders arrived. Most of the buildings were destroyed in repeated attacks, but enough survives to ensure the ruins are a striking and evocative sight. The site sprawls, so stop by the visitor center at the entrance to pick up a map. Each of the many walking trails traversing the area takes in different hidden ruins tucked away amid the lakes and hills. Highlights include the oldest ruins, the **Teampall na Skellig,** across the lake at the foot of towering cliffs (unfortunately there's no boat service and they cannot be visited), and the cave known as **Kevin's Bed,** believed to be where St. Kevin lived when he first arrived at Glendalough. Follow the path from the upper lake to the lower lake to walk through the remains of the monastery complex. There's a nearly perfect round tower, 31m (102 ft.) high and 16m (52 ft.) around the base, as well as hundreds of timeworn Celtic crosses and several chapels. One of these is St. Kevin's Chapel, often called **St. Kevin's Kitchen,** a fine specimen of an early Irish barrel-vaulted oratory with a miniature round belfry rising from a stone roof. Climb the hills to take in the beauty of this extraordinary site from above.

Signposted from R756, 2km (1.3 miles) west of Laragh, Co. Wicklow. www.glendalough. ie. ℐ **040/445-352.** Admission €4 adults; €2 students and children; €10 families. Mid-Mar to mid-Oct daily 9:30am–6pm; mid-Oct to mid-Mar daily 9:30am–5pm; last admission 45 min. before closing.

Mount Usher Gardens ★★ GARDENS   Spreading out on 8 hectares (20 acres) at the edge of the River Vartry, this peaceful and romantic site was once an ancient lake. Since 1868 it's been a riverside garden, designed in a distinctively informal style, with fiery rhododendrons, fragrant eucalyptus trees, giant Tibetan lilies, and snowy camellias competing for your attention. Attuned to their natural setting, these gardens have an almost untended feel—a sort of floral woodland. A spacious cafe, run by the fantastic Avoca chain, overlooks the river and gardens. The courtyard at the entrance to the gardens contains an interesting assortment of shops selling seeds, gardening supplies, and books.

Ashford, Co. Wicklow (off the N11). www.mountushergardens.ie. ℐ **040/440-205.** Admission €7.50 adults; €6.50 seniors and students; €3.50 children 4–16; free for children under 4. Daily 10am–5pm; last admission 30 min. before closing. Avoca Garden Café: Mon–Fri 9:30am–5pm; Sat–Sun 10am–5pm.

The Powerscourt Estate ★★★ GARDENS/HISTORIC HOUSE   The 20th century was not kind to this magnificent estate; abandoned and then gutted by fire, it took more than 30 years for the Palladian house to be restored to its former glory. The gardens, however, are magnificent, with classical statuary, a shady grotto made of petrified moss, a peaceful Japanese garden, and a massive, over-the-top fountain from which statues of winged horses rise. Landscaper Daniel Robertson designed the gardens between 1745 and 1767. Legend has it that due to crippling gout, he oversaw the work while being carted around in a wheelbarrow, sipping port as he went. When the bottle was dry, work was done for the day. At the garden center, you can learn everything there is to know about the plants that thrive here and pick up seeds to take home (although beware of Customs rules for such things). A few rooms of the house are open to the public, though only one or two days a week, so check ahead. There's also a playground and gift shops. If you feel

walk this way: HIKING IN COUNTY WICKLOW

Loved by hikers and ramblers for its peace, isolation, and sheer beauty, the **Wicklow Way** is a 132km (82-mile) signposted walking path that follows forest trails, sheep paths, and country roads from the suburbs south of Dublin, up into the Wicklow Mountains, and down through country farmland to Clonegal. It takes about 5 to 7 days to walk its entirety, with overnight stops at B&Bs and hostels along the route. Most people, however, choose to walk sections as day trips. (**Tip:** The southern section, through Tinahely, Shillelagh, and Clonegal, is much gentler and less hilly.) You can pick up information and maps at the Wicklow National Park center at Glendalough, or get more information on the Wicklow Way at **www.irishways.com**.

St. Kevin's Way, an ancient pilgrims' route more than 1,000 years old, has recently been restored. The path runs for 30km (19 miles) through scenic countryside from Hollywood to Glendalough, following the route taken by pilgrims who visited the ancient monastic site. As it winds through roads, forest paths, and open mountainside, it visits many of the historical sites associated with St. Kevin, as well as areas of geological interest and scenic beauty.

Leaflets containing maps and route descriptions for other walks can be found at tourist offices. Folks who prefer less strenuous walking may enjoy the paths around the lakes at **Glendalough** (see p. 106).

energetic, follow the well-marked path over 7km (4 miles) to the picturesque **Powerscourt Waterfall**—the highest in Ireland at 121m (397 ft.). Or you can drive, following signs from the estate. Powerscourt is only about 20km (12½ miles) south of Dublin, and can be reached by city buses 44 or 185 to Enniskerry village, approximately a 25-minute walk from the estate.

On R760, Enniskerry, Co. Wicklow. www.powerscourt.ie. © **01/204-6000. Gardens:** €8.50 adults (€6.50 Nov–Feb), €7.50 seniors and students, €5 children under 16, €25 families. **Waterfall:** €5.50 adults, €5 seniors and students, €2.50 children under 16, €16 families. **Gardens:** Daily 9:30am–5:30pm (or at dusk if earlier). **Garden Pavilion:** Mon–Sat 9:30am–5:30pm; Sun 10am–5:30pm. **Ballroom and Garden Rooms:** May–Sept Sun-Mon 9:30am–1:30pm; Oct–Apr Sun 9:30am–1:30pm. **Powerscourt Waterfall:** May–Aug 9:30am–7pm; Mar–Apr and Sept–Oct 10:30am–5:30pm; Nov–Feb 10:30am–4:30pm.

Russborough House ★★ ARCHITECTURE   Sprawling low across the green landscape, this somber greystone villa was built between 1741 and 1751. The designer was Richard Cassels, the same man who designed the much more fanciful Powerscourt House (see above). Today, however, Russborough is known not for its architecture but for housing a small but mighty art gallery. In the 1950s, the house was bought by Sir Alfred Beit, a member of the De Beers diamond family, specifically to hold his massive personal art collection, and it displays one of the most exquisite small rural art collections you're likely to find anywhere. Although many of the most valuable paintings have been moved to other museums after a series of robberies, the collection still includes works by Vermeer, Gainsborough, and Rubens. You can see the house only by guided tour, and there is certainly a lot to see—ornate plaster ceilings by the Lafranchini brothers, huge marble mantelpieces, and fine displays of silver, porcelain, and furniture. Kids will be amused by a fiendish maze, a "fairy trail" on the grounds that tells the story of Russborough's resident fairy, and sheepdog demonstrations daily at 2pm (in good weather). The grounds also contain traditional craft workshops where artisans can be watched in action, including a blacksmith and a candlemaker.

Signposted from N81, 3.2km (2 miles) south of Blessington, Co. Wicklow. www.russ boroughhouse.ie. ⓒ **045/865-239.** House: €12 adults; €9 seniors and students; €6 children 6–15; children 5 and under free. Maze: €3, or €10 family. Family ticket for house plus maze: €30. Sheepdog demonstration €5. Fairy trail €3. Mar–Sept daily 10am–6pm (tours hourly); Oct–Dec Mon–Fri tours 1 and 2pm; Sat, Sun, and holiday Mon tours noon, 1, 2, and 3pm.

Wicklow Mountains National Park ★★★ NATURE SITE Sprawling around Glendalough, this hilly national park is popular with hikers walking the Wicklow Way, a hiking trail that cuts across the park (see above). In the high season, you'll find an information station at the Upper Lake at Glendalough where you can get maps and route guides. Behind the center is a sweet little "sensory garden" (free admission), containing a variety of plants chosen for their scent, texture, and even the sounds of the wildlife they attract. The closest parking is at Upper Lake, where you'll pay a couple of euro per car; or just walk up from the visitor center at Glendalough (p. 106), where the parking is free. *Note:* The Irish National Parks and Wildlife Service warns that ticks carrying Lyme disease are known to live in the hills. Although the risk of contracting the disease is small, you should dress in long sleeves, wear a hat, avoid hiking in shorts, and check for ticks afterward.

Glendalough, Co. Wicklow. www.wicklowmountainsnationalpark.ie. ⓒ **040/445-325.** Free admission. Glendalough Visitor Centre €3 adults, €2 seniors, €1 students and children, €8 families. Park open 24 hours. Visitor Centre mid-Mar to mid-Oct daily 9:30am–6pm; mid-Oct to mid-Mar daily 9:30am—5pm; last admission to center 45 min. before closing.

THE SOUTHEAST

Dramatic coastline, misty mountains, and evocative historic monuments characterize the lush counties south of Dublin. The area also has a distinctive, musical dialect, peppered with unique words and phrases—remnants of the ancient Yola language that was once spoken here. The three main tourist centers of the Southeast—Waterford, Wexford, and Kilkenny—are close enough together that you could use any as a base for exploring the region by car. In only a few minutes, you really start to feel like you've left the city behind and entered the real countryside. But "city" is a relative term out here: Waterford, the biggest town in the region, has a population of just 46,000.

ESSENTIALS

Arriving

BY BUS Bus Éireann (www.buseireann.ie; ℂ **01/836-6111**) operates direct service several times a day from Dublin's central bus station (Busáras), into Kilkenny, Wexford, and Waterford. The journey to Kilkenny takes upwards of 2 hours; to Wexford and Waterford, closer to 3.

BY TRAIN Irish Rail (www.irishrail.ie; ℂ **1850/366-222**) operates several trains daily between Dublin and Kilkenny, Wexford, and Waterford. The journey to Kilkenny takes about 90 minutes; to Waterford, a little over 2 hours; and to Wexford, 2½ hours.

BY FERRY Ferries from Britain sail to Rosslare Harbour, 19km (12 miles) south of Wexford Town. Call **Irish Ferries** (www.irish ferries.ie; ℂ **0818/300-400**) or **Stena Line** (www.stenaline.com; ℂ **01/204-7777**) for information. Irish Ferries also sail to Rosslare from northern France.

BY CAR The journey from Dublin to Kilkenny, Waterford, or Wexford is nearly all via motorway. From Dublin to Wexford, take N11 south. For Kilkenny, take E20, then M7 southwest out of Dublin, then split off onto M9. If you're heading to Waterford, stay on M9 for another 50km (31 miles) after the turnoff for Kilkenny. The drive to Kilkenny is about 1½ hours, and to Waterford or Wexford about 2 hours, but considerably longer if you're caught in Dublin's terrible rush hour traffic.

BY PLANE The British budget airline **Flybe** (www.flybe.com) flies a few times a week into tiny **Waterford Airport** in Killowen (www.waterfordair port.ie; © **051/846-600**), 9km (5⅔ miles) south of Waterford Town. The Belgian budget airline **VLM** (www.flyvlm.com) flies here a few times per week from Birmingham and London's Luton airport in the U.K.

Getting Around

It's relatively simple to travel between Kilkenny, Wexford, or Waterford by public transport; however, as with most rural areas in Ireland, getting *around* the countryside by public transport once you're here is extremely challenging. Unless you're sticking to the big towns, your best option is to rent a car.

BY BUS Direct buses connect Waterford and Wexford every couple of hours; most journeys take an hour. A handful of buses per day run between Kilkenny and Waterford; the journey takes 1 to 2 hours, depending on if you have to change buses (which you almost always do). No convenient bus routes connect Kilkenny and Wexford; you'll have to go through Waterford.

BY TRAIN A half-dozen or so trains daily go between Kilkenny and Waterford; the journey takes 35 minutes. Getting from Kilkenny or Waterford to Wexford by train involves multiple changes and can take all day; avoid this route if at all possible and take a bus to Wexford.

BY CAR To rent a car from Dublin, try **Hertz** (www.hertz.ie) at Dublin Airport (© **01/844-5466**); or 2 Haddington Rd., Dublin 4 (© **01/668-7566**). **Europcar** also has branches at Dublin Airport (© **01/812-2800**) and Mark St. (off Pearse St.), Dublin 2 (© **01/648-5900**). In Kilkenny, try **Enterprise-Rent-A-Car** at the Kilkenny Car Complex, Dublin Rd. (www.enterprise.ie; © **056/775-3318**). **Hertz** has a branch in Wexford Town, on Ferrybank (© **053/915-2500**), or you can try **Budget Car Rental** at Rosslare Ferryport (www.budget.ie; © **053/913-3318**). In Waterford, Enterprise has a branch on Cork Rd. (www.enterprise.co.uk; © **051/304-804**).

BY FERRY Driving between Waterford and Wexford involves a circuitous route via New Ross—unless you cut the distance in half by taking the handy car ferry from the poetically named **Passage East,** about 12km (7½ miles) east of Waterford (www.passageferry.ie; © **051/382-480**). Regular crossings run April to September, Monday to Saturday 7am to 10pm, Sunday and public holidays 9:30am to 10pm; October to March, Monday to Saturday 7am to 8pm, Sunday and public holidays 9:30am to 8pm. Tickets per car are €8 one-way, €12 round-trip.

WHERE TO STAY

Waterford and Kilkenny both have some high-quality, reasonably priced accommodations within the town centers. In Wexford, choice in town is limited; you're much better opting for a place in the countryside, where there is a satisfying mixture of bucolic farmhouses and luxurious getaways.

Where to Stay in Waterford City

Granville Hotel ★★ With its elegant Sienna-colored frontage, this welcoming hotel was built in the late 1700s and has been in business continuously since 1865. The interior retains a manor-house feel, with rich color schemes, deep-red carpeting, and antique furniture. Guest rooms are comfortable and reasonably spacious—although not all have air-conditioning, so request this when you book if it's important to you. Some rooms overlook Waterford Quay, with its field of gently bobbing yacht masts. The hotel bar is popular with locals, and the modern Irish **Bianconi Restaurant** is excellent. Staff could hardly be friendlier or more helpful. You can book a relaxing (and reasonably priced) massage treatment in the Therapy Room.

Meagher's Quay, Waterford, Co. Waterford. www.granville-hotel.ie. ℂ **051/305-555.** 98 units. €119–€149. Parking at nearby lots (no discount) €3.50–€5 overnight; €5–€17 for 24 hr. Breakfast not included in lower rates. Dinner, bed and breakfast packages available. **Amenities:** Wi-Fi (free); restaurant; bar; room service; A/C.

Samuel's Heritage ★★ This charming B&B on the outskirts of Waterford (just a little too far to be within walking distance from the center) overlooks open fields on one side and the River Suir on the other. Sally, Des, and their family has converted their home into a modern, well-equipped lodging. (How often do you find a countryside B&B with its own mini-gym and infrared sauna?) Bright and cheery guest rooms have ample space, plus extras like flatscreen TVs and free Wi-Fi. Family rooms sleep up to four. Delicious breakfast options include smoked salmon and eggs from their own hens.

Halfway House, Dunmore Rd., Waterford, Co. Waterford. www.samuelsheritage.com. ℂ **051/875094.** 6 units. €80–€90. Breakfast included in rates. Free parking. **Amenities:** Wi-Fi (free); gym; sauna.

Waterford Marina Hotel ★ This well-run, modern hotel overlooking the River Suir isn't particularly characterful, but it's in a great location, a short walk from the center of Waterford. Rooms are clean and have everything you need, with comfortable beds. Family rooms are an exceptionally good value—they sleep up to four, usually for just €10 or so more than the standard double rates. (You'll pay a €25 supplement for kids btw. 12 and 16.) Some bedrooms have lovely views over the water. Special offers often listed on the website include packages that cover dinner in the excellent restaurant. *Tip:* Ask for an upper floor room, for better views and (since there can be street noise at night, particularly on weekends) to be above the ruckus.

Canada St., Waterford, Co. Waterford. www.waterfordmarinahotel.com. ℂ **051/856-600.** 81 units. €70–€158. Free parking. Breakfast not included in lower rates. **Amenities:** Wi-Fi (free); restaurant; bar; room service; accessible rooms.

Where to Stay in County Wexford

Monart Spa ★★★ A luxurious, restorative, grown-up retreat, Monart is consistently named among the top spas in Ireland—and for good reason. It's a sumptuous, impeccably designed place, set beside a lake and a verdant forest. Guest rooms are surrounded by woodland, and some have little

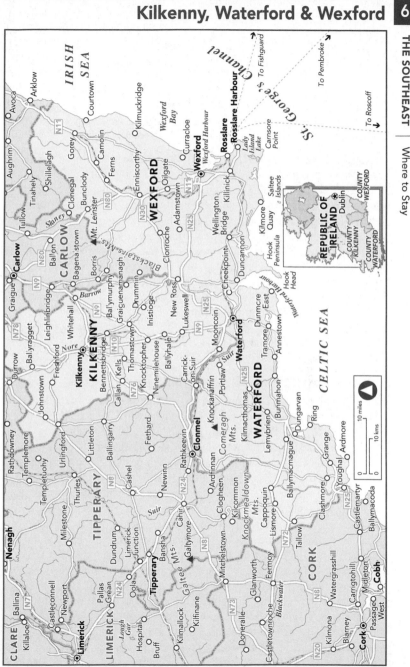

balconies overlooking the grounds. The restaurant is excellent, though expensive (€40 for three courses, and many dishes cost extra). The heavenly spa has a thermal suite (free to use for guests) equipped with two pools, a salt grotto, indoor and outdoor saunas, and an aroma steam room. Check the website for package deals, particularly midweek specials. To maintain the air of serenity, no children are allowed at Monart.

On L6124, The Still, about 5km (3 miles) W of Enniscorthy, Co. Wexford. www.monart. ie. ℰ **053/923-8999.** 70 units. €218–€238. Free parking. Rates include breakfast. Dinner, bed and breakfast, and spa treatment packages available. **Amenities:** Wi-Fi (free); 2 restaurants; bar; room service; afternoon tea; cafe; spa; pool.

Riverbank House Hotel ★★ This cozy midsize hotel just outside the town center in Wexford has lovely views of the River Slaney. Rooms overlooking the river have suitably huge picture windows. Beds are comfortable and very large; some are four-poster. Family rooms cost just €30 more than doubles (though they are not that much bigger, with one double and one single bed). The bar and restaurant are pleasant spaces, filled with natural light. The casual pub-style food is good too—unfussy, international dishes of the something-for-everyone variety—and in good weather you can dine on the terrace overlooking the river. The genuinely cheerful staff helps things run smoothly. All in all, this is a thoroughly decent, near-budget option about a 10-minute walk from central Wexford.

The Bridge, Wexford Co. Wexford. www.riverbankhousehotel.com. ℰ **053/912-3611.** 23 units. €80–€110. Free parking. Breakfast not included in lower rates. **Amenities:** Wi-Fi (free); restaurant; bar; room service.

Where to Stay in County Kilkenny

Lawcus Farm Guesthouse ★★★ Perfect peace and tranquility await you at this gorgeous farmyard B&B, deep in the Kilkenny countryside. Make no mistake that this is the real deal ("helping us on the farm at feeding time is greatly appreciated," says the website), but hosts Mark and Anne Marie go out of their way to welcome guests. The early-19th-century farmhouse has been beautifully renovated. Guest rooms are cozy and decent-sized, with plenty of natural light. Some have original fireplaces; one has exposed greystone walls and an antique-style brass bed. It's a pastoral setting to die for—you're right next to a river, where you can go wild water swimming, or even try your hand at fishing for trout. Home-cooked breakfasts are delicious, but you have to fend for yourself at dinner. (Luckily, your hosts can recommend a string of nearby places.) They've opened a self-contained lodge for couples, the Tree House, which sits on a rocky outcrop down by the river—what romantic bliss!—and costs €250 for 2 nights, including breakfast in the main house. The only snag in this rural idyll? Lawcus Farm doesn't accept credit cards or checks, so make sure you're able to pay in cash.

Stoneyford, Co. Kilkenny. From the R713, pass Stoneyford sign and turn to the right of the small bridge; follow signs to B&B. www.lawcusfarmguesthouse.com. ℰ **086/603-1667.** 5 units. €100. Free parking. Rates include breakfast. Discounts for stays of 2 or more nights. Children under 5 free (1 per party). **Amenities:** Wi-Fi (free).

Rosquil House ★★   Comfortable and friendly, this modest little B&B is great value for money. No, it's not fancy, but it was custom-built by the owners, so bedrooms are spacious and well-proportioned (one is accessible for travelers with disabilities). And the same care that went into the design of the home goes into the hospitality: hosts Rhoda and Phil greet guests with genuine warmth and enthusiasm, making them feel immediately at home. Public areas, including a large guest lounge, are tastefully decorated in color schemes of chocolate and cream with polished wood floors. The breakfasts cooked by Phil are delicious. The only downside is that you're a little far from the action, with central Kilkenny about a 15-minute walk away.

Castlecomer Rd., Kilkenny, Co. Kilkenny. www.rosquilhouse.com. ⓒ **056/772-1419.** 7 units. €70–€90. Parking at nearby lots (no discount) €3.50–€5 overnight; €5–€16 for 24 hr. Rates include breakfast. **Amenities:** Wi-Fi (free).

WHERE TO EAT
Where to Eat in County Waterford

Bodega! ★★ MODERN IRISH/EUROPEAN   A restaurant with an exclamation point in the name isn't really the sort of place you'd expect to sit up straight, and Bodega! certainly does its best to cultivate a funky vibe. Order a cocktail and nibble on a tasting platter, or go all out on a full meal; smoked and local-market fish cooked in ginger beer batter, for instance, or local pork served with homemade sauerkraut. The word "local" appears reassuringly often on the menu; even the burgers come with a delicious smoked farmhouse cheese that's travelled barely an hour to get here. The long cocktail list should help maintain the buzz.

54 John's St., Waterford City. www.bodegawaterford.com. ⓒ **051/844-177.** Tasting platters €13–€25. Main courses €16–€28. Closed Sun.

The Munster ★ BISTRO   This cozy bar, across the street from the House of Waterford Crystal visitor center (p. 120), serves a smallish menu of unpretentious, traditional pub grub—think sandwiches, Irish stew, seafood pie, and an enormous house burger. The early-evening menu has a few slightly more ambitious choices, such as chicken breast with chorizo and Parmesan cream, or salmon fishcake served with chili jam. It may lack frills, but everything's well prepared.

Bailey's New St., Waterford City. www.themunsterbar.com. ⓒ **051/874-656.** Main courses €12–€14. Mon 12:30am–2:30pm; Tues–Fri 12:30–2:30pm and 5–9pm; Sat 5–9pm; Sun 4–8pm.

Richmond House ★★★ MODERN IRISH   The grounds of this 18th-century mansion hide away a bountiful produce patch, where the chef gets most of the fruit and vegetables for the restaurant's kitchen. This is something of a dining destination for people in this part of Ireland, and it's easy to see why—the menu is a hugely successful combination of Irish and Continental flavors. Menus change daily, according to what's fresh and in season, but you're likely to find locally sourced lamb, beef, and seafood served with sides like *champ* (mashed potato and spring onion) or something freshly picked from the garden. The wine list includes a better-than-average selection of wines by the glass—a relief, given the price of dinner. Those wanting to sample some of this sumptuous home cooking on a budget may want to check out the early bird menus (€28–€33) served until 7:30pm. They also have a few guest rooms (around €120–€150 per night) if you like it so much you don't want to leave.

Singposted from N72, Cappoquin, Co. Waterford. www.richmondhouse.net. © **058/54278.** Fixed-price menus €28–€55. Daily 6–9pm. Closed Dec 22–Jan 10.

Where to Eat in County Wexford

Aldridge Lodge ★★★ IRISH   This wonderful restaurant near the village of Duncannon has been wowing diners for over a decade. The menu very much depends on what's in season, but specialties of the talented chef, Billy Whitty, include Kilmore Quay scallops with a deliciously sweet red-onion marmalade; slow-cooked lamb; and lobster fresh from Hook Head. The tasting menu is a delight, bucking the trend for an endless procession of bite-size plates in favor of four balanced and well-designed courses (thoroughly reasonable, too, at just €30 per head). Aldridge Lodge also has three elegant bedrooms for €90 per night; dinner, bed and breakfast packages are excellent value for money.

Duncannon, near New Ross, Co. Wexford. www.aldridgelodge.com. © **051/389-116.** Set menus €30–€40. Reservations essential. Wed–Sat 6–9:30pm; Sun 1–2pm, dinner seatings 5:30 and 8:30pm.

Cistin Eile ★★ MODERN IRISH   Gaelic words painted on the dining room wall translate to "hunger makes a great sauce"—a wry nod to tradition that nicely sums up this place. Wexford native and rising star chef Warren Gillen deeply embraces the flavors of his home region, yet gives them a contemporary twist. Fish straight from the market, local meats and game—all are elegantly presented without a hint of pretension. One of the nicest things about Cistin Eile is how relaxed it feels; Warren often greets guests at the door personally and chats to them at their tables. *Tip:* Lunch here is surprisingly affordable.

80 South Main St., Wexford, Co. Wexford. © **053/912-1616.** Main courses €9–€17. Reservations recommended. Mon–Tues noon–3pm; Wed–Fri noon–9pm; Sat 12:30–9pm. Closed Sun.

Mary Barry's Bar ★ PUB FOOD   Straight-up pub food is the order of the day in this cheerful pub opposite the village church in Kilmore. Tasty, filling plates of burgers, fresh seafood (from Kilmore Quay, naturally), and overflowing sandwiches are more than enough for a satisfying lunch on the road. You can eat in the large garden if it's a sunny day—kids will appreciate the play area, complete with giant inflatables. After 5:30pm, Mondays to Thursdays, they do a great-value set menu, with three courses for just €20.

On R739, Kilmore, Co. Wexford. www.marybarrys.ie. © **051/913-5982.** Main courses €11–€25. Mon–Wed noon–8:30pm; Thurs, Sun noon–9pm; Fri–Sat noon–9:30pm.

The Yard ★★ BRASSERIE There are two sides to this place; drop in at lunchtime for a hearty but informal meal (beer-battered cod and chips, perhaps, or a tasty burger), or come in the evening for a more elaborate brasserie-style menu, combining traditional Irish flavors with global influences. Specials could include eggrolls made with Bluebell Falls goats' cheese, or seabass filets served with lime-and-chile butter and a fresh pico de gallo. Come on Thursday or Friday night for the great value set menu—four courses for just €27, plus free entry to the **Centenary Stores** (www.thestores.ie; *©* **053/912-4424**), a popular nightclub on Charlotte Street. Open Thursday to Saturday evenings, the **Little Yard** is an alternative dining space, part bar, part tapas restaurant. It's also open Sunday nights on holiday weekends.

3 Lower Georges St. www.theyard.ie. *©* **053/914-4083.** Main courses €17–€30. Mon–Sat noon–10pm.

Where to Eat in Kilkenny Town

Campagne ★★★ BISTRO The chef at this outstanding French-Irish restaurant, about a 10-minute walk from Kilkenny Castle, used to run the kitchen at the superlative **Chapter One** in Dublin (see p. 64). The dining room is sleek and atmospherically lit, with colorful modern art on the walls. The menu is short but subtly inventive: wild seabass with Jerusalem artichoke and porcini mushroom butter, or perhaps filet of free range pork with black pudding and celery gratin. A full vegetarian menu is always available. For dessert, try the warm caramelized pear with cinnamon ice cream. While this place is quite pricey, plenty of locals will tell you it's their go-to for a special dinner. The extensive wine list is well chosen, with particularly strong French options.

5 The Arches, Gashouse Lane, Kilkenny Town. www.campagne.ie. *©* **056/777-2858.** Main courses €29–€32. Tues–Thurs 6–10pm; Fri–Sat 12:30–2:30pm, 6–10pm; Sun 12.30–2:30pm. Closed Sun for dinner except public holiday weekends; closed Tues nights after public holiday Mondays.

Gourmet Store ★ DELI/CAFE Very good for a quick lunch on the go, this cafe in the center of Kilkenny is popular with local workers who come for tasty sandwiches and bagels. There's a great stock of deli goods, so you can put together your own picnic basket, or the folks behind the counter can do it for you—perfect for when you need to snatch a quick bite on the road. A lot of the off-the-shelf products are local and small-brand, including jams and chutneys that make great gifts and edible souvenirs.

56 High St. www.thegourmetstorekilkenny.com. *©* **056/777-1727.** All items €4–€10. Mon–Sat 8am–6pm.

Kyteler's Inn ★ PUB In business for over 6 centuries, this atmospheric old inn serves decent pub food—sandwiches, Irish stew, burgers, fish and chips—but it's the atmosphere you really come for. With all the exposed flagstones and cozy nooks, it's hard to think of a more satisfyingly Irish-looking pub. The place is named after former resident and noted hellraiser, Alice Kyteler, who died in 1324. She poisoned at least three of her husbands, ran the

Inn as a den of debauchery, and was sentenced to be burned as a witch. But she escaped, and nobody saw or heard from her again. Unless, that is, you believe some of the more colorful tales about this place after dark . . .

Kieran St., Kilkenny Town. www.kytelersinn.com. © **056/772-1064.** Main courses €8–€24. Daily noon–around midnight (food served until about 10pm).

Rinuccini ★★★ ITALIAN   This extremely popular restaurant, opposite Kilkenny Castle (see p. 125), packs in diners for its delicious Italian food with an Irish accent. The basement-level dining room gets very busy, but the food more than makes up for it. The homemade pasta is as good as you'd expect, and on the specials board, local produce really comes into its own—prawns and black sole from Kilmore Quay, finished with cream sauce or white wine; Silver Hill duck baked with sweet aurum (an Italian orange liqueur); or maybe just a fresh-as-can-be catch of the day. Desserts are equally good—try the homemade chocolate tart served with honey ice cream, or the tasty cheese plate, filled with selections imported from Italy. Due to Rinuccini's popularity, you should make reservations if you're coming on a weekend.

1 The Parade, Kilkenny Town. www.rinuccini.com. © **056/776-1575.** Main courses €17–€29. Mon–Fri noon–2:30pm, 5–10pm; Sat noon–3pm, 5–10pm; Sun noon–9pm.

Where to Eat near the Rock of Cashel

Chez Hans ★★ EUROPEAN   Located in a converted church building—which, rather wonderfully, was bought in the 1860s with a 1,000-year lease on terms of one shilling per year—Chez Hans is one of the most reliably good restaurants in Cashel. Menus change several times a week, based on what's freshest and best. Seafood features heavily (Kilmore Quay scallops with salad Niçoise perhaps, or organic salmon served with seasonal vegetables), or you could opt for some local lamb with an herb crust, or monkfish with butternut puree. The dining room is a beautiful space, redolent of the building's past life. Reservations are recommended. The restaurant is a 2-minute walk from the Rock of Cashel.

Rockside, Cashel, Co. Tipperary. www.chezhans.net. © **062/61177.** Main courses €24–€38. Tues–Sat 6–10pm.

EXPLORING COUNTY WATERFORD

Waterford City's unprotected proximity at the edge of the ferocious Atlantic Ocean makes it Ireland's Windy City, as a sea breeze is always blowing here. Not only is it the main seaport of southeast Ireland, its oceanside location has a lot to do with its status as the oldest city in the country, founded by Viking invaders in the 9th century.

VISITOR INFORMATION   The **Waterford Discover Ireland Centre** is at 120 Parade Quay, Waterford (www.waterfordtourism.com; © 051/875-823). It's open Monday to Friday, 9am to 5:15pm (sometimes later in summer), and on weekends in summertime only.

Top Attractions in Waterford City

Bishop's Palace ★★ MUSEUM   One of three separate museums known collectively as *Waterford Treasures,* the Bishop's Palace focuses on life in the city from 1700 until the mid-20th century. The collection covering the 18th century is by far the most impressive, including furniture, art, fashion, and some exquisite glass and silverwork. The Georgian drawing room is dominated by Willem Van der Hagen's 1736 landscape painting of Waterford City—the oldest landscape of an Irish city in existence—depicting long-vanished Waterford landmarks such as the medieval Christ Church Cathedral, demolished in 1773. Appropriately enough, given its close proximity to the famous factory (see below), the museum also holds the earliest surviving piece of Waterford Crystal, a decanter dating from 1789. The Bishop's Palace, an elegant example of Georgian architecture, was built by Richard Cassels (1690–1751), architect of **Leinster House** in Dublin (see p. 84).

The Mall, Waterford City. www.waterfordtreasures.com/bishops-palace. *©* **051/849-650.** Admission €7 adults; €6 seniors and students; children under 14 free. Combined ticket with Medieval Museum €10 adults; €9 seniors and students. Mon–Fri 9:15am–6pm; Sat 9:30am–6pm; Sun and public holidays 11am–6pm (closes at 5pm Sept–May).

Christ Church Cathedral ★ CATHEDRAL   Waterford's most important church building is a beautiful example of late-18th-century architecture. The Italianate style that so enthralled the Georgians is plain to see—so much so that the interior looks almost like a stately home rather than a place of worship. Corinthian columns top grand marble plinths, rising up to meet the grand stucco, with its delicate filigreed detail. The current building, one of two cathedrals in the city designed by John Roberts, was finished in 1773, replacing one built by the Vikings in the 11th century. (Only a solitary pillar remains from the original building.) This was where Strongbow, the first English lord to invade Ireland, married an Irish princess—thus gaining a permanent foothold into the Irish nobility. Christ Church's Catholic counterpart, Holy Trinity Cathedral (also designed by John Roberts), is on Barronstrand Street (see below).

Cathedral Square. www.christchurchwaterford.com. *©* **051/858-958.** Free admission. Easter–Oct Mon–Sat 10am–5pm. Oct–Easter Mon–Sat noon–3pm.

Garter Lane Arts Centre ★ ARTS COMPLEX   One of Ireland's largest arts centers, the Garter Lane occupies two buildings on O'Connell Street. Number 5 holds exhibition rooms and artists' studios, and no. 22a, a former Friends Meeting House, is home of the Garter Lane Theatre, along with an art gallery and outdoor courtyard. The gallery showcases works by contemporary and local artists, plus a varied program of music, dance, and films.

O'Connell St., Waterford City. www.garterlane.ie. *©* **051/855-038.** Many events and exhibitions free; ticketed events around €5 to €20. Tues–Sat 11am–10pm; Sun 7–10pm; individual performance times vary.

Holy Trinity Cathedral ★ CATHEDRAL   Waterford has two impressive cathedrals, one Catholic and the other Protestant, both built by one

THE rock OF CASHEL

Worth the long drive it takes to get here from almost anywhere useful, this is one of Ireland's most iconic—and most impressive—medieval ruins. The extraordinary, dramatic outline of this craggy abbey, atop a hill in the center of Cashel, dominates views for miles around.

An outcrop of limestone reaching some 60m (197 ft.) into the sky, the so-called "Rock" tells the tales of 16 centuries. It was the seat of the kings of Munster at least as far back as A.D. 360, and it remained a royal fortress until 1101, when King Murtagh O'Brien granted it to the church. Among Cashel's many great moments was the legendary baptism of King Aengus by St. Patrick in 448. Remaining on the rock are the ruins of a two-towered chapel, a cruciform cathedral, a 28m (92-ft.) round tower, and a cluster of other medieval monuments. Inside the cathedral, extraordinary and detailed ancient carvings survive in excellent condition. The views of and from the Rock are spectacular.

Cashel is located 72km (45 miles) northeast of Waterford on R688. Entry to the Rock costs €7 adults, €5 seniors, €3 children and students, and €17 families. It's open mid-March to early June daily 9am to 5:30pm; early June to mid-September daily 9am to 7pm; mid-September to mid-October daily 9am to 5:30pm; and mid-October to mid-March daily 9am to 4:30pm. Last admission is 45 minutes before closing. For more information see www.heritageireland.ie or call ✆ **062/61437.**

equal-opportunity architect, John Roberts (the other being Christ Church Cathedral in Cathedral Square). This is the Catholic version; the only baroque cathedral in Ireland, complete with 10 unique Waterford crystal chandeliers. Roberts lived 82 years (1714–96), fathered 22 children with his beloved wife, and built nearly every significant 18th-century building around Waterford.

Barronstrand and Henrietta sts., Waterford City. www.waterford-cathedral.com. ✆**051/875-166.** Free admission. Open daily; hours can vary but generally 7:30am–7pm.

House of Waterford Crystal ★ FACTORY TOUR One of the best-known Irish brands in the world, Waterford Crystal has been made in the city (with significant periods of hiatus) since 1783. In 2009, the company filed for bankruptcy—perhaps Ireland's most high-profile victim of the global financial crisis—and for a while it looked like this iconic brand might disappear for good. But new owners were soon found, and with them came this shiny, purpose-built factory and visitor center, right in the heart of Waterford. You can tour the factory to watch the glittering products being molded, blown, cut, and finished, mostly using traditional methods that have changed little in 200 years. Or, if you'd rather just drop in for sparkly souvenirs, you can visit the enormous gift shop without taking the tour.

The Mall, Waterford City. www.waterfordvisitorcentre.com. ✆ **051/317-000.** Admission €14 adults; €10 seniors and students; €5 children 6–18; children under 6 free; €30 families. **Tour:** Apr–Oct Mon–Sat 9am–4:15pm; Sun 9:30am–4:15pm. Nov–Dec Mon–Fri 9:30am–3:15pm. Jan–Feb Mon–Fri 9am–3:15pm. Mar Mon–Sat 9am–3:15pm; Sun 9:30am–3:15pm. **Store:** Mar–Oct 9am–6pm; Sun 9:30am–6pm. Nov–Dec Mon–Fri 9:30am–5pm; Sun noon–5pm. Jan–Feb daily 9:30am–5pm.

Medieval Museum ★★ MUSEUM The latest addition to the multi-site **Waterford Treasures,** the Medieval Museum has some beautiful artifacts from the city's medieval period, including richly embroidered cloth-of-gold vestments, intricate metal badges worn by pilgrims to the Holy Land, and the lavishly illustrated 1373 Charter Roll of Waterford. The building itself is as much of a treasure as the items on display. Closed off for years, the impressive 13th-century Chorister's Hall with its vaulted stone ceiling now forms one of the main areas of the museum, together with a 15th-century wine vault.

Cathedral Sq., Waterford City. www.waterfordtreasures.com/medieval-museum. ℂ **051/849-501.** Admission €7 adults; €6 seniors and students; children under 14 free; combined ticket with Bishop's Palace €10 adults; €9 seniors and students. Mon–Fri 9:15am–6pm, Sat 9:30am–6pm, Sun 11am–6pm (closes at 5pm Sept–May). Last admission 40 min. before closing.

Reginald's Tower ★★ MUSEUM Claimed to be Ireland's oldest building that's still in day-to-day use, Reginald's Tower was built around the year 1000 by the Viking invaders who founded the city. Today it houses a museum devoted to that period in Waterford's history; while much of it is interpretive in nature, with plaques that tell the story in absorbing detail, a surprising number of actual items are on display too. Highlights include fragments of Viking pottery, coins, and jewelry, including a stunning ornamental clasp, intricately patterned with fine threads of gold and silver. Be careful when climbing the old stone staircase—in order to confound attackers, these "stumble steps" were designed to be deliberately uneven, hence easy to trip over (also oriented in such a way to make wielding a sword impossible if you're right-handed—so better leave yours behind).

The Quay, Waterford City. www.waterfordtreasures.com/reginalds-tower. ℂ **051/304-220.** Admission €3 adults, €2 seniors, €1 students and children. Late Mar to mid-Dec daily 9:30am–5:30pm. Jan to early Mar Wed–Sun 9:30am–5pm. Last admission 30 min. before closing.

Farther Afield in County Waterford

Ardmore High Cross ★ RELIGIOUS SITE Ardmore (Irish for "the great height") is a very ancient Christian site—St. Declan, its founder, is said to have been a bishop in Munster as early as the mid-4th century, well before St. Patrick came to Ireland. Tradition has it that the small stone oratory in a cemetery high above Ardmore marks his burial site. St. Declan's Oratory is one of several stone structures composing the ancient monastic settlement. The most striking is the perfectly intact 30m-high (98-ft.) round tower. On site are also ruins of a medieval cathedral and, nearby, St. Declan's well and church. Ardmore is near the border with County Cork, about 70km (43 miles) southwest of Waterford City.

On R673, Ardmore. Free admission. Daily dawn–dusk. From the main N25 road, turn onto R673 and follow signs to Ardmore.

Lismore Castle Gardens ★ GARDENS High above the River Blackwater, this turreted medieval fortress dates from 1185, when Prince John of England (later the infamously bad King John who signed the Magna Carta) established a castle on this site. The grounds, surrounded by thick defensive walls dating from 1626, are spread across nearly 3 hectares (7 acres). They're peaceful and quite lovely to walk around, dotted with sculptures and with views of the massive castle. You're free to wander the whole 3,200-hectare (7,904-acre) estate of gardens, forests, and farmland —but not the castle itself, which is privately owned. Lismore. www.lismorecastlegardens.com. © **058/54061.** Admission €8 adults; €5 seniors, students, and children. Apr–Sept daily 10:30am–5:30pm; last admission 1 hr. before closing. From Cappoquin, take N72 6.5km (4 miles) west.

EXPLORING COUNTY WEXFORD

Although it's within easy reach of County Wexford, Dublin might as well be hundreds of miles away—the countryside in this area feels so bucolic and peaceful. Wexford is known for its long stretches of pristine beaches and for the evocative historic monuments in Wexford Town and on the Hook Head Peninsula. The modern English name of Wexford evolved from *Waesfjord*, which is what the Vikings called it when they invaded in the 9th century. The Normans captured the town at the end of the 12th century, and you can still see remnants of their fort at the Irish National Heritage Park.

VISITOR INFORMATION The Wexford Tourist Office on Crescent Quay, Wexford (www.visitwexford.ie; © **053/912-3111**) is open Monday to Saturday from 9:15am to 5:30pm. From late July to mid-August it's also open on Sundays from 10:30am to 5pm.

Top Attractions in County Wexford

Hook Lighthouse & Heritage Centre ★★ LIGHTHOUSE The Hook Head Peninsula is one of southern Ireland's loveliest drives, full of captivating vistas and hidden byways to discover. Nestled at the end of it all is this picturesque old lighthouse, the oldest part of which dates from the 13th century, making it the world's oldest lighthouse still in continuous use. Guided tours do an excellent job of telling the history of the lighthouse and the surrounding peninsula, which has been occupied since at least the 5th century A.D. There is an active program of special events, from art courses to ghost tours. *Tip:* The drive from Waterford is drastically shorter if you take the Passage East car ferry; see p. 111 for details. The lighthouse is 30km (18⅔ miles) southeast of Waterford and 47km (29 miles) southwest of Wexford.

Hook Head, Co. Wexford. www.hookheritage.ie. © **051/397-055.** Admission €6 adults; €4.50 seniors and students; €3.50 children 5–16; children under 5 free; €18–€20 families. Visitor center: June–Aug daily 9:30am–6pm; May and Sept 9:30am–5:30pm; Oct–Apr 9:30am–5pm. Lighthouse tours: June–Aug half-hourly 10am–5:30pm; Sept–May hourly 10am–5pm.

Irish Agricultural Museum and Famine Exhibition ★★ MUSEUM This deeply affecting museum on the grounds of the 14th-century Johnstown Castle illuminates how important agriculture has been to the history of this region. Exhibits are devoted to, among other things, dairy farming, country furniture, traditional crafts, and historic machinery. Of course no farming museum in Ireland would be complete without mention of its greatest catastrophe—the Great Famine, which killed about a million people in the mid-19th century (and was responsible for the emigration of a million more). A special section puts it all into perspective in a thought-provoking way.

Johnstown Castle Estate, Bridgetown Rd., off Wexford-Rosslare Rd. (N25), Wexford, Co. Wexford. www.irishagrimuseum.ie. © **053/918-4671. Gardens and museum:** €8 adults; €6 seniors; €4 children; €24 families. **Museum only:** €6 adults; €5 seniors; €4 children; €20 families. **Gardens only** (Mar–Oct): €3 adults; €2 seniors; €1 children; €8 families. **Gardens only** (Nov–Feb) free. **Museum:** June–Aug Mon–Fri 9am–6pm; Sat–Sun and public holidays 11am–6pm. Mar–May and Sept–Oct Mon–Fri 9am–5pm; Sat–Sun and public holidays 11am–5pm. Nov–Feb Mon–Fri 9am–4pm; Sat–Sun and public holidays 11am–4pm. **Gardens:** July–Aug daily 9am–6:30pm; Mar–June and Sept–Oct daily 9am–5:30pm; Nov–Feb daily 9am–4:30pm.

Irish National Heritage Park ★★ HERITAGE SITE   On the banks of the River Slaney, just outside of Wexford Town, this 14-hectare (35-acre) living-history park provides a fun introduction for visitors of all ages to life in ancient Ireland, from the Stone Age to the Norman invasion. Each reconstructed glimpse into Irish history has its own natural setting and wildlife. There's also a nature trail and interpretive center, complete with gift shop and cafe. Kids can easily be amused for half a day here.

Ferrycarrig (about 4.8km/3 miles west of Wexford, signposted from N11), Co. Wexford. www.inhp.com. © **053/912-0733.** Admission €9.50 adults; €8 seniors and students; children under 5 free; €23–€25 families. May–Aug daily 9:30am–6:30pm (last admission 5pm); Sept–Apr 9:30am–5:30pm (last admission 3pm).

SS *Dunbrody* Famine Ship ★★ HISTORIC SITE   This huge, life-size reconstruction of a 19th-century tall ship is exactly the kind of vessel on which a million or more people emigrated from Ireland to escape the Great Famine. An interpretive history center, the SS *Dunbrody* offers an engaging way to learn about that history—particularly for youngsters, who will find it less stuffy than a conventional museum. Actors in period dress lead the tours, describing in great detail what life on board was like for the passengers. The SS *Dunbrody* is in New Ross, 36km (22⅓ miles) west of Wexford.

The Quay, New Ross, Co. Wexford. www.dunbrody.com. © **051/425-239.** Admission €10 adults; €8 seniors; €6 students and children; €22–€30 families. Daily 9am–6pm. First tour 9:45am; last tour 5pm.

Tintern Abbey ★ RELIGIOUS SITE   In a lovely rural setting overlooking Bannow Bay, Tintern Abbey was founded in the 12th century by William Marshall, the Earl of Pembroke, as thanks to God after he nearly died at sea. The parts that remain—nave, chancel, tower, chapel, and cloister—date from the early 13th century, though they have been much altered since then. The grounds are extraordinarily beautiful and include a stone bridge spanning a narrow sea inlet. Although it's a poetic enough spot in its own right, this is not the Tintern Abbey that William Wordsworth wrote about in his famous poem of the same name; the monks who named this abbey were Cistercians from the other Tintern, which is in Wales, and they simply gave this one the same name.

Saltmills, New Ross. © **051/562-650.** Free admission. Mid-May to late Sept daily 10am–5pm. Signposted 19km (12 miles) south of New Ross off of R733.

Wexford Walking Tours ★★ TOUR   Proud of their town's ancient streets and antique buildings, the people of Wexford began conducting guided tours for visitors more than 30 years ago. Now the tourism office runs the tours on a more formal basis, but they're still led by locals, whose knowledge of the town and its history is unrivaled. The regular 90-minute historical tour runs March to October, Monday to Saturday, and costs €5 per person. It departs at 11am from the Tourist Office (see p. 122), which also handles booking. They also offer ghost tours and a walk of the surviving sections of the medieval town walls.

Departs from the Wexford Tourist Office on Crescent Quay. www.wexfordwalkingtours. net. © **086/352-6133.** Tour €4. Mar–Oct Mon–Sat 11am.

EXPLORING COUNTY KILKENNY

Like so many Irish towns, Kilkenny Town stands on the site of an old monastery from which it takes its name. A priory was founded here in the 6th century by St. Canice: In Gaelic, *Cill Choinnigh* means "Canice's Church." In medieval times, it was a prosperous walled city. Much of its medieval architecture has been skillfully preserved, including long sections of the medieval wall. Farther afield from the county seat, the gentle countryside is full of captivating old ruins, from the majestic Kells Priory to the haunting remains of Jerpoint Abbey.

VISITOR INFORMATION   The Kilkenny Tourist Office at Shee Alms House, Rose Inn Street, Kilkenny (www.visitkilkenny.ie; © **056/775-1500**) is open May to September, Monday to Saturday 9am to 6pm, Sunday 10:30am to 4pm; October to April, Monday to Saturday 9:15am to 5pm.

Top Attractions in County Kilkenny

Jerpoint Abbey ★★ RELIGIOUS SITE   About 18km (11 miles) southeast of Kilkenny, this outstanding Cistercian monastery dates from the 12th century. Highlights of the atmospheric ruins, which are preserved in a peaceful country setting, include a sculptured cloister arcade, Romanesque architecture in the north nave, and unique stone carvings on the medieval tombs (some of which supposedly have traces of original paint on them, but we've never been able to find it). The staff is quite friendly and knowledgeable about the local area. Ask for details of where to find the mysterious, ghostly ruins of the **Church of the Long Man,** about 16km (10 miles) away. If you're lucky, they'll be able to direct you—it's nigh on impossible to find otherwise, and a local secret you may find yourself sworn to keep. *Tip:* If you're here in spring or autumn, plan your visit for toward the end of the day. Wandering around these ancient places as the setting sun blushes the walls in shades of peach and gold is an unforgettable experience.

On N8, 2.5km (1½ miles) southwest of Thomastown, Co. Kilkenny. www.heritageireland. ie. © **056/772-4623.** Admission €4 adults; €3 seniors; €2 students and children; €10 families. Early Mar to Sept daily 9am–5:30pm; Oct daily 9am–5pm; Nov to early Dec daily 9:30–4pm. Closed early Dec to early Mar (except to pre-booked tours).

Kells Priory ★★RELIGIOUS SITE   With its encompassing fortification walls and towers, Kells is a glorious ruined monastery enfolded into the sloping south bank of the King's River. In 1193, Baron Geoffrey FitzRobert founded the priory and established a Norman-style town beside it. The current ruins date from the 13th to 15th centuries. The priory's wall has been carefully restored, and it connects seven towers, the remains of an abbey, and foundations of chapels and houses. You can tell by the thick walls that this monastery was well fortified, and those walls were built for a reason—it was frequently attacked. In the 13th century, it was the subject of two major battles and burned to the ground. (Despite the similar name, this is not the same monastery where the famous **Book of Kells,** see p. 68, was stored for years before being moved to Dublin in the 1650s. That monastery is in County Meath, just off the M3, about 65km/40 miles north of Dublin.) The priory is less than a half-mile from the village of Kells, so if you have some time to spare, cross the footbridge behind it, which takes you on a beautiful stroll across the river and intersects a riverside walk leading to a picturesque old mill.

Kells, Co. Kilkenny. ℂ056/775-1500. Free admission. Take N76 south from Kilkenny, follow signs for R699/Callan and stay on R699 until you see signs for Kells.

Kilkenny Castle ★★★CASTLE   Standing majestically beside the River Nore on the south side of Kilkenny City, this landmark medieval castle was built in the 12th century and remodeled in Victorian times. From its sturdy corner towers to its battlements, Kilkenny Castle retains the imposing lines of an authentic fortress and sets the tone for the city. The exquisitely restored interior includes a library, drawing room, and bedrooms, all decorated in 1830s style. The former servants' quarters are now an art gallery. The 20-hectare (49-acre) grounds include a riverside walk, extensive gardens, and a well-equipped children's playground. Entry is prefaced by an informative video on the rise, demise, and restoration of the structure. This is a very busy site, so arrive early (or quite late) to avoid waiting.

The Parade, Kilkenny Town. www.kilkennycastle.ie. ℂ 056/770-4100. Admission €7 adults; €5 seniors; €3 students and children; children under 6 free; €17 families. June–Aug 9am–5:30pm; Apr–May, Sept 9:30am–5:30pm; Oct–Feb 9:30am–4:30pm; Mar 9:30am–5pm. Guided tours only Nov–Jan. Last admission 30 min. before closing (45 min. Nov–Jan).

Kilkenny Walking Tours ★★TOURS   Local historian Pat Tynan leads you through the streets and lanes of medieval Kilkenny on this lively walking tour. Tall-sounding (true) tales are really Pat's strong point; he's a mine of trivia, much of it rather sensational. (His own website sells the tour with promises of "black death, whippings, burnings, crime, jails, theft and prostitutes." How's *that* for a pitch?) Tours depart daily from the tourist office, Rose Inn Street, and last about 70 minutes.

C/o Kilkenny Tourist Office, Rose Inn St., Kilkenny Town. www.kilkennywalkingtours.ie. ℂ087/265-1745. Tickets €7 adults; €6.50 seniors and students. Mid-Mar to Oct Mon–Sat 10:30am, 12:15, 3pm; Sun 11:15am, 12:30pm.

COUNTY CORK

T he largest of Ireland's counties, Cork is also one of its most diverse. It encompasses a lively capital city, quiet country villages, rocky hills, picturesque beaches, and long stretches of flat, green farmland. Here, modern tourism (this is where you find Blarney Castle, after all) meets workaday Irish life, and somehow they manage to coexist gracefully. St. Fin Barre founded Cork in the 6th century, when he built a monastery on a swampy estuary of the River Lee, giving the place the rather generic Gaelic name of *Corcaigh*—which, unromantically, means "marsh." Range beyond Cork City to visit the pretty harbor town of Kinsale, famous for spearheading Ireland's gourmet food scene in the '90s and '00s; the storied seaport of Cobh in East Cork; or the barren beauty of Cape Clear Island in craggy West Cork.

ESSENTIALS

Arriving

BY PLANE **Cork Airport,** Kinsale Road (www.corkairport. com; ✆ **021/413-131**), is served by **Aer Lingus** and **Ryanair,** and a handful of other budget airlines. Now Ireland's third-busiest airport, after Dublin and Belfast, it has direct flights to and from several European countries, including nine cities in the U.K. and seven in France. However, it has stopped running any scheduled flights to other airports within Ireland.

BY BUS From Dublin Airport, **AirCoach** (www.aircoach.ie; ✆ **01/844-7118**) runs a regular direct service from Dublin to Cork City. You can catch the bus either at Dublin Airport or Westmoreland Street, in the center of Dublin; from there, the journey to Patrick's Quay in the center of Cork takes 3 hours. Buses leave at 25 minutes past the hour from Terminal 2 (starting at 6:25am), 5 minutes later from Terminal 1, and then on the hour from Westmoreland Street, with the final bus of the day leaving the city at midnight. One-way tickets are €17 adults, €10 children; round-trip tickets are €27 adults, €20 children. In Cork City, **Bus Éireann** (www.buseireann.ie; ✆ **021/450-8188**) runs from the Parnell Place Bus Station to all parts of the Republic. Bus 249 connects Cork with Kinsale. Buses also arrive on Pier Road.

BY TRAIN Iarnród Éireann/Irish Rail (www.irishrail.ie; ✆ 185/036-6222) travels to Cork City from Dublin and other parts of Ireland. Trains arrive at Kent Station, Lower Glanmire Road, in eastern Cork City (✆ 021/455-7277). Kinsale does not have a train station.

BY FERRY There are no longer any direct ferry routes into Cork from Britain. However, **Brittany Ferries** (www.brittany-ferries.com; ✆ 021/427-7801) sail once a day between Roscoff, in France, and Cork's Ringaskiddy Ferryport.

BY CAR Cork is reachable on the N8 from Dublin, N25 from Waterford, and N22 from Killarney. To hire a car in Cork, try **Enterprise Rent-A-Car,** Kinsale Road (✆ 021/497-5133) or **Hertz** at Cork Airport (✆ 021/496-5849).

Visitor Information

The **Cork Discover Ireland Centre** is at the appropriately named Tourist House at 42 Grand Parade, Cork (www.corkcity.ie; ✆ 021/425-5100). The **Kinsale Tourist Office** is on Pier Road, Kinsale (www.kinsale.ie; ✆ 021/477-2234). The **Cobh Tourist Office** is in the Sirius Arts Centre, the Old Yacht Club Building, Lower Road, Cobh (✆ 024/481-3612). **Seasonal tourist offices** operate at the Jameson Centre, Midleton (✆ 021/461-3702), and Market Square, Youghal (✆ 024/20170).

[FastFACTS] CORK CITY

ATMs/Banks In Cork City, try **Ulster Bank** (88 Patrick St.; ✆ 021/427-0618).

Dentists For dental emergencies, your hotel will usually contact a dentist for you; otherwise, a good option is **Smiles Town Dental,** 112 Oliver Plunkett St., Cork (✆ 021/427-4706).

Doctors For medical emergencies, dial ✆ 999. For non-emergencies, your hotel should call you a

doctor. Otherwise, you could try the **Patrick Street Medical Centre,** 9 Patrick St., Cork (✆ 021/427-8699).

Emergencies For police, fire, or other emergencies, dial ✆ 999.

Internet Access **Cork City Library** at 57 Grand Parade (✆ 021/492-4900) has Internet terminals that nonmembers can use for €1 per half-hour.

Pharmacies In Cork, there's **Murphy's Pharmacy,**

48 North Main St. (✆ 021/427-4121) or **Marian Pharmacy** on Friar's Walk (✆ 021/496-3821).

Post Office The main post office is on Oliver Plunkett Street (✆ 021/485-1032).

Taxis The main taxi ranks in Cork are along St. Patrick's Street, along the South Mall, and outside major hotels. You can also call **ABC Taxis** (✆ 021/496-1961), or **Cork Taxi Co-Op** (✆ 021/427-2222).

WHERE TO STAY

Cork City is filled with B&Bs and small hotels, particularly along Western Road. They vary in quality, but among them are some interesting, decently priced options. Away from the city, the pretty harbor town of Kinsale contains several elegant, high-quality B&Bs and boutique-style accommodations.

Where to Stay in Cork City

MODERATE

Imperial Hotel ★ This city center hotel is surprisingly affordable for the amenities it offers, with elegantly restored public areas that are redolent of a much more expensive kind of hotel altogether. The guest rooms are perhaps a little plain by comparison, and the most basic rooms are small, but upgrading just a little gets you ample space and a bit more style. There are four restaurants, including **Lafayettes,** which does a great afternoon tea, and the Escape Spa offers a long list of indulgent, revitalizing treatments, starting at about €75 for a 45-minute facial. Check the website for dinner, bed and breakfast packages, and inclusive spa deals too.

76 South Mall. www.flynnhotels.com. ✆**021/427-4040.** 130 units. €118–€197. Parking at nearby lot (€9 per 24 hours, discounted rate only valid from 3pm on day of arrival to noon on day of departure). Rates include breakfast. **Amenities:** Wi-Fi (free); restaurant; bar; room service; spa.

Lancaster Lodge ★ Another small hotel on Western Road, Lancaster Lodge is modern, well run, and a good value for your money. The purple color scheme in some of the public areas might be a bit garish for some, but guest rooms are big, with contemporary furnishings. Suites, which aren't a great deal more than the standard doubles, come with Jacuzzi baths. Breakfast is better than you might expect from a budget hotel, and while they don't serve dinner, central Cork is only a short walk away.

Lancaster Quay, Western Rd. www.lancasterlodge.com. ✆ **021/425-1125.** 48 units. €113–€156. Free parking. Breakfast not included in lower rates. **Amenities:** Wi-Fi (free); room service.

River Lee Hotel ★★ A 5-minute walk from the city center, this shiny, modern hotel overlooks the River Lee. Guest rooms are quietly chic, with an understated modern style and huge windows that make the best of city views. Executive rooms have fancy extras such as Nespresso coffee machines and access to a private lounge with panoramic views of the city. The **Vanilla Browns** spa is an excellent value—a half-hour massage costs €45, and all but a handful of treatments are under €100. The attached health club includes a (nearly) Olympic-size indoor swimming pool. The substantial breakfast buffet (€14) offers much more than the usual options.

Western Rd. www.doylecollection.com/hotels/the-river-lee-hotel. ✆ **021/425-2700.** 182 units. €130–€180. Free parking (underground lot). Breakfast not included in lower rates. Dinner, bed and breakfast packages available. **Amenities:** Restaurant; room service; spa; swimming pool; Wi-Fi (free).

INEXPENSIVE

Ambassador Hotel ★ The impressive redbrick exterior of this hilltop 1870s mansion on the northeast outskirts of Cork gives way to a glossy lobby, with black-and-white checkered floors and twinkly chandeliers. Guest rooms are modestly decorated with traditional-style furnishings—pay the extra for an upper-floor room with a city view. There's a pleasant bar, filled with

Cork City

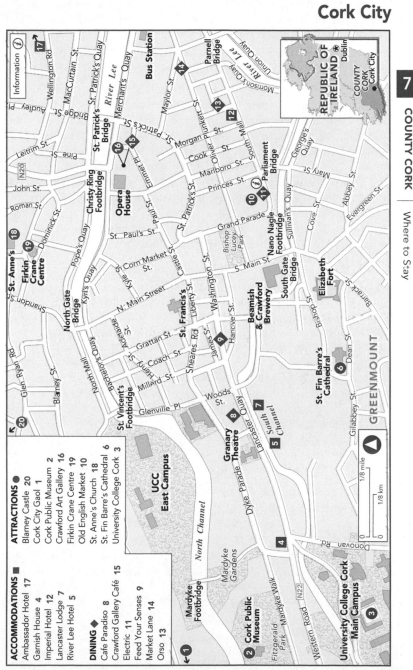

ACCOMMODATIONS ■
Ambassador Hotel **17**
Garnish House **4**
Imperial Hotel **12**
Lancaster Lodge **7**
River Lee Hotel **5**

DINING ◆
Cafe Paradiso **8**
Crawford Gallery Café **15**
Electric **11**
Feed Your Senses **9**
Market Lane **14**
Orso **13**

ATTRACTIONS ●
Blarney Castle **20**
Cork City Gaol **1**
Cork Public Museum **2**
Crawford Art Gallery **16**
Firkin Crane Centre **19**
Old English Market **10**
St. Anne's Church **18**
St. Fin Barre's Cathedral **6**
University College Cork **3**

Information ⓘ

REPUBLIC OF IRELAND ✪
Dublin
COUNTY CORK
Cork City

129

floor-to-ceiling book cases, and a restaurant too—handy when you're a mile or so from the center of town, although it's hardly a trek by taxi. Be aware that the Ambassador can get quite booked up by wedding parties in the summer.

Military Hill. www.ambassadorhotel.ie. © **021/453-9000.** 70 units. €80–€105. Free parking. Rates include breakfast. **Amenities:** Wi-Fi (free); restaurant; bar; room service; gym.

Garnish House ★★ One of several B&Bs and hotels in the Western Road neighborhood, Garnish House is a sweet and friendly place to stay. You're hardly through the door before being offered an afternoon tea, complete with delicious homemade scones. Guest rooms are pleasant with well-sized beds, and some rooms even have Jacuzzi baths. Breakfasts are outstanding; in addition to the usual hearty "full Irish" options, you could have French toast, pancakes, lentil ragout, stuffed tomatoes, salmon-and-dill tarts, scrambled eggs with avocado—more choices than plenty of restaurants around here would offer at dinner.

1 St. Mary's Villas, Western Rd. www.garnish.ie. © **021/427-5111.** 14 units. €81–€100. Free parking. Rates include breakfast. **Amenities:** Wi-Fi (free).

Where to Stay in Kinsale
MODERATE

Actons Hotel ★ Built in the mid-19th century, this pleasant, well-run property looking out over Kinsale Harbour has been a hotel since the 1940s, though a recent renovation has smoothed out a few wrinkles. Guest rooms aren't huge, but they're nicely designed, with very large beds and lovely harbor views. In a town where it's easy to find accommodations with character but not particularly modern conveniences, you'll welcome the few extras such as an elevator (you'd be surprised how rare that is around here) and a swimming pool. The hotel's two restaurants are good, but you've also got Kinsale and its wonderful restaurants on your doorstep.

Pier Rd. www.actonshotelkinsale.com. © **021/477-9900.** 74 units. €120–€180. Free parking. Rates include breakfast. Dinner, bed and breakfast packages available. **Amenities:** 2 restaurants; bar; room service; gym; pool; accessible rooms; Wi-Fi (free).

Blue Haven Hotel ★★ There's something wonderfully old-school about this chic town house hotel in the middle of Kinsale. The rooms are traditionally decorated with antique-style furniture and heritage print wallpaper. The friendly staff runs things very professionally, and the in-house seafood restaurant, the **Fishmarket,** is popular. Dinner, bed and breakfast packages are available for around €110 to €150. The only snag is that you can get street noise here, so ask for an upper-floor room if you're a light sleeper.

3-4 Pearse St. www.bluehavenkinsale.com. © **021/477-2209.** 17 units. €110–€170. Parking at nearby lots (no discount) around €1.40 per hour. Rates include breakfast. Dinner, bed and breakfast packages and 2-night midweek and weekend deals available. **Amenities:** Wi-Fi (free); 2 restaurants; bar; room service.

Desmond House ★★ This lovely, historic B&B is one of the best places to stay in Kinsale. Desmond House was built in the mid-18th century, and,

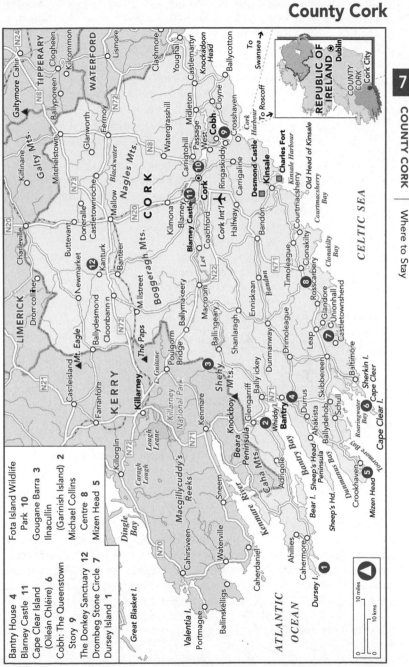

Bantry House **4**
Blarney Castle **11**
Cape Clear Island
(Oileán Chléire) **6**
Cobh: The Queenstown
Story **9**
The Donkey Sanctuary **12**
Drombeg Stone Circle **7**
Dursey Island **1**

Fota Island Wildlife
Park **10**
Gougane Barra **3**
Ilnacullin
(Garinish Island) **2**
Michael Collins
Centre **8**
Mizen Head **5**

TIPPERARY
WATERFORD
LIMERICK
KERRY
CORK
REPUBLIC OF
IRELAND
COUNTY
CORK
Cork City
Dublin

CELTIC SEA
ATLANTIC OCEAN

131

according to host Michael McLaughlin, is one of the oldest and best-preserved Georgian buildings in town. Michael is a genuine and charming man; his policy of charging American visitors according to whichever exchange rate works out best with the euro—on the day you booked or the day you check out—is a particularly considerate gesture. Guest rooms are generous with big, comfortable beds, and the modern bathrooms are furnished with whirlpool tubs. Many of the ingredients for the delicious breakfasts come straight from the **Old English Market ★★** in Cork (see p. 139).

42 Cork St. www.desmondhousekinsale.com. ℂ**021/477-3575.** 4 units. €145. Parking at nearby lots around €1.40 per hour. Rates include breakfast. **Amenities:** Wi-Fi (free).

Pier House ★★ There's something wonderfully bright and cheerful about this sweet place in Kinsale. Hosts Pat and Anne have done a beautiful job in converting the 19th-century town house into a B&B, with chic color schemes and subtle splashes of modern art. A few of the bedrooms have little balconies, and guests are welcome to bring wine back with them if they want to spend a leisurely hour admiring the views of the harbor or garden. Breakfasts are delicious and plentiful. You'll have to fend for yourself at dinner, but this is hardly a chore in foodie-friendly Kinsale.

Pier Road. www.pierhousekinsale.com. ℂ**021/477-4169.** 10 units. €100–€140. Parking for bikes and motorbikes only; car parking at nearby lots around €1.50 per hour. Rates include breakfast. **Amenities:** Wi-Fi (free).

WHERE TO EAT

Cork's reputation as a kind of cultural "Dublin South" is burnished by its restaurant scene, smattered with trendy eateries. However, it's Kinsale where the county really goes to let its collective belt out. Over the last 20 years, the town has transformed itself from a sleepy fishing village into one of Ireland's premier food destinations.

Where to Eat in Cork City

Cafe Paradiso ★★★ VEGETARIAN   An inventive, classy vegetarian restaurant on the Western Road strip, Cafe Paradiso does such magnificent things without meat that even passionate carnivores will find plenty to love. Start with parsnip tortellini with ginger butter, before tucking in to some sweet chile-glazed tofu with bok choi, or a delicious feta and pistachio nut couscous cake served with cilantro yoghurt. Desserts are heavenly; if it's on the menu, try the dark chocolate mousse with salted caramel popcorn. The excellent wine list is reasonably priced. If you can't quite afford dinner here, come before 6:30pm on Monday to Friday for the early bird menu (€23 for two courses, €29 for three). For those who prefer to roll straight from table to bed, they also have guest rooms for €220 per couple, per night.

16 Lancaster Quay. www.cafeparadiso.ie. ℂ **021/427-7939.** Fixed-price menus: two courses €33, three courses €36–€40. Mon–Fri 5:30–10pm; Sat noon–2:30pm, 5:30–10pm. No children after 7pm.

a tuneful pint: CORK'S MOST MUSICAL PUBS

Cork has a deserved reputation as home to some of Ireland's best pubs for live, traditional music. It's virtually a rite of passage to catch a session while enjoying a pint or two (and it's stout in these parts, by the way—Murphy's or Beamish, not Guinness—if you really want to fit in). You can just follow your ears to find the best places, but here are a few of the most respected to get you started. **An Bodhran** (the name refers to a type of drum made from goatskin) at 42 Oliver Plunkett St. (© **021/427-4544**) has live sessions nightly, as does the cozy **An Spailpín Fánach** (which means "The Wandering Migrant Worker") at 27 South Main St. (© **021/427-7949**). **Sin é** (literally, "That's It"), 8 Coburg St. (© **021/450-2266**) has been one of Cork's top live-music pubs for decades, long before it became a popular tourist activity. They have sessions most nights, but those on Tuesdays, Fridays, and Sundays tend to be particularly good. And if you've had enough live music at the atmospheric **Long Valley** (www.thelongvalleybar.com; © **021/427-2144**), you could go upstairs to watch a poetry slam. They are generally held on Monday nights, along with a lively program of spoken-word events; see www.obheal.ie for more details.

Crawford Gallery Café ★★ CAFE A big step up from the average cafe tacked onto an art gallery, the Crawford is as much a great little bistro as it is a convenient spot for a coffee or light nibble. It's open for breakfast, which certainly provides some excellent options if you can't face another hotel morning meal. You'll find spiced scones, American-style pancakes, and delicious eggs Florentine with organic spinach on the menu. Lunchtime is when this place gets busiest, though, and the line-up changes regularly with plenty of daily specials like chorizo bean cassoulet or smoked salmon salad with horseradish dressing.

At the Crawford Gallery, Emmet Place. www.crawfordartgallery.ie. © **021/427-4415.** Breakfast: €3–€11; lunch: €11–€15. Mon–Sat 8:30am–4pm.

Electric ★★ SEAFOOD/MODERN IRISH With a dining room overlooking the river and the city skyline beyond, you could easily get swept up in the romantic atmosphere of this trendy but unpretentious restaurant. The menu isn't large, but it's well done, focusing on upscale comfort food; roast chicken with honey roast vegetables and champ mash (made with potato and spring onion), chicken and chorizo stew with sourdough, and a juicy house burger topped with Irish blue cheese. In addition to the main restaurant is the **Fish Bar** (evenings only), where you can eat super-fresh seafood while perched on bar stools overlooking the river. The Fish Bar takes reservations for two sittings only, at 7 and 9pm.

41 South Mall. www.electriccork.com/restaurant. © **021/422-2990.** Main courses €15–€28. Wed–Sat noon–10pm, Sun–Tues noon–9pm. Fish Bar evenings only; no children in the Fish Bar.

Feed Your Senses ★★ SPANISH   This intimate restaurant just west of the city center has a warm and casual vibe. The cozy dining room is decorated in a rustic taverna style. The food is billed as tapas, but plates are really quite generously proportioned. Try a fluffy tortilla, with a serving of *albondigas* (Spanish meatballs, though made with Irish beef and pork), or maybe some *chorizos con vino* (fried chorizo sausage cooked in red wine). There's a good wine list, although the lusty, full-bodied house red is a delicious enough accompaniment by itself.

27 Washington St. ℃ **021/427-4633.** Main courses €7–€12. Tues–Wed 4–9:30pm; Thurs–Fri 4–10:30pm; Sat 1–10:30pm; Sun 1–9:30pm. Closed Mon.

Market Lane ★★ IRISH   This friendly, informal downtown restaurant serves Irish-inflected bistro food. It's a let-your-hair-down kind of place, and the menu consists mostly of traditional, unpretentious cooking, done very well. Comfort food staples such as roast chicken might come served with mashed potato and a homemade stuffing; or you could find yourself tempted by a plate of salmon with spiced arancini balls, or coconut and ginger curry. The early bird menu is outstanding value at just €23 for three courses (Mon–Thurs 5–7pm, and Sun 1–7pm).

5–6 Oliver Plunkett St. www.marketlane.ie. ℃ **021/427-4710.** Main courses €12–€18. Mon–Thurs noon–10pm; Fri–Sat noon–10:30pm; Sun 1–9pm (10pm on public holidays).

Orso ★★★ IRISH/MEDITERRANEAN   This place is like a ray of warm Mediterranean sunshine in downtown Cork City. Traditional flavors of southern Europe are mixed with Irish influences, and the result is nothing short of delightful. It's open all day, so you can pop in for a breakfast of banana flatbread with cinnamon and lime zest, or a traditional Moglai bread stuffed with bacon, egg, and cheese. The lunch menu is long and varied, but it's really at dinnertime when the excellent cooking comes into its own. Plates include seared scallops with samphire and sumac, or chicken served with plum and rhubarb relish. Nearly everything on the wine list is available by the glass, and the small cocktail menu is intriguing—try the delicious house Bellini.

8 Pembroke St. www.orso.ie. ℃ **021/243-8000.** Main courses €8–€20. Mon 8:30am–6pm; Tues–Thurs 8:30am–10pm; Fri–Sat 8:30am–10:30pm; Sun (Dec only) 1–10pm. Closed Sun, Jan–Nov.

Where to Eat in Kinsale

Crackpots ★★★ SEAFOOD/MODERN IRISH   A happy marriage of designer pottery shop and outstandingly good restaurant, Crackpots specializes in fresh, delicious seafood. The ingredients are all locally sourced, so exactly what appears on the menu depends on what's freshest—grilled langoustine with spinach and lime pesto; fried king prawns with garlic and chorizo; or maybe some Oysterhaven scallops with an herb crust and citrus-infused crème fraiche. The menu always includes a few non-seafood items like roast duck, lamb, or a simple steak served in a brandy-pepper sauce, plus

THE GREAT GOURMET GATHERING: kinsale food festival

Food lovers from all over Ireland—and even farther afield—descend on Kinsale for a weekend each October when the Kinsale Gourmet Festival takes over town. The event's calendar changes every year, but there are always plenty of cooking demonstrations and other lively activities. Restaurants join in the fun by hosting parties, special tastings, "meet the chef" events, and other culinary goodies. Many of them are free, although some of the bigger events and banquets charge about €20 to €100 per ticket. It's magnificent, Bacchanalian fun. Learn more and book tickets at www.kinsalerestaurants.com.

a vegetarian option or two. Every Friday night, you can dine to the sound of a local pianist.

3 Cork St., Kinsale. www.crackpots.ie. ⓒ **021/477-2847.** Main courses €10–€29. Mon–Sat 6–9pm; Sun 12:30–3pm. No dinner Sun.

Finn's Table ★★★ MODERN IRISH   The menu here is ambitious without being overly complicated and with plenty of space to let the ingredients breathe. As you'd expect from Kinsale, the seafood on the menu comes directly from the harbor, so you never know exactly what will end up in the kitchen. However, on a typical night you could find a filet of John Dory with fennel croquettes, or turbot with baby leeks and lime. While the standout dishes tend to be seafood, there's plenty more to choose from, and the meats are all sourced from the owner's parents, who run a butcher shop in nearby Mitchelstown.

6 Main St., Kinsale. www.finnstable.com. ⓒ **021/470-9636.** Main courses €22–€33. Wed–Mon 6–10pm. Closed Tues.

Fishy Fishy ★★★ SEAFOOD   Widely respected, hugely popular, and yet brilliantly simple, the Fishy Fishy is one of the best restaurants in Kinsale. The owners also have a gourmet store and fish-and-chip shop on Guardwell Street, but this is their flagship. The skillfully prepared, fresh seafood comes from a small number of trusted local suppliers. And we do mean local: Shane catches the cod and turbot; Maurice provides the crab; Christy, David, and Jimmy catch the prawns—you get the idea. Exactly what's cooking that day depends on the catch, but you can expect to find the signature Fishy Fishy pie of salmon and shellfish in a creamy sauce with a breadcrumb topping, and a plate of classic fish in tempura batter with homemade chips. Reservations are only taken for dinner, so this place gets packed during lunchtime.

Crowleys Quay, Kinsale. www.fishyfishy.ie. ⓒ **021/470-0415.** Main courses €19–€27. Mar–Oct daily noon–9pm; Nov–Feb Sun–Wed noon–4pm, Thurs–Sat noon–9pm. Closed Jan.

Max's ★★★ MODERN IRISH   A husband-and-wife team has run Max's since the '90s, and they're still effortlessly adept at making diners feel welcome.

The menu changes seasonally, but the main flavors are all local—meat from Kilbrittan, a little village down the coast, and shellfish that were caught close enough that they could have been carried to the door. There's also a full vegetarian menu and plenty of kids' options. The early bird menu (a thoroughly reasonable €30 for three courses) is served until 7:30pm and 7pm on Saturdays.

48 Main St. www.maxs.ie. ✆ **021/477-2443.** Main courses €24–€30. Daily 6–10pm. Closed Jan.

Poet's Corner Cafe ★★ CAFE   Drop in for a freshly baked scone, a cup of herbal tea (the choice is huge), or a cup of coffee and a toasted sandwich. As the name suggests, this place styles itself as a "reading cafe"; not only can you buy books here, bring them two books in good condition and they'll let you swap it for another one from their second-hand collection. The "Irish Corner" is filled with interesting books and other information about the area.

44 Main St. www.poetscornerkinsale.com. ✆ **086/227-7276.** Lunch items €5–€7. Daily 9:30am–6pm.

The Spaniard ★★ BISTRO   The portrait on the sign of this atmospheric old inn shows Don Juan de Aguila, the Spanish commander who led a force of 4,000 men, assisted by local Irish revolutionaries, against the English at the Battle of Kinsale in 1601. The English won, but Don Juan became a hero in local folklore. The present inn dates from around 50 years after the battle, and it's still a satisfying place with an old-world look. They serve excellent, homey pub food in the restaurant, but the bar menu is just as good, and cheaper, too. Try the house special chowder, followed by a plate of fresh brill with leek and fennel, or a hearty beef rib in red wine gravy. An eclectic program of live music features everything from straight-up Irish folk to Russian Gypsy bands.

Junction of Scilly and Lower Road. www.thespaniard.ie. ✆ **021/477-2436.** Main courses €14–€25. Daily 9:30am–9pm.

The Steakhouse ★★ GRILL   In a town full of wonderful restaurants noted mostly for its seafood, devoted carnivores will be glad to discover this truly excellent grill. The restaurant sources its beef from the southwest region—particularly the Cork native Dexter breed, which lends itself particularly well to rib-eye—served with delicious comfort food sides. It's not all about the beef, with daily seafood, chicken, and duck specials. Leave room for the house special chocolate pudding with whipped cream.

18 Lower O'Connell St. www.thesteakhouse.ie. ✆ **021/470-9850.** Main courses €16–€29. Mon–Fri 5:30–9pm; Sat 5:30–10pm; Sun 1–3pm and 5:30–10pm.

EXPLORING COUNTY CORK

A busy, artsy hub where urban conveniences are seasoned by an appreciation for rural life, **Cork City** is also home to a major university, which keeps the population young, the creative class dynamic, the pubs interesting, and the number of affordable restaurants plentiful. Not far from the city, Blarney Castle is an impressive sight—although it would take a starry-eyed medievalist indeed to claim that the experience wasn't somewhat marred by the touristy atmosphere. Meanwhile, 25km (15½ miles) to the south of the city, the adorable harbor town of **Kinsale** is both an attractive hideaway and a major restaurant destination. To the east of Cork City, the two great attractions are **Fota Island,** a brilliantly designed wildlife park, and **Cobh,** which was the last port of call in Ireland for millions of emigrants in the 19th and early 20th centuries.

Top Attractions in Cork City

Cork City might as well be called Dublin South. It's far smaller than the capital, with 125,000 residents, but it's a busy, attractive, cultured place. Cork also has traffic congestion and can feel gritty and crowded, but for its fans, these flaws merely underscore the sense that it's a real working city.

Blarney Castle ★ CASTLE   Though a runaway favorite for the hotly contested title of "cheesiest tourist attraction in Ireland," Blarney Castle is an imposing edifice. Constructed in the late 15th century, it was once much bigger; the massive square tower is all that remains of the original medieval structure. This is where you'll find its most famous attraction, and probably the most disappointing magical rock you'll ever kiss, the eponymous "Blarney Stone." Whoever first decided that this particular slab had mystical powers certainly didn't have the convenience of visitors in mind; after trudging up a series of poorly lit narrow staircases, you'll find it wedged underneath the battlements, far enough to make it uncomfortable to reach, but not so far that countless tourists cannot lie down, stick their heads outside, and kiss it in hopes of achieving lifelong loquaciousness. There's no extra charge for kissing the Blarney Stone, though it's customary to tip the attendant who holds your legs (you might want to do it *before* they hang you over the edge). Also check out the dungeons penetrating the rock at the base of the castle. If you need a break from the masses, the gardens are pretty and much less crowded. On the grounds is the later **Blarney House,** built in 1874 in the then-fashionable Scottish Baronial style with filigreed turrets and imposing grey stone that resemble a mini-Hogwarts. You can tour the interior from June to August only, Monday to Saturday, from 10am to 2pm. Blarney Castle is 8km (5 miles) outside Cork City on R617. You can easily get here by bus; the number 215 stops about twice an hour (once per hour on Sundays). Ask the driver to let you off at the stop nearest the castle.

Blarney, Cork. www.blarneycastle.ie. ⓒ **021/438-5252.** Admission €13 adults; €11 seniors and students; €5 children 8–16; €32 families. June–Aug Mon–Sat 9am–7pm; Sun 9am–6pm. May, Sept Mon–Sat 9am–6:30pm; Sun 9am–6pm. Apr Mon–Sat 9am–6pm; Sun 9am–6pm. Oct, Mar Mon–Sat 9am–6pm, Sun 9am–5pm. Public holiday hours same as Sun. Last admission generally 30 min. before closing; closes at dusk if earlier.

Cork City Gaol ★ HISTORIC SITE   Like something out of a Victorian novel, this early-19th-century jail is an austere and highly atmospheric building. Opened in 1824 as a women's prison, its famous inmates included the

THE GUINNESS CORK jazz festival

Held every year since 1978, this is Ireland's biggest and most prestigious jazz festival. Big names such as Ella Fitzgerald, Oscar Peterson, and Stephane Grappelli have played here over the years, and more than 1,000 performers from all over the world take part annually. It's held at various citywide venues in late October. Visit www.guinnessjazzfestival.com for details. Tickets go on sale in early September; prices vary and some events are free.

extraordinary Constance Markievicz (1868–1927), the first woman elected to the British parliament, who was sentenced to execution after she took part in the 1916 Easter Rising (her sentence was eventually commuted). After the Irish War of Independence, she became the first female cabinet minister anywhere in the world. Earlier in its history, the jail was the last place in Ireland many convicts were held before being shipped off to Australia. This colorful history is well presented, with the (perhaps inevitable) aid of costumed mannequins. Somewhat incongruously, in 1927, after the building ceased to be used as a prison, it became the site of Ireland's first radio station. A small museum tells this story, complete with a restored studio from the period.

Convent Avenue, Sunday's Well, Cork. www.corkcitygaol.com. ℭ **021/430-5022.** Admission €8 adults; €7 seniors and students; €5 children; €25 families. Radio Museum €2. Mar–Oct daily 9:30am–5pm; Nov–Feb daily 10am–4pm.

Cork City Tours ★ TOURS Riding around on open-top buses, you can hop on and off to explore the sights of Ireland's second city. They run all day in a loop from March through October (as frequently as every half-hour in July and Aug). Tour highlights include the Cork City Gaol, St. Anne's Church, and UCC (University College, Cork). While the tour begins at the tourist office (42 Grand Parade), you can buy a ticket on the bus at several stops; check out the route on the Cork City Tours website.

www.corkcitytour.com. ℭ **021/430-9090.** Tickets €15 adults; €13 seniors and students; €5 children 5–18; children under 5 free; €35 families. Mar–Oct daily, with hours and number of tours reflecting seasonal demand (usually 9:30am–4:30pm).

Cork Public Museum ★ MUSEUM This simple, rather endearing civic museum is a good place to get an overview of the city's history. Displays include a few objects from Cork's ancient past—including an Iron Age helmet and some of the oldest tools ever discovered in Ireland—but it's strongest when it comes to the traditional crafts made in the city during the 19th and 20th centuries, including silverware and intricate lace from the Victorian period. There are also very good collections relating to the lives of local revolutionaries, including Michael Collins (see p. 142).

Fitzgerald Park, Cork. www.corkcity.ie. ℭ **021/427-0679.** Free admission. Mon–Fri 11am–1pm, 2:15–5pm; Sat 11am–1pm, 2:15–4pm; Sun 3–5pm. Oct–Mar closed Sun.

Crawford Art Gallery ★★★ MUSEUM   One of the best art galleries in Ireland, the Crawford has impressive collections of sculpture and painting. The Irish School is particularly well represented, with works from John Butts (1728–65), including his fine 1755 panorama of Cork City, and Dublin-born Harry Clarke (1889–1931), one of the most celebrated illustrators of the early 20th century, who also produced some extraordinary, early Deco-influenced stained glass. There's a strong collection of works by female Irish artists from the mid-19th century onward; check out the extraordinary abstract work of Mainie Jellet (1897–1944) and the Cubist painter Norah McGuinness (1901–80). The gallery also has a program of temporary exhibitions. The Crawford Gallery Café (see p. 133) is a good spot for a light lunch.

Emmet Place, Cork. www.crawfordartgallery.ie. ℰ **021/480-5042.** Free admission. Mon–Wed, Fri–Sat 10am–5pm; Thurs 10am–8pm. 2nd floor closes 4:45pm daily. Closed public holidays.

The Firkin Crane Cultural Centre ★ PERFORMING ARTS   Named after two Danish words for measurements of butter, the Firkin Crane is one of Ireland's major centers for contemporary dance, hosting touring companies in addition to showcasing new talent. Many performances are free. The only down-side is that performances are infrequent—usually just a handful per month.

John Redmond St., Shandon, Cork. www.firkincrane.ie. ℰ **021/450-7487.** Ticket prices and performance times vary by event.

Old English Market ★★ MARKET   The name of this bustling food market harks back to the days of English rule—it was first granted a charter in 1610 during the reign of King James I. The current market building dates from 1788, although it was redesigned after being gutted by fire in the 1980s. Inside is a cornucopia of fresh produce, including super-traditional Cork del-icacies—some of them tempting, others less palatable to outsiders. (Tripe, anyone? How about pig's trotters?) Happily, more modern refreshments and takeaway snacks are readily available.

Grand Parade; enter from Patrick St., Grand Parade, Oliver Plunkett St., or Princes St. www.englishmarket.ie. ℰ **085/763-2259.** Free admission. Mon–Sat 8am–6pm Closed public holidays.

St. Anne's Church ★ CHURCH   Cork's most recognizable landmark, also known as Shandon Church, is famous for its giant pepper-pot steeple and eight melodious bells. No matter where you stand in the downtown area, you can see the stone tower crowned with a gilt ball and a unique fish weathervane. The clock, added in 1847, made it the first four-faced clock tower in the world (beating London's Big Ben by just a few years). Until fairly recently, due to a quirk of clockworks, it was known as "the four-faced liar" because each side showed a different time—except on the hour when they all somehow managed to synchronize. Disappointingly, perhaps, that charming quirk has now been repaired. Climb the 1722 belfry for a chance to ring the famous Shandon Bells.

If you continue on the somewhat precarious climb past the bells, you'll be rewarded with spectacular views over the surrounding countryside.

Church St., Shandon, Cork. www.shandonbells.ie. © **021/450-5906.** Free admission. Clock tower €5 adults; €4 seniors and students; €2.50 children; €12 families. June–Sept Mon–Sat 10am–5pm; Sun 11:30am–4:30pm. Mar–May, Oct Mon–Sat 10am–4pm; Sun 11:30am–4pm. Nov–Feb Mon–Sat 11am–3pm; Sun 11:30am–3pm. Last entry to tower 20 min. before closing.

St. Fin Barre's Cathedral ★ CHURCH   With its three soaring spires dominating the Cork skyline, this Church of Ireland cathedral sits on the very spot St. Finbarre chose in A.D. 600 for his church and school. A much smaller medieval tower was demolished to make way for the current building, which dates from the early 1860s—there's nothing left of the earlier original, although a few pieces of decorative stonework were salvaged and can be viewed inside. The architect, William Burges (1827–81), won a competition staged to create a new Anglican cathedral in the city; his design embraced the French Gothic style that was popular at the time. The interior is highly ornamented with some stunning mosaic work. The bells were inherited from a 1735 church that also previously stood on this site. The Cathedral hosts occasional exhibitions; check the website for listings of what's on.

Bishop St. www.corkcathedral.webs.com. © **021/496-3387.** Admission €5 adults; €4 seniors; €3 students and children. Mon–Sat 9:30am–5:30pm, Sun 12:30–5pm (Dec–Mar closed Sun). Closed certain public holidays; call to check.

University College Cork and Glucksman Gallery ★★ UNIVERSITY   Part of Ireland's national university, with about 7,000 students, this center of learning is housed in a pretty quadrangle of Gothic Revival–style buildings. Colorful gardens and wooded grounds grace the campus. An audio tour of the grounds takes in the Crawford Observatory, the Harry Clarke stained-glass windows in Honan Chapel, a landscaped garden, and the Stone Corridor, a collection of stones inscribed with the ancient Irish *ogham* written language. You can also join an hour-long guided tour, given by students, leaving from the visitor center at 3pm from Monday to Friday, or noon on Saturdays. Also on the campus, the innovative **Lewis Glucksman Gallery** (www.glucksman.org; © **021/490-1844**) has an excellent program of exhibitions. Expect to see cutting-edge photography, painting, sculpture, and a few items from the university's ever-expanding permanent collection. A good cafe and shop are also on site. Admission to the Glucksman is free, though a donation of €5 per person is requested.

Visitor Centre: North Wing, Main Quad, Western Rd. www.ucc.ie/en/visitors/centre. © **021/490-1876.** Visitor Centre: Mon–Fri 9am–5pm, Sat noon–5pm. Glucksman Gallery: Tues–Sat 10am–5pm; Sun 2–5pm (closed Mon).

Top Attractions in Kinsale

This former fishing village is enchanting, with its narrow, winding streets, well-kept 18th-century houses, imaginatively painted shop fronts, window boxes overflowing with colorful flowers, and a harbor full of sailboats.

THE scilly WALK

Technically a separate village, Scilly is effectively a miniscule suburb of Kinsale, located across the harbor, but it retains a strong sense of its own identity. Pronounced "silly," its name is thought to hark back to fishermen from the Scilly Isles (off the coast of Cornwall, England) who settled here during the 17th century.

Pick up maps at the Kinsale Tourist Office to follow this signposted pedestrian path that runs along the sea from Scilly to Charles Fort. Take the right-hand road around the village, skirting along the coast, and join the marked pedestrian trail by the waterside. Along here there are lovely views across to Kinsale, and across the harbor you'll see the stout remains of **James Fort**. Named for King James I, it was built by the English shortly after the 1601 Battle of Kinsale to guard the entrance to the port and ensure against further insurrection. It was captured by the forces of the (Protestant) King William I during his war with the deposed (Catholic) James II in 1690—part of the same conflict that is still commemorated today by the Protestant "Orange marches" in Northern Ireland.

Another tiny hamlet on the outskirts of Kinsale, **Summer Cove** is as sweet a place as its halcyon name suggests. Black-and-white toy town houses, with splashes of green and red, face the harbor as gulls circle overhead and the waves froth and bubble along the harbor walls. A short walk uphill from Summer Cove lies **Charles Fort** (see below), which faces James Fort across the harbor.

Kinsale has a more eventful history than you might think, however. In 1601, it was the scene of a major sea battle between Protestant England and Catholic Spain—one in which Irish rebels played a covert part. You can learn all about this fascinating conflict on one of local man Don Herlihy's absorbing "Historic Strolls" (see p. 142).

Charles Fort ★ HISTORIC SITE   Southeast of Kinsale, at the head of the harbor, this coastal landmark dating from the late 17th century was named for Charles II, who was king of England and Ireland at the time it was built. A classic star-shaped fort, it was constructed to replace medieval Ringcurran Castle, which had been reduced to rubble by the English army. After a lengthy fight, the allied Irish and Spanish troops were defeated by the English army, who reduced Ringcurran to rubble. In 1678, this impressive fortress was built to reinforce the defenses of James Fort across the harbor. Charles Fort remained in use as a barracks until the end of British rule in the early 20th century. Extensively damaged during the civil war, it has only recently been restored.

Summercove, Kinsale. www.heritageireland.ie.✆ **021/477-2263.** Admission €4 adults, €3 seniors, €2 students and children, €10 families. Mid-Mar to Oct daily 10am–6pm; Nov to mid-Mar daily 10am–5pm.

Desmond Castle ★ CASTLE   This small, squat stone fortress doesn't really look like a castle, in part because it incongruously sits halfway up a residential street. It was built around 1500 as the Customs house for Kinsale Harbour. In the late 17th century it was turned into a prison, at which time its

who was **MICHAEL COLLINS?**

Among the heroes of Ireland's struggle for independence, Michael Collins seems to be Cork's favorite native son. Affectionately referred to as "the Big Fella," Collins was the commander in chief of the army of the Irish Free State, which finally won the Republic's independence from Britain in 1921.

Collins was born in 1890 and, along with seven brothers and sisters, he was raised on a farm in Sam's Cross, just outside the little town of **Clonakilty.** He emigrated to England at 15, like many other young Irish men seeking work in London. In his 20s, he joined the Irish revolutionary group, the Irish Republican Brotherhood (I.R.B.) and first came to fame in 1916 as one of the planners and leaders of the Easter Rising (see p. 18). Although it aroused passions among the population, the Rising was in fact a military disaster, and Collins—young but clever—railed against its amateurism. He was furious about the seizure of prominent buildings—such as Dublin's General Post Office (see p. 84)—that were impossible

to defend, impossible to escape from, and difficult to get supplies into.

After the battle, Collins was arrested and sent to an internment camp in Britain, along with hundreds of other rebels. There his stature within the I.R.B. grew, and by the time he was released, he had become one of the leaders of the Republican movement. In 1918, he was elected a member of the British Parliament, but like many other Irish members, he refused to go to London, instead announcing that he would sit only in an Irish parliament in Dublin. Most of the rebel Irish MPs (including Eamon de Valera) were arrested by British troops for their actions, but Collins avoided arrest, and later helped de Valera escape from prison. Over the subsequent years, de Valera and Collins worked together to create an Irish state.

After lengthy political wrangling and much bloodshed (Collins orchestrated an assassination that essentially wiped out the British secret service in Ireland), Collins was sent by de Valera in 1921 to negotiate a treaty with the British

---

history took several dark detours, including a fire that gutted the building in 1747, roasting alive 54 French soldiers who were imprisoned within. Later, during the potato famine, it was used as a workhouse. There's an unusual but interesting little museum inside, detailing the story of the Irish exiles who helped transform the global wine trade from the 17th century onward.

Cork St., Kinsale. www.heritageireland.ie. © **021/477-4855.** Admission €4 adults, €3 seniors, €2 students and children, €10 families. Apr to late Sept daily 10am–6pm. Closed last week of Sept–Mar.

Kinsale Historic Stroll ★★★ TOUR   One of the most pleasant ways to spend an hour in these parts is to take local resident Don Herlihy's excellent walking tour—or "Historic Stroll," as he prefers to call it—of Kinsale town. Don and his fellow guide, Barry Moloney, have been leading visitors around the main sights since the mid-1990s, and their local knowledge is second to none. Highlights include the 12th-century St. Multose Church; a walk past Desmond Castle (see p. 141); and the harbor, where the 17th-century Battle of Kinsale is recounted with an enthusiasm only found in people who really

government. In the meeting, British Prime Minister David Lloyd George agreed to allow Ireland to become a free republic, as long as that republic did not include the largely Protestant counties of Ulster, which would stay part of the United Kingdom. Knowing he could not get more at the time and determined to end the violence, Collins reluctantly agreed to sign the treaty, hoping to renegotiate later. After signing the document Collins said, "I have just signed my death warrant."

As he'd expected, the plan tore the new Republic apart, dividing the group now known as the IRA into two factions—those who wanted to continue fighting for all of Ireland, and those who favored the treaty. Fighting soon broke out in Dublin, and the civil war was underway.

Collins had learned many lessons from the Easter debacle, and now his strategy was completely different. His soldiers operated as "flying columns," waging a guerrilla war against the enemy—suddenly attacking, and then just as suddenly withdrawing, thus minimizing their losses and leaving the opposition baffled.

The battles stretched on for 10 months. In August 1922, Collins, weary of the war, was on a peace mission in his home county. Stopping at a pub near his mother's birthplace, he and his escort were on the road near Béal na Bláth when Collins was shot and killed. Precisely who killed him—his own men or the opposition—was never known. On his rapid rise to the top, he'd made too many enemies. He was 31 years old.

The **Michael Collins Centre** (www.michaelcollinscentre.com; © **023/884-6107**), located on the farm where he grew up, is a good place to learn more about the man. In addition to an hour-long tour, featuring a film and a visit to the actual ambush site, the center runs in-depth guided trips around the local area. (These last 3½ hours and are probably for Collins devotees only.) The center is signposted off N71, 5.6km (3½ miles) west of Clonakilty. It's open mid-June to mid-September, Mondays to Fridays from 10:30am to 5pm, and Saturdays from 11am to 2pm. Admission is free.

love their subject. Don asserts that the battle was perhaps the most significant turning point in Irish history, and when you hear his argument firsthand, you're inclined to agree. You pay at the end or, in their words, "drop out for free if you're not delighted." That probably doesn't happen very often.

Departs from Kinsale Tourist Office, Pier Road, Kinsale. www.historicstrollkinsale.com. © **021/477-2873** or 087/250-0731. Tours €6 adults; €1 children. May–Sept Mon–Sat 9:15, 11:15am, Sun 11:15am. Mar–Apr, Oct daily 11:15am. Nov to mid-Mar prebooking only.

Kinsale Pottery and Arts Centre ★ STORE This excellent ceramics workshop on the outside of Kinsale sells beautiful, original items of pottery from delicate tea sets and tableware to ornamental masks. The shop is full of surprises, and prices aren't too steep for the quality of what's for sale. A two-floor gallery always has some interesting pieces on display.

Ballinacurra, Kinsale. www.kinsaleceramics.com. © **021/477-2771.** Free admission. Daily 10am–6pm. From Kinsale: From Pearse St., turn left at the junction with the Blue Haven hotel on your right, then follow signs to Bandon and Innishannon. Take this road up the big hill, past Woodlands B&B and the Kinsale GAA sports ground, then look for signs to Kinsale Pottery after about ⅓km (⅕ mile) on the left.

Out from Cork & Kinsale

Farther afield from the county's two most visited hubs, the verdant County Cork countryside is a place of natural beauty—yet many of its most impressive sites are little known outside Ireland. Beauty spots such as Gougane Barra and Mizen Head have a real sense of drama, as do ancient sites such as the Drombeg Stone Circle. Meanwhile, a more recent past can be explored in the bittersweet museum at Cobh—once was the main point of departure for Irish people emigrating to the New World. And if you don't mind treading a well-beaten path on the tourist trail, County Cork is also home to one of Ireland's most famous attractions: Blarney Castle.

Bantry House ★★ HISTORIC HOME   Built around 1750 for the earls of Bantry, this Georgian house holds furniture and *objets d'art* from all over Europe, including Aubusson and Gobelin tapestries said to have been made for Marie Antoinette. The gardens, with original statuary, are beautifully kept—climb the steps behind the building for a panoramic view of the house, gardens, and Bantry Bay. There is also an informative exhibition on the ill-fated Spanish Armada, led by the Irish rebel Wolfe Tone, which attempted to invade the country near Bantry House in 1769. Fully guided tours (included in the ticket price) take place daily at 2pm; otherwise, you're free to wander around yourself. And if you really love it here, you can spend the night (rooms €170–€200).

Bantry, Co. Cork. www.bantryhouse.com. ✆ **027/50047.** Admission €12 adults; €9 seniors and students; €3 children 6–16; children under 6 free; €27 families. Gardens only €5. July–Aug daily 10am–5pm; mid-Apr to May and Sept–Oct, Tues–Sun 10am–5pm. Closed Nov to mid-Apr.

Cape Clear Island (Oileán Chléire) ★★ ISLAND   The southernmost inhabited point in Ireland, 13km (8 miles) off the mainland, Cape Clear Island has a permanent population of just a hundred residents. It is a bleak place with a rock-bound coastline and no trees to break the rush of sea wind, but it's also starkly beautiful. In early summer, wildflowers brighten the landscape, and in October, passerine migrants, some on their way from North America and Siberia, fill the air. Seabirds are abundant during the nesting season, especially from July to September. You can get to the island by ferry (see below) and explore it all at your own pace; alternatively, **Fastnet Tours** (www.fastnettour.com; ✆ **028/39159**) run a twice-weekly tour from the pier in Baltimore (June–Aug, Wed and Sat at 11am; €32 per person). After visiting the island's tiny heritage center, you're taken out for a boat ride around **Fastnet Rock,** a craggy outcrop in the Atlantic. Home to nothing but a weather-beaten lighthouse, Fastnet was traditionally known as "Teardrop Island," not for its shape, but because it was the last piece of Ireland that emigrants saw on their way to America.

Cape Clear Island, Co. Cork. www.oilean-chleire.ie. **Ferry:** ✆ **028/39159** or 41923. Return-trip tickets €16 adults, €8 children 13 and under, €40 families. Generally 4 times daily, sometimes less in winter. Schedule may change according to weather.

The Donkey Sanctuary ★ SANCTUARY   A real heartbreaker, this one: a charity that rescues abandoned and abused donkeys and nurses them back to

point of departure: A DAY IN COBH

If you're a foreigner with an Irish surname, this bustling seaside town could be more important to you than you realize. Cobh (pronounced *cove*, meaning "haven") used to be called Queenstown, and it was once Ireland's chief port of emigration. During the early 20th century, several transatlantic liners departed from here every week. It was also the last port of call for the RMS *Titanic* before it sank in April 1912. That story is expertly told at **Cobh: the Queenstown Story** (Deepwater Quay; www.cobhheritage.com; ✆ **021/481-3591**). Part of the Cobh Heritage Centre, the exhibition is open April to October daily from 9:30am to 6pm; and the rest of the year, from 9:30am to 5pm. Last admission is 1 hour before closing. It opens 11am on Sunday and public holidays, year-round. Tickets cost €9.50 adults, €7.50 seniors and students, €5 children, and €25 families.

A short walk from St. Colman's Cathedral, the **Lusitania Memorial** (Casement Sq.) commemorates the British passenger liner sunk by a German U-boat on May 7, 1915, killing 1,198 passengers, including several victims buried in Cobh cemetery. Across Casement Square from the memorial, the **Titanic Experience** (www.titanicexperiencecobh.ie; ✆ **021/481-4412**) is more of a themed attraction than a museum—it's just a few recreated rooms from the ship and a series of exhibits about the ill-fated voyage, emptying into a very busy gift shop. It's open daily from 9am to 6pm, with "tours" every 15 minutes. Entry costs €9.50 adults €7.50 seniors and students, €5.50 children, and €24 families.

Frankly, your time would be better spent climbing the hill to the handsome neo-Gothic **St. Colman's Cathedral** (www.cobhcathedralparish.ie; ✆ **021/481-3222**). Started in 1868, the cathedral was the country's most expensive religious building of its time. The largest of its 47 bells weighs 3½ tons, and the organ has nearly 2,500 pipes. The interior is vast and ornate, including a beautiful nave and precipitously high chancel arch. It is also a popular venue for concerts and recitals.

If you want to discover more about Cobh's role in the *Titanic* story, an hour-long **walking tour** visits several related sites, putting it all into the context of the town's maritime history. In truth this is a general historical tour of the town with just a couple of *Titanic* connections, but it's informative nonetheless. The tour departs from the Commodore Hotel, 4 Westbourne Place, at 11am and 2pm daily. (From Oct to Mar, the tour only runs if there are pre-bookings.) It costs €9.50 adults, €4.75 children. For bookings, call ✆ **021/481-5211,** or visit **www.titanic.ie**.

health. A few of the beasts of burden here have been voluntarily relinquished by owners who are no longer able to care for them, but the majority have sadder histories. The donkeys live out their days at this quiet and bucolic place, where they receive medical aid and plenty of TLC. Visitors can meet the gentle patients and learn their stories. The emphasis is on happy endings.

Liscarroll, nr. Mallow, Co. Cork. www.thedonkeysanctuary.ie. ✆ **022/48398.** Free admission. Mon–Fri 9am–4:30pm; Sat, Sun, and public holidays 10am–5pm.

Drombeg Stone Circle ★★ HISTORIC SITE This ring of 13 standing stones is the finest example of a megalithic stone circle in County Cork. The circle dates from 153 B.C., and little is known about its ritual purpose.

However, the remains of two huts and a cooking place, just to the west of the circle, give some clue; it is thought that heated stones were placed in a water trough (which can be seen adjacent to the huts), and the hot water was used for cooking. This section has been dated to sometime between A.D. 368 and 608. While you're out this way, consider stopping at the charming little village of **Ballydehob (Béal** Átha **Dá Chab).** An arty place with an ancient stone bridge and some brightly painted houses, it's one big photo opportunity. Ballydehob is also signposted from R597 between Rosscarbery and Glandore.

Off R597 between Rosscarbery and Glandore, Co. Cork. No phone. Free admission (open site). The turning for Drombeg Stone Circle is signposted just after the sign for Drombeg (if approaching from Rosscarbery); if approaching from Glandore, it's about 0.5km (⅓ mile) after the whitewashed church in Drombeg village.

Dursey Island ★★ HERITAGE/NATURE SITE This is a real adventure—a barren promontory extending into the sea at the tip of the Beara Peninsula. The island offers no amenities for tourists, but the adventurous will be rewarded with beautiful seaside walks, a 200-year-old signal tower, and a memorable passage from the mainland via cable car. To get there, take R571 past Cahermore to its terminus. As you sway wildly in the wooden cable car, you'll wonder whether or not to be reassured that someone saw fit to place the text of Psalm 91 inside ("If you say 'the Lord is my refuge,' and you make the Most High your dwelling, no harm will overtake you"). You may even be sharing your car with sheep or cows, as it's also used to transport livestock to and from the island. At this point, you might wonder whether a ferry would have been a wiser option. It wouldn't. Apparently the channel between the island and mainland is just too treacherous to permit regular crossing by boat. Cables run all year, Monday to Saturday, from 9:30 to 11am, 2:30 to 5pm and 7 to 8pm, and Sunday from 9 to 10:30am, 1 to 2:30pm, and 7 to 8pm (7–8pm crossings for return journeys only). Summertime has extended hours; from June to September they sometimes run continuously all day. The cable runs back and forth constantly between the listed times and can't be prebooked—it's always first come, first served. However, it's essential to check return times with the operator before you go, because the island has no shops, pubs, restaurants, or lodging of any kind (save for a few cottages for rent, by prebooking only; see the website for details). Bring food, water, and warm clothing. For up-to-date information on changes to the schedule, call the Skibbereen Tourist Office at ✆ **028/21766.**

Dursey Island. www.durseyisland.ie. No phone. Cable car round-trip €8 adults; €4 children. About 21km (14 miles) west of Castletown-Bearhaven (follow R572).

Fota Island & Wildlife Park ★★ ZOO If only all zoos were like this thoughtfully designed park. Most of the animals are free to roam without any apparent barriers, mingling with each other and human visitors. Many of the park's residents—including kangaroos, macaws, and lemurs—have the run of 16 hectares (40 acres) of grassland; only the more dangerous animals, such as cheetahs and gibbons, are behind conventional fencing. Besides close contact with a menagerie of exotic creatures, kids can be entertained by a tour train, picnic area, toddler playground, and gift shop.

Fota Island, Carrigtwohill. www.fotawildlife.ie. ℭ **021/481-2678.** Admission €16 adults; €11 seniors and students; €10 children 3–15 and under; children under 3 free; €46–€60 families. Mon–Sat 10am–6pm; Sun 10:30am–6pm. Last entry 4:30pm.

Gougane Barra ★★ ISLAND One of Western Ireland's most beautiful spots, Gougane Barra (which means "St. Fin Barre's Cleft") is the name of both a tiny old settlement and a forest park a little northeast of the Pass of Keimaneigh, 24km (15 miles) northeast of Bantry, and well signposted off R584, about half-way between Macroom and Glengarriff. Its loveliest feature is a dark, romantic lake, the source of the River Lee. This is where St. Fin Barre founded a monastery, supposedly on the small island connected by a causeway to the mainland. Though nothing remains of the saint's 6th-century community, the setting is idyllic, with rhododendrons spilling into the still waters where swans glide by.

7km (4½ miles) west of Ballingeary, Co. Cork (signposted off R584).

Ilnacullin (Garinish Island) ★★ ISLAND Officially known as Ilnacullin, but usually referred to as Garinish (or "Garnish"), this little island is a beautiful and tranquil place. It used to be little more than a barren outcrop, its only distinguishing feature a Martello tower left over from the Napoleonic Wars. Then, in 1919, the English landscaper Harold Peto was commissioned to create an elaborately planned Italianate garden, with classical pavilions and myriad unusual plants and flowers. The island can be reached for a round-trip fee of €10 per person (€5 children age 6–15) on a covered ferry operated by **Blue Pool Ferry,** the Blue Pool, Glengarriff (www.bluepoolferry.com; ℭ **027/63333**), or **Harbour Queen Ferries,** the Harbour, Glengarriff (www.harbourqueenferry.com; ℭ **027/63116**). Boats run back and forth about every 20 to 30 minutes. *Note:* The Harbour Queen doesn't take credit cards. The nearest ATMs are in Bantry.

Glengarriff, Co. Cork. www.garnishisland.com. ℭ **027/63040.** Admission (gardens) €4 adults; €3 seniors; €2 students and children; €10 families. June Mon–Sat 10am–6pm, Sun 11am–6pm. July–Aug Mon–Sat 9:30am–6pm, Sun 11am–6pm. May and Sept Mon–Sat 10am–6pm, Sun noon–6pm. Apr Mon–Sat 10am–5:30pm; Sun 1–6pm. Oct Mon–Sat 10am–4pm; Sun 1–5pm. Last landing 1 hr. before closing. No landings Nov–Mar.

Mizen Head ★★★ VIEWS At Mizen Head, the very extreme southwest tip of Ireland, the land falls precipitously into the Atlantic breakers in a procession of spectacular 210m (689-ft.) sea cliffs. You can cross a suspension bridge to an old signal station, now a visitor center, and stand on a rock promontory at the southernmost point of the mainland. The sea view is spectacular, and it's worth a trip regardless of the weather. A huge renovation in the early 2010s added new bridges, viewing platforms, and a simulated ship's bridge. On the way out to Mizen Head, you'll pass Barleycove Beach, a gorgeous stretch of sand and rock.

Mizen Head. www.mizenhead.ie. ℭ **028/35115** or 35225. Admission €6 adults; €4.50 seniors and students; €3.50 children 5–11; children under 5 free; €18 families. June–Aug daily 10am–6pm; mid-Mar to May and Sept–Oct daily 10:30am–5pm; Nov to mid-Mar Sat–Sun 11am–4pm. From Cork take N71 to Ballydehob, then R592 and R591 to Golleen and follow signs to Mizen Head.

COUNTY KERRY

Known for rolling green fields, vibrant little towns, and craggy ocean vistas, County Kerry is one of those places visitors to Ireland always have at the top of their lists. Charming villages like colorful Kenmare and bustling historic towns like Killarney make perfect stops on any Irish tour. Its peaceful green valleys are just what you hope for when you come to Ireland. Unfortunately, this cuts both ways: With massive popularity come massive crowds of tourists. The height of summer is incredibly busy here—if it's peace you want, ideally, you should hit these hills in the late spring or fall. But there's an antidote for even the busiest times: Should you find that the tour-bus traffic on the **Ring of Kerry** is getting to you, simply turn off onto a small country lane, and within seconds you'll find yourself virtually alone in the peaceful Irish countryside.

ESSENTIALS

Arriving

BY BUS Bus Éireann (www.buseireann.ie; ℭ **064/663-0011**) operates regularly scheduled service into Killarney and Dingle from all parts of Ireland.

BY TRAIN Trains from Dublin, Cork, and Galway arrive daily at the Killarney Railway Station (www.irishrail.ie; ℭ **064/663-1067**), Railway Road, off East Avenue Road. Kenmare and Dingle do not have train stations.

BY CAR Unless you join an organized tour (see p. 150), a car is the only feasible way to get around the Ring of Kerry. Getting to Killarney from Cork is easy—just head northeast out of Cork City on N22; the distance is about 85km (53 miles). To get to Killarney from Dublin, take M7 southwest to Limerick, then N21 (which also leads to Tralee, gateway to the Dingle Peninsula), and N22 to Killarney. The total journey is about 310km (193 miles). Kenmare and Killarney are connected by the main N71 Ring of Kerry Road; they're only 33km (20½ miles) apart, but allow plenty of time due to the winding nature of the road (and, in summer, tour-bus traffic). To hire a car in Killarney, try **Budget** at the International Hotel on Kenmare Place (www.budget.ie; ℭ **064/663-4341**) or **Enterprise** on Upper Park Road (www.enterprise.ie; ℭ **066/711-9304**).

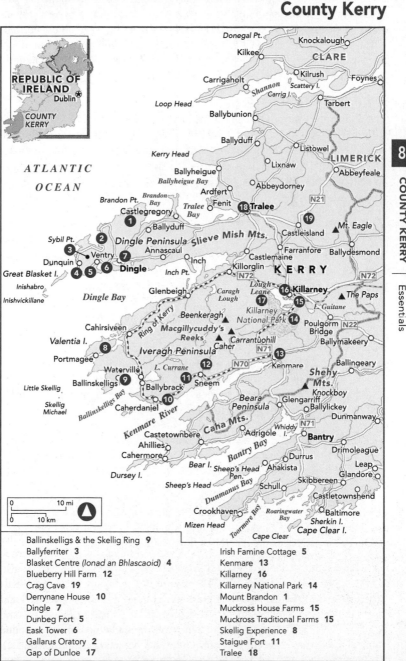

BY PLANE Aer Lingus (www.aerlingus.com; ✆ 081/836-5000) has two flights per day from Dublin into the miniscule Kerry County Airport in Farandole (www.kerryairport.ie; ✆ 066/976-4644), about 16km (10 miles) north of Killarney. There are also a couple of flights a week from London's Luton and Stanstead Airports; they're all operated by **Ryanair** (www.ryanair.com; ✆ 0871/246-0000 in the U.K. or 1520/444-004).

Visitor Information

The **Killarney Tourist Office** is at the Discover Ireland Centre, Beech Road, Killarney (www.killarney.ie; ✆ 064/663-1633). The **Kenmare Tourist Office** is at the Kenmare Heritage Centre, Market Square, Kenmare (www.kenmare.ie; ✆ 064/664-1233). The **Tralee Tourist Office** is at the Ashe Memorial Hall on Denny Street, Tralee (✆ 066/712-1288). And the **Dingle Tourist Office** is on the Quay, Dingle (www.dingle-peninsula.ie; ✆ 066/915-1188). All stay open year-round.

Organized Tours

If you're not confident in renting a car and driving yourself around County Kerry's tourist-clogged roads, plenty of companies will take you to see the major sights on organized bus tours. Most depart from **Killarney,** the most popular base for exploring the Ring (see p. 161). Prices vary enormously according to what you choose, but expect to pay somewhere in the region of €20 to €40 per person. Two recommended operators are **Corcoran's Chauffeur Tours,** 8 College St. (www.corcorantours.com; ✆ 064/663-6666); and **Doro's Tours,** 22 Main St. (www.derostours.com; ✆ 064/663-1251 or 663-1567). Both run full-day tours of the Ring of Kerry, tours to Dingle and the Slea Head Peninsula, and a variety of tours centered around Killarney National Park.

WHERE TO STAY

As the main tourist hub of County Kerry, it should come as no surprise that Killarney offers the greatest choice of accommodations. However, if you have the freedom of a car, consider nearby Kenmare as an alternative base. It's quieter and just as convenient for exploring the Ring of Kerry. If the somewhat less-traveled Dingle Peninsula is your destination, base yourself in the town of Dingle, which has some delightful B&Bs and small hotels.

Where to Stay Around the Ring of Kerry

EXPENSIVE

Aghadoe Heights ★★★ This seductive retreat just north of Killarney is worth the splurge; luxurious and welcoming, it's a relaxing spa escape. The large, modern guest rooms are decorated in soothing tones of white, gray, and oatmeal. Beds are extremely comfortable and bathrooms impeccable. It's worth spending a little extra to get a room at the front to appreciate the stunning views of the Lower Lake in Killarney National Park. There is a huge list of treatments in the opulent spa (they even have a "precious stone chamber" for some of the more exotic options), and the thermal suite is full of high-tech touches such as showers infused with essential oils. On site are two excellent restaurants and a bar overlooking the lake.

About 5km (3 mi) NW of Killarney, signposted off N22; Ard Na Be Rd., Aghadoe. www. aghadoeheights.com. © **064/663-1766.** 74 units. €230–€300. Free parking. Breakfast included. Spa and dinner, bed and breakfast packages available. **Amenities:** 2 restaurants; bar; pool; spa; room service; Wi-Fi (free).

Cahernane House ★★★
A neo-Gothic mansion on the outskirts of Killarney National Park, Cahernane was once home to the Earls of Pembroke, and it's still evocative of bygone days. The public areas, in particular, have the feel of a traditional gentlemen's club filled with antique furniture, stag heads on the wall, and roaring fires in the open grates. Guest rooms are more modern, though no less elegant, and some bathrooms come with deep claw-foot tubs. Many rooms have private patios. Cahernane has two restaurants: the excellent, formal **Herbert Room,** and the more relaxed **Cellar Bar,** set in an old wine cellar. Fields and farmland surround the hotel, and the misty mountains of the park rise in the distance. Check the website for special offers, including dinner, bed and breakfast deals.

Muckross Rd., Killarney. www.cahernane.com. © **064/663-1895.** 38 units. €140–€185. Free parking. Breakfast included. **Amenities:** Restaurant; bar; room service; Wi-Fi (free).

Park Hotel Kenmare ★★★
The noble greystone house holding the elegant Park Hotel was described by the Irish *Independent* newspaper as, "as close as you'll get to Downton Abbey without going on set." And that's about right. The circa 1897 building rambles through large, perfectly decorated rooms, each more glorious than the last, with open fireplaces, grand oil paintings, and imposing staircases galore. All around are spectacular views of mirror-like lake and green, rolling hills. Staff are polite but not snobbish and will help arrange anything you need, including sightseeing excursions and horse-riding expeditions. However, the extraordinary Samas spa might prove so distracting you forget to go sightseeing at all. Bedrooms are quiet and unusually spacious for Ireland; all are impeccably decorated, some with four-poster beds, complete with heavy fabric curtains and warm bed covers, perfect for cold nights. The in-house restaurant is known for its Irish-European cuisine and formal atmosphere; prices are about as high as you'd expect for this kind of service.

Kenmare High Street, Kenmare. www.parkkenmare.com. © **064/664-1200.** 46 units. €250–€420. Free parking. Breakfast included. **Amenities:** Wi-Fi (free); restaurant; bar; room service; spa.

MODERATE
Derrynane Hotel ★
The view from this place is striking—perched on a promontory overlooking Kenmare Bay, guests look out across a dramatic coastal inlet streaked with tiny green islands and a smattering of pleasure boats cruising around the coast. Accommodations have few frills; some are

nicely designed, if rather spartan, and others could do with an upgrade. Package deals include "Golden Breaks" with special discounts for seniors. This place is really geared toward family groups, with standard rooms that actually sleep up to three; handy extras include an indoor playroom and child-friendly menus at dinner. Other amenities include a small outdoor pool, sauna, and a seaweed-bath treatment room. A small herb garden on the grounds provides ingredients for the in-house restaurant.

Caherdaniel (signposted from N70 Ring of Kerry Rd.). www.derrynane.com. ⓒ**066/947-5136.** 70 units. €58–€118. Free parking. Breakfast not included in lower rates. **Amenities:** Restaurant; bar; room service; pool; gym; treatment room; Wi-Fi (free).

Earls Court House ★★ Just outside the center of Killarney, on a quiet street with views of the mountains, Earls Court House is a pleasingly old-fashioned B&B. Guest rooms are simple but elegant, featuring polished wood furniture and buttermilk-colored walls. A few have canopy or four-poster beds. Flatscreen TVs mounted to the walls add a modern touch. You can take afternoon tea in one of the two guest lounges (included in the price of your room), and light suppers are served until early evening. The excellent, varied breakfasts include fresh, home-baked bread and pastries. Check the website for special seasonal offers.

Woodlawn Rd., Killarney. www.killarney-earlscourt.ie. ⓒ **064/663-4009.** 24 units. €120–€130. Free parking. Breakfast included. 2-night minimum on some summer weekends. **Amenities:** Wi-Fi (free); guest lounges; library.

Friars Glen ★★★ Nestled in the cleft of a lush and verdant glen inside Killarney National Park, this delightful B&B could hardly be friendlier or better run. Hosts John and Mary (and their two dogs) welcome guests like old friends; they really enjoy what they do and take pride in helping visitors plan their explorations of the park and the Ring of Kerry. They will even organize tours on your behalf and can provide babysitting in the evenings with a bit of notice. The building itself looks like an old farmhouse (exposed stone, woodsy feel), but it is actually recently built. Guest rooms are cozy and simple, boasting knotted-wood furniture and decent-size bathrooms. The views of the surrounding glen are inspiring. Breakfast is served until a very civilized 10am. Dinner isn't offered, but the place is only a short drive south of Killarney. From the N71, turn east just south of the Jarvey's Rest pub.

Mangerton Rd., Muckross, Killarney. www.friarsglen.ie. ⓒ **064/663-7500.** 10 units. €100–€110. Free parking. Breakfast included. **Amenities:** Wi-Fi (free). From N71, turn west just south of the Jarvey's Rest pub. The turning for Friar's Glen is on the right immediately after the Muckross Garden Centre.

Iskeroon ★★★ In a spectacularly beautiful setting on the Ring of Kerry, looking out across the Derrynane coast and out to the Skellig Islands, this extraordinary bed and breakfast is a serene and special place to stay. Built in the 1930s, the house isn't large, but this merely adds to the feeling of special care and attention you experience from the moment you walk through the door. The two suites, with stone floors, king-size beds, handmade furniture, and beautiful pieces of art, have been elegantly renovated. Fresh ingredients are provided for breakfast, but you prepare it yourself in the kitchenette that comes with your suite—and there's no better location to enjoy a leisurely breakfast than your balcony overlooking the sea. The only downside is the 3-night minimum stay, but it hardly feels like a negative once you're here. Needless to say, it can get booked up far in advance. The former coach house on the grounds is rented out as a full self-catering accommodation for €400 to €450 per week (depending on the time of year). From the Scariff Inn, follow signs for Bunavalla Pier, then signs to Iskeroon.

Bunavalla (halfway between Waterville and Caherdaniel). www.iskeroon.com. ℰ **066/947-5119.** 2 units. €100. Free parking. Breakfast included. 3-night minimum stay. **Amenities:** DVD player and library; kitchenette; Wi-Fi (free).

Sallyport House ★★   An extremely good value for the money, this peaceful 1930s mansion-turned-B&B in Kenmare is filled with interesting antiques, lending a touch of old-school luxury to its already traditional charms. (Thanks to a wealthy industrialist ancestor, there's a story behind most of them.) Guest rooms are comfortable and spacious. A few rooms have intricately carved antique four-poster beds. The house is surrounded by beautiful countryside, and some rooms look out over an idyllic lake. Breakfasts are delicious, and the service is warm and accommodating without ever being intrusive.

Shelbourne St., Kenmare (just south of junction with Pier Rd.). www.sallyporthouse. com. ℰ **064/664-2066.** 5 units. €110–€130. Free parking. Breakfast included. **Amenities:** Wi-Fi (free).

Shelburne Lodge ★★   This cozy 18th-century house was originally the country home of William Petty, the Lord Shelburne (1737–1805), a Dublin-born landowner who was responsible for building much of the modern town of Kenmare. He later became Prime Minister of Great Britain and Ireland, and in 1783 he signed the Treaty of Paris that formally ended the American War of Independence, bringing peace between Britain and the U.S. His home is in good hands nowadays, thanks to wonderful hosts Tom and Maura Foley. Rooms have an old-fashioned air with antique furniture, huge beds, and color schemes of yellow and peach. Public areas have a similar feel—the guest sitting room is so packed with handsome furniture that it's like walking through an antique shop. A lovely, manicured lawn is out back, and the center of Kenmare is only a short walk away.

Cork Rd., Kenmare. www.shelburnelodge.com. ℰ **064/664-1013.** 9 units. €100–€160. Free parking. Breakfast included. **Amenities:** Wi-Fi (free).

INEXPENSIVE

Coffey River's Edge ★   A bright, cheery building overlooking the River Laune in the center of Killorglin, Coffey's is an exceptional value for the money. Most rooms are decently sized (one upstairs is quite small, though), with double beds and contemporary wood furniture. Breakfasts are served in a dining room overlooking the river and picturesque stone bridge, or in fair weather, on a large guest balcony and deck. No evening meal is served, but pretty Killorglin is just a short stroll away. Owners Finbarr and Anne are both keen golfers and will happily arrange for you to have a game at a local course.

The Bridge, Killorglin. www.coffeysriversedge.com. © **066/976-1750.** 11 units. €60–€70. Free parking. Breakfast included. **Amenities:** Wi-Fi (free).

Larkinley Lodge ★★ A great option just a few blocks from the center of Killarney, Larkinley Lodge is a stylish, modern B&B in a beautifully converted town house. Toni and Danny Sheehan are gregarious hosts, with an eye for detail. Guest rooms are small, but just the right mix of traditional and modern, with minimal clutter and muted color schemes. Don't miss the home-baked scones at breakfast. The location is only about a 10-minute walk into central Killarney, not far from great pubs and restaurants. However, it's in a quiet neighborhood, so you can easily escape the evening street noise that can sometimes be a problem in this lively town.

Lewis Rd., Killarney. www.larkinley.ie. © **064/663-5142.** 6 units. €80–€90. Free parking. Breakfast included. **Amenities:** Wi-Fi (free).

QC's ★★ More of a restaurant-with-rooms than a small hotel, QC's is nonetheless a stylish and unique place to stay on the Ring of Kerry. Bedrooms are open-plan contemporary spaces with a minimalist vibe: polished wood floors, huge skylights, and claw-foot tubs next to the bed, with a few high-tech extras such as Bose stereos. The guest lounge looks as if it's tumbled from the pages of a decor magazine, featuring deep velvet sofas and a cozy, wood-burning stove. The superb downstairs restaurant specializes in fresh seafood. They take pride in local flavors cooked to perfection, such as roast hake with samphire and lemon risotto, or local meats served with seasonal vegetables and delicious sauces.

Main St., Cahersiveen. www.qcbar.com. © **066/947-2244.** 5 units. €73–€110. Free parking. Breakfast included. **Amenities:** Wi-Fi (free).

Sea Shore Farm ★★ A modern house overlooking Kenmare Bay and the mountains beyond, this is a special place to stay. Big floor-to-ceiling windows take full advantage of the magnificent surroundings. The guest rooms are large (very large in some cases) and tastefully furnished. The guest lounge has a library of travel books, though you may find yourself too distracted by the views to concentrate. Kenmare is a short drive away or just a captivating, 15-minute walk through the countryside—the better to work off those indulgent breakfasts. Hosts Mary and Owen make everything run smoothly and are always full of helpful suggestions for things to do. They have an encyclopedic knowledge of the local area.

Sea Shore, Tubrid, Kenmare. www.seashorekenmare.com. © **064/664-1270.** 5 units. €90–€130. Free parking. Breakfast included. **Amenities:** Wi-Fi (free).

Where to Stay in Dingle & Tralee
MODERATE
Ballygarry House ★★ On the outer edge of Tralee, this pleasant country inn is ensconced amid lush gardens. Built as a manor house in the 18th century,

plenty of its original features have been retained. Elegant guest rooms maintain the country mansion air; superior rooms are surprisingly spacious, with king-size beds. Family rooms are an excellent value at (usually) the same price as doubles. The in-house spa is a relaxing, revitalizing hideaway (as is the outdoor hot tub). Special inclusive spa offers change monthly—massage, facial, and access to the spa facilities for around €80 to €100 is the kind of deal you can expect. The Brooks restaurant serves excellent, modern Irish food.

Signposted off N21, Leebrook, approx. 3.3km (2 miles) west of central Tralee. www.ballygarryhouse.com. ℰ **066/712-3322.** 46 units. €92–€148. Free parking. Breakfast included. **Amenities:** Wi-Fi (free); spa; restaurant; bar.

Castlewood House ★★★ Overlooking the glassy expanse of Dingle Bay, this lovely whitewashed house is filled with art and antiques. Its location is exceptional, and views of the shimmering water, framed by distant mountains, are breathtaking. Guest rooms are chic and comfortable, with neutral tones, designer furniture, and well-chosen art. Bathrooms have Jacuzzi tubs. Breakfasts (in fact all meals here) are outstanding—porridge with a dash of whiskey, homemade breads, oranges in caramel, kippers with scrambled egg, or a light and fluffy omelet with smoked salmon. Despite the beautifully rural feel to the location, Dingle Marina is only a 10-minute walk away.

The Wood, Dingle Town. www.castlewooddingle.com. ℰ **066/915-2788.** 14 units. €138–€156. Free parking. Breakfast included. **Amenities:** Wi-Fi (free).

Greenmount House ★★★ A luxurious B&B overlooking Dingle Bay, Greenmount House is one of the best places to stay in the area. The view from the front is like a cliché of what you might imagine all of Ireland to be like; rolling green slopes fall gently into the sea at Dingle Bay as the streets of quaint Dingle Town curve around the coastline below. The public areas are arranged at the front as much as possible so that you can admire the view from the guest lounge or breakfast room. The garden has an enclosed hot tub where you can savor a glass of wine. Guest rooms are bright and spacious; some have polished wood floors and others have skylights, letting the daylight pour in. Breakfasts are delicious and plentiful (a fave: tasty smoked salmon and scrambled eggs). Hosts Mary and John are incredibly friendly and will even arrange personal tours of the area, escorted by a member of their own family.

Upper John St., Dingle Town. www.greenmounthouse.ie. ℰ **066/915-1414.** 14 units. €100–€155. 2-night minimum on summer weekends. Free parking. Breakfast included. **Amenities:** Wi-Fi (free).

WHERE TO EAT

Though relatively light on standout first-class restaurants, Kerry has a wide variety of options—including great pubs and family-friendly eateries. Kenmare and Killarney take the lion's share of the best places, but the countryside has some enticing surprises. Dingle is one of the best places in Ireland for gourmet seafood, not to mention its more low-rent (but delicious) cousin, fish and chips.

Where to Eat Around the Ring of Kerry

EXPENSIVE

Bricin ★★ IRISH   Rather incongruously located above a craft shop, this is a longstanding favorite of the Killarney dining scene. *Bricin* means "little trout" in Gaelic, and seafood is one of the strong points of their traditional Irish menu. Locally reared meat is also often on the menu, served with interesting sauces—rack of roast lamb with Madeira and rosemary sauce, for example, or steak with brandy, bourbon, and pepper. However, it's the house specialty for which this place is renowned: boxty, a classic pancake stuffed with several different types of filling. The dining room is an old-fashioned kind of place, complete with stained-glass windows and an open fireplace. Bricin serves a great-value early bird menu (€22 for two courses) until 6:45pm.

26 High St. www.bricin.com. ☏ **064/663-4902.** Fixed-price menus €29 and €35. Tues–Sat 6–9pm. Closed early Jan to early Mar.

Jack's Coastguard Restaurant ★★★ SEAFOOD/MODERN IRISH   This cheery restaurant lists "Water's Edge" as its address. That's not so much a street name as a description; it's right on the harbor in Cromane, a tiny village near Killorglin. The dining room is a bright, modern space boasting beautiful views of the bay, while a pianist plays away in the corner. The fixed-price menus hit elegant notes with choices like salmon fillet with samphire, or rib-eye with horseradish fondant potatoes. For dessert, try the strawberry–and–balsamic vinegar homemade ice cream. The restaurant is attached to a popular local pub, and live music plays every Monday night in summer.

Water's Edge, Cromane Lower, Killorglin. www.jackscromane.com. ☏ **066/976-9102.** Three-course fixed-price menus €36. May–Sept Wed–Mon noon–9pm; Oct Wed–Sun noon–9pm; Nov–Apr Thurs–Sun noon-9pm. Closed Jan.

The Lime Tree ★★ MODERN IRISH   This internationally praised restaurant in a charming, historic building offers an elegant twist on casual cuisine. The menu is smart and varied without being overly complicated, with plenty of locally sourced ingredients. You might start with Sneem black pudding with crispy fried potato cakes, or the deconstructed prawn cocktail with Cognac-infused sauce, then go on to entrees such as pan-fried sirloin with grilled mushrooms, or breast of free-range duck with rhubarb chutney. Desserts are upscale comfort food: a rich terrine of white and dark chocolate with black currant sorbet, or crepes with butterscotch sauce and praline. The wine list is excellent, with plenty of very affordable choices.

Shelbourne St., Kenmare. www.limetreerestaurant.com. ☏ **064/664-1225.** Main courses €18–€28. Daily 6:30–9:30pm.

Nick's Restaurant and Piano Bar ★★ SEAFOOD/IRISH   The rather Rat Pack feel to this restaurant's name says everything about its old-school credentials. Nick's is quite famous in this part of Ireland—it's been here since 1978—and although you won't find cutting-edge modern cuisine here, it still deserves its reputation as one of the better places to eat along the Ring of

Kerry. Choose from two dining areas: a formal restaurant or the bar, where a simpler (and less expensive) selection is served in more relaxed surroundings. On the main menu are several catches of the day (naturally), as well as dishes such as grilled sole and a classic seafood platter. You can also order grilled steaks and lamb. The bar menu is more of the fish and chips or steak sandwich variety, but it's still good and fresh. Everything is served to the gentle melodies of a live piano accompaniment. The same as it ever was.

Lower Bridge St., Killorglin. www.nicks.ie. © **066/976-1219.** Main courses €22–€34. Tues–Sun 5:30–10pm.

Packie's ★★ IRISH Packie's has been a local favorite in Kenmare for years. The candlelit dining room is atmospheric, and the crowd is as much residents as visitors. And it's easy to understand why—the food is unpretentious but delicious, using a bounty of local ingredients. You might choose to sample steak, lamb, or perhaps super-fresh seafood, all simply prepared but melt-in-your-mouth tasty. Desserts are worth leaving room for. The reasonably priced wine list offers plenty of choices available by the glass.

Henry St. www.kenmare.com/packies. ©**064/664-1508.** Main courses €17–€28. Tues–Sat 6–10pm. Closed Feb.

MODERATE

The Blind Piper ★ IRISH This friendly, lively pub is one of the top places to eat in Caherdaniel. The high-quality bar menu strikes a nice line between straightforward traditional pub grub and something a little more sophisticated—Guinness stew with fresh soda bread, scampi and chips, pasta, or burgers made with locally sourced beef. The charming staff makes you feel right at home, and the bar is enlivened by live traditional music sessions on Thursday nights from 9:15pm. The Blind Piper is a bit hard to find, partly because it doesn't have a proper street address. Take the main N70 road through Caherdaniel, and then take the turn next to the big red building in the center of the village. (There's usually a handmade sign here pointing you in the right direction.) The pub is painted bright yellow.

Off main Ring of Kerry Road (N70), Caherdaniel. www.blindpiperpub.com. ©**066/947-5126.** Main courses €11–€17. Mon–Thurs 11am–11:30pm (food served noon–4pm); Fri–Sat 11am–midnight (food served noon–8pm); Sun noon–11pm (food served 12:30–8:30pm).

The Boathouse Bistro ★ BISTRO/SEAFOOD This casual seafood bistro at Dromquinna Manor has an outside seating area overlooking Kenmare Bay, making it perfect for a warm summer night. The menu serves dishes like pan-seared salmon or the house-special fishcakes with mango salsa. Or you could just have a burger and sea-salted French fries while you take in the wonderful view. This is a good stop for lunch on a sunny day, especially when the weather's fine and you can sit outside. It closes for much of the off-season.

On N70, 5km (3 miles) west of Kenmare. www.dromquinnamanor.com. ©**064/664-2888.** Main courses €11–€25. July–Aug daily 12:30–9pm; May–June and Sept Tues–Sun 12:30–9pm; Oct Thurs–Sun 12:30–9pm; Mar–Apr weekends 12:30–9pm. Closed Nov–Feb.

The Jarvey's Rest ★ IRISH This popular pub is not nearly as old as it tries to appear, with a roomful of exposed beams and rows of tankards on the ceiling, as if any moment now a crowd of jolly drinkers may swipe them down and roar a drunken toast. But it has charm, and a recent change of owners has given the place a welcome overhaul. The menu is crowd-pleasing stuff—smoked chowder, fish and chips, or a juicy burger served in a Waterford *blaa* (a kind of soft white roll). For dessert, try the sticky toffee pudding (a kind of moist steamed cake made with dates and brown sugar) with butterscotch sauce. During summer there's a lively show of traditional Irish music and dancing on certain nights—call for dates.

At the Muckross Park Hotel, Muckross Rd. www.muckrosspark.com. ⓒ **064/662-3400.** 3-course fixed-price menu €29. Mid-Mar to Oct daily 12:30pm–midnight (food served until 9:30pm); Nov to mid-Mar Fri–Sun 12:30pm–11pm (food served until 6pm).

Kate Kearney's Cottage ★ INTERNATIONAL Unofficially considered the gateway to the Gap of Dunloe, this cheerful pub is hugely popular. It's a little touristy (a dead giveaway is the in-house souvenir shop), but the atmosphere is upbeat and traditional, and the stick-to-your-ribs pub food is pretty tasty. Think steaks, ribs, burgers, and bistro-style classics, all washed down with a restorative pint. The pub is named after a feisty local woman who carved out a reputation as a maker of illegal *potcheen* (moonshine) that she called Mountain Dew.

Gap of Dunloe, Beaufort, signposted from N72 (Ring of Kerry Rd.). www.katekearneyscot tage.com. ⓒ **064/664-4146.** Main courses €13–€18. Daily noon–11pm (food 6:30–9:30pm).

The Laurels ★ INTERNATIONAL The menu at this busy pub in the center of Killarney is populist fare. Starters include deep-fried brie with red currant sauce and chicken wings, while entrees range from a generous steak served with peppercorn sauce and French fries to traditional Irish dishes such as Irish stew, and traditional potato cakes with gravy. They also serve a massive seafood platter that must be seen to be believed. The lunch menu is much simpler, serving "doorstep" (very thick-cut) sandwiches, burgers, salads, and the like. In summer, the pub features lively music sessions several times a week.

Main St. www.thelaurelspub.com. ⓒ **064/663-1149.** Main courses €16–€29. Mon–Thurs 10:30am–11:30pm; Fri–Sat 10:30am–12:30am; Sun 12:30–11pm. (Food served until about 9:30pm.)

Quinlan's Seafood Bar ★ SEAFOOD This casual fish-focused eatery is where the locals go when they're craving fish. With a seafood counter up front, selling straight from the boat, the fare here is simple and straightforward—fish and chips, with a light batter and a giant portion of chunky fries, come straight from the fryer. Have it with mushy peas, and you're deep into a true Irish dinner. If you fancy more sophisticated dishes, their menu obliges, with scallops in butter, boiled Irish lobster, lemon sole in a buttery sauce, or prawns so fresh they all but crawl off the plate. The white, clean dining room is nothing fancy, but it does the job.

77 High Street. www.kerryfish.com. ⓒ **064/662-0666.** Main courses €11–€22. Daily noon–9pm.

TAKING A (moon) shine TO POTCHEEN

"Keep your eyes well peeled today, the excise men are on their way, searching for the mountain tay, in the hills of Connemara . . ."

—From "The Hills of Connemara"

Potcheen is a potent form of Irish moonshine, traditionally brewed from grain or potatoes. It was banned by the English crown in 1661, an act that effectively criminalized thousands of distillers overnight. Unsurprisingly, that didn't stop people from making the stuff, and after 336 years on the wrong side of the law, potcheen was finally made legal again in 1997.

One 17th-century writer said of potcheen that "it enlighteneth ye heart, casts off melancholy, keeps back old age and breaketh ye wind." Its usefulness didn't stop there, evidently, as history records the drink being used as everything from a bath tonic to a substitute for dynamite.

Potcheen has long been used in fiction as a symbol of Irish nationalism, its contraband status rich with rebellious overtones. The traditional folk song "The Hills of Connemara" describes potcheen being secretly distributed under the noses of excise men.

In 2008, the European Union awarded the drink "Geographical Indicative" protection. This means that only the genuine Irish product is allowed to carry the name (the same status enjoyed by champagne and Parma ham).

You'll find potcheen for sale in a few souvenir stores. Like most liquors it can be drunk straight, on the rocks, or with a mixer, but at anything from 80 to a massive 180 proof, potcheen packs a mean punch, so enjoy . . . cautiously.

Smuggler's Inn ★ SEAFOOD/IRISH   Overlooking the beach in Waterville, this is a popular option for lunch. The menu is mostly seafood caught fresh from Ballinskelligs Bay—think oysters, black sole, and seafood chowder. Local seafood is a specialty—black sole from Ballinskelligs, or Dolus Head baked cod—or you could go for some roast duck or a tender steak. The conservatory dining room has sweeping views of the bay, or you can sit outside and take in the full glory of it all. The Smuggler's Inn also does bed-and-breakfast accommodations for around €70 to €110 per night.

Cliff Rd., Waterville. www.the-smugglers-inn.com. © **066/947-4330.** Main courses €15–€30. Daily noon–3pm, 6–9pm. No children after 8pm. Closed Nov–Easter.

INEXPENSIVE

The Blue Bull ★ IRISH   This great little pub in tiny, picturesque Sneem serves traditional fare in a couple of cozy dining spaces. The menu doesn't deviate too far from Irish pub classics, but it does it all very well—fish and chips, mussels in garlic sauce, steaks, sandwiches, and salads. The crowd, a good mix of hungry tourists and easygoing locals settling down at the bar, makes for a congenial atmosphere. This is a straight-up traditional pub with a bar area in the front separate from the dining rooms. It's a great spot for eavesdropping on a few conversations, and possibly being asked your opinion about the topic of the day.

South Square, Sneem. © **066/947-5126.** Main courses €6–€18. Mon–Sat 11am–around midnight; Sun noon–11pm (food until about 9pm).

Purple Heather ★IRISH   This sweet lunch spot in Kenmare serves simple, unpretentious meals. It's also rather dark (the euphemism would be "cozy"), but that shouldn't deter you; this cafe is popular with locals. Start with a leisurely pint of Guinness at the bar in front, before venturing toward the little dining area at the back for a lunch of toasted sandwiches, fluffy omelets, homemade soups, or a bowl of chowder.

Henry St., Kenmare. www.thepurpleheatherkenmare.com. © **064/664-1016.** Main courses €7–€18. Mon–Sat 11am–5:30pm. Closed bank holidays.

Wharton's Traditional Fish & Chips ★★FISH & CHIPS   Proof that not all the best dining experiences come with a hefty price tag, Wharton's is an outstanding "chipper." The menu is traditional—who would have it any other way with fish and chips?—although asking if you'd prefer your fish battered or fried in breadcrumbs is a nice twist. It's nothing too fancy, but that's half the point—this is real Irish fast food. They have a few seats inside or in the little courtyard at the front, or you can get everything to go.

Main St., Kenmare. ©**064/664-2622.** Main courses €6–€10. Daily 11am–9pm.

Where to Eat in Dingle & Tralee
EXPENSIVE

The Chart House ★★IRISH   This friendly restaurant on the outskirts of Dingle is one of the most popular places to indulge in the local bounty. The menu is short but impeccably judged, filled with regional flavor and a hint of global influences. Expect European-influenced Irish dishes like black pudding hash with soft-boiled egg, hake served with mashed parsnip and carrot, and roast lamb with garlic potatoes. Almost everything on the menu is sourced from providers within the Dingle Peninsula. You can choose from certain dishes on the menu as a €33 prix-fixe deal, and the three-course early bird special has almost as much choice as the evening service for €27.

The Mall, Dingle. www.thecharthousedingle.com. © **066/915-2255.** Main courses €18–€27. Daily 6–10pm. Times may vary in winter. Closed Jan to mid-Feb.

Doyle's Seafood Bar ★★★SEAFOOD   Doyle's is simply one of the best places in the region for top-notch seafood. As you'd expect from a place like this, what you find on the menu will depend on the catch of the day; most likely this will include oysters on the half-shell, fresh and delicious. Specialties include fish stew made with white wine and saffron, turbot with red pepper and chive sauce, or black sole with a lemon and parsley butter. Carnivores are taken care of with grilled steak or lamb. The wine list is extensive, and the early bird menu is served until 7:30pm (€30 for three courses).

4 John St., Dingle Town. www.doylesofdingle.ie. © **066/915-2674.** Main courses €23–€33. Mon–Sat (and Sun on public holiday weekends only) 5–9:30pm. Closed Jan.

MODERATE
Denny Lane ★ BISTRO   A good option for a quick lunch in Tralee, Denny Lane serves tasty soups, salads, sandwiches, and light lunch specials. It's nothing fancy, but the food is good and the atmosphere congenial. They

also do breakfast until a very civilized noon (or brunch until 2pm). Dinner on weekends includes a selection of steaks, seafood, burgers, and other favorites all mixed up with a popular tapas menu.

11 Denny St., Tralee. www.dennylane.ie. ℂ **066/712-9831.** Lunch main courses €5–€11. Dinner main courses €16–€26. Mon–Thurs 10am–4pm; Fri–Sat 10am–11pm (last orders 9pm).

INEXPENSIVE

Reel Dingle Fish ★★ FISH & CHIPS My favorite "chipper" in Dingle, this spot cooks everything the traditional way: fish in batter, with piping-hot chips, and no messing around. But there's a greater-than-average choice of fresh fish to choose from, including hake, monkfish, pollock, and locally smoked haddock. They also sell homemade burgers crafted from local beef.

Bridge St., Dingle Town. ℂ**066/915-1713.** €5–€12. Daily noon to around 11pm.

EXPLORING THE RING OF KERRY

Undoubtedly Ireland's most popular scenic route, the Ring of Kerry winds its way along a panorama of rugged coastline, tall mountains, pristine lakes, and beautiful small towns and villages. The Ring of Kerry is both the actual name of the road—or, if you want to be pedantic, a section of the N70, N71, and N72 highways—and the collective name given to the many attractions in the area. Nearly all of County Kerry's most popular sights are either on or within a short distance of the Ring. Its largest hub, **Killarney,** is best known for its glorious surroundings, in particular the spectacular landscapes of **Killarney National Park,** which includes the **Killarney Lakes** and the scenic **Gap of Dunloe.** The town of **Kenmare** makes for a more charming (and certainly more quiet) base.

What you won't find along the Ring of Kerry road, at least in the summertime, is much in the way of peace. Bicyclists avoid the route because of the scores of tour buses thundering down it from early morning until late in the day. You can drive either way along the Ring of Kerry, but a counterclockwise route gives you the most spectacular views. Very large vehicles are always meant to travel this way to avoid accidents and nasty traffic jams around the Ring's perilously narrow bends.

Top Attractions in Killarney

Killarney's ample stock of restaurants, pubs, and hotels keeps it buzzing with visitors throughout the year. Given this, tourism is a bit more in-your-face here than perhaps anywhere else in Kerry, with leprechaun-laden souvenir shops on every corner. In the summer its narrow streets are prone to tour-bus traffic jams. That aside, though, it has much to offer, and plenty of beauty to go with the bustle.

Still, the main attraction is the valley in which Killarney nestles—a verdant landscape of mist-wreathed lakes and rugged hills so spectacular that author and playwright Brendan Behan once said, "Even an ad man would be

killarney NATIONAL PARK

A huge, rambling wilderness with breath-taking scenery just steps from the hub-bub of Killarney, this national park is an essential stop along the Ring of Kerry. Cars are banned from most of the trails that traverse the park, so hike or hire a **"jarvey,"** or "jaunting car"—an old-fashioned horse-and-buggy available at not-too-steep prices. The drivers congregate behind the visitor center at Muckross House (see p. 165).

Within the park's limits are two estates, **Muckross** and **Knockreer** (see p. 164). The main visitor center for the park is in **Muckross House** (✆ **064/663-1440**) and is clearly signposted. Drop by here to pick up maps before you get started. The visitor center is open daily from 9am to 5:30pm; hours may vary in winter.

Three lakes dot the park. The largest, the **Lower Lake,** is sometimes called Lough Leane or Lough Lein, translated as "the lake of learning." It's more than 6km (3¾ miles) long and holds 30 small islands that seem to rise from the mist. The most celebrated of Killarney's islands, the lovely **Innisfallen** (see p. 163), can be found on Lower Lake. Nearby are the **Middle Lake** or Muck-ross Lake, and the smallest of the three, the **Upper Lake.**

Here are three walks you could take to explore the best of Killarney Park:

Blue Pool Nature Trail: Starting behind the Muckross Park Hotel, this trail winds for a relaxing 2.3km (1.5 miles) through coniferous woodland beside a small lake. The trail is named for the lake's unusually deep blue-green color, a result of copper deposits in the soil. Incorporated into a small section of the Blue Pool trail is the **Cloghereen Nature Trail,** a walk fully accessible to blind visitors. A guide rope leads you along the route, lined by plants identifiable by scent and touch. An audio guide is available from the Muckross House visitor center for a small deposit.

Mossy Woods Nature Trail: One of the park's gentler trails, this route starts from Muckross Lake and runs just under 2km (1¼ miles). The moss-covered trees and rocks it passes are a major habitat for bird life. You'll also see several strawberry trees (*Arbutus*), something of a botanical mystery, along the route. They're commonplace around these parts but found almost nowhere else in Northern Europe. The route offers some incredible views of the Torc Mountains and MacGillycuddy's Reeks.

Torc Mountain Walk: This moderately difficult 10km (6-mile) trail starts at the Torc Waterfall parking lot, about 6km (3¾ miles) south of Killarney. Follow the trail to the top of the falls, then, at a T-intersection, turn left toward the top parking lot, then right onto Old Kenmare Road, following a stream along the south slopes of Torc Mountain. After leaving the woods, you'll see Torc Mountain on your right. Look for a crescent-shaped gouge in the side of the road with a small cairn at its far edge; this marks the path to the ridge top, where you'll get spectacular views of the Killarney Lakes and nearby MacGillycuddy's Reeks. It's also accessible on a 4.5km (2.8-mile) looped walking trail from Muckross House.

For more information on the park, visit **www.killarneynationalpark.ie**.

---

ashamed to eulogize it." Escaping the crowded streets to explore the quiet rural splendor of the 65-sq.-km (25-sq.-mile) **Killarney National Park** could hardly be easier. The main visitor center is just 7km (4½ miles) south of the city, or you could merely walk to the cathedral and keep going—it backs onto the **Knockreer Estate** ★ (sce p. 164), which is itself a section of the park.

Killarney National Park

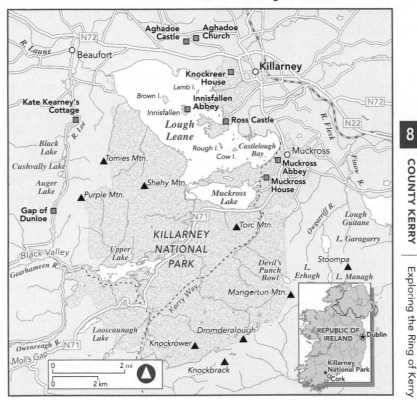

Gap of Dunloe ★★ VIEWS   A narrow pass between the Purple Mountains and MacGillycuddy's Reeks, the winding Gap of Dunloe rises through mountains and wetlands on the western side of Killarney National Park. The route through the gap passes craggy hills, meandering streams, and deep gullies, and it ends in the park at the Upper Lake. Some of the roads can be difficult around here, so many people choose to explore by bicycle (try **Killarney Rent-a-Bike,** Lower New Street; www.killarneyrentabike.com; ⓒ **064/663-1282**) or by "jarvey." These can be booked at the National Park Visitor Centre at Muckross House (see box above) or from **Killarney Jaunting Cars,** Muckross Close (www.killarneyjauntingcars.ie; ⓒ **064/663-3358**).

Signposted from N72 (Ring of Kerry Rd.), Killarney.

Innisfallen ★★ ISLAND   Shrouded in forest, this small island appears to float peacefully on Killarney National Park's Lower Lake. Behind the trees is what's left of a monastery that was founded in the 7th century and flourished for 1,000 years. It's thought that Brian Boru, the great Irish chieftain, and St.

163

Brendan the Navigator were educated here. From 950 to 1320, the "Annals of Innisfallen," a chronicle of early Irish history, was written at the monastery. You can reach Innisfallen by rowboat, available for rental at Ross Castle (see **Killarney Lakes Cruise ★**, below).

Lower Lake, opposite Ross Castle, Ross Rd., (signposted from N71, Ring of Kerry Rd.), Killarney.

Killarney Grand ★ PUB/LIVE MUSIC   This hugely popular pub in Killarney—officially known as Sheehan's Bar, although the signs out front say both—is one of the best places in the region to hear traditional Irish music. There are lively sessions nightly at 9pm; after 11pm it turns into a nightclub. The atmosphere gets pretty raucous, and the crowds can really pack in here (definitely standing room only), but the music is always good. Some of the biggest names in Irish music have played here over the years, and you never know when you might catch the next big thing. A "neat" dress code is enforced at the door. In other words, you don't have to wear your best duds, but don't be too scruffy, either.

Main St., Killarney. www.killarneygrand.com. © **064/663-1159.** Admission free until 11pm; price varies after that, according to who's playing. Mon–Sat 7:30pm–2:30am; Sun 7:30pm–1:30am.

Killarney Lakes Cruise ★ TOUR   From the harbor at Ross Castle (see p. 166), the **MV Pride of the Lake** takes you on an hour-long waterborne cruise. The covered boat ride is a little on the touristy side—and very popular, so you might want to make reservations—but the views of the park from the lake are gorgeous. You can also take a tour that combines a lake cruise with a "jaunting car" ride around the park. *Tip:* You can get to the pier by Ross Castle on a free shuttle bus from Killarney town center. It leaves Scotts Street (by the junction with East Avenue Rd.) a quarter of an hour before each sailing. Lake cruises are strictly limited to 80 people, so you may want to book at busy times—but be sure to bring a printout of the confirmation or they won't let you board.

The Pier, Ross Castle, Ross Rd., off N71 (Ring of Kerry Rd.), Killarney. www.killarneylake tours.ie. © **064/662-7737.** Tickets €10; children under 3 free. May–Sept sailings 12:30 and 2:30pm, Apr and Oct 2:30pm only. Times may change according to weather.

Knockreer Estate ★ GARDENS   The grand old house that once stood here burned down in the early 20th century. A modern building of the same name on the same site serves as the park's education center, while the lovely old gardens of the estate still exist. Here, 200-year-old trees mix with sweet wildflowers and azaleas to fragrant effect. A signposted walk takes you past beautiful views of the Lower Lake and the valley; a pathway leads down to the River Deenagh. Main access to Knockreer is through Deenagh Lodge Gate, opposite St. Mary's Cathedral in Killarney town.

Main entrance near St. Mary's Cathedral on Cathedral Place, off New St., Killarney. Free admission.

Muckross House & Gardens ★★ HISTORIC HOME This elegant, neo-Gothic Victorian house at the entrance to Killarney National Park was built in 1843. The rooms are presented much as they would have been in the mid-19th century, from the grand, *Downton Abbey*–like formal dining room to the stark contrast of the Victorian kitchens and servants' quarters below the stairs. The landscaped gardens are beautiful and a riot of color in high summer. The pleasant cafe, overlooking some manicured flowerbeds, is a lovely spot to linger over a cup of tea. A traditional weavers' and craft shop is also on the grounds, along with the evocative ruin of the 15th-century **Muckross Abbey,** founded about 1448 and burned by Cromwell's troops in 1652. The abbey's central feature is a vaulted cloister around a courtyard that contains a huge yew tree, thought to be as old as the abbey itself. William Makepeace Thackeray once called it "the prettiest little bijou of a ruined abbey ever seen."

On N71 (Ring of Kerry Rd.), 6km (3.6 miles) south of Killarney. www.muckross-house.ie. ℂ **064/667-0144.** Admission €9 adults; €7.50 seniors and students; €6 children under 15; €28–€32 families. Joint ticket with Muckross Traditional Farms: €15 adults; €13 seniors and students; €11 children under 15; €45–€50 families. July–Aug daily 9am–7pm; Sept–June daily 9am–5:30pm. Last admission 1 hr. before closing.

Muckross Traditional Farms ★★ LIVING HISTORY PARK Not far from the Muckross House estate, these farms demonstrate traditional life as it was in previous centuries in County Kerry. It's cleverly done—the farmhouses and barns are so authentically detailed that you feel as if you've dropped in on the real deal. In a way, you have. Work really happens here: Farmhands work the fields while the blacksmith, carpenter, and wheelwright ply their trades. Women draw water from the wells and cook meals in historically accurate kitchens. There's also a petting zoo, where kids can handle some of the animals. A coach constantly circles the grounds, ferrying those with mobility problems between different areas of the farm. *Note:* A combination ticket allows you to visit Muckross House & Gardens for a small extra fee.

Kenmare Rd. (N71), Killarney, County Kerry. www.muckross-house.ie. ℂ **064/663-0804.** Admission €9 adults; €7.50 seniors and students; €6 children under 15; €28–€32 families. Joint ticket with Muckross House: €15 adults; €13 seniors and students; €11 children under 15; €45–€50 families. June–Aug daily 10am–6pm; May and Sept daily 1–6pm; Mar–Apr and Oct, Sat–Sun and public holidays 1–6pm. Last admission 1 hr. before closing. Closed Nov–Apr.

Ross Castle ★ CASTLE   Just outside Killarney Town, this 15th-century fortress still guards the edge of the Lower Lake. Built by the O'Donoghue chieftains, the castle was the last stronghold in Munster to surrender to Cromwell's forces in 1652. But it could not withstand time and the English army: All that remains of it today is a tower house surrounded by a fortified *bawn* (walled garden) with rounded turrets. The tower has been furnished in the style of the late 16th and early 17th centuries. Although you can wander the grounds at will, you can only see inside the castle on a guided tour. The tours can be a bit tedious, as the guides seem to scrounge around for facts interesting enough to justify the ticket price. In good weather, the best way to reach the castle is via a lakeside walk (it's 3km/2 miles from Killarney). From the castle, you can take boat tours of the lake (see p. 164).

Ross Rd., signposted from N71 (Ring of Kerry Rd.), Killarney. www.heritageireland.ie. *©* **064/663-5851.** €4 adults, €3 seniors, €2 students and children, €10 families. Mid-Mar to Oct daily 9:30am–5:45pm. Last admission 45 min. before closing. No photography.

St. Mary's Cathedral ★ CHURCH   If you think this limestone cathedral looks more Castle Dracula than parish church, it may be because New Street was once the home of Bram Stoker, who spent summers in Killarney while he was a student at Trinity College, Dublin. Officially known as the Catholic Church of St. Mary of the Assumption, it's designed in the Gothic Revival style and laid out in the shape of a cross. Construction began in 1842, was interrupted by the Famine, and finally concluded in 1855 (although the towering spire wasn't added until 1912).

Cathedral Place, off New St., Killarney. *©* **064/663-1014.** Free admission. Daily 10:30am–6pm.

Top Attractions in Kenmare

Originally called *Neidin* (pronounced Nay-deen, meaning "little nest" in Irish), Kenmare is indeed a little nest of verdant foliage and colorful buildings nestled between the River Roughty and Kenmare Bay. It's an enchanting place with flower boxes at every window, sparkling clean sidewalks, and great shops.

Kenmare Druid Circle ★ ANCIENT SITE   On a small hill near the market square, this large, Bronze Age druid stone circle is magnificently intact, featuring 15 standing stones arranged around a central boulder that still bears signs (circular holes, a shallow dent at the center) of having been used in ceremonies. To find it, walk down to the market square and follow signs on the left side of the road. There's no visitor center, and no admission fee; it's just sitting in a small paddock, passed by the traffic of everyday life.

Off the Square, Kenmare.

Kenmare Farmer's Market ★ MARKET   If you're visiting midweek, be sure to check out this small but lively open-air market held every Wednesday in Kenmare's main square. The emphasis is on food from small, artisan producers from across the region and beyond. You'll also find rustic crafts. Traders can come here from quite far afield to sell their wares, although the

ALL'S fair IN KENMARE ON AUGUST 15TH

One day of the year, Kenmare is no less overrun with visitors than Killarney: August 15, **Fair Day.** This is a working agricultural market, and the streets are taken over by farmers selling all manner of livestock, while a small army of onlookers descends on the town to witness the picturesque congregation. Stalls and other amusements provide fresh food, souvenirs, and even fortune-telling.

bulk of what's for sale is locally sourced. It's a fun and lively market to browse your way through.

The Square, Kenmare. Wed 10am–4pm. Some stalls may close in bad weather.

Seafari ★★ TOUR   A good option for families, this 2-hour cruise aboard a 15m (49-ft.) covered boat makes for an engaging introduction to Kenmare Bay and its wildlife—specifically the dolphins, sea otters, and gray seals you'll most likely see frolicking nearby. Boats depart from the pier next to the Kenmare suspension bridge. The family ticket includes coffee, tea, cookies, lollipops for the kids, and a drink of rum for the grown-ups. They'll also lend you a pair of binoculars if you need one. Live entertainment sometimes follows you on board, from kid-friendly puppet shows to traditional Irish music. Reservations recommended.

3 The Pier, Kenmare. www.seafariireland.com. (C) **064/664-2059.** Tour €20 adults; €18 students; €16 teenagers; €13 children 11 and under; €61 families. Apr–Oct, two sailings daily; call or check website for departure times.

Top Attractions on the Ring of Kerry Drive

As the scenic Ring of Kerry drive winds around cliffs and the edges of mountains, with nothing but the sea below, you'll probably average only 50kmph (31 mph) at best, but the views make it worth taking your time. The counterclockwise drive follows N70 north out of Killarney along the north coast of the Iveragh peninsula. Between **Killorglin** and **Glenbeigh,** you'll pass **Carrantuohill,** Ireland's tallest mountain at 1,041m (3,414 ft.). Bleak views of open bog land fill the landscape, with remnants of many stone cottages dating from the mid-19th-century Great Famine, when this hard-hit area lost three-quarters of its population. At **Cahersiveen,** you can zip across to the little island of **Valentia,** a smugglers' haven in the 18th century, nowadays the ferry port for excursions to **Skellig Michael** (see box p. 168). At the end of the peninsula, the beach resort of **Waterville** was for years a favorite retreat of Charlie Chaplin (1889–1977); there's a statue of him near the beach. Farther south, in **Caherdaniel,** is Derrynane, home to 19th-century Irish leader Daniel O'Connell (see p. 169). As the road loops back along the south coast, you'll pass through the colorful village of **Sneem,** its houses painted in vibrant colors—blue, pink, yellow, and orange—that burst out on a rainy day like a little touch of the Mediterranean. The following points of interest are listed alphabetically, though all are on, or within easy reach of, the route described above.

GREAT, mysterious WONDER: A TRIP TO THE SKELLIG ISLANDS

"Whoever has not stood in the graveyard on the summit of that cliff, among the beehive dwellings and beehive oratory, does not know Ireland through and through . . . "

–George Bernard Shaw

The craggy, inhospitable Skellig Islands rise precipitously from the sea. Here, gray skies meet stormy horizons about 14km (8 miles) off the coast of the Iveragh Peninsula. From the mainland, Skellig Michael and Little Skellig appear impossibly sharp-angled and daunting even today, even though the mere act of getting there isn't perilous, as it was in the 6th and 7th centuries. Back then, a group of monks built a community on the steepest, most wind-battered peaks. Over time, they carved 600 steps into the cliffs and built monastic buildings hundreds of feet above the ocean. The

complex is now a UNESCO World Heritage Site.

Landing is only possible on **Skellig Michael ★★★,** the largest of the islands. There is something tragic and beautiful about the remains of the ancient oratories and beehive cells there. Historians know very little about these monks and how they lived, although they obviously sought intense isolation. Records relating to the Skelligs indicate that even here, all but completely hidden, the Vikings found the monastery and punished it as they did all the Irish monastic settlements. Monks were kidnapped and killed in attacks in the 8th century, but the settlement always recovered. To this day, nobody knows why the monks finally abandoned the rock in the 12th century. Skellig Michael recently gained worldwide attention for its appearance at the end of *Star Wars: The*

Ballinskelligs and the Skellig Ring ★★ HISTORIC SITE West of Waterville, across a small bay, the coastal village of **Ballinskelligs** contains the absurdly picturesque ruins of St. Michael Ballinskelligs, a medieval priory overlooking the sea. A sandy beach also features the remnants of a 16th-century castle. Ballinskelligs is a starting point for the so-called **Skellig Ring,** a stunning coastal drive that takes in some of the best views of the mysterious Skellig Islands (see box above). It also passes through some of the most spectacular scenery in the county, and with the merest fraction of the traffic that can clog the Ring of Kerry. However, be warned: Its very remoteness means this route can be tough going, and the roads are very mountainous in places. This is also the edge of Gaeltacht territory, where Irish is the primary language on road signs. To find the Ring, head south through Ballinskelligs. About 0.5km (⅓ mile) after the pink An Post building, you'll come to a crossroads. The Skellig Ring (*Morchuaird na Sceilge* in Gaelic) is signposted to the right. The signs continue throughout the route.

Visitor Information Point: Barbara's Beach Café, Ballinskelligs Beach, Ballinskelligs, Co. Kerry. **Tourist Office:** Cahersiveen Community Centre, Church St., Cahersiveen, Co. Kerry. www.visitballinskelligs.ie. ℂ **066/947-2589** (Cahersiveen, summer only).

Force Awakens. The next *Star Wars* movie was also allowed to film on the ancient monument for several weeks in 2016—not without controversy in Ireland.

Start your exploration at the **Skellig Experience** (www.skelligexperience.com; (C) **066/947-6306**) on Valentia Island, which is reached via a road bridge from Portmagee. The well-designed visitor center tells you all about the extraordinary history of these ancient edifices and also offers boat trips out to see the islands. It's open daily 10am to 7pm in July and August, and 10am to 6pm in May, June, and September; in March, April, October, and November, it's open weekdays only from 10am to 5pm. Last entry is 45 minutes before closing. Admission costs €5 adults, €4 seniors and students, €3 children, and €14 families; if you add a cruise to the Skelligs,

the cost is €30 adults, €28 seniors and students, €18 children, and €85 families. Note that, at present, the visitor center's boat trips only cruise *around* the Skelligs, and **do not make landfall.** If you want to see the ruins on Skellig Michael up close, you have to go with one of the independent boat operators who work the route. A list of endorsed skippers is on the Skellig Experience website; if you use **Des Lavelle** ((C) **066/947-6124** or 087/237-1017) or **Eoin Walsh** ((C) **066/ 947-6327** or 087/283 3522) the fee includes visitor center entry. Both charge €50 per person.

There are also "unofficial" ways of reaching the islands, completely at your own risk. For a negotiated fee, you can usually find a fisherman willing to take you over, wait, and bring you back. The crossing will be rougher but certainly more adventurous.

Blueberry Hill Farm ★★ FARM   Looking for a way to amuse younger children for half a day? Try this working farm that still follows traditional farming methods. As part of the half-day tours, you can help milk cows, make butter, and take part in a treasure hunt. Children get to interact with the animals and can help out at feeding time. There's a cafe selling fresh, homemade scones and other treats. The whole experience is very friendly, authentic, and can be delightful for the little ones. Book ahead in the high season, as tours are limited to small groups. Full-day courses in such skills as basket weaving, blacksmithing, food preserving, and beekeeping are available for adults.

Signposted from R568 (Sneem-Killarney Rd.), Sneem. www.blueberryhillfarm.ie. (C) **086/356-1150** or 086/316-0224. Admission €20 adults and children. Tours start at 10am and 3pm.

Derrynane House National Historic Park ★★ MUSEUM   Irish political leader and Parliament member Daniel O'Connell (1775–1847) became known as "the Great Liberator" for his successful campaign to repeal the laws that barred Catholics from holding office. He became particularly famous in his lifetime for his so-called "monster meetings," vast public rallies held across the country (one, on the Hill of Tara, was reckoned to have been

KILLORGLIN: THE puck STOPS HERE

The first major stop on the Ring of Kerry northward from Killarney, **Killorglin** is a sleepy little town—until August 10, at least, when the annual **Puck Fair** (www.puckfair.ie) incites a 3-day explosion of merrymaking and pageantry.

One of Ireland's last remaining traditional fairs, it's technically an agricultural show; the apex of the event involves capturing a mountain goat (which symbolizes the *puka* or *puki*, a mischievous Celtic sprite) that is then declared *King Puck* and paraded around town on a throne, wearing a crown. It's bonkers but quite a lot of fun.

Nobody knows how the fair began, but one story dates it to Cromwell's invasion of Ireland in the mid-17th century. English soldiers were foraging for food in the hills above the town and tried to capture a herd of goats. One escaped to Killorglin and alerted the villagers to mount a defense. Others say the fair is pre-Christian, connected with the Pagan feast of Lughnasa on August 1.

For the rest of the year, Killorglin is a pretty, quiet town, well worth a wander. The River Laune runs straight through the town center. As you cross the old stone bridge, look out for the whimsical statue of the goat on the eastern side—and know that it stands in honor of this town's love for the *puka*.

attended by nearly a million supporters). His house, at Caherdaniel, is open to the public. It contains a museum devoted to his life featuring various artifacts and items from his personal archives. Not everything will be of interest to those who aren't already familiar with his story, but a few pieces—such as the gilded carriage from which he triumphantly greeted crowds after a brief spell as a political prisoner—are definitely worth seeing. The vast grounds are a scenic spot to wander through.

Signposted from N70 (Ring of Kerry Rd.), approx. 2.5km (1½ miles) from Caherdaniel. www.heritageireland.ie. ℰ **066/947-5113.** Admission €4 adults; €3 seniors; €2 students and children; €10 families. Apr–Sept daily 10:30am–6pm; late Mar and Oct Wed–Sun and public holidays 10am-5pm; Nov to mid-Dec Sat-Sun 10am–4pm.

Staigue Fort ★★ HISTORIC SITE This well-preserved, surprisingly large prehistoric fort is built of rough stones without mortar of any kind. The walls are 4m (13 ft.) thick at the base. Historians are not certain what purpose it served—it may have been a hilltop fortress or just a kind of prehistoric community center—but experts think it probably dates from around 1000 B.C. It's an open site with no visitor center. Look for signs, and hike up the path through the field.

4km (2½ miles) off N70 just outside Castlecove on a small farm road (follow signs).

Shopping

Kenmare is one of the best towns in the region for local crafts. In addition to the places listed below, check out the town's regular farmer's market, held in the town square every Wednesday (see p. 166).

Avoca at Moll's Gap ★ Creative, colorful, and with what must be one of the world's best-appointed parking lots, this branch of Avoca is on a mountain pass just off the main Ring of Kerry Road, north of Kenmare. Though quite small, it sells a good selection of the crafts, knitwear, and upscale knickknacks for which the Wicklow-based company is famous. (See p. 87 for a review of their flagship store in Dublin.) The cafe upstairs is also a handy stop for a light lunch or restorative cup of tea and slice of cake. Moll's Gap (on R568, signposted from main N71 Ring of Kerry Rd.), Kenmare. www.avoca.ie. © 064/663-4720. Mon–Fri 9:30am–5:30pm; Sat–Sun and public holidays 10am–6pm. Cafe closes 5pm.

De Barra Jewellery ★ Young jewelry designer Shane de Barra runs this exquisite boutique in the center of Kenmare. His creations in gold and other precious materials have a unique, subtle beauty. He has an especially deft touch with freshwater pearls that he forms into lovely necklaces strung together with tiny threads of gold. Prices aren't too high, considering the quality. A true original. Main St., Kenmare. © **064/664-1867.** Mon–Sat 9:30am–6pm.

Lorge Chocolatier ★★★ Benoit Lorge makes his exquisite artisanal chocolates at this workshop, 10km (6 miles) south of Kenmare on the N71 road. They're wonderful creations, elegantly presented—his gift boxes are little works of art in themselves. Too bad their precious, tasty cargo must be eaten. All of it. Right now. N71, Bonane, nr. Kenmare. www.shop.lorge.ie. © **064/667-9994.**

Quills Woollen Market ★ Housed in a delightfully multicolored row of shops in the center of Kenmare, this longstanding business specializes in traditional Irish knitwear—particularly heavy knit Aran sweaters, coats, and cardigans. They also sell Irish tweeds, shawls, linens, and various home decor pieces like plush sheepskin rugs. It's a great place to stock up on authentic souvenirs. Other branches of Quills are in Killarney, Glengarriff, Ballingeary, and Sneem. Main St. www.irishgiftsandsweaters.com. © **064/664-1078.**

EXPLORING THE DINGLE PENINSULA

At the western end of the county, the less visited Dingle Peninsula also has much to offer. To call it "undiscovered" would be too generous—in the summer, Dingle Town is packed with travelers—but it's not as ruthlessly jammed as the Ring of Kerry. And from time to time, even in the high season, you can find yourself blissfully alone amid its natural beauty.

Dingle *(An Daingean)*—a charming, brightly colored little town at the foot of steep hills—makes a good base for exploring the area. From Dingle town, head west by car along R559 and you'll encounter the **Slea Head Drive,** a spectacular stretch of road known for its collection of ruined abbeys and old forts (tourist information centers can give you a guide). Looping around the western tip of the Dingle Peninsula, this scenic drive offers rugged coastal vistas, unspoiled islands, and mossy archaeological sites—picture-postcard Ireland at its best. *Note:* This is serious Gaeltacht territory, so by law, all signs—even road hazard signs—are in Gaelic only.

Top Attractions on the Dingle Peninsula

The Blasket Islands ★★ ISLANDS   Overshadowed by the more famous Skelligs (see p. 168), the Blaskets are another group of mysterious, abandoned islands off the Kerry coast, but with more recent stories to tell. For hundreds of years, these were home to an isolated community with a rich tradition of storytelling and folklore—all in traditional Gaelic, of course—that was well documented in the late 1800s. In 1953, however, the Irish government ordered a mandatory evacuation when the islands were considered too dangerous for habitation. The individual islands have wonderfully evocative names like **The Sleeping Giant** and **Cathedral Rocks,** but the only island you can actually visit is the largest, **Great Blasket,** where a few crumbling buildings and skeletal edifices remain—an eerie ghost town in an outstandingly beautiful setting. See it all in a stunning 13km (8-mile) walking route that stretches to the west end of the island, passing sea cliffs and beaches of ivory sand. You can pick up maps and other information from the **Blasket Centre** on the mainland in Dunquin. Trips aboard the *Peig Sayers* (www.greatblasketisland.net; ✆ **066/057-2626**), a nippy, rigid inflatable vessel, include a 3-hour stop on Great Blasket *and* a detour to look out for Fungie the Dingle Dolphin (see below); they leave from Dingle Marina at 12:30pm every day and cost €35 adults, €20 children. Alternatively, **Marine Tours** (www.marinetours.ie; ✆ **086/335-3805**) runs half-day tours leaving Ventry at 10:30am and returning at 5pm daily. Their tour includes 3 hours on Great Blasket; the rest of the time is spent cruising around the other islands without making landfall. The cost of this tour is €50.

The Blasket Centre (Ionad an Bhlascaoid): Dunquin (Dún Chaoin). www.blasketislands. ie.✆ **066/915-6444.** Admission €4 adults; €3 seniors; €2 children; €10 families. Mid-Mar to Oct daily 10am–6pm. Last admission 45 min. before closing.

Dingle Dolphin Boat Tours ★★ TOUR   The story of Fungie the Dingle Dolphin is curious and heartwarming, although its veracity is unknown. According to lore, the bottlenose dolphin was first spotted by Dingle's lighthouse keeper in 1983, as it escorted fishing boats out to sea and then back again at the end of their voyages day after day. The sailors named him, and he became a harbor fixture. Fishermen took their children out to swim with him, and he seemed to love human contact. Now people come from miles around to have a few minutes' time with Fungie, and the fishermen ferry them out to meet him. Trips last about 60 minutes and depart roughly every two hours in low season, as often as every half-hour in high season. Fungie swims right up to the boats that stay out long enough to afford views of the picturesque bay. You can also take an early morning trip (8am–10am) in a smaller RIB (rigid inflatable boat) craft that holds only 10 people. On the morning trips only, you have the option of hiring a wetsuit and getting in the water with Fungie—but you'll need to book in advance (and tell them that you'll want a wetsuit, which costs extra). The skippers take great lengths to stress that the trips are on Fungie's terms—they don't chase him, and have no control over whether he puts in an appearance (although he usually does). On the standard trips, you don't pay if he doesn't show. However, while

what's in a name: A GRUESOME TALE IN BALLYFERRITER

The unassuming village of **Ballyferriter (Baile an Fheirtearaigh)**, part of the Slea Head Drive, is named after a local rebel named Piaras Ferriter. He was a poet and soldier who fought in the 1641 rebellion and ultimately became the last area commander to surrender to Oliver Cromwell's English troops.

Just north of the village, you can follow signs to the moody ruins of the **Dún an Oir Fort,** a defensive citadel dating from the Iron Age. There's also a small memorial to 600 Spanish and Irish troops who were massacred here by the English in 1580. Most were beheaded—a fact commemorated by the highly gruesome local names for two adjacent fields nearby. The first, where the executions were carried out, is called "the Field of the Cutting." The second, where their partial remains were buried, is "the Field of the Heads."

the little fella is still packing in the crowds at the time of writing, nobody quite knows how old Fungie is. So before you get the little ones too excited, you might want to check ahead . . . discreetly.

The Pier, Dingle. www.dingledolphin.com.© **066/915-2626.** Tour starts at €16 adults, €8 children 11 and under. Daily, around 11:30am–4pm, weather permitting.

Dunbeg Fort (Dun Beag) ★ RUINS   Sitting atop a sheer cliff just south of Slea Head, outside the village of Ventry, this 5th-century fort's stony walls rise from the cliff edge as if they were always part of it. The round Iron Age structure's stone walls are still mostly sturdy, although part of the fort has fallen into the sea. Walk around the fort to see where other fortifications and "beehive" huts were built inside the walls thousands of years ago. There's also a mysterious underground passage. You can get information on the history of the fort in the modern visitor's center, and stop for a cup of tea and some hearty soup in the little on-site cafe.

Dunbeg Fort, Slea Head Drive. www.dunbegfort.ie.© **066/915-9070.** Admission €3 adults; €2 children. Daily 9:30am–6pm.

Eask Tower ★ VIEWS   Built in 1847 as a Great Famine relief project, this is a remarkable edifice, a 12m (39-ft.) tower built of solid stone nearly 5m (16-ft.) thick with a wooden arrow pointing to the mouth of Dingle's harbor. It is certainly interesting to look at, but the main reason for making the 1.6km (1-mile) climb to the summit of Carhoo Hill is not to see the tower, but the incredible views of Dingle Harbour, Connor Pass, and, on the far side of the bay, the peaks of the Iveragh Peninsula. Save a trip here for a clear day.

Carhoo Hill, Dingle. From Dingle, follow Slea Head Rd. 3.2km (2 miles), turn left at road signposted for Coláiste Ide, and continue another 3.2km (2 miles).

Gallarus Oratory ★ HISTORIC SITE   This small, beehive-shaped church is one of the best-preserved pieces of early Christian architecture in Ireland. Built between the 7th and the 9th centuries A.D., its walls and roof are made entirely from dry stones without mortar—yet the interior stays remarkably dry. (Not quite

day hike: HIGH ATOP MOUNT BRANDON

It'll take a full day to scale **Mount Brandon,** Ireland's second-tallest mountain, but the views of ocean and gorgeous countryside are extraordinary.

The approach from the west is a more gradual climb, but the walk from the eastern, Cloghane side is far more interesting, taking in a pastoral vista of the **Paternoster Lakes.** The road to the trail head is signposted just past Cloghane on the road to Brandon town; drive about 5km (3 miles) on this road to a small parking lot and the **Lopsided Tea House.** Be sure to bring plenty of water and food, gear for wind and rain, and a good map. The trail climbs through fields, past an elaborate grotto, and along the slope of an open hillside where red-and-white poles clearly mark the way. As you round the corner of the high open hillside, the Paternoster Lakes and Brandon come into view.

The only seriously strenuous leg is the climb out of this valley to the ridge, a short but intense scramble over boulders and around ledges. Once you reach the ridge top, turn left and follow the trail another .4km (.25 miles) or so to the summit. You can return the way you came or continue south along the ridge, returning to Cloghane on the **Pilgrim's Route,** an old track that circumnavigates the Dingle Peninsula. Although this is a day hike (about 4 hr. to the summit and back), and very well marked, it shouldn't be taken lightly and certainly isn't for amateurs—bring all necessary supplies and let someone know when you expect to return.

Information on routes and weather conditions is available at the Cloghane visitor center.

dry enough, sadly, to avoid minor damage during heavy floods that hit Ireland in 2014.) The small visitor center features displays on the history of the Oratory, plus the obligatory information film. Nearby is the single surviving tower of 15th-century **Gallarus Castle.** Tours of the castle can be pre-booked with the visitor center (not that there's much to see inside).

4.8km (3 miles) east of Ballyferriter. www.heritageireland.ie. © **064/663-2402.** Free admission. May–Aug daily 10am–6pm. Signposted down small farm road off R559, either 11.8km (7⅓ miles) northeast of Dingle or 4.8km (3 miles) east of Ballyferriter.

Irish Famine Cottage ★ HISTORIC SITE
This cottage isn't a replica; it's a real dwelling, maintained as it would have been at the time it was abandoned during the Great Famine years of the mid-19th century. The humble stone building, scattered with pieces of furniture, is a stark and haunting sight, perched on a windswept cliff overlooking the coast. Sheep and horses graze nearby, adding to the feeling of wildness and isolation. You can't go inside, but looking in through the windows gives a powerful enough impression of what life was really like for the rural poor. The ticket price includes a bag of feed you can take up with you for the curious farm animals who watch your approach. *Note:* The cottage is a 2-minute walk uphill from the parking lot, so it may not be suitable for those with mobility problems.

Signposted from R559, Ventry. www.famine-cottage.com. © **066/915-6241.** €4 adults, €3 children. Apr–Oct daily 10am–6pm. If approaching from the west, sign is just after the turn for Dunbeg Fort.

Shopping

Brian de Staic Jewellery Workshop ★ A highly respected jewelry designer, Brian de Staic has built up quite a following since he first appeared on the scene over 30 years ago. He specializes in modern interpretations of ancient Celtic motifs, and you'll find everything from pendants and brooches to earrings, bracelets, and crosses. Some of his work is based on instantly recognizable designs; others are more subtle and abstract. It's all exquisite. Green St., Dingle Town. www.briandestaic.com. ℂ **066/915-1298.** Mon–Sat 9am–5:30pm.

Louis Mulcahy Workshop ★ A big name in designer Irish pottery, Mulcahy designs everything on sale in this shop, and personally crafts many of the pieces—chances are you'll be able to come away with a true original. It's all beautifully made, from Deco-influenced vases to kitchenware, tea sets, and ornaments. Considering what a name he is, Louis's prices are pretty reasonable too. The workshop also has a handy cafe. Clogher is 16.5km (10⅓ miles) northwest of Dingle on R559. On R559, Clogher, Ballyferriter, near Dingle. www.louismulcahy.com. ℂ **066/915-6229.** Workshop: May–Sept Mon–Fri 9am–7pm, Sat–Sun 10am–7pm; Oct–Feb Mon–Fri 9am–5:30pm, Sat–Sun 10am–5:30pm; Mar–Apr Mon–Fri 9am–6pm, Sat–Sun 10am–6pm.

Elsewhere in County Kerry

Crag Cave ★★ CAVES Although they are believed to be more than a million years old, these limestone caves were not discovered until 1983. The guides accompany you 3,753m (12,310 ft.) into the well-lit cave passage on a 40-minute tour revealing massive stalactites and fascinating caverns. It's very touristy, but interesting nonetheless; if need be, you can get your souvenir fix at the crafts shop. There is also a children's play area (endearingly called **Crazy Cave**), although it costs extra. The Garden Restaurant is a useful stop for lunch if you need a quick bite. On the same site is the **Kingdom Falconry** center, where you can watch birds of prey fly and be guided by handlers.

College Rd., Castleisland (turn left off N21 onto Main St., then left onto College Rd.). www.cragcave.com. ℂ **066/714-1244. Caves:** €12 adults; €9 seniors and students; €5 children; €25–€30 families. **Kingdom Falconry:** €8 adults, seniors, and students; €5 children. **Crazy Cave:** €8 per child for 2 hr. play (accompanying adults free); 3 children €20. **Combination tickets:** €20 adults; €17 seniors and students; €18 children (includes Crazy Cave). Apr–Dec daily 10am–6pm; Dec–Mar Sat–Sun 10am–6pm. **Tour times:** May–Aug, every ½ hr.; Sept–Apr 10:45am, noon, 2:30, 4, and 5:25pm.

COUNTIES CLARE & LIMERICK

North of County Kerry, the west coast of Ireland charms and fascinates with a varied and stunning landscape. From County Limerick's lush, emerald-green farmland edging the Shannon River, you can head north to County Clare's vast and breathtaking Cliffs of Moher and the lunar landscape of the extraordinary Burren National Park. However far you go, there's something wonderful to catch your eye. County Clare is a wild and beguiling county, with landscapes full of high drama and majestic beauty. This is where Ireland begins to get wild.

ESSENTIALS

Arriving

BY PLANE   Several of the big airlines operate regular scheduled flights into **Shannon Airport,** off the Limerick-Ennis road (N18), County Clare (www.shannonairport.com; ℰ **061/712-000**), 24km (15 miles) west of Limerick. Although not as busy as it used to be, due to many of its short-haul routes having moved to Cork, Shannon is still one of Ireland's major points of arrival and departure for transatlantic flights.

BY BUS   **Bus Éireann** (www.buseireann.ie; ℰ **061/313-333**) provides regular bus service from all parts of Ireland to **Colbert Station,** Limerick's railway station, on Parnell Street. In County Clare, most of the small towns and countryside attractions listed in this chapter are all accessible on Bus Éireann, although service isn't frequent in the most rural areas.

BY TRAIN   **Irish Rail** operates direct trains from Dublin, Cork, and Killarney, with connections from other parts of Ireland, to Limerick's **Colbert Station,** Parnell Street (www.irishrail.ie; ℰ **061/315-555**).

BY CAR   Although several of the major sights in this region can be reached on public transportation, you really need a car for the more remote places. Shannon Airport has offices of: **Avis** (www. avis.ie; ℰ **061/715-600**), **Budget** (www.budget.ie; ℰ **061/471-361**), and **Hertz** (www.hertz.ie; ℰ **061/471-369**). Several local firms also maintain desks at the airport; among the most reliable is **Dan**

Dooley Rent-A-Car (www.dan-dooley.ie; ℭ **061/471-098;** also in Limerick City at ℭ **062/53103**).

Visitor Information

The **Burren Centre** in Kilfenora (ℭ **065/708-8030**) is the place to go for information on the Burren region. In addition, visitor information points are on Main Street in **Ballyvaughan** (ℭ **065/707-7464**) and at the **Cliffs of Moher** (ℭ **065/708-6141**).

The **Limerick Tourist Information Centre** on Arthur's Quay, Limerick (ℭ **061/317-522**) is open Monday to Friday 9am to 5pm; in summer, it's often open weekends, too (call to check). Another office inside the **Adare Heritage Centre,** Main Street, Adare (www.adareheritagecentre.ie; ℭ **061/396-666**) is open daily, year-round, from 9am to 6pm.

WHERE TO STAY

County Clare contains the most unique and special places to stay in the region. That said, it's perhaps a little surprising that there aren't more of them to be found. Fortunately there are some real gems among their number. Meanwhile, Limerick City's economic growth spurt in the 1990s and 2000s led to the construction of several large, impersonal chain hotels there. But why would you bother? The real finds are to be had in the rural parts of County Limerick, where you can hide away in a lovely old cottage on a tranquil farm, or splurge on a night in a grand country-house retreat.

Where to Stay in County Clare

Aran View Country House ★   The clue's in the name at this small and friendly hotel in Doolin: The house looks across an expanse of lawn and sea, out to the Aran Islands in the distance. It was built in the mid-17th century and has good-sized guest rooms that maintain a traditional feel. The bar wisely takes full advantage of the amazing view out front, making this a lovely spot for an early evening pint as the sun goes down. Breakfasts are good too. Doolin is about a 10-minute drive up the coast from the Cliffs of Moher.

Coast Rd., Doolin, Co. Clare. www.aranview.com. ℭ **065/707-4061.** 13 units. €125–€140. Free parking. Breakfast included. **Amenities:** Restaurant; bar; Wi-Fi (free).

Fergus View ★★   More breathtaking views are to be had at this sweet B&B near Corofin, one of the gateways to the Burren. You could sit for ages marveling at the long vista of rolling fields and rambling hills, joined by the wonderful owner, Mary, as she brings you a fortifying tray of tea to sip by the open fire. Mary is also an expert on the Burren and all this area has to offer visitors, and will happily share her encyclopedic knowledge. Guest rooms are small and simple, but the beds are comfortable. On the grounds is a self-catering lodge that sleeps five. Fergus View is closed from November to Easter.

On R476 in Kilnaboy, 3.2km (2 miles) north of Corofin, Co. Clare. www.fergusview.com. ℭ **065/683-7606.** 6 units. €76. Discounts for 2 nights or more. Free parking. Breakfast included. **Amenities:** Wi-Fi (free).

LOVED-UP IN lisdoonvarna

If you've been looking for love in all the wrong places, clearly you've never been to Lisdoonvarna. This County Clare town lives for *l'amour*. There's a Matchmaker Pub on the main street (inside the Imperial Hotel); two local residents call themselves professional matchmakers (Willie Daly, a horse dealer, and James White, a hotelier); and every autumn, the town hosts the month-long **Lisdoonvarna Matchmaking Festival** (www.matchmakerireland.com). Thousands of love-lorn singletons come in search of The One, and locals cheer them on. Up and down each street, every atmospheric corner is used for mixers and minglers. Residents stir the pot by hosting romantic breakfasts, dinners, games, and dances. So good are their intentions and so charming is their belief in true love—in the idea that there really is somebody out there for everybody, and that they should all come together in a far-flung corner of western Ireland to find one another—that you may just fall for it. Lisdoonvarna can be found on the main N67 road, between Ballyvaughan and Ennistimon.

Gregans Castle Hotel ★★★ An elegant 18th-century house in an extraordinary setting, Gregans is not in fact even remotely castle-like, but don't let that bother you. This unique place is one of the most peaceful hotels in Ireland. Manager Simon Haden is the second generation of hoteliers in his family to run this place, although it's been a hotel for much longer—famous guests of the 20th century included J. R. R. Tolkien, who was apparently so inspired by the otherworldly views of the surrounding Burren that he drew on them to describe Mordor in *The Lord of the Rings*. Guest rooms are design-magazine chic, with modern furnishings and bay windows. Televisions are banned in the hotel, to enable guests to get maximum benefit from the tranquil surroundings. Even if you can't stretch to the cost of a night here, consider booking a table in the superb restaurant, **Gregans Castle ★★★** (see p. 182). Chef David Hurley's modern Irish cooking is utterly superlative—though if you don't want to splurge, the excellent bar food menu is much cheaper. Check the website for some attractive dinner, bed and breakfast packages, and midweek deals.

Ballyvaughan, Co. Clare. www.gregans.ie. © **065/707-7005.** 22 units. €179–€258. Free parking. Breakfast included. **Amenities:** Restaurant; bar; Wi-Fi (free).

Moy House ★★★ An extraordinary squat tower house built in the 19th century, overlooking the crashing waves of the Atlantic Ocean, Moy House is a unique place. You can climb the four-story central tower for the best view out to sea, although the view from some of the guest rooms is almost as good. (The cheaper ones have views of the grounds, not the sea.) Rooms are designed in a muted, contemporary style, with large beds and modern bathrooms. In what has to be a one-of-a-kind feature, one bathroom even has an original, glass-covered well. You can walk down to the beach for a stroll along the dramatic shoreline, or relax in the drawing room—the house is packed with bookshelves. The restaurant is excellent, with a very strong emphasis on

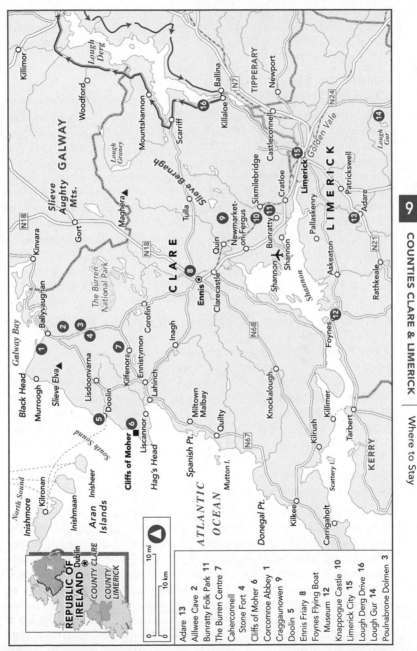

Killimor

Lough Derg

Woodford

GALWAY

Slieve Aughty Mts.

Kinvara

Gort

Ballyvaughan

Galway Bay

Black Head

Murroogh

Slieve Elva▲

Lisdoonvarna

Doolin

5

6

Cliffs of Moher

South Sound

North Sound

Kilronan

Inishmore

Inishmaan

Inisheer

Aran Islands

ATLANTIC OCEAN

Hag's Head

Spanish Pt.

Mutton I.

Liscannor

Lahinch

Ennistymon

Kilfenora

Corofin

Inagh

Miltown Malbay

Quilty

Donegal Pt.

Knockalough

Kilkee

Carrigaholt

Scattery I.

Kilrush

Killimer

Tarbert

KERRY

1 **2** **3** **4** **7**

The Burren National Park

CLARE

Ennis ⦿ **8**

Clarecastle

Quin

Tulla

Newmarket-on-Fergus

9

Maghera▲

Slieve Bernagh

Lough Graney

Mountshannon

Scarriff

Killaloe

16

Ballina

N7

TIPPERARY

Newport

N24

Castleconnell

Cratloe

Sixmilebridge

10 **11** Bunratty

Shannon ✈

Shannon

Shannon

Pallaskenry

Askeaton

Rathkeale

N21

Foynes

12

N68

N67

N18

N18

Limerick **15**

Golden Vale

LIMERICK

Patrickswell

Adare **13**

14

Lough Gur

REPUBLIC OF IRELAND ⊛ Dublin

COUNTY CLARE

COUNTY LIMERICK

10 mi

10 km

0
0

Adare 13
Aillwee Cave 2
Bunratty Folk Park 11
The Burren Centre 7
Caherconnell
  Stone Fort 4
Cliffs of Moher 6
Corcomroe Abbey 1
Craggaunowen 9
Doolin 5
Ennis Friary 8
Foynes Flying Boat
  Museum 12
Knappogue Castle 10
Limerick City 15
Lough Derg Drive 16
Lough Gur 14
Poulnabrone Dolmen 3

179

seasonal produce, but it's certainly not cheap at €55 per person for a five-course, fixed-price menu. Check the website for good deals, including dinner, bed and breakfast packages.

On N67, 1.6km (1 mile) south of Lahinch, Co. Clare. www.moyhouse.com. ℂ **065/708-2800.** 9 units. €141–€224. Free parking. Breakfast included. **Amenities:** Restaurant; Internet in public rooms (free).

Where to Stay in County Limerick

Adare Manor ★★★ Surrounded by a whopping 340 hectares (840 acres) of landscaped grounds, on the very edge of charming Adare village, this luxurious resort looks impressively Victorian Gothic from the outside. Indoors, you'll find a beautifully restored and converted manor house; it's mostly 19th-century, although check out the elaborately carved 15th-century doors on the ground floor. Adare Manor is renowned as a golf destination, with a highly rated 18-hole championship course. Archery, clay-pigeon shooting, and horseback riding can all be easily arranged. The **Oak Room ★★★** restaurant is one of the best in the area (see p. 184). *Note: At this writing, Adare Manor was closed for a major refurbishment, adding more guest rooms, a spa, and a cinema. It is scheduled to reopen in July 2017.*

Adare, Co. Limerick. www.adaremanor.com. ℂ **061/605-200.** 62 units. €480–€995. 2-night minimum stay in villas. Free parking. Breakfast included. **Amenities:** 2 restaurants; bar; room service; spa; pool; gym; golf course; Wi-Fi (free).

Courtyard Cottage ★ A former cowshed may not sound like the height of glamour, but this is a beautifully converted elegant space, a short drive east of Foynes. You really feel away from the herd (no pun intended), with 202 hectares (500 acres) of farmland between you and civilization. And what could be more civilized than going up to the manor house, where the charming owner and family resides, for dinner—or even having it brought to your door if you prefer? (€25; or you can fend for yourself in the cottage's own kitchen.) You can rent this place as a fully self-catering option, or as a B&B, with tasty Irish breakfasts cooked every morning up at the house.

Askeaton, Co. Limerick. ℂ **061/392-112** or 087/213–3698. 2 units. €100–€160 B&B; €550–€650 per week self-catering. Free parking. Breakfast included in B&B rate. **Amenities:** Dinner on request (notice required); kitchen; tennis court; no Wi-Fi.

Echo Lodge ★★ This place was once a convent, before being converted into a chic and stylish hotel. Bedrooms are reasonably small, but decorated in such a way that they could be described as "traditional," only without the acres of chintz that usually implies—instead they use vintage print wallpapers, tasteful color schemes, and pleasantly eccentric *objets d'art* touches here and there, such as mini-Ionic columns for bedside tables. The **Mustard Seed ★★★** restaurant is one of the best in the region (see p. 183). There's usually a good handful of special offers on the website, including dinner, bed and breakfast packages.

Ballingarry, Co. Limerick (13km/8 miles south of Adare). www.mustardseed.ie. ℂ **069/68508.** 76 units. €104–€244. Free parking. Breakfast included. **Amenities:** Restaurant; bar; room service; Wi-Fi (free in public areas only).

Fitzgerald's Woodlands House Hotel ★★ The bedrooms at this pleasant, modern hotel aren't particularly fancy, but they're enormous—rare for a place with such moderate per-night rates. The hotel makes a big deal out of how good its beds are, thanks to a full 10cm (4 in.) down mattress topper on each of the beds. The in-house Revas Spa offers relaxation treatments and a thermal suite to while away the last hint of travel fatigue; you can book couples' packages that include massages and afternoon tea for two for around €280. Deals include dinner, bed and breakfast packages and seniors discounts.

Adare, Co. Limerick. www.woodlands-hotel.ie. ℂ **061/605-100.** 94 units. €102–€174. Free parking. Breakfast included. Dinner, bed and breakfast packages available. **Amenities:** Restaurant; bar; room service; spa; Wi-Fi (free).

WHERE TO EAT

Dutifully demolishing the rule of thumb that the best restaurants are usually found in cities, the rural byways of Counties Claire and Limerick contain several places to eat that would be serious contenders on any "best of" lists for Ireland.

Where to Eat in County Clare

Bay Fish & Chips ★ FISH & CHIPS Close to the Cliffs of Moher, the Bay serves fresh, tasty fish and chips. There's nothing fancy here—battered seafood and chunky, steaming chips, always to "take away"—but it's the simplicity of this dish that makes it such a staple in this part of the world. Specials always include a fresh catch of the day. Portions are formidable. To get here from the Cliffs, just head south on R478 for a little over 5.5km (3½ miles). It's on the main street as you drive through Liscannor—look for the small white building with a blue wave painted on one end.

Main St., Liscannor, Co. Clare. ℂ **083/112-3351.** Fish and chips €5–€10. Daily noon–around 11pm.

The Cherry Tree ★★★ MODERN IRISH Overlooking a lake in the sweet village of Killaloe, the Cherry Tree has raked in awards over the years, and with good reason. The menu, which uses plenty of local ingredients, is simple yet sophisticated, wisely giving space for those local flavors to come to the fore. A starter of scallops from West Cork could lead on to John Dory fillet served with roasted pepper and baby spinach, or a rack of Wicklow lamb. The early bird menu, served from 6pm to 9pm Tuesday to Thursday, and from 6pm to 7:30pm on Friday and Saturday, is great value at €26 for three. Reservations are advisable.

Lakeside, Ballina, Killaloe, Co. Clare. www.cherrytreerestaurant.ie. ℂ **061/375-688.** Main courses €15–€27. Tues–Sat 12:30–3pm, 6–10pm; Sun 12:30–3pm.

Durty Nelly's ★ IRISH/PUB FOOD You don't walk into a pub called Durty Nelly's expecting haute cuisine, but some welcome surprises are to be found here. They serve appetizing pub food—fish and chips, steak

THERE ONCE WAS A poet FROM LIMERICK . . .

So how did a genre of bawdy pub poetry come to be associated with this unassuming Irish town? The answer seems buried nearly 300 years in the past. Nobody really knows who wrote the first sharply worded, five-line poem, but the format became popular in the 18th century, due to a group of poets who lived in the town of Croom in County Limerick. Known as the *Fili na Maighe*, or the "Gaelic poets of the Maigue," the poets wrote sardonic, quick-witted poems in Irish that soon became all the rage. Their style was adopted across the region, and within a century, everybody was doing it. Anthologies on the subject list 42 poets and Irish scholars in the county in the 19th century, whose limerick-style compositions covered a range of topics—romance, drinking, personal squabbles, and politics.

But it's possible that the scathing, satiric limerick style we know today rose from an 18th-century battle of wills between a poet and pub owner, Sean O'Tuama, and his friend Andrias Mac-Craith. Boyhood friends O'Tuama and MacCraith grew up in County Limerick. After a spectacular falling-out (nobody quite remembers over what), they vented their wit in a series of castigating verses about each other. As these became enormously popular, the modern limerick was born. In retrospect, they're kind of cute, although the meter was sometimes a little stretched. As MacCraith once wrote:

O'Tuama! You boast yourself handy,
At selling good ale and bright brandy
But the fact is your liquor
Makes everyone sicker,
I tell you this, I, your good friend, Andy.

sandwiches, burgers, and salads. Those who don't mind a bit of cheesy tourist novelty can have their picture taken while pouring their own pint of Guinness. The proximity to **Bunratty Castle ★★** (see p. 185) will mean that most travelers will probably see it as more of a lunch spot than a dinner destination, but there are actually three dining rooms here—the more refined Oyster and Loft restaurants offer an upmarket version of the same food (good steaks, Thai curries, fresh seafood, and so on). And if you're wondering about the name, "Durty Nelly" was a somewhat ribald heroine of Irish folklore, said to have invented the magical cure-all (and highly alcoholic) variety of moonshine, "potcheen" (see p. 159).

Next to Bunratty Castle, Bunratty, Co. Clare. www.durtynellys.ie. ✆ **061/364-861.** Lunch main courses €11–€25. Mon–Thurs 10:30am–11:30pm; Fri–Sat 10:30am–12:30am; Sun noon–11pm. Bar food served noon–10pm daily. **Oyster restaurant:** Daily noon–10pm. **Loft restaurant:** Daily 5:30–10pm.

Gregans Castle ★★★ MODERN IRISH   The hugely talented David Hurley is the head chef at the exceptional in-house restaurant of the **Gregans Castle Hotel ★★★** in Ballyvaughan (see p. 178). His menus are exquisite; easily the equal of top-level restaurants in major cities. The seven-course tasting menu forms the entirety of the dinner service, although a slightly cheaper, three-course dinner menu is available in the Corkscrew Bar until 7:30pm on Sundays and Wednesdays. A typical meal could start with a few expertly prepared canapés, followed by caramelized scallops, lamb with bok choi, or perhaps some impeccably presented local seafood. Desserts are sumptuous; blackcurrant soufflé with buttermilk custard, for instance. If you love Gregans so much that you don't want to leave (and that would be perfectly understandable), rooms start at around €179 per night during high season.

Ballyvaughan, Co. Clare. www.gregans.ie. ☎ **065/707-7005.** Fixed-price menu €70. Mon–Tues, Thurs–Sat, 6–9pm. No dinner Wed and Sun (except bar food). Children under 7 only allowed at 6pm sharp.

Vaughan's Anchor Inn ★★ SEAFOOD   A 10-minute drive from the Cliffs of Moher, this excellent pub specializes in top-notch seafood. If you've really worked up an appetite, or possibly have been locked in a room without food for a month, go straight for the gigantic platter of local seafood. Otherwise, try a delicious plate of crab claws with garlic butter, or some traditional fish and chips. There are always a couple of meaty choices on the menu too. At lunchtime, they offer a few sandwiches and nibbles alongside the heartier options. Vaughan's Anchor Inn is on the main street in Liscannor; look out for the long white building with the small parking lot on the right, not long after you round the bend and see the small town center ahead of you.

Main St., Liscannor, Co. Clare. ☎ **065/708-1548.** Main courses €18–€26. Daily 12:30–9pm.

Where to Eat in County Limerick

Mortell's ★★ SEAFOOD/DELI   This great little deli restaurant is an excellent lunch option if you're in Limerick City and need a place to have lunch. The seafood (much of it local) is beautifully prepared, and cooked right in front of your eyes. There's always a choice of at least three different catches of the day, although you could also opt for a burger or simply a cup of coffee and a sandwich. The lively, chatty staff keep everything running smoothly.

40 Roaches St., Limerick, Co. Limerick. www.mortellsseafoodrestaurant.weebly.com. ☎ **061/415-457.** Lunch main courses €5–€14. Mon–Sat 8:30am–4:30pm.

The Mustard Seed ★★★ MODERN EUROPEAN   The in-house restaurant of the excellent **Echo Lodge** ★★ hotel (p. 180) is one of the best-loved, and most widely known, in the region. The restaurant has its own kitchen garden that supplies many of the ingredients. The four-course menus are imaginative and scintillating; after a starter of monkfish with pistachio puree, you could go for filet of John Dory with artichoke fricassee, or beef ribeye with creamed corn and tarragon. There's an eight-course tasting menu for €75, or come before 7:30pm any night except Saturday for the Twilight Dinner, a slightly pared-down version of the main menu for €46. Dinner, bed and breakfast deals are usually offered on the website.

At the Echo Lodge hotel, Ballingarry, Co. Limerick (13km/8 miles south of Adare). www.mustardseed.ie. ☎ **069/68508.** Fixed-price 4-course dinner €60. Mon–Sat 6:30–9:30pm; Sun 6–9pm.

The Oak Room ★★★ MODERN IRISH   Another superb hotel restaurant, the Oak Room is part of **Adare Manor** ★★★ (see p. 180). The high stone windows and silver candelabra of the dining room here should leave no doubt that this is a place where you're expected to sit up straight—gentlemen, a tie if you please. The food certainly lives up to the promise of being something special. Herb-and-citron-marinated salmon makes a deliciously piquant starter before a main course of beef filet with cracked pepper jus, or rack of lamb with a wild-garlic crust. *Note: At this writing Adare Manor, including the Oak Room, was closed for a major renovation. It is scheduled to reopen in July 2017.*

Adare, Co. Limerick. www.adaremanor.com. ✆ **061/605-200.** Main courses €25–€35. Daily 6:30–10pm.

The Wild Geese ★★★ MODERN IRISH   What is it about Adare that breeds superlative restaurants? The Wild Geese, in the center of the village, mixes fresh, local ingredients with global accents. An entree might be roast chicken stuffed with soft Bluebell Falls goat cheese, a specialty from County Clare; or some Atlantic salmon flavored with lemon and tarragon, served in a prawn sauce. There's also a vegetarian menu. Sunday lunch, which often features dishes seen on the evening menu, is significantly cheaper than dinner service, at just €20 for two courses.

Adare, Co. Limerick. www.thewild-geese.com. ✆ **061/396-451.** Fixed-price menus €30–€37. Tues–Sat 6:30–9:30pm, Sun 12:30–3pm. Closed most of Jan.

EXPLORING COUNTY CLARE

With its miles of pasture and green, softly rolling fields, Clare seems, at first, a pleasantly pastoral place. But head to the coast and a dramatic landscape awaits you, with plunging cliffs and crashing waves. Turn north, and you'll find visual drama of a different kind, courtesy of the otherworldly landscapes of **the Burren National Park,** the county's greatest attraction. Clare is an excellent place for those fascinated by the country's ancient history, because it's littered with historic and prehistoric sites, from the **Poulnabrone Dolmen** to **Bunratty Castle,** with its better-than-expected folk park. And traditional Irish music is always on heavy rotation in Clare, especially in the charming village of **Doolin.**

Top Attractions in County Clare

Aillwee Cave ★★ CAVES   The story of how this deep cave system came to be discovered starts with a curious dog. In 1944, a local farmer followed his dog into a small opening in the hillside. He was astonished to find that it opened out into a huge cavern with 1,000m (3,280 ft.) of passages running straight into the heart of a mountain. The publicity-shy farmer kept it to himself for decades before eventually spreading the word. Professional cave explorers later uncovered its magnificent bridged chasms, deep caverns, a frozen waterfall, and hollows created by hibernating brown bears (which have been extinct in Ireland for 10,000 years.) Guided tours are excellent here, usually led by geology students from area universities. Enjoy the scary moment when they turn out the lights for a minute so you can experience the depth of the darkness inside. Tours last approximately 30 minutes, and are conducted continuously. On the same site, the **Burren Birds of Prey Centre** is a working aviary designed to mimic the natural habitat of the buzzards, falcons, eagles, and owls that live there. For €70 per person, you can take a private "Hawk Walk," where a handler shows you the birds up close and teaches you how to handle a hawk for yourself. It culminates in a guided forest walk, where you learn how to release the bird and call it back. (Tickets for the Hawk Walk, which include admission to the cave and the Birds of Prey Center, must be booked in advance.) There are also a couple of craft shops on site, where among other things, you can buy Aillwee's own brand of cheese. *Tip:* Buy your tickets online for substantial discounts.

Off R480, near Ballyvaughan, Co. Clare. www.aillweecave.ie. ℂ**065/707-7036.** Admission to caves: €12 adults; €6 children; €35 families. Birds of Prey Centre: €10 adults; €8 children; €25 families. Combined ticket: €18 adults; €10 children; €50 families. Open daily, July–Aug 10am–6:30pm, Mar–June and Sept–Oct 10am–5:30pm, Nov–Feb 10am–5pm (no flying displays Nov–Dec). Times given are first and last tour.

Bunratty Castle & Folk Park ★★ HERITAGE SITE Built in 1425

and restored in the 1950s, Bunratty is an impressive early-15th-century castle, and home to two major tourist attractions: a "living history" recreation of a 19th-century village, and a riotous nighttime medieval banquet. You can tour the interior of the castle, which is surprisingly complete, including a fine collection of medieval furniture and art. The restored walled garden is a beautiful place to meander. However, the folk park is probably the bigger draw here. Actors in period costume wander around as you walk through the authentic-looking village center, complete with everything from a post office and schoolroom to a doctor's office. You can go inside each one and chat to the occupants. Meanwhile, professional craftspeople work their trades, using traditional methods. There's even a Victorian-style pub. It's all great fun, and a brilliant way to imbue kids with a sense of history. In the evenings, the medieval banquet takes over the castle's Great Hall. After a full, sit-down meal, there's a lively show of music, dancing, and folk stories—all performed by actors and musicians in medieval garb. There are two sittings nightly, at 5:30 and 8:45pm. Booking is essential.

Signposted from N18 (Shannon-Limerick Rd.), Bunratty, Co. Clare. www.shannonheritage.com. ℂ**061/361-511.** Admission €15 adults; €9 seniors, students, and children 6–12; children under 6 free; €34–€38 families. **Medieval banquet:** €54 adults; €37 children 10–12; €25 children 6–9; children under 6 free. **Castle:** daily 9am–5:30pm. Last admission to castle 1 hr. before closing; last admission to park 45 min. before closing.

The Burren National Park ★★★ PARK Carved by nature from bare

carboniferous limestone, this stark, otherworldly landscape spreads across 1,653 hectares (4,083 acres) and continually acquires more land as it becomes available. It's a remarkable rocky land, dotted with picturesque ruined castles, tumbling cliffs, rushing rivers, lakes, barren rock mountains, and plant l

...at defies all of nature's conventional rules. Amid the rocks, delicate wildflowers somehow find enough dirt to thrive, and ferns curl gently around boulders, moss softens hard edges, orchids flower exotically, and violets brighten the landscape. Formed 300 million years ago, when shells and sediment were deposited under a tropical sea, over centuries the land was eroded by Irish winds and rains, as well as poor prehistoric farming methods, creating the desolate beauty you see today. The park is particularly rich in archaeological remains from the Neolithic through the medieval periods—dolmens and wedge tombs (approximately 120 of them), ring forts (500 of those), round towers, ancient churches, high crosses, monasteries, and holy wells. Centered at Mullaghmore Mountain, the park has no official entrance points—and like all National Parks in Ireland, it's completely free to enter. (Certain attractions within the park's boundaries—such as **Caherconnell Stone Fort,** below, and **Aillwee Caves,** p. 184—do charge admission, but others such as Corcomroe Abbey, p. 187, and the Poulnabrone Dolmen, p. 189, are open sites with no admission fee.) **The Burren Centre,** on R476 to Kilfenora, provides an informative overview with films, landscape models, and interpretive displays. A craft shop and tearoom are also on site and local guide **Tony Kirby** (www.heartofburrenwalks.com; ℂ **065/682-7707**) leads 2½-hour guided walks from outside the center at 2:15pm, Tuesday and Wednesday, and 10:30am Thursday to Sunday. The cost is €20, including entry to the exhibition. The center is next to the ruins of **Kilfenora Cathedral,** which contains some interesting wall carvings—look for the heads above what's left of the doors and windows.

Visitor center: Kilfenora, Co. Clare. www.theburrencentre.ie. ℂ **065/708-8030.** Admission €6 adults, €5 seniors and students, €4 children 6–16, €20 families, children 5 and under free. Jun–Aug daily 9:30am–5:30pm; mid-Mar to May and Sept–Oct daily 10am–5pm.

Caherconnell Stone Fort ★ ANCIENT SITE

Built sometime around the year 950 A.D., this rugged, early medieval ring fort was used as a defensive structure for at least 200 years. It's one of the best-preserved ruins of its kind in Ireland; the dry stone walls are around 3 meters (9¾ ft.) tall in places, and equally as thick. Today, it's partly under the care of an archaeology school, so you'll often see students at work. There's a visitor center with a cafe and an exhibition focusing on the Burren's forts, dolmens, and other ancient monuments. More entertainingly, you can also see sheepdog demonstrations at the fort from March to October; visit the website to find out when.

On R480, 1km (3/4 mile) north of the Poulnabrone Dolmen (see p. 189), near Carran, Co. Clare. www.caherconnell.com. ℂ **065/708-9999.** Admission to fort €7 adults; €6 seniors and students; €4 children under 12; €17 families. **Sheepdog demos:** €5 adults; €3 children under 12; €15 families. **Joint ticket for fort and demos:** €9.60 adults; €8 seniors and students; €5.60 children under 12; €25 families. July–Aug 10am–6pm; May–June and Sept 10am–5:30pm; Mar–Apr and Oct 10:30am–5pm; closed Nov–Feb.

Cliffs of Moher ★★ NATURAL SITE

The cries of nesting seabirds are faintly audible amid the roar of the Atlantic crashing against the base of these breathtaking cliffs. Undulating for 8km (5 miles) along the coast, the cliffs tower as high as 214m (702 ft.) over the sea. In bad weather, access is (understandably)

walk this way: THE BURREN WAY

With its unique terrain and meandering walking paths, the Burren lends itself beautifully to walking. The **Burren Way** is a 42km (26-mile) signposted route stretching from Ballyvaughan to Liscannor, incorporating old "green roads": unpaved former highways that crisscross the Burren landscape in inaccessible areas. (Most were created during the Great Famine as work projects for starving locals.) An information sheet outlining the route is available from any tourist office. You can also contact **Guided Walks and Hikes** (www.burrenguided walks.com; *℗* **065/707-6100**) for guided walks and hikes of varying lengths.

limited, as the wind can blow very hard here; when the weather is fine, a guardrail offers you a small sense of security as you peek over the edge. (Some foolhardy visitors always insist on climbing over it for a better view of the sheer drop—needless to say, this is completely against the rules.) On a clear day, you can see the Aran Islands in Galway Bay as misty shapes in the distance. Look the other way, however, and you'll see a constant throng of tour groups, coaches, and cars. The enormous visitor center houses gift shops, a high-tech "Cliffs of Moher Experience," and various other exhibits that feel designed to wring every last euro out of the entirely natural wonder. Furthermore, the visitor center has the only (legal) car park, which you can't use without buying entry tickets to the whole center—effectively turning it into a steep *per person* parking charge. (You may see places beside the narrow road where you could illegally park and walk straight up to the cliffs without paying a cent, but we can't recommend that.) Head up the path beside the visitor center to **O'Brien's Tower** for the best view of the cliffs. The 19th-century tower is a knockout spot for photos, although—surprise!—you have to pay an extra €2 to climb the stairs.

Nr. Liscannor, Co. Clare. www.cliffsofmoher.ie. *℗* **065/708-6141.** Admission €6 adults; €4 disabled, seniors and students; children 15 and under free. Price includes parking and visitor center admission. July–Aug daily 9am–9pm; June Mon–Fri 9am–7:30pm, Sat–Sun 9am–8pm; May and Sept Mon–Fri 9am–7pm, Sat–Sun 9am–7:30pm; Apr Mon–Fri 9am–6:30pm, Sat–Sun 9am–7pm; Mar and Oct Mon–Fri 9am–6pm, Sat–Sun 9am–6:30pm; Nov–Feb daily 9am–5pm. Tower and cliffs may be inaccessible in bad weather.

Corcomroe Abbey ★★ RELIGIOUS SITE/RUINS

Set jewel-like in a languid green valley bounded by rolling hills, the jagged ruins of this Cistercian abbey are breathtaking. Donal Mór O'Brien founded the abbey in 1194, and his grandson, a former king of Thomond, is entombed in the structure's northern wall. There are some interesting medieval and Romanesque carvings set in the stone, including one of a bishop with a crosier. Corcomroe is a lonely spot, except for Easter morning, when people come from miles around to celebrate Mass. It's meant to be quite a sight. Look for a mound, surrounded by trees, beside the road on the way out—it's the remains of an ancient ring fort.

Signposted from L1014, near Oughtmama, Co. Clare. No phone. Free admission (open site).

Craggaunowen ★★ HERITAGE SITE   Following the successful castle-plus-open-air-museum template of **Bunratty Castle** (p. 185), Craggaunowen focuses on what life would have been like for the Bronze Age inhabitants of Ireland. A reconstructed "crannog" shows how Celts lived, worked, and defended themselves from the Iron Age right through to the middle of the first millennium. (Records indicate, in fact, that scattered communities lived like this as late as the 1600s.) Other reconstructions to explore here include a 4th-century ring fort and underground passages known as souterrains, thought to have been used for cool storage. (Incidentally, some archaeologists believe there are real souterrains at **Caherconnell Stone Fort**—see p. 186—that have yet to be excavated.) Costumed historian-guides provide demonstrations of the techniques inhabitants of such settlements would have used to cook, build, weave, and so on. Also on display is the Brendan Boat, a replica vessel of the kind Vikings are believed to have sailed to America; it was built in 1976 by explorer Tim Severin, who used it to do just that—a 4,500-mile journey that took him and his crew just over a year. The 16th-century **Craggaunowen Castle** is also on the grounds (included in the price).

Kilmurray, near Quin, Co. Clare. www.cliffsofmoher.ie. ℂ**061/360788.** Admission €9 adults; €5.50 children aged 6–16, children under 6 free, €22–€25 families. Easter to mid-Sept daily 10am–5pm. Closed mid-Sept to Easter.

Doolin ★★ VILLAGE   Doolin's old pubs and restaurants ring with the sound of fiddle and accordion all year long, earning this secluded fishing village a reputation as the unofficial capital of Irish traditional music. Most famous among them is **Gus O'Connor's Pub** (Fisher St.; www.gusoconnorsdoolin.com; ℂ **065/707-4168**), set among a row of thatched fisherman's cottages, about a 10-minute walk from the seafront. Great though the craic is here, the pub's fame inevitably draws crowds, and it can get packed to the rafters on a busy night. If you're looking for something a little more authentic, head up the road to **McGann's** (Main St.; www.mcgannspubdoolin.com; ℂ **065/707-4133**); it's less well known and not so unrelentingly jammed as Gus O'Connor's. In fact, on many nights, there are no locals in Gus's at all—they're all here, downing pints of Guinness and listening to the fiddles. Feel free to join them. Doolin is on R479, about 7.8km (4¾ miles) west of Lisdoonvarna.

Tourist Information Point: at the Hotel Doolin, Fitz's Cross, Doolin, Co. Clare. ℂ**065/707-4111** or 086/856-9725.

Ennis Friary ★ RELIGIOUS SITE/RUINS   When you walk around what's left of Ennis Friary, it can be hard to get a sense of its original scale. Records show, however, that in 1375 it was the home and workplace for no less than 350 friars and 600 students. Founded in 1241, this Franciscan abbey was a famous seat of learning in medieval times, making Ennis a focal point of Western Europe for many years. It was finally forced to close in 1692, and thereafter fell into ruin, but it's been partly restored, and contains many beautifully sculpted medieval tombs, decorative fragments, and carvings, including the famous McMahon tomb, with its striking representations of the Passion. The nave and chancel are the oldest parts of the friary, but other structures, such as the 15th-century tower, transept, and sacristy, are also rich in architectural detail.

Abbey St., Ennis, Co. Clare. www.heritageireland.ie. ✆ 065/682-9100. Admission €4 adults; €3 seniors; €2 children and students; €10 families. Easter–Sept daily 10am–6pm; Oct daily 10am–5pm. Last admission 45 min. before closing.

Knappogue Castle & Walled Gardens ★★ CASTLE   Midway between Bunratty and Ennis, this regal castle was built in 1467 as the home of the MacNamara clan—who, along with the O'Briens, dominated the area for more than 1,000 years. Oliver Cromwell used the castle as a base in the mid-17th century while pillaging the countryside, which is why, unlike many castles, it was largely left intact. The original Norman structure also has elaborate late-Georgian and Regency wings, added in the early and mid-19th century. Later, in the 20th century, it fell into disrepair, but was rescued by Texan Mark Edwin Andrews (1903–1992), a former U.S. Assistant Secretary of the Navy. He and his wife, Lavone, an architect, worked closely with area historical societies and returned the castle to its former glory, even furnishing it with 15th-century furniture. The Andrews family then turned Knappogue over to the Irish people. The peaceful walled gardens have been meticulously restored to their Victorian condition—look for the wonderful statue of Bacchus. The gardens supply herbs for the **medieval banquets,** held nightly at 6:30pm, from April to October. Banquet tickets cost €48 adults, €33 children 9–12, €22 children 6–8 (free for children under 6). Reservations are essential. *Note:* There is no cafe or restaurant on site during the day.

Quin, Co. Clare. www.shannonheritage.com. ✆ 061/360-788. Admission €6.50 adults; €4 seniors; €3.50 children 5–16; children under 6 free; €17–€20 families. Castle: May–Aug daily 10am–4:30pm. Last admission 45 min. before closing.

Poulnabrone Dolmen ★ ANCIENT SITE   This portal tomb is an exquisitely preserved prehistoric site, made all the more arresting by the alien Burren landscape in which it sits. Its dolmen (or stone table) is huge, and surrounded by a natural pavement of rocks. The tomb has been dated back 5,000 years. When it was excavated in the 1980s, the remains of 16 people were found. And yet, the greatest mystery remains how the gigantic boulders were moved and lifted—the capstone alone weighs 4½ tonnes (5 tons). In the summer, you probably won't have much trouble finding this sight—just look for all the tour buses. At times they literally block the road.

On R480, 1km (¾ mile) south of Caherconnell Stone Fort (see p. 186), near Carran, Co. Clare. Free admission (open site).

Sports in County Clare

One of Ireland's most famous golf courses is at **Lahinch Golf Club,** Lahinch (www.lahinchgolf.com; ✆ 065/708-1003). Of its two 18-hole links courses, the "Old Course"—the longer championship links course—is the one that has given Lahinch its worldwide repute. This course's elevations, especially at the 9th and 13th holes, make for great views, but they also make wind an integral part of

LIMERICK CITY: worth A VISIT?

It is synonymous the world over with a type of lively, often lewd verse, but spend much time in Limerick's eponymous capital and you might find yourself making up a few off-color rhymes of your own. With a population of 100,000, it's the Republic's third-largest city (only Dublin and Cork are bigger), with a gritty, crime-ridden urban feel usually associated with much bigger cities. In 2008, it suffered the ignominy of being named the murder capital of Europe, while the same report declared Ireland to be Europe's safest country overall. In more recent years, it has been the backdrop for a notorious, ongoing gang feud.

Simply put, Limerick just isn't very nice. That said, there have been genuine efforts to make things better. The tourist board is doing its part to clean the place up, with a certain amount of success. A prime example is **King John's Castle ★** (Nicholas Street; www.shannonheritage. com; ✆ **061/360-788**). This stern riverside fortress, dating from 1210, is the centerpiece of Limerick's historic area. But rarely has a historic building been so poorly treated in the modern age; during the 1950s, in an astonishing act of government vandalism, it even had a public housing project built within its central courtyard. Thankfully that's long gone, but the big, modern, visitor-center building that went up in its place still

rather spoils the effect. However, a recent renovation has greatly improved the visitor facilities, including high-tech interactive displays. Admission to the castle costs €10 adults, €8 seniors and students, €5.25 children ages 6 to 16 (free for children under 6), €22 to €25 families. It's open April to September from 9:30am to 5:30pm, and October to March from 9:30am to 4:30pm (last admission 1 hr. before closing).

Located in an 18th-century Customs building with a fine Palladian front, the **Hunt Museum ★★** (Rutland Street; www.huntmuseum.com; ✆ **061/312833**) has exhibits on ancient Greece and Rome, and paintings by Picasso and Renoir. Admission costs €5.50 adults, €4.50 seniors and students, €3.50 children, and €14 families. It's open Monday to Saturday from 10am to 5pm, Sunday and public holidays from 2 to 5pm. For more modern art, try the **Limerick City Gallery of Art ★**, in People's Park at the corner of Perry Square and Mallow St. (www.gallery.limerick.ie; ✆ **061/310-633**). Besides regularly changing contemporary art exhibitions, the gallery's permanent collection includes work by Irish painters Jack B. Yeats and Sir John Lavery. It's open Monday to Saturday 10am to 5:30pm (and until 8pm on Thurs), Sunday noon to 5:30pm (closed on public holidays). Admission is free.

play. Watch the goats, Lahinch's legendary weather forecasters: If they huddle by the clubhouse, it means a storm is approaching. Visitors are welcome to play, especially on weekdays; greens fees are €50 to €170 for the Old Course and a more affordable €20 to €35 for the newer Castle Course. Meanwhile, the bling quotient is high at the **Trump International Golf Links,** Doonbeg (www. trumpgolfireland.com; ✆ **065/905-5600**), owned since 2014 by American reality TV star Donald Trump. Before Trump plastered his name over everything, this was a respected course designed by golf pro Greg Norman; its magnificent 15th hole ends in a funnel-shaped green surrounded by sky-high dunes. The complex includes a country club, hotel, and cottages, and (no surprise) greens fees are quite high; expect to pay around €180 per person.

EXPLORING COUNTY LIMERICK

The majority of County Limerick is peaceful, pleasant farmland. The picture-postcard village of Adare is definitely worth a visit, as are Lough Gurr and Rathkeale. Sadly, the same cannot be said of Limerick City; despite the best efforts of the Tourist Board to shake up its image (see box above), the city remains a rather gritty, unpleasant place.

Top Attractions in County Limerick

Adare ★★ TOWN   *"O sweet Adare,"* wrote the poet Gerald Griffin (1803–40), *"O soft retreat of sylvan splendor/Nor summer sun nor morning gale/E'er hailed a scene more softly tender."* Like a town plucked from a book of fairy tales, Adare has thatched cottages, black-and-white timbered houses, lichen-covered churches, and romantic ruins, all strewn along the banks of the River Maigue. Unfortunately, all of this means that Adare has been seriously discovered by the tour-bus crowds—even by May, which is still officially off-season, the roads can get clogged at times—but it's still absolutely worth a stop. Drop in at the **Adare Heritage Centre** on Main Street, roughly in the middle of the village. Part visitor center, part museum on the history of the town, it also has a small craft store and a shop selling Irish woolens. From June to September the center also runs bus tours to Desmond Castle (see p. 141), costing €6 adults, €5 seniors, students and children, and €20 families.

Adare, Co. Limerick. Heritage Centre. www.adareheritagecentre.ie. © **061/396-666.** Historical Exhibition: €5 adults; €3.50 seniors, students, and children. Free admission. Daily 9am–6pm.

Foynes Flying Boat Museum ★★ MUSEUM   When Shannon Airport was just a remote patch of undeveloped farmland, this was the center of international aviation in Europe. The first commercial flight from the U.S. to Europe touched down at Foynes Airport one hot July morning in 1937; five years later this became one end of the first-ever regular service between the two continents. (In the same year, Foynes was also the birthplace of the Irish coffee: After a particularly violent storm turned back a New York–bound flight, the bartender was asked to serve something that would both warm up and calm down the rattled passengers—so he served hot coffee and threw shots of whiskey in for good measure.) At this engaging museum, you can see a replica of the original Pan Am "flying boat," which may make you swear never to complain about a modern flight again. You can also tour the actual terminal building, kept as it was when the airport closed in 1945, and experience a replica 1940s cinema.

Foynes, Co. Limerick. www.flyingboatmuseum.com. © **069/65416.** Admission €12 adults; €10 seniors and students; €7 children 5–13; children under 5 free; €30 families. Open daily, June–Sept 9:30am–6pm, mid-Mar to May 9:30am–5pm, Oct to mid-Nov 9:30am–5pm. Last admission 1 hr. before closing. Closed Mid-Nov to mid-Mar.

Lough Gur ★★ LAKE/ ANCIENT SITE   Occupied continuously from the Neolithic period to late medieval times, this lovely lake's shores hold an unusual

THE lough derg DRIVE

At the meeting point of Counties Clare, Limerick, and Tipperary, the Shannon River's largest lake, Lough Derg—virtually an inland sea—creates a stunning waterscape 40km (25 miles) long and almost 16km (10 miles) wide. The road that circles the lake for 153km (95 miles), the **Lough Derg Drive,** is one of Ireland's great scenic drives, a continuous photo opportunity with panoramas of glistening waters, gentle mountains, and hilly farmlands unspoiled by commercialization.

The drive is also a collage of colorful shoreline towns, starting at the lake's south end with **Killaloe,** County Clare, and **Ballina,** County Tipperary. They're so close that they are essentially one community—only a splendid 13-arch bridge over the Shannon separates them. In the summer, its pubs and bars fill with weekend sailors. **Killaloe** is a picturesque town with lakeside views at almost every turn and restaurants and pubs perched on the shore. **Kincora,** on the highest ground at Killaloe, was traditionally said to be the royal settlement of Brian Boru and the other O'Brien kings, although no trace of any buildings survives.

Memorable little towns and harborside villages like **Mountshannon** and **Dromineer** dot the rest of the Lough Derg Drive. Some towns, like **Terryglass** and **Woodford,** are known for atmospheric old pubs where spontaneous sessions of traditional Irish music are likely to break out. Others, like **Puckane** and **Ballinderry,** offer unique crafts. On the north shore of the lake in County Galway, **Portumna** is worth a visit for its forest park and castle.

The best way to get to Lough Derg is by car or boat. Since the area has limited public transportation, you will need a car to get around the lake. Major roads that lead to Lough Derg are the main Limerick-Dublin road (N7) from points east and south, N6 and N65 from Galway and the west, and N52 from the north. The Lough Derg Drive, which is well signposted, is a combination of R352 on the west bank of the lake and R493, R494, and R495 on the east bank.

preponderance of ancient sites. Most of the sights are well signposted on the R512, the drive that skirts around the lake's edge. Archaeologists have uncovered foundations of a small farmstead built around the year 900, a lake island dwelling built between 500 and 1000, a wedge-shaped tomb that was a communal grave around 2,500 B.C., and the extraordinary **Grange Stone Circle,** a 4,000-year-old site with 113 upright stones forming the largest prehistoric stone circle in Ireland. An interesting Heritage Centre helps put it all into context. The center underwent a half-million euro renovation in 2015, with new exhibits dedicated to explaining why Neolithic people chose this area to settle. To find the center, turn east off R512 at Reardons Pub in Holycross, take the first left afterward, and follow Lough Gur Road. The lake itself is a great place to explore and have a picnic.

11km (6¾ miles) SE of Limerick City on R512, Lough Gur, Co. Limerick. www.loughgur.com. ✆ **061/385-386.** Free access to Lough Gur itself; Heritage Centre €5 adults; €4 seniors and students; €3 children; €15 families. Heritage Center open Mar–late Oct Mon–Fri 10am–5pm; Sat–Sun and public holidays noon–6pm. Late Oct–late Nov and late Dec–Feb Mon–Fri 10am–4pm, Sat–Sun and public holidays noon–4pm.

COUNTY GALWAY

For many travelers to Ireland, Galway is the farthest edge of their journey. Part of the reason they draw the line here is because the depths of the county look so forbidding—with its bleak bogs, heather-clad moors, and extraordinary light—they think that it must be the end of all that's worth seeing in Ireland. It isn't, of course, but Galway *is* just far enough west to escape much of the touristy bustle of Kerry or Cork. And that's a compelling part of its attraction—here you can climb hills, catch fish, explore history, and get away from it all in the Irish countryside. With its misty, mountain-fringed lakes, rugged coastline, and extensive wilderness, County Galway is a wild and wooly area. And yet, nestled just outside its most dramatic and unkempt part—the windswept, boggy expanse of Connemara—is one of Ireland's most sophisticated towns. Though small, Galway City has long been a center for the arts, and the winding, medieval streets of its oldest quarter have a seductively bohemian air.

ESSENTIALS

Arriving

BY BUS   Buses from all parts of Ireland arrive daily at **Bus Éireann Travel Centre,** Ceannt Station, off Eyre Square, Galway, County Galway (www.buseireann.ie; ✆ **091/562-000**). They also provide daily service to Clifden. Buses to rural areas sometimes run only a handful of times per day, however, and remote sites may be completely inaccessible without a car.

BY TRAIN   Direct trains from Dublin and Limerick arrive daily at Ceannt Station in Galway City, off Eyre Square.

BY CAR   Galway City is on the main N18, N17, N63, N67, and M6 roads. Journey time from Dublin is about 2 hours; from Killarney it's about 3 hours; and from Cork it's about 2½ hours. Outside of Galway City, which is easily accessible by public transportation, your options in this region get pretty limited if you don't have a car.

To hire one in Galway, try **Budget,** 12 Eyre Square (www.budget.ie; ✆ **091/564-570**) or **Europcar** at Motorpark, Headford Road (www.irishcar rentals.com; ✆ **091/741-150**).

BY PLANE Galway has an airport, but as of this writing it has not been used for regular scheduled flights since 2011. There were a small handful of commercial flights from the airport in 2014 and 2015, but none on a regular basis, or with major airlines. There's a possibility they will resume in future, though, so it may be worth checking www.galwayairport.com for updates.

Visitor Information

The **Galway Tourist Office** is on Forster Street, Galway City (www.galway. ie; ✆ **091/537-700**). The city also has a smaller tourist information point on Eyre Square. Out in Connemara, the **Clifden Tourist Office** is on Galway Road, Clifden (✆ **095/21163**). The Clifden office is closed in winter.

[FastFACTS] GALWAY CITY

ATMs/ Banks In Galway City, there's a **Bank of Ireland** (✆ **091/567-321**) and an **AIB** (✆ **091/561-151**) on Eyre Square. ATMs are frustratingly rare the farther you get into the countryside, so make sure you get cash when you can.

Dentists For dental emergencies, your hotel should contact a dentist for you; otherwise, try **Eyre Square Dental Clinic** on Prospect Hill, Eyre Square (✆ **091/562-932**).

Doctors For medical emergencies, dial ✆ **999.** For non-emergencies, your hotel should call you a doctor. Otherwise, in Galway City visit the **Crescent Medical Centre,** 1 The Crescent (✆ **091/587-213**).

Emergencies For police, fire, or other emergencies, dial ✆ **999.**

Internet Access Chat & Net, 2 Eyre Square (✆ **091/539-896**) offers Internet access and low-cost international calls.

Pharmacies Lloyds Pharmacy is at 13 Forster Street (✆ **091/567-740**). If you need a drugstore after hours, the **University Late Night Pharmacy,** at the University Halls of Residence, 1 Newcastle Road (✆ **091/520-115**) is open until 9pm weekdays, though it doesn't stay open late on weekends.

Taxis Try **Abbey Cabs** (✆ **091/533-333**) or **Galway Taxis** (✆ **091/561-111**).

WHERE TO STAY

Galway City has a handful of good, reasonably priced accommodations, although, as with many Irish cities, you'll get more for your money by staying in the 'burbs—in this case, pretty Salthill, a mile or two to the west of the center. Farther afield from the region's main hub, the countryside is scattered with exceptionally beautiful and interesting places to stay.

Where to Stay in and Around Galway City

The G ★★★ Chic designer flourishes and contemporary art grace this modern, luxurious hotel overlooking the glassy waters of Lough Atalia and Galway Bay, about a 5-minute drive northeast of the city center. Many bedrooms have floor-to-ceiling windows to take full advantage of those views,

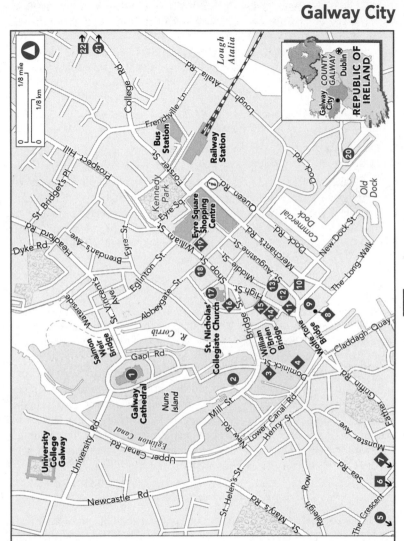

ATTRACTIONS ●
Druid Theatre **13**
Ferry to the Aran Islands **20**
Galway Arts Centre **2**
Galway Atlantaquaria **5**
Galway Cathedral **1**
Galway City Museum **9**
Galway Irish Crystal Centre **21**
Hall of the Red Earl **12**
Lynch's Castle **18**
St. Nicholas' Collegiate
  Church **17**

ACCOMMODATIONS ■
The G **22**
The House Hotel **10**
Marless House **6**
Sea Breeze Lodge **6**

RESTAURANTS ◆
Aniar **3**
Ard Bia at Nimmo's **8**
G.B.C. **19**
Gourmet Tart Company **7**
Kirwan's Lane **14**
Martine's Quay Street **11**
Oscars Seafood Bistro **4**
The Pie Maker **15**
Sheridan's Cheesemongers **16**

 Information

195

flooding the place with natural light. Service is outstanding, with charming and attentive staff. Treatments in the beautifully designed spa aren't cheap, but check for special offers—you can sometimes find deals that include a massage, use of the thermal suite, and dinner. Talking of food, **Gigi's** restaurant serves good modern Irish cuisine, with plenty of local meats and seafood. The four set menus cover different bases, price-wise—Delight, for example, will set you back €30 for two courses, while Indulge is a pricier €42.

Wellpark, Galway City. www.theghotel.ie. ℰ **091/865-200.** 101 units. €113–€189. Free parking. Breakfast included. **Amenities:** Restaurant; bar; room service; spa; gym; Wi-Fi (free).

The House Hotel ★★   In the heart of Galway City, this upbeat, funky hotel has a modern vibe, with public areas filled with playful design statements, from polka-dot chairs to hot-pink sofas. Guest rooms, however, are far more muted and restful, with oatmeal, white, or green color schemes, and the slightest hint of a retro theme. The restaurant is good, and surprisingly reasonable for a hotel of this size in the center of the city. The in-house cocktail bar is a lively nightspot. That said, you're spoiled for choice when it comes to nightlife in this neighborhood—Galway's buzzing Latin Quarter is literally on your doorstep.

Spanish Parade, Galway, Co. Galway. www.thehousehotel.ie. ℰ **091/755-111.** 134 units. €129–€229. Discounted parking at nearby lot (€8 for 24 hr.). Breakfast not included in lower rates. **Amenities:** Wi-Fi (free); restaurant; bar; room service.

Marless House ★   This pleasant, friendly B&B in Salthill, a small seaside commuter town immediately to the west of Galway, is an exceptionally good value for the money. Guest rooms are spacious and spotlessly clean, though some have slightly overwhelming floral color schemes. Mary and Tom are thoughtful hosts; they have arrangements with several local tour companies, so if you want to book an organized trip to one of the major sights in the region—including the Aran Islands or the Cliffs of Moher—the tour bus will come and pick you up directly from here, and drop you back at the end of the day. Mary is also a fount of sightseeing information, and will cheerfully help you draw up an itinerary. Breakfasts are delicious and filling.

8 Threadneedle Rd., Salthill. www.marlesshouse.com. ℰ **091/523-931.** 6 units. €70–€90. Free parking. Breakfast included. **Amenities:** Wi-Fi (free).

Sea Breeze Lodge ★★   Another good option in Salthill, just outside Galway City, this stylish little B&B overlooks Galway Bay. Guest rooms are spacious and contemporary, with polished wood floors and big windows, looking out over the bay or garden. Beds are enormous—the larger ones are super kingsize (the European equivalent of an American king-size), and all have luxurious memory-foam mattresses. Breakfasts are served in a pleasant little conservatory overlooking the garden. The hotel can arrange tours of the major sights in the area, including an all-day trip to the Aran Islands for €25 per person. There's no restaurant, but the center of Galway is only about 5km (3 miles) by car or taxi.

9 Cashelmara, Salthill. www.seabreezelodge.org. ℰ **091/529-581.** 6 units. €122–€178. Free parking. Rates include breakfast. **Amenities:** Wi-Fi (free).

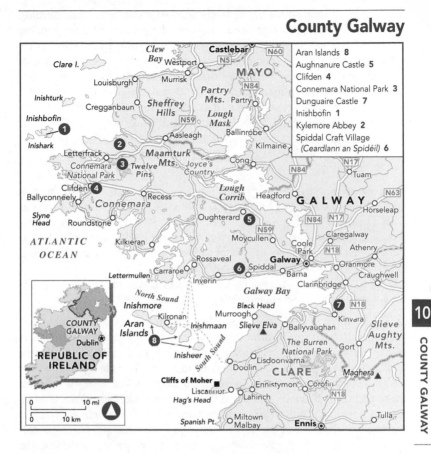

Aran Islands **8**
Aughnanure Castle **5**
Clifden **4**
Connemara National Park **3**
Dunguaire Castle **7**
Inishbofin **1**
Kylemore Abbey **2**
Spiddal Craft Village
(Ceardlann an Spidéil) **6**

Where to Stay in the Aran Islands

Kilmurvey House ★★   This lovely guesthouse, overlooking Dún Aengus Fort, is probably the best of the (admittedly few) accommodations to choose from on the Aran Islands. Austere outside, inside it's all cheerful, bright rooms and polished wood floors. Owner Teresa Joyce is extremely welcoming, and her home-cooked breakfasts are delicious (try her porridge made with whiskey). Guest rooms are enormous. She also offers a babysitting service if parents are in the mood for an island date night.

Kilronan, Inishmore, Aran Islands, Co. Galway. www.aranislands.ie/kilmurvey-house. ✆ **099/61218.** 12 units. €100–€120. Free parking. Rates include breakfast. **Amenities:** Wi-Fi (free).

Where to Stay in Connemara

The Anglers Return ★   Surrounded by beautiful gardens, this lovely, artsy retreat was built as a hunting lodge in the 19th century; today it's run with charm by Lynn Hill, a talented artist. Bedrooms are simple and modestly furnished with antiques. The views over the grounds and nearby river are gorgeous. The only downside is that none of the rooms have private bathrooms—you have to use one of two bathrooms located down the corridor, although robes are thoughtfully provided. Guests are free to wander the gardens, which are practically an attraction by themselves. Those wanting more seclusion, and a touch of adventure, may want to rent a yurt on the grounds. The Anglers Return doesn't accept credit cards; it's cash or check only.

Toombeola, Roundstone, Co. Galway. www.anglersreturn.com. © **095/21204.** 3 units. €110. Free parking. Breakfast included. Closed Dec–Jan. **Amenities:** Restaurant; guest lounge; Wi-Fi (free).

Currarevagh House ★ This elegant Italianate manor house, built in 1842, sits just outside tiny Oughterard, at the edge of the clear blue waters of Lough Corrib. The house is a perfect retreat—its spacious lounges have fires crackling at the hearth, ideal for relaxing on a rainy day. Rooms are large, with floral curtains, and beds are comfortable. Meals in the pink-hued dining room are excellent, and often feature the day's catch.

Oughterard, Co. Galway. www.currarevagh.com. © **091/552-312.** 12 units. €170 double. Breakfast included. **Amenities:** Restaurant; bar; Wi-Fi (free).

Delphi Lodge ★★★ This vine-covered 18th-century country house on a 1,000-acre lakefront estate is one of Ireland's best small hotels. Guest rooms are spacious and masculine, furnished with an informally elegant touch, all with peaceful lake and mountain views. The library and lounge are warmed by wood-burning fireplaces. There's an honor bar where you make your own cocktails in the evening, and a snooker bar where you can retire to practice your steady hand. Dinners here are excellent, with an emphasis on the catch of the day, and eaten at a long dining table to encourage conversation. Owner Peter Mantle can supply you with everything you need to fish—permits, licenses, and equipment rental. The staff is friendly and helpful.

The Delphi Estate and Fishery, Leenane, County Galway. www.delphilodge.ie. © **095/42222.** 12 units. €230–€320. Rates include full Irish breakfast. Closed Christmas and New Year's holidays. **Amenities:** Restaurant (guests only); honor bar; Wi-Fi (free).

Dolphin Beach House ★★★ All in all, this is one of our favorite guesthouses on the Emerald Isle. A splendidly restored early-20th-century homestead, Dolphin Beach House has awe-inspiring views of the bay at Clifden. The guest rooms are huge and light-filled, with handmade wood beds and high ceilings. The dining room looks out across acres of green fields, giving way to the azure sea beyond. Delicious evening meals are served here, such as local lamb or a catch of the day. The vegetables for the table are grown in the house's own organic garden. Breakfasts are good, too. Fearghus Foyle is an easy, charming host and a passionate environmentalist; the house is almost entirely powered by renewable energy sources, and there's a rainwater collection and recycling system. Check the website for midweek discount deals. *Note:* Dinner must be booked in advance, before you arrive.

Lower Sky Rd., Clifden, Co. Galway. www.dolphinbeachhouse.com. 🕾 **095/21204.** 4 units. €130–€180. No children under 12. Free parking. Breakfast included. 3-course dinner €40. **Amenities:** Wi-Fi (free); restaurant.

Doonmore Hotel ★   On Inishbofin Island (see p. 210), this waterfront hotel might not be fancy, but the views are extraordinary—from every window you see stunning vistas of the sea and High Island. Guest rooms are quite basic, but families will be pleased to find the spacious units with children's bunk beds. Rooms in the modern extension are furnished with pine furniture and flooded with light. Older rooms in the main house are a little worn but still pleasant. Staff are cheerful, and the restaurant offers good, unpretentious cooking.

Inishbofin Island, Co. Galway. www.doonmorehotel.com. 🕾 **095/45804.** 25 units. €80–€100. Rates include full breakfast. Closed Nov–Mar. **Amenities:** Restaurant; bar; Wi-Fi (free).

Errisbeg Lodge ★   This mountainside lodge near the little town of Roundstone feels more isolated than it is. Tucked away between the wild countryside and the ocean, its setting is glorious, and makes for wonderful, windy walks down to the sandy beach. Guest rooms are simply decorated with pine furniture and floral bedding. All have exquisite mountain or ocean views. This is not a five-star hotel by any means, but the hosts are very friendly and the scenery is breathtaking.

Just over 1.6km (1 mile) outside of Roundstone on Clifden Rd., Roundstone, Co. Galway. www.errisbeglodge.com. 🕾 **095/35807.** 5 units. €90–€100 double. Breakfast included. No credit cards. Closed Dec–Jan. **Amenities:** Smoke-free rooms; Wi-Fi (free).

Renvyle House Hotel ★★   This grand old house on the rocky edge of the Atlantic Ocean seems truly in the middle of nowhere, although it is near Connemara National Park (see p. 210). Still, it's worth the journey, and not just for these breathtaking windswept views. There are miles of pristine Irish wilderness to explore around it. The poet W. B. Yeats honeymooned here when it was a family home; Winston Churchill was also a regular guest. Lounges are sprawling and wood-floored, warmed by open fires. Guest rooms vary in size and decor, some are grand and spacious, others are small and cozy. Most have tasteful, masculine decor. The in-house restaurant offers divine, European-inspired Irish cooking.

Renvyle, Co. Galway. www.renvyle.com. 🕾 **095/43511.** 65 units. €135–€240. Rates include full breakfast. Closed Jan–Feb. **Amenities:** Restaurant; bar; 9-hole golf course; outdoor pool; 2 tennis courts; Wi-Fi (free).

WHERE TO EAT

Cosmopolitan Galway City is naturally the focus of the western region's culinary scene. That's not to say that the range of options is particularly varied, but there are some excellent places—particularly if you're after fresh, local seafood. The rest of the county is not without a few top-notch places either, plus a liberal smattering of cheap and cheerful lunch spots.

Where to Eat in Galway City

Aniar ★★★ MODERN IRISH This Michelin-starred restaurant in the center of Galway City is one of the best, and most fashionable, places to eat in the region. Head chef Ultan Cooke has won as many fans for his passionate slow-food ethos as for his delicious food. Well, almost as many . . . okay, it's mainly the food. The menu is tiny, but always designed firmly according to what's in season and best that day. Mussels might be served with scurvy grass—a kind of wild herb native to the region—or monkfish with celeriac and black garlic. The only downside is the cost. This is not a cheap night out, although the tasting menus are less expensive than you might expect from a place this trendy—choose from six courses for €70, all the way up to ten courses for €100. Needless to say, reservations are essential.

53 Lower Dominick St. www.aniarrestaurant.ie. ✆ **091/535-947.** Tasting menus €70–€100. Tues–Thurs 6–10pm, Fri–Sat 5:30–10pm. Closed Sun and Mon.

Ard Bia at Nimmo's ★★ SEAFOOD/BISTRO/CAFE The pleasantly rustic dining room at this fashionable restaurant in Galway City doubles as a popular cafe during the day. At any time, the emphasis is the same: delicious, homey flavors, with local and seasonal produce. Stop in for some tasty, creative sandwiches at lunch, or maybe some fresh hummus with roasted vegetables. In the evening, expect local fish with harissa and mussel broth, or perhaps some pheasant with pancetta-crushed potatoes. The wine list is excellent, and reasonably priced—you can drop in for a glass or two without eating, if you don't mind perching on a barstool. They also do a popular brunch on weekends.

Spanish Arch, Long Walk, Galway City. www.ardbia.com. ✆ **091/561-114.** Lunch main courses: €7–€13. Dinner main courses: €20–€27. Mon–Fri 10am–3:30pm (lunch served from noon), 6–10pm; Sat–Sun 10am–3:30pm (brunch only), 6–10pm.

G.B.C. (Galway Bakery Company) ★★ BAKERY/BISTRO Hugely popular with locals, this cheerful bakery and cafe also has a busy bistro restaurant upstairs. The downstairs cafe serves breakfast, fresh bakery goods, and light meals all day; it's a buzzing spot for a cup of coffee and a mid-afternoon treat. Meanwhile, upstairs is a proper sit-down restaurant, albeit a pleasantly informal one, serving steak, roast chicken, fajitas, pasta, and fresh fish. The evening set menu offers much the same hearty kind of fare, but the early bird menu tends to have a couple of different options—such as burgers, open sandwiches, and even an extremely late-in-the-day full Irish breakfast.

Williamsgate St. www.gbcgalway.com. ✆ **091/563-087.** Lunch: €10–€12. Dinner main courses €11–€17. Cafe: daily 8am–9pm. Restaurant: daily 8am–10pm.

Gourmet Tart Company ★★ BAKERY/INTERNATIONAL A French-style bakery and patisserie with a restaurant attached, the Gourmet Tart Company is very popular with locals for snacks, light meals, and sweet treats. The home-baked cakes, tarts, and pastries make for a tempting mid-afternoon snack or a breakfast on the go. (The cafe also does a very good sit-down breakfast if you want to linger.) At lunch they sell sandwiches and assorted deli items to take out. At night, however, a full menu of delicious, international fare at very reasonable prices suddenly appears—filet of sole with new potatoes; Thai curry with coconut rice; or perhaps a salad of Parma ham, pears, and Cashel blue cheese. Brunch is popular on Sundays. The Gourmet Tart Company also has smaller (deli/bakery only) branches on Abbeygate Street and Headford Road in Galway City.

Salthill Upper (opposite Salthill Church), Salthill. www.gourmettartco.com. © **091/861-667.** Breakfast: €2–€9. Lunch main courses: €9–€12. Dinner main courses €9–€18. Mar–Dec Sun–Thurs 7:30am–7pm; Fri–Sat 7:30pm–11pm. (Last food orders 6pm Mon–Thurs, 9pm Fri–Sat, 6pm Sun.) Jan–Feb daily 7:30am–7pm (no dinner).

Kirwan's Lane ★★ MODERN IRISH/SEAFOOD The exposed stone walls of the elegant downstairs dining room at this popular restaurant speak to the building's medieval origins. Open the menu, however, and everything suddenly seems bang up to date—this is one of the most popular and reliable restaurants in Galway City for modern Irish cuisine. Seafood is a specialty— langoustine and lamb linguine with chili, lemon, and garlic; or a cold platter of smoked salmon, prawns, and oysters. Carnivores are not overlooked, with a good selection of meat dishes too (try the steak with horseradish potatoes).

Kirwan's Lane. www.kirwanslane.com. © **091/568-266.** Main courses €17–€25. Mon–Sat 12:30–2:30pm, 6–10pm; Sun 6–9:30pm.

Martine's Quay Street ★★ BISTRO A friendly, cozy restaurant and bar in the center of Galway City, Martine's serves excellent, Irish-influenced bistro style cooking, with just a hint of an international accent. The menu is short but well judged: dishes like tempura of hake or salmon fish cakes, followed by a juicy steak, cooked in a charcoal oven, or catch of the day. They take their meat seriously here: The specials board includes a "cut of the day," according to what's best. The "Not so Early Bird" menu has limited options, but is a snip at just €20 for two courses, or €25 for three. (The "not so" is because it's actually available all night, every night.) Martine's is also a good choice for a simple but delicious lunch of salads, sandwiches, and a few larger plates, all for around €10 or less.

21 Quay St. www.winebar.ie. © **091/565-662.** Main courses €14–€30. Daily 11am–3:30pm, 5–10:30pm.

Oscars Seafood Bistro ★★★ SEAFOOD Another standout spot for seafood in Galway City, Oscar's is a cheerful, relaxed kind of place. The dining room is filled with modern art, as fabric drapes across the ceiling add a bohemian touch. You could start with some prawns, cooked simply in garlic and butter, then try some Clare Island salmon with seasonal vegetables; seared scallops with lime drizzle; or a plate of crab claws and prawns, dripping with local cheese. Ingredients are sourced from local producers and farmers' markets. The two-course fixed-price menu is great value, just €19 (Mon–Thurs until 7:30pm).

Dominick St. www.oscarsbistro.ie. © **091/852-180.** Main courses €15–€26. Daily noon–9pm.

COUNTY GALWAY

Where to Eat

The Pie Maker ★★ PIES   Just try and beat *this* for an authentic Irish food experience. With its old-style red-and-gold frontage and dimly lit, quirkily decorated dining room, it's a cozy and atmospheric place. The menu consists of pies, pies, and more pies, in light, fresh pastry crusts. There are a couple of sweet options, but most are savory with hot, fresh fillings of meat and vegetables, such as roast beef, curried chicken, chicken and mushroom, or sausage and mozzarella. Super-traditional sides come in the form of creamy mashed potatoes and garden peas. And if by some miracle you have room for dessert, try the amazing Banoffee pie, a heavenly combination of whipped cream, banana, and toffee, with a crumbly base. Pies can also be ordered to go. *Note:* The Pie Maker doesn't take credit cards.

10 Cross St. Upper. ☎ **091/513-151.** Main courses €6–€13. Daily noon–10pm.

Sheridan's Cheesemongers ★★ DELI/WINE BAR   Well, this is an unusual idea—an artisan cheese shop and deli, doubling up as a bar where you can order a glass of wine and some nibbles. Food comes in the form of delicious cheeseboards and charcuterie, much of it locally produced. So simple, so delicious, and hugely popular too—you might struggle to get one of the few tables during busy times. This is a really good alternative to heavy restaurant food when all you really want is a chat and a sophisticated snack. Oh, and the selection of cheeses is sensational.

Church Yard St., Galway City. www.sheridanscheesemongers.com. ☎ **091/564-832** or 091/564-829 (shop). Main courses €5–€10. **Wine bar:** Tues–Fri 1pm–midnight; Sat noon–midnight; Sun 4pm–midnight. Wine bar closed Mon. **Shop:** Mon–Fri 10am–6pm; Sat 9am–6pm; closed Sun.

Where to Eat in the Aran Islands

Teach Nan Phaidi ★★ CAFE/IRISH   The Aran Islands aren't exactly awash with fine restaurants, and so as a captive audience you might be forgiven for lowering your expectations. But this little cafe-restaurant near the Dún Aengus Fort is nothing short of delightful. The Irish country cottage interior is atmospheric, with exposed wood beams and jauntily painted furniture. The menu is straightforward and unfussy but quite delicious: cakes, stews, sandwiches, and soups—comfort food, in other words, and incredibly welcome after a blustery day on the island. Most of the ingredients are locally sourced, and there's a special children's menu, too. The homemade desserts, particularly the cakes, are absolutely delicious. Service is upbeat and cheerful.

Kilmurvey, Inis Mor, Aran Islands, Co. Galway. ☎ **099/20975.** Main courses €5–€14. Daily 11am–5pm.

Where to Eat in Connemara

O'Dowd's ★★ SEAFOOD   There's not much room in this tiny pub in tiny Roundstone, which means you'll be fighting for space with dozens of hungry locals. But trust them, because they know exactly what they're here for: extremely good, fresh seafood, simply and beautifully prepared. There's nothing complicated about the menu, and that's part of the appeal—Connemara

FOLLOWING IN THE footsteps OF POETS

In the early 1900s, every summer the area southeast of Galway City became a sort of Bloomsbury Society West, as Dublin's greatest literary minds decamped to a cluster of nearby manor homes. About 36km (22⅓ miles) southeast of Galway City, near the northern border of the Burren (see chapter 9), you'll see signs to the beautiful **Coole Park National Forest** (www.coolepark.ie; ☏ **091/631804**). This was once a country home of the dramatist and arts patron Lady Augusta Gregory (1852–1932), who, along with W. B. Yeats and Edward Martyn, founded the **Abbey Theatre** ★ in Dublin (see p. 90). Sadly, her house no longer stands, but her influence is memorialized in a tree on the grounds on which the following people carved their initials while visiting with her: George Bernard Shaw, Sean O'Casey, John Masefield, Oliver St. John Gogarty, W. B. Yeats, and Douglas Hyde, the first president of Ireland. Clearly, she was an exceptional woman, and this is an exceptional place. The visitor center shows a number of films on Lady Gregory and Coole Park, and has a tearoom, picnic tables, and some lovely nature trails. The visitor center is open daily, 10am to 6pm from June to August; it's open 10am to 5pm in April, May, and September (closed last weekend in Sept). Admission is free.

Not too far from the home of his friend, the great poet W. B. Yeats (1865–1939) had his own summer home in Gort at **Thoor Ballylee**. The restored 16th-century Norman tower house served as the inspiration for his poems "The Winding Stair" and "The Tower."

In the interpretive center, an audiovisual presentation examines the poet's life. Also on the grounds are the original Ballylee Mill, partially restored, and a bookshop specializing in Anglo-Irish literature. The tower suffered serious flood damage in 2014, but has now been restored by a local community group, who run it as a cultural center. There are exhibitions and regular events, such as poetry readings—see **www.yeatsthoorballylee.org** for a current schedule. From mid-June to August the center is open daily 11am to 6pm; in September, it's open Monday to Friday 10am to 1pm, Saturday and Sunday noon to 4pm. Opening times for the rest of the year are patchy at the moment, while the center finds its feet; go on-line or call ☏ **091/631-436** to check. The site is on the N18 at Gort.

Also near Yeats's and Lady Gregory's summer homes, **Dunguaire Castle** (www.shannonheritage.com; ☏ **061/360-788**) sits on the south shore of Galway Bay, between Gort and Kilcolgan in Kinvara. Once the royal seat of the 7th-century King Guaire of Connaught, the castle was taken over by Oliver St. John Gogarty (1878–1957), Irish surgeon, author, poet, and wit; his great friends Yeats and Lady Gregory were frequent guests. Today, you can enjoy exquisite views from its battlements of the nearby Burren and Galway Bay, and stay for a **medieval banquet** on a summer evening (Apr–Oct). There are two sittings nightly, at 5:30 and 8:45pm; the banquet costs €48 adults, €33 children 9 to 12, and €22 children 6 to 8. Reservations are essential. For more information, go to www.shannonheritage.com.

salmon or seafood medley, served in a white wine and cream sauce, or a steaming bowl of beef and Guinness stew to keep carnivores happy. Try the delicious chowder if it's on offer. Needless to say, booking is advisable.

Roundstone, Co. Galway. www.odowdsseafoodbar.com. ☏ **095/35809.** Main courses €13–€29. Mon–Sat 10am–midnight; Sun noon–11pm (food served until about 9:30pm summer, 9pm winter).

addy Coyne's Pub ★★★ IRISH   It can be hard to find this lovely pub in tiny, blink-and-you'll-miss-it Renvyle—just outside blink-just-a-little-bit-longer-and-you'll-miss-it-too Tully—but it's worth the trek. Aside from the postcard-worthy frontage, dating from 1811, this doesn't *look* like the kind of place that's likely to wow you with its cooking. But the numbers of people making their way here for dinner should provide a clue. There's nothing pretentious about the cooking—it's just wonderful, classic Irish fare, done extremely well. Seafood is a specialty—the daily specials are chalked up outside, but expect hake, salmon, mussels, or maybe some Clew Bay oysters, served as they come or with a tasty cheese crumble topping. Burgers are juicy and tender, and the steaks are big enough for three people. Wash it all down with a pint of expertly poured Guinness. Desserts are avowedly traditional (try the homemade trifle). They don't take reservations, though, so arrive early or be prepared to wait.

Tully Cross, Renvyle, Co. Galway. www.paddycoynespub.com. ℂ **095/43499.** Reservations not accepted. Main courses €12–€25. Daily 6–9:30pm (but times vary—call to check).

The Steam Café ★ CAFE   This cute and simple little cafe is one of the best places in Clifden for lunch. The menu isn't fancy, but it's all good—wraps, sandwiches, light meals, and daily specials, all made with quality ingredients. Salads come from the cafe's own organic vegetable garden. The soups are particularly tasty, with ever-changing daily specials; you may find minestrone, tomato and herb, or even carrot and orange. They also do tasty cakes and desserts—great to wash down the excellent coffee. Also on site is **Veldon's Seafarer** ★★ (below), and at the rear of the hotel, from May to September you'll find a more upscale dinner-only option, the **Station House Restaurant** (ℂ **095/21699;** main courses €15–€25; closed Mon and Tues).

Station House Hotel courtyard, off N59 (Galway Rd.), Clifden, Co. Galway. ℂ **095/30600.** Main courses €4–€12. Mon–Sat 10am–5:30pm. Closed Sun.

Veldon's Seafarer ★★ SEAFOOD   The fishermen's nets, captain's wheels, and assorted sailing paraphernalia plastered across the polished wooden walls of this friendly bar and restaurant leaves you in no doubt as to what the specialty of the house is. You can eat from a fairly simple bar menu—traditional fish and chips, hamburgers, Irish stew—or retreat to the pleasant restaurant area, where you could start with some tasty calamari, or crab claws, fresh from nearby Cleggan. Follow that up with a plate of haddock filet with a sweet potato coulis, perhaps, or just take a deep breath and tackle the enormous seafood platter.

N59, Letterfrack, Co. Galway. www.veldons.ie. ℂ **095/41046.** Bar food €5–€16. Main courses €14–€16. Mon–Thurs 10am–11:30pm, Fri–Sat 10am–12:30am, Sun 10am–11pm; food generally served until about 9pm.

EXPLORING COUNTY GALWAY

The majority of top attractions in County Galway are split between two regions: the area around busy Galway City, and the wild, untamed landscapes to the west known as Connemara. Here you'll find windswept, boggy countryside peppered with breathtaking views, dramatic old buildings, and charming little towns.

A DAY AT THE races

"As I went down to Galway Town/To seek for recreation . . ." So goes the famous folk song "Galway Races," and the **Galway Races** are still a big deal in the Irish horse-racing calendar—and almost as big a social event as a sporting one.

People dress up in posh frocks and big hats, and the crowds cheer enthusiastically as competing racehorses pound the turf. Horse lovers and high rollers pour in from around the country for the race weeks, in July, September, and October. The animals are the best around, and the atmosphere is electric.

Since 1869, the action has taken place at the **Galway Racecourse** (www.galwayraces.com; ℂ **091/753-870**), just outside of Galway City in Ballybrit, less than 3km (2 miles) northeast of town. Ticket prices vary depending on the event and day of the week, but expect to pay from around €20 to upwards of €40 for a ticket. Multi-day and season tickets are also available.

Top Attractions in and Around Galway City

A small but thriving and cultured city, Galway still has its winding medieval lanes, but it also has a cosmopolitan core. The city's hub is busy Eyre Square (pronounced *Air* Square), which is a few minutes' walk from everywhere. The charming, artsy medieval district is a tiny, tangled area; getting lost is half the fun of going there. Close to the city docks, you can still see the area where long ago Spanish merchants unloaded cargo from their galleons. The **Spanish Arch** was one of four arches built in 1594, and the **Spanish Parade** is a small open square, which, like Eyre Square, is great for people-watching.

Druid Theatre ★★ PERFORMING ARTS   Highly respected across Ireland and beyond for its original, cutting-edge productions, the Druid has been one of the region's foremost arts institutions since the 1970s. It's particularly known for premiering new work from up-and-coming writers, so expect to find challenging, intelligent material staged here. They also produce new versions of classic plays by Irish, British, and European dramatists. Shows can sell out some time in advance, however, and are often out on the road (the Druid is a touring company), so check out what's on and make reservations as far ahead as possible. Ticket prices range from around €15 to €45.

Flood St., Galway City. www.druid.ie. ℂ **091/568-660.** Ticket prices and performance times vary.

Galway Arts Centre ★★ ARTS COMPLEX   Once the home of W. B. Yeats's patron, Lady Gregory, this attractive town house housed local governmental offices for many years. Today, it offers an excellent program of concerts, readings, and exhibitions by Irish and international artists—returning the house to a purpose that Lady Gregory would have appreciated. Usually two or three exhibitions run at any one time.

47 Dominick St., Galway City. www.galwayartscentre.ie. ℂ **091/565-886.** Free admission. Mon–Thurs 10am–5:30pm; Fri 10am–5pm; Sat noon–5pm.

Galway Atlantaquaria ★ AQUARIUM   Also known as the National Aquarium of Ireland (it's the largest in the country), this is a fantastic change of pace for kids who are tired of trudging around historic ruins. One's imagination is captured right from the first exhibit– a dramatic "splash room," where a large, 1-ton-capacity tank goes off every minute or so with a giant splash, which is designed to imitate the natural movement of waves on the Galway coast. Highlights of the thoughtful exhibits include an enormous two-story ocean tank, housing a couple hundred sea creatures (including small sharks); a wreck tank that's home to dangerous conger eels; and touch pools in which kids can handle tame starfish and hermit crabs, under supervision from the aquarium staff. There's also the opportunity to tickle some inquisitive rays, though make sure your hands are wet first or your touch can burn their sensitive skin. Free talks accompany daily feeding times—check out the schedule as you enter to find out who's being fed when and where.

The Promenade, Salthill. www.nationalaquarium.ie. ⓒ **091/585-100.** €12 adults; €8 seniors and students; €7.50 children 3–16; €22–€33 families. Wed–Fri 10am–5pm; Sat–Sun 10am–6pm. Closed Mon–Tues.

Galway Cathedral ★ CHURCH   Officially the "Cathedral of Our Lady Assumed into Heaven and St. Nicholas," Galway's cathedral has an impressive domed exterior that looks suitably Romanesque in style, although it was actually built in the 1960s. The striking interior has rows of symmetrical stone archways and dramatic lighting. Contemporary Irish artisans designed the statues, colorful mosaics, and stained-glass windows. The limestone for the walls was cut from local quarries, while the polished floor is made from Connemara marble.

University and Gaol rds., Galway City (by west end of the Salmon Weir Bridge), Galway City. www.galwaycathedral.ie. ⓒ **091/563-577** (select option 4). Free admission; donations welcome. Daily 8:30am–6:30pm.

Galway City Museum ★ MUSEUM   Overlooking the Spanish Arch, built in 1594 by the docks where Spanish galleons used to unload their cargo, this rather endearing little museum is a good place to acquaint yourself with the city's history. Permanent galleries downstairs relate to Galway's prehistoric and medieval periods, while the upper levels deal with the city's more recent past, including its relationship with the arts. Highlights include a large collection of intricate embroidered textiles, made by a local order of nuns between the 17th and 20th centuries, and some engaging exhibits relating to the history of cinema in the city. A lively program of special events includes talks, touring exhibitions, and hands-on arts workshops.

Spanish Parade, Galway City. www.galwaycitymuseum.ie. ⓒ **091/532-460.** Free admission. Easter–Sept Tues–Sat 10am–5pm, Sun noon–5. Oct–Easter Tues–Sat 10am–5pm.

Galway Irish Crystal Heritage Centre ★ FACTORY TOUR   Not as well-known as its feted Waterford rival, Galway Crystal is just as distinctive and beautiful. At this modern visitor center, you can observe the master craftspeople at their work, from blowing the molten glass to cutting the finished

THE aran islands

"I have heard that, at that time, the ruling proprietor and magistrate of the north island used to give any man who had done wrong a letter to a jailer in Galway, and send him off by himself to serve a term of imprisonment."

–J. M. Synge

When you see their ghostly shapes floating 48km (30 miles) out at sea like misty Brigadoon, you instantly understand why the sea-battered and wind-whipped Aran Islands have been the subject of fable and song for thousands of years.

The three islands—**Inis Mor** (Inishmore), **Inis Meain** (Inishmaan), and **Inis Oirr** (Inisheer)—are outposts of Gaelic culture and language. All the islands are rather strange looking, with a ring of rocks around their outer edges and, inside, small farms surrounded by soft green grass and wildflowers. Life on the islands is deeply isolated. To this day, many of the 1,500 inhabitants maintain a somewhat traditional life, fishing from *currachs* (small crafts made of tarred canvas stretched over timber frames), living in stone cottages, relying on pony-drawn wagons to get around, and speaking Gaelic. They still wear the classic creamy handmade *bainin* sweaters that originated here, as there's nothing better for keeping out the chill.

Of the islands, **Inishmore** is the largest and easiest to reach from Galway. Its easy transport means you can escape the crowds if you wish. Most visitors debark from the ferries at **Kilronan,** Inishmore's main town (though it's only the size of a village). It's an easy enough place in which to arrange or rent transportation. The mode is up to you: Horse-drawn buggies can be hailed like taxis as you step off the boat, minivans stand at the ready, and bicycle-rental shops are within sight. Drop in at **Oifig Fáilte** (Aran Island Tourist Information) in Kilronan to pick up walking maps, ask questions, and generally get yourself going here.

There are some excellent geological sights on the islands, including the magnificent **Dún Aengus ★★,** a vast 2,000-year-old stone fortress on Inishmore on the edge of a cliff that drops 90m (295 ft.) to the sea. Its original purpose is unknown—some think it was a military structure, others say it was a vast ceremonial theater. From the top, there are spectacular views of Galway Bay, the Burren, and Connemara.

Aran Island Ferries (www.aranisland ferries.com; ✆ **091/568-903**) runs daily service to Inishmore and Inishmaan. Boats leave from Rossaveal (Ros a' Mhíl) 37km (23 miles) west of Galway City. The crossing takes 40 minutes. There are usually three crossings a day, at 10:30am, 1pm, and 6:30pm in summer, 10:30am and 6pm in winter, but always call to check the schedule. The booking office is at 4 Forster Street in Galway; a shuttle bus goes from nearby Queen's Street to the ferry port (to take the shuttle, you must check in at the booking office at least 90 minutes before sailing time). The round-trip crossing costs €25 adults, €20 seniors and students, €13 children. The shuttle bus costs €7 adults, €6 seniors and students, €4 children.

product (weekdays only, although the center is open daily). However, most people just come to browse the huge factory shop, with its glittering array of crystal and other craft items, such as Belleek pottery.

East of the city on the main Dublin Rd. (N6), Merlin Park, Co. Galway. www.galwaycrys tal.ie. ✆ **091/757-311.** Free admission. Mon–Fri 9am–5:30pm, Sat 10am–5pm, Sun and public holidays noon–5pm.

GONE TO THE bogs

If you spend enough time in Ireland, you'll get used to the strong, smoky smell of burning turf—dried bricks of peat taken from bogs. Fully a third of the Connemara countryside is classified as bog, and these stark and beautiful boglands—formed over 2,500 years ago—have long been an important source of fuel. (During the Iron Age, the Celts also found other use for the bogs, using them to store perishable foods, such as butter.) Although no longer the lifeline it once was, cutting and drying turf is still an integral part of the rhythm of the seasons in Connemara.

Cutting requires a special tool, a spade called a *slane*, which slices the turf into bricks about 46cm (18 in.) long. The bricks are first spread out flat to dry, and then stacked in pyramids for further drying.

You can always tell when turf is burning in a home's fireplace—the smoke coming out of the chimney is blue and sweet-scented. It's such a quintessentially Irish smell, it may provoke feelings of intense nostalgia among those who grow to love it. Regrettably the bricks are a little bulky to make good souvenirs, but you may find turf-scented incense and candles in craft stores.

Hall of the Red Earl ★★ ANCIENT SITE   This fascinating site is what's left of a baronial hall from the Middle Ages, built by the powerful de Burgh family, Anglo-Norman earls who essentially ruled this region in the 13th century. In the late 1200s, they erected what must have been a lavish hall in which to hold court, receive subjects, settle disputes, and generally live it up in true medieval style. The earls were eventually overthrown by local tribes and the building was abandoned. Time slowly covered any trace of the building, until the foundations were discovered during building work in 1997. You can tour them on glass gangways and view some of the thousands of artifacts that were also unearthed during the excavation.

Custom House, Druid Lane, Galway City. © **091/564-946.** Free admission. May–Sept Mon–Fri 9:30am–4:45pm; Sat 10am–1pm. Oct–Apr Mon–Fri 9:30am–4:45pm. Closed Sat Oct–Apr and Sun year-round.

Lynch's Castle ★ CASTLE   Dating from 1490 and renovated in the 19th century, this impressive structure was once home to the Lynch family, who ruled the city for many years. It's one of the oldest medieval town houses in Ireland and is now a branch of the Allied Irish Bank. The stern exterior is watched over by a handful of amusing gargoyles; inside is a small display telling the building's history.

Abbeygate and Shop sts., Galway City. Free admission. Mon–Fri 10am–4pm (until 5pm on Thurs).

Spiddal Craft Village (Ceardlann an Spidéil) ★★ ARTS COMPLEX   On the main road as you enter Spiddal from Galway, this is a fantastic collection of cottage-style crafts stores and workshops. The artists in residence here change, but selection is always diverse. At this writing, they include a basket maker; a couple of wonderful contemporary ceramicists; a jeweler specializing in pieces made from pre-euro Irish coins (you can pick them out by your birth year); a traditional weaver; and a stained-glass artist. Plenty of the work is affordable without stretching the budget too far. Even if you're not buying, it's an inspiring place to browse. The on-site **Builín Blasta Café** sells delicious bakery goods, snacks, and light meals, in addition to takeaway deli items. You can contact the individual artists via the main website.

About 15km (9.3 miles) west of Galway on R336, Spiddal, Co. Galway. www.spiddal crafts.com. ✆ **086/806-7352.** Daily 10am–6pm.

St. Nicholas' Collegiate Church ★★ CHURCH   Galway's oldest church—it's claimed that Christopher Columbus prayed here in 1477 before one of his early attempts to reach the New World—St. Nicholas' was established about 1320. Over the centuries, it has changed from Roman Catholic to Church of Ireland and back again at least four times. Currently, it's under the aegis of the Church of Ireland. Inside are a 12th-century crusader's tomb with a Norman inscription, a carved font from the 16th or 17th century, and a stone lectern with barley-sugar twist columns from the 15th century. You can arrange guided tours conducted by a knowledgeable and enthusiastic church representative. Call or ask at the church for details.

Jcn. of Mainguard and Lombard sts., Galway City. www.stnicholas.ie. ✆ **086/389-8777.** Free admission (donations requested). Mar–Dec daily 9am–7pm; Jan–Feb daily 9am–5pm. Opening times may vary in winter. No tours Sun morning.

Top Attractions in Connemara

If you look for Connemara on road signs, you may be looking forever, because it's not a city or county, but rather an area or region. The boundaries are a bit hazy, but most agree that Connemara is west of Galway City, starting at Oughterard and continuing toward the Atlantic. You know it when you see it—it's an area of heartbreaking barrenness and unique beauty, with dark bogs and tall, jagged mountains punctuated by curving, glassy lakes dotted with green islands. The desolate landscape is caused, in part, by an absence of trees that were felled and dragged off long ago for building ships, houses, and furniture. Connemara is part of the **Gaeltacht,** or Irish-speaking area, so many signs are in Gaelic only.

Aughnanure Castle ★ CASTLE   Standing on an outcrop of rock surrounded by forest and pasture, this sturdy fortress is a well-preserved Irish tower castle, with an unusual double *bawn* (fortified enclosure) and a still-complete watchtower that you can climb. It was built around A.D. 1500 as a stronghold of the "Ferocious" O'Flaherty clan, who dominated the region and terrified the neighbors in their day. The castle's fireplaces are so big that you could fit a double bed in them. The ruined banqueting hall contains the remains of a dry harbor. *Note:* At this writing, access was limited to the grounds only, due to long-term maintenance work. It's expected to be open as normal by 2017.

Oughterard, Co. Galway. www.heritageireland.ie. ✆ **091/552-214.** Admission adults, €3 seniors, €2 children, €10 families. Mid-Mar to late Oct daily 9:30am–6pm

Clifden (An Clochán) ★ TOWN   This pretty little seaside town has an enviable location at the edge of the blue waters of Clifden Bay, where miles of curving, sandy beaches skirt the rugged coastline. It's a small, attractive place with colorful Victorian shop fronts and church steeples thrusting skyward through a veil of trees. With its plentiful restaurants, shops, hotels, and pubs, there's plenty to keep you amused here for a few hours. Though undeniably handsome and worth a visit, the downside is that Clifden is also quite touristy. If you prefer somewhere more off the beaten path, take a detour to **Roundstone** *(Cloch na Rón)* on your way out of town. About 24km (15 miles) south on R341, it's a smaller, sleepier fishing port, with pristine beaches. To reach Clifden from Galway City, take N59; the stunning drive, which takes just over 1 hour, passes through the heart of Connemara National Park (see below).

Clifden, Co. Galway.

Connemara National Park ★★★ PARK   This gorgeous national park encompasses over 2,000 hectares (4,940 acres) of mountains, bogs, grasslands, and hiking trails. Some of the best lead through the peaceful *Gleann Mór* **(Big Glen),** with its River Polladirk, or up to the **Twelve Bens** (also called the Twelve Pins), a small, quartzite mountain range north of the Galway-Clifden road. Nearby are the lesser-known, equally lovely **Maumturk** range and the breathtaking **Killary Fiord**—the only fiord in Ireland, indeed this entire region of Europe. None of the Twelve Bens rises above 730m (2,392 ft.), which makes their summits quite accessible to those who don't mind walking at a steep incline. Frequent rainfall produces dozens of tiny streams and waterfalls, and the views are spectacular. The excellent visitor center south of the crossroads in **Letterfrack** dispenses general information on the park, as well as providing sustenance in the form of tea, sandwiches, and fresh baked goods.

Visitor Centre: Signposted from N59, Letterfrack, Co. Galway. www.connemaranation alpark.ie. ℅ **095/41054** or 076/100-2530. Free admission. Visitor Centre: Mar–Oct 9am–5:30pm. Park open daily, year-round.

Inishbofin ★★ ISLAND   A place of seclusion and spectacular beauty, this small emerald-green gem lies 11km (6¾ miles) off the northwest coast of Connemara. Try to come here on a day when the skies are clear enough to deliver the unforgettable views of and from its shores. Once the domain of monks, then the lair of pirate queen Grace O'Malley (see p. 223), later Cromwell's infamous priest prison—you can still see his original, star-shaped barracks—Inishbofin is currently home to just 180 year-round human residents, a seal colony, and a sea bird sanctuary. Numerous ferries to the island operate from the port of Cleggan (13km/8 miles northwest of Clifden off N59) daily April through October. **Inishbofin Island Discovery** (www.inishbofinislanddiscovery.com; ℅ **095/45819** or 086/171-8829) sails twice a day, or three times a day in summer. Round-trip fares

CONNEMARA pony TREKKING

The sturdy yet elegant Connemara pony is the only horse breed native to Ireland, though it has received an infusion of Spanish blood over the centuries. Often raised in tiny fields with limestone pastures, the ponies are known for their stamina and gentleness, which make them ideal for amateur riders and young people. Born and bred to traverse the region's rugged terrain, they are adept at scaling short, steep hills and delicately picking their way along rocky shores.

Because much of the countryside is well off the beaten track, pony trekking is actually a fantastic way to cover ground. It gets you off the busy roads and out into the countryside, even onto the white-sand beaches near Roundstone and elsewhere along the coast. The **Cleggan Beach Riding Centre,** Cleggan (www.clegganridingcentre.com; *©* **095/44746**) offers beach and mountain treks, the most popular being a 3-hour ride to Omey Island at low tide. And near Loughrea, the **Aille Cross Equestrian Centre** (www.connemara trails.com; *©* **091/843-968**) can set you up with guided treks for all levels of ability.

are €20 adults, €10 children 5 to 18, and €5 children under 5. *Note:* Reservations are essential, and evening sail times are liable to be brought forward in bad weather—so make sure you keep an eye on the hour.

Inishbofin, Co. Galway.

Kylemore Abbey ★★ HISTORIC SITE   As you round yet another bend on the particularly barren stretch of country road around Kylemore, this extraordinary neo-Gothic abbey looms into view, at the base of a wooded hill across the mirror-like Kylemore Lake. The facade of the main building—a vast, crenelated 19th-century house—is a splendid example of neo-Gothic architecture. In 1920, its owners donated it to the Benedictine nuns, and the sisters have run a convent boarding school here ever since. You can see a little of the interior, but it's disappointingly plain; the exterior and the grounds are the real reason to visit, especially that breathtaking view across the lake. The highlight is the restored Gothic chapel, an exquisite cathedral in miniature with a plain, somber cemetery to one side; and don't miss the lavish Victorian walled garden, and the breathtaking views of it all from across the lake. The complex includes a decent restaurant that serves produce grown on the nuns' farm, as well as tea and good scones; a shop with a working pottery studio; and a visitor center. The abbey is most atmospheric when the bells are rung for midday office or for vespers at 6pm.

Kylemore, Co. Galway (follow signs from N59). www.kylemoreabbeytourism.ie. *©* **095/52011.** Admission €13 adults; €10 seniors; €9 students and children 11–17; children under 11 free; €26–€35 families. July–Aug daily 9am–7pm; Mar–June and Sept–Oct daily 9:30am–5:30pm; Nov–Feb daily 10am–4:30pm.

NORTHWEST IRELAND: MAYO, SLIGO & DONEGAL

The strikingly beautiful landscape of Galway segues into the strikingly beautiful landscape of southern Mayo without any fanfare. Like Galway, Mayo is a land of dramatic scenery, with rocky cliffs plunging down into the opaque blue waters of the icy sea. If you head farther north, you'll reach the smooth pastures of County Sligo, the classic landscape that inspired the great Irish poet William Butler Yeats. The main appeal here is not its towns, which tend to be functional farm communities, but the countryside itself. Though the region is dotted with fairy-tale castles and mysterious prehistoric sites, its biggest gift to the visitor is tranquility.

ESSENTIALS

Arriving

BY BUS   **Bus Éireann** runs daily bus service to Sligo Town from Dublin, Galway, and other points including Derry in Northern Ireland. It provides daily service to major towns in Mayo. The bus station in Sligo is on Lord Edward Street.

BY TRAIN   Trains from Dublin and other major points arrive daily at Westport in Mayo, and Sligo Town in Sligo. The train station in Westport is on Altamont Street; about a 10-minute walk from the town center; in Sligo it's on Lord Edward Street, next to the bus station.

BY CAR   Mayo can be reached by four major highways: N84 from Galway; the north-south N59 from Connemara on up to Sligo; and N5 and N60 from the east, connecting to Dublin-bound roads. Four other major routes lead to Sligo: N4 from Dublin and the east, N17 from Galway and the south, N15 from Donegal to the north, and N16 from Northern Ireland.

BY PLANE **Ireland West Airport Knock** in Charlestown, County Mayo (www.knockairport.com; ☏ 094/936-8100) is becoming quite a popular hub for budget airlines from the U.K. **Aer Lingus** (www.aerlingus.com; ☏ 081/836-5000) and **Ryanair** (www.ryanair.com; ☏ 0871/246-0000 in the U.K. or 152/044-4004) run daily scheduled flights from London, Liverpool, Edinburgh, and Bristol. **Flybe** (www.flybe.com; ☏ 087/1700-2000 in the U.K. or 0044/1392-683-152) also offers daily flights from Manchester and a few flights per week from Birmingham. There are no flights to the airport from other points in Ireland.

Visitor Information

The main tourist information center for County Mayo is the **Westport Tourist Office,** Bridge Street, Westport (www.mayo.ie; ☏ 098/25711). There is also an office on Pearse Street in **Ballina** (☏ 096/72800). The **Sligo Tourist Office** is on the ground floor of the Old Bank Building, O'Connell Street, Sligo Town (www.sligotourism.ie; ☏ 071/916-1201).

WHERE TO STAY

This region of Ireland is not the most stocked with top-notch places to stay; even the major towns have only a smattering of decent B&Bs and small hotels. However, some gems are to be found in the deepest reaches of the countryside. It takes effort to get to these places, but the journey will be worth it.

Where to Stay in County Mayo

Ashford Castle ★★★ This extraordinary, fairytale-like castle has entertained plenty of famous guests over the years—Grace Kelly, Ronald Reagan, Brad Pitt, Pierce Brosnan, and Tony Blair to name just a few. It also has a list of awards and commendations as long as your arm, including best hotel in Ireland, and third best in Europe overall, from *Condé Naste Traveller* in 2012. Ashford Castle was built in the 13th century and still looks every inch the palatial abode, thanks to the suits of armor and priceless antiques lining the walls and the huge four-poster beds filling the sumptuous guest rooms. The grounds are stunning—the castle overlooks Lough Corrib, and there are acres of forest and landscaped gardens. A luxurious range of spa treatments is on hand to soothe and pamper guests. The restaurant is as excellent as you'd expect (don't even think about dressing down), although a less formal eatery is on the grounds too. Of course, you'll also need a chest full of solid gold treasure to afford a night here—although, if it makes any difference at all, the dinner, bed and breakfast packages are pretty good. Check the website for special deals, especially in the off-season.

On R346, on the eastern approach to Cong, Co. Mayo. www.ashford.ie. ☏ 094/954-6003. 83 units. €550–€675. Free parking. Breakfast included. **Amenities:** Restaurants (2); bar; gym; massage treatments; estate sports including golf; fishing; and clay-pigeon shooting; Wi-Fi (free).

The Bervie ★★★   Overlooking the Atlantic Ocean on Achill Island (see p. 225), reached by a road bridge across Achill Sound, the Bervie is an inspiring place to stay. Husband-and-wife hosts Elizabeth and John Barrett spent years lovingly restoring the building. Elizabeth actually grew up in the house; it's been a B&B since the 1930s, although today it's a far more sophisticated place than she remembers from her childhood. Guest rooms are large and spacious, with well-chosen furniture (most of it made locally) and tasteful art. Some rooms directly overlook the sea—and what a view! You can see some of the other islands dotted around the bay from certain rooms, while others have a dramatic view of cliffs. Light pours in from huge windows, and the whispering of the waves soothes you off to a restful sleep. Elizabeth's home-cooked breakfasts are to die for, and after years of being advance notice–only, the outstanding dinners are now a permanent fixture. Think roast chicken with lemon and thyme, black sole with Clare Island salmon, or rib-eye steak with onion marmalade and blue cheese mushrooms—all with excellent use of local ingredients. There's a good (and reasonably priced) wine list too. On weekends there's a 2-night minimum, but the higher rate also includes dinner.

The Strand, Keel, Achill, Co. Mayo. (Take N59 to Achill Island, then R319 to Keel.) www. bervie-guesthouse-achill.com. ⓒ **098/43114.** 14 units. €110–€140. Weekend dinner, bed and breakfast €300–€340 (2 nights inclusive). Free parking. Breakfast included. Dinner €45. **Amenities:** Restaurant; Wi-Fi (free).

Enniscoe House ★★   Flanked by Mount Nephin on one side and the shimmering waters of Lough Conn on the other, Enniscoe is a stunningly restored mid-18th-century mansion. Very little has been significantly altered from the original structure, so the place is overflowing with wonderful period details (one room even has its original silk wallpaper). Bedrooms are oversized, with big windows and antique, half-canopied beds. Bathrooms are modern and elegantly designed. Susan Kellett and her son, DJ, run the place with a natural flair for hospitality. Susan is a great cook, too; make sure you book one of her excellent dinners. The grounds are big, and with enough to do that you could spend a day here without ever stepping back into the outside world, should you wish. They're open to the public, with a cafe and a Heritage Centre, complete with a local history museum, genealogical service, and a small antiques shop. The Enniscoe estate also has a couple of self-catering cottages if you want more privacy.

Castlehill, Ballina, Co. Mayo. www.enniscoe.com. ⓒ **096/31112.** 6 units. €160–€240. Dinner €50. Free parking. Breakfast included. **Amenities:** Guest lounge.

Windmill Cottages ★★   Your host, Pierre Blezat, so fell for the charms of County Mayo when he first visited that he left his native France to run Windmill Cottage as a B&B. He restored the small complex of farm buildings personally, and each displays a personal touch. The effect is like a series of cozy, contemporary country cabins; exposed pine walls, modern art on the walls, and up-to-date furniture. The cottages are a stone's throw (literally)

ACCOMMODATIONS ■
Ashford Castle **4**
The Bervie **1**
Enniscoe House **10**
Windmill Cottages **6**

DINING ◆
An Port Mór **5**
The Beehive **2**
Dillons Bar & Grill **11**
The Helm **5**
Wilde's at the Lodge at Ashford **4**

ATTRACTIONS ●
Ballintubber Abbey **8**
Céide Fields **12**
Clare Island **3**
National Museum of Ireland:
  Country Life **9**
Westport House
  and Pirate Adventure Park **7**

from the sea, and the views of the water, with mountains in the distance, are seductive. The breakfast room takes full advantage of the view and sometimes doubles as a dining room in the evenings, when Pierre serves delicious French-Irish meals that must be booked in advance (€32 per person, including a pre-dinner drink). Pierre can also arrange a chauffeur service to Westport train station for €15; transfers from farther afield are possible, too.

Carraholly, about 2km (1¼ miles) west of Westport Golf Club, Co. Mayo. www.wind mill-cottage.com. © **098/56006.** 6 units. €110–€160. Dinner €32. Free parking. Breakfast included. Closed Oct–Mar. **Amenities:** Bike hire; sauna; hot tub; Wi-Fi (free).

Where to Stay in County Sligo

The Glasshouse ★   A solid, modern option overlooking the River Garavogue in Sligo Town, The Glasshouse resembles a gleaming, modern ship from the outside. The public areas inside either look bold and funky or like an explosion in a kitsch factory, depending on your point of view: multicolored circles on the carpet, misshapen blue sofas, and a bright orange signature color in the towering atrium. Bedrooms are a little more refined, with muted tones and modern art on the walls. There is an in-house restaurant, although you could certainly eat more cheaply in town. The appropriately named View Bar looks out over Sligo Town and has live music (if you are sensitive to noise, ask for a room away from the bar when you book).

Swan Point, Sligo, Co. Sligo. www.theglasshouse.ie. ✆ **071/919-4300.** 116 units. €72–€136. Free parking. Breakfast not included in lower rates. **Amenities:** Internet (broadband/via TV); restaurant; bars (2); room service; A/C (some rooms).

Ross Farmhouse ★★   Not far from Carrowkeel (see p. 226), Ross Farmhouse is a restored 1880s cottage, surrounded by acres and acres of rolling farmland. The cheerful owners, Nicholas and Oriel Hill-Wilkinson, see this place as their pride and joy, and it shows in the wholehearted welcome they give guests. Bedrooms are reasonably sized, with simple, unfussy furnishings. One is a family room, and another is fully accessible to wheelchairs. Downstairs are two lovely guest lounges filled with antiques. An open peat-fire warms the hearth in winter. Breakfasts are good, and they'll cook for you in the evenings if you book in advance (very reasonable at €35 per person; there's a good wine list, too, or you can bring your own). In addition to all countryside walks, ancient ruins, and sweet little towns, the area has some of the best horseback riding in Ireland—ask if you'd like recommendations for local riding centers. *Note:* Not all bedrooms have a private bathroom, so specify when you book if you want one.

Riverstown, Co. Sligo. (Follow signs from Drumfin on N4 or Coola on R284.) www.ross farmhousesligo.com. ✆ **071/916-5140.** 6 units. €90. Free parking. Breakfast included. **Amenities:** Wi-Fi (free).

Sligo Park Hotel ★   A pleasant little park surrounds this convenient, cheap-ish hotel in Sligo Town. Guest rooms are simply furnished in a contemporary style, with muted color schemes of gray and brown, and good-size bathrooms. One or two rooms could do with some TLC around the edges, though the public areas are sleek and well designed. Family rooms only cost around €10 more than doubles. This hotel won't win any awards for heart-of-Ireland atmosphere, but as a clean, modern base, it's a good option in a region that's short on choice. One word of caution: The hotel is also a popular venue for weddings and other events, so noise can sometimes be a problem on weekends. You might want to ask for a room as far away from the bar as possible.

Pearse Rd., Sligo Town. www.sligoparkhotel.com. ✆ **071/919-0400.** 136 units. €69–€121 double. Free parking. Breakfast not included in lower rates. **Amenities:** Restaurant; bar; room service; sauna; pool; Wi-Fi (free).

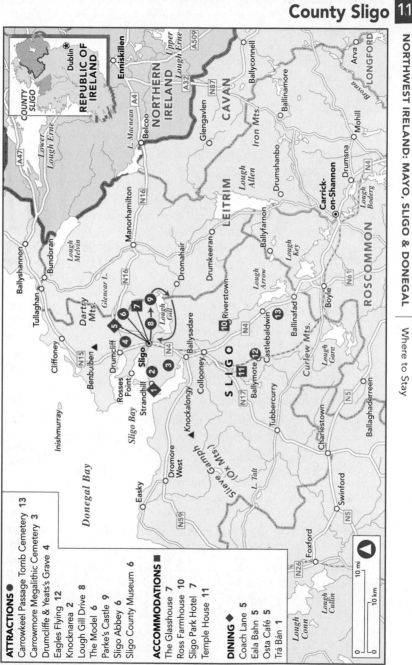

REPUBLIC OF IRELAND

COUNTY SLIGO

Dublin

Enniskillen

NORTHERN IRELAND

Lower Lough Erne

Upper Lough Erne

L. Macnean

Belcoo

CAVAN

Ballyconnell

Arva

LONGFORD

Mohill

Drumsna

Carrick-on-Shannon

ROSCOMMON

Ballinamore

Glengavlen

Drumshanbo

Lough Boderg

N87

A509

A32

A4

N16

Manorhamilton

Dromahair

Drumkeeran

LEITRIM

Lough Allen

Ballyfarnon

Lough Key

Boyle

N61

N4

Ballyshannon

Bundoran

Tullaghan

Cliffoney

Lough Melvin

Glencar L.

Darty Mts.

N16

Riverstown

Lough Arrow

Ballinafad

Curlew Mts.

Lough Gara

N15

Drumcliff

Benbulben

Lough Gill

Ballysadare

N4

SLIGO

Castlebaldwin

N4

Rosses Point

Strandhill

Sligo

Ballymote

N17

N5

Inishmurray

Sligo Bay

Knocklalong

Colloony

Tubbercurry

Charlestown

Ballaghaderreen

Donegal Bay

Dromore West

Slieve Gamph (Ox Mts.)

L. Talt

Ballycurry

N59

Easky

N26

Foxford

Swinford

N5

Lough Conn

Lough Cullin

0   10 mi
0   10 km

ATTRACTIONS ●

Carrowkeel Passage Tomb Cemetery 13
Carrowmore Megalithic Cemetery 3
Drumcliffe & Yeats's Grave 4
Eagles Flying 12
Knocknarea 2
Lough Gill Drive 8
The Model 6
Parke's Castle 9
Sligo Abbey 6
Sligo County Museum 6

ACCOMMODATIONS ■

The Glasshouse 7
Ross Farmhouse 10
Sligo Park Hotel 7
Temple House 11

DINING ◆

Coach Lane 5
Eala Bahn 5
Osta Café 5
Trá Bán 1

Temple House ★★★ This is quite simply *the* place to stay in the northwest if you're after a truly unique and historic B&B experience. Temple House is not full of five-star extras, but you'll find it hard to beat for historical authenticity, beautiful surroundings, and sheer charm. The 1665 manor house has been restored, bit by painstaking bit, by the amiable young custodians of the estate, Roderick and Helena Perceval. The place is dripping with history; once a thriving country estate, it fell slowly into near-ruin during the turbulent years of the 20th century. The huge guest rooms are packed with interesting antiques, yet have completely modern, recently renovated bathrooms. Nightly dinners are more akin to parties, with all guests seated around an enormous old table enjoying outstanding food. Breakfasts hit the spot too, with plenty of homemade treats. The beautiful grounds include a boating lake, a walled garden, and even a ruined Knights Templar castle. Supposedly there are a couple of resident ghosts roaming around, although they must be of a very Bacchanalian kind, with such a welcoming and convivial atmosphere as this. There is also a self-catering cottage on the grounds.

Ballymote, Ballinacarrow, Co. Sligo. www.templehouse.ie. ✆ **071/918-3329.** 6 units. €100–€210. Dinner €45. Free parking. Breakfast included. Closed Dec–Mar. No dinner Sun. **Amenities:** Wi-Fi (free).

WHERE TO EAT

Standout restaurants in this part of the country are few and far between. However, they often can be found in hotels and the better B&Bs. Westport, in County Mayo, has some good, reliable choices, and the dining scene in Sligo Town has improved dramatically over the last couple of years.

Where to Eat in County Mayo

An Port Mór ★★ SEAFOOD/MODERN IRISH This multi-award-winning seafood restaurant in Westport specializes in seafood. Local catches dominate the menu, so you could easily find Clew Bay crab cakes and scallops, or blue trout (yes, *blue*) from Curran served with tarragon and canola. The seafood is excellent, but it's not all that's on offer; expect to find a juicy sirloin served with red-onion marmalade, or perhaps some local lamb. Service is excellent, too.

Bridge St., Westport, Co. Mayo. www.anportmor.com. ✆ **098/26730.** Main courses €15–€28. Tues–Sun 6pm–midnight.

The Beehive ★ CAFE There aren't many places to eat on Achill Island, and this homey craft store–cum–cafe is one of the best. (Technically, they say, this is a "Craft Coffee Shop.") Stop and refuel on excellent sandwiches and cakes, or a bowl of homemade soup (the chowder is particularly good). The craft store isn't bad either. The Beehive overlooks the beach at Keel, and you can sit outside with your food on a warm day.

Keel, Achill Island, Co. Mayo. ✆ **086/854-2009.** €5–€12. Daily 9:30am–6pm. Closed Nov–Easter.

farther afield: COUNTY DONEGAL

Just a few miles north of Sligo Town, roads twist and corkscrew and the landscape opens up into great sweeping views of steep hills and barren shores, as a freezing mist blows off the sea. This is Donegal.

The austere beauty of this far-flung county is bleak yet unforgettable. This is where you go to get away from other travelers. Its roads are rarely bothered by tour buses, and even gas stations are scarce.

To the north of Donegal Town, you'll find breathtaking scenery around **Donegal Bay.** Follow the main road (N56) west out of Donegal Town, then branch off on coastal R263 for a slow, spectacularly scenic drive to the towering **Slieve League** sea cliffs. They're almost three times the height of their famous southern cousins, the Cliffs of Moher—and at Slieve League you won't have to joust for space to get the awesome views. (*And* parking is free.) It's a long, steep

climb to the top, but the visitor center runs a shuttle bus to the best view point.

The coast north of here, known as the **Atlantic Highlands,** offers some stunning scenery as well. Stop off in the adorable village of **Ardara (**Árd *an* **Rátha)** to poke around antiques stores and shops selling local wool blankets before following N56 north, turning off whenever a beach or tiny village catches your eye.

East of the Highlands, the wild beauty of the **Inishowen Peninsula** awaits. To drive around the Inishowen is to traverse desolate seascapes, intimidating mountains, restful valleys, and thick woodlands. If you've made it this far, well done! You can join the few tourists to have stood on Malin Head and felt the icy mist come in on a wind that hits you like a fist. You can feel the satisfaction of knowing you've come as far as you can go. And now you can truly say that you have *done* Ireland.

Dillon's Bar & Restaurant ★ GRILL This friendly, bustling eatery tucked away in a courtyard is a great find. Hugely popular with locals for its welcoming atmosphere and sizeable portions, it's a warm and relaxing place to enjoy a casual meal of unpretentious food at reasonable prices. The restaurant itself is spacious, in what seems to be an old warehouse, with high, hammered copper ceilings. But the hearty food is the main attraction. Locals swear by the grilled sirloin steak, but there's also Cajun chicken; Chinese-style roast duck; and a hearty, creamy local seafood pie. If you're lucky, there might be traditional music later on—you wouldn't be the first to come for dinner and stay for a dance or two. Dillon's has recently added some B&B rooms, costing upwards of €75 per room, per night.

Dillon Terrace, Ballina, Co. Mayo. www.dillonsbarandrestaurant.ie. ℂ **096/72230.** Main courses €14–€23. Mon–Sat 5pm–midnight; Sun 1–9pm.

The Helm ★ SEAFOOD/BISTRO Portions are huge at this relaxed Westport bar-restaurant that specializes in local seafood—tackle the delicious fisherman's platter only if very hungry. Rich seafood chowder is a particular specialty. Main dishes also include steaks, rack of lamb, and pork chops, in addition to the fishy options. Lunch service is heartier and more traditional, with Irish stew alongside lasagna and chips. Desserts are all comfort food, like

WHEN hollywood CAME TO MAYO

When director John Ford descended on the sweet little town of **Cong** in County Mayo to make his classic 1951 film *The Quiet Man,* starring John Wayne and Maureen O'Hara, the town's profile skyrocketed. Tourists were soon visiting in the tens of thousands, and Cong was transformed.

Surprisingly, visitors still flock here on Quiet Man pilgrimages, even though the film is well over half a century old. The **Quiet Man Museum,** Circular Road (www.quietman-cong.com/cong-museum; ✆ **094/954-6089**) is a charming little thatched cottage that has been transformed into an exact replica of John Wayne's house in the movie, right down to the right furniture. (Sadly, the actual cottage used in the film was torn down, stone by stone, by souvenir hunters.)

From April to October, it's open daily from 10am to 4pm. Admission costs €5 adults; €4 seniors, students, and children; and €15 families. They usually run tours of the village every day at 11am, and other times if demand is high.

Just around the corner on Abbey Street are the ruins of **Cong Abbey.** Founded in 623, it was rebuilt in the 12th century, then comprehensively destroyed by Henry VIII in the 1540s. Even here there's a reminder of this town's Hollywood moment: The **Quiet Man Statue,** a full-size bronze of Maureen O'Hara being whisked off her feet by John Wayne. It's become an almost obligatory focal point for souvenir selfies.

Cong is roughly halfway between Galway and Westport, on R344, R345, and R346.

pies, crumbles, and even jelly and ice cream. The Helm is also a B&B with a few self-catering apartments available, too.

The Harbour, Westport, Co. Mayo. www.thehelm.ie. ✆ **098/26398.** Main courses €17–€23. Sun–Thurs 8am–11:30pm; Fri–Sat 8am–12:30am. Food served until about 9:30pm.

Wilde's at the Lodge at Ashford ★★★ MODERN IRISH   If, like the other 99% of us, you can't quite swing a night at **Ashford Castle** ★★★ (see p. 213), then you might find this a viable alternative for a slice of Irish upper crust glamour. Lisloughrey Lodge was once home to the estate managers of Ashford, but now it's run as a boutique hotel with a fantastic restaurant. Wilde's is overseen by Jonathan Keane, an up-and-coming star of the Irish culinary world. His modern Irish cooking is deliciously inventive; just a glance at the menu is enough to give you an idea of his celebratory approach to food. From the tasting menu (or "Menu of Discovery") you might be offered king crab with sea urchin and eucalyptus, duck with hay, wild turbot with monk's beard (we presume the Tuscan vegetable), and, to finish, a piquant parfait of rhubarb and pink peppercorns. Many of the same dishes are available in larger portions as an a la carte selection. The dining room has a fantastic view of Lough Corrib. If you want to spend the night, doubles start at around €185.

On the grounds of Ashford Castle, Cong, Co. Mayo. www.lisloughreylodge.com. ✆ **094/954-5400.** Main courses €23–€29. Tasting menu €10 per course. Mar–Oct Mon–Sat 6:30–9pm; Sun 1–3:30pm, 6:30–9pm. Nov–Feb Wed–Sat 6:30–9pm, Sun 1–3:30pm, 6:30–9pm.

Where to Eat in County Sligo

Coach Lane at Donaghy's Bar ★★ IRISH/INTERNATIONAL   A very popular spot with Sligo residents, Coach Lane has two dining rooms: a bar, serving easy crowd pleasers such as burgers, fish and chips, and shepherd's pie; and a more upmarket, gastropub-style restaurant. Most ingredients are regionally sourced, and the seafood is particularly good here. Try the queen scallop and spinach tart, then dive into a hearty plate of steak and chips, or some cod served with samphire (a salty green vegetable that grows only by the sea) and white-wine butter.

1-2 Lord Edward St., Sligo Town, Co. Sligo. www.coachlane.ie. © **071/916-2417.** Main courses €17–€25. Bar food: Daily 3–10pm. Restaurant: Daily 5:30–10pm.

Eala Bhan ★★ INTERNATIONAL   Local meats and seafood are featured at this popular brasserie in Sligo Town. The menu takes traditional brasserie classics and adds a light touch of creative flair—tender steak filet comes with mashed potatoes, red-onion marmalade, and bacon crisp, while the sea bass is balanced by a piquant pea-and-lemon risotto and a rich champagne cream sauce. Three-course set menus are a good value, and feature many dishes from the main menus. The early bird menu (served until 6:20pm daily) is just €20 for three courses. The lunch menu is almost as extensive as dinner, with a few lighter options such as poached chicken salad or seafood chowder.

Rockwood Parade, Sligo Town, Co. Sligo. www.ealabhan.ie. © **071/914-5823.** Main courses €19–€26. Mon–Sat noon–3pm, 5–9:30pm; Sun 12:30–3pm, 5–9:30pm.

Osta Café and Wine Bar ★★ CAFE   The owners of this sweet cafe overlooking the river in Sligo are big believers in the slow food and organic movements, and it's reflected in their delicious, healthful food that makes superb use of ingredients from small local producers. There are usually only a few dishes offered each day, but you're virtually guaranteed to find something authentically Irish—boxty, perhaps, or omelets made from smoked Gubbeen cheese and potato. Soups are a specialty too. Even the sandwiches qualify as local, because they're made with deliciously fresh bread from a nearby bakery. In the early evening on Thursday to Saturday, the food switches to a simple but tasty tapas menu. *Insider tip:* A Gaelic speaking group meets here every Friday evening, so if you drop by then, you can eavesdrop on some of the language being used.

Garavogue Weir, off Stephen St., Sligo Town, Co. Sligo. www.osta.ie. © **071/914-4639.** Main courses €5–€11. Mon–Wed 8am–7pm; Thurs–Sat 8am–8pm; Sun 9am–5pm.

Trá Bán ★★ MODERN IRISH   Another fine place for steaks and seafood, Trá Bán is above a popular bar in Strandhill, a little seaside town about 8km (5 miles) west of Sligo Town. Crab cakes, chicken wings, and "sea and shore" (an Irish version of surf 'n' turf) are complemented with an occasional, more adventurous choice, like stuffed plaice paupiette served with prawn mousse and a lemon-and-dill risotto. If you order a steak, try "reefing the beef" (their phrase, not ours) by adding a couple of garlic-butter scallops on top. They also offer a special children's menu (three courses for €14). The atmosphere is relaxed and easygoing, with a cheery and efficient staff. Reservations are recommended, especially on weekends.

Above the Strand Bar, Strandhill, Co. Sligo. www.trabansligo.ie. ✆ **071/912-8402.** Main courses €18–€24. Tues–Sun 5–9:30pm. Closed Mon.

EXPLORING COUNTY MAYO

Serenely beautiful, County Mayo sits in the shadow of its more famous neighbor, Galway, and doesn't seem to mind. For experienced Ireland travelers, Mayo is a kind of Galway Lite—its rugged coastal scenery is similar to that of Galway, but it has less of the traffic or tourist overload from which Galway suffers in the summer. This is peaceful, pleasant Ireland, with striking seascapes and inland scenery that ranges from lush and green to stark, desert-like, and mountainous. It's an unpredictable place, where the terrain changes at the turn of a steering wheel.

Because it's a rural county with no major cities or many large towns, County Mayo feels a bit like a place without a center. Towns like **Westport** *(Cathair na Mart)* and **Ballina** *(Béal an Átha)* make good bases. Of the two, Westport is the more attractive; it's also home to one of the county's biggest (and most touristy) attractions, **Westport House.** Ballina, meanwhile, is within easy reach of some atmospheric historical sites—including **Céide Fields,** a superbly preserved and explicated footprint of an advanced Stone Age farming community.

Top Attractions in County Mayo

Ballintubber Abbey ★★ CHURCH   This abbey is a real survivor—one of only a few Irish churches in continuous use for almost 800 years. Founded in 1216 by Cathal O'Connor, king of Connaught, it has endured fires, numerous attacks, pestilences, and anti-Catholic pogroms. Although Oliver Cromwell's forces thoroughly dismantled the abbey—they even carried off its roof in 1653 in an effort to suppress it—clerics continued discreetly conducting religious rites. Today, it's an impressively restored church, with 13th-century windows on the right side of the nave and a doorway dating to the 15th century. Guided tours are available weekdays from 9:30am to 5pm; there's no charge, but donations of €4 per person are requested. The **Celtic Furrow** visitor center illuminates the abbey's troubled and fascinating history, as part of a wider examination of spiritual life in Ireland dating back 5,000 years.

Off the main Galway-Castlebar Rd. (N84), about 21.5km (13½ miles) east of Westport, Ballintubber, Co. Mayo. www.ballintubberabbey.ie. ✆ **094/903-0934.** Free admission. Daily 9am–midnight. Celtic Furrow: June–Aug daily 10:30am–5pm.

Céide Fields ★★ ANCIENT SITE   In a breathtaking setting above huge chalk cliffs that plunge hundreds of feet down into a deep blue sea, an ancient people once lived, worked, and buried their dead. However, nobody knew this

local hero: GRACE O'MALLEY, THE PIRATE QUEEN

By all accounts, Grace O'Malley—aka the "Pirate Queen"—was a woman ahead of her time. Born in 1530 on **Clare Island ★★** (see p. 224), she grew up to be an adventurer, pirate, gambler, mercenary, traitor, chieftain, noble-woman, and general badass. And while she is remembered now with affection, at the time she was feared and despised in equal measure.

Even as a child, Grace was fiercely independent. When her mother refused to let her sail with her father, she cut off her hair and dressed in boys' clothing. Her father called her *"Grainne Mhaol,"* or "Bald Grace," later shortened to Granuaile (pronounced Graw-nya-wayl), a nickname she'd carry all her life.

At 16, Grace married Donal O'Fla-herty, second in line to the O'Flaherty clan chieftain, who ruled all of Connacht. Her career as a pirate began a few years later when the city of Galway, one of the largest trading posts in northern Europe, refused to do business with the O'Fla-hertys. Grace used her fleet of fast gal-leys to waylay slower vessels on their way into Galway Harbour. She then offered safe passage for a fee in lieu of pillaging the ships.

She is most fondly remembered for refusing to trade her lands in return for an English title, a common practice of the day.

When the English captured her sons in 1593, she went to London to try to secure their release. In an extraordinary turn of events, she actually secured a meeting with Queen Elizabeth herself. History records that the two women got on quite well (although legend has it that Grace initially tried to smuggle a knife in with her, in case things went differently). A deal was struck; Elizabeth agreed to release Grace's sons and to return some captured lands, if Grace would agree to renounce piracy. This she did and returned to Ireland triumphantly.

The truce did not last, however. Grace got her sons back, but not her prop-erty—so she took up piracy again and continued her legendary seafaring career until her death from natural causes in the 1600s.

until the 1930s, when a local farmer noticed the stones in his fields were piled in strange patterns. More than 40 years later, his archaeologist son explored the discovery further. Under the turf, he found Stone Age fields, megalithic tombs, and the foundations of a village. Standing amid it now, you can see a pattern of farm fields as they were laid out 5,000 years ago (predating the Egyptian pyramids). Preserved for millennia beneath the bog, the site is both fascinating and inscrutable. To a casual observer, it's little more than piles of stones, but the visitor center makes it meaningful in a series of displays, films, and tours. The pyramid-shaped center itself is designed to fit in with the dra-matic surroundings—you can see the building from miles away.

On R314, 8km (5 miles) west of Ballycastle, Co. Mayo. www.heritageireland.ie. ☏ **096/43325.** Admission €4 adults; €3.50 seniors; €2 students and children; €10 fam-ilies. June–Sept daily 10am–6pm; Apr–May and Oct daily 10am–5pm; last tour 1 hr. before closing. Closed Nov–Mar.

Clare Island ★★ ISLAND   Floating about 5km (3 miles) off the Mayo coast, just beyond Clew Bay, Clare Island is a place of unspoiled splendor. Inhabited for 5,000 years and once quite populous—1,700 people lived there in the early 19th century—Clare is now home to only about 150 year-round islanders, plus perhaps as many sheep. But the island is best known as the haunt of Grace O'Malley, the "Pirate Queen," who controlled the coastal waters 400 years ago (see box p. 223). O'Malley's modest castle and the partially restored Cistercian abbey where she is buried are among the island's few attractions. The rest of the draw is its remote natural beauty. Two ferry services operate out of Roonagh Harbour, 29km (18 miles) south of Westport: **O'Malley's Ferry Service** (www.omalleyferries.com; ✆ **098/25045**); and **Clare Island Ferries** (www.clareislandferry.com; ✆ **098/23737**). The round-trip fare for the 15-minute journey is around €15 to €20.

Co. Mayo.

The National Museum of Ireland: Country Life ★★ MUSEUM   The
countryside outpost of Ireland's multisite national museum (the others are all in Dublin, see chapter 4), this one specializes in Irish life, trade, culture, and tradition since the mid-19th century. Absorbing and informative exhibitions deal with folklore; the natural environment and how local communities have relied on it for survival; political and social upheaval, particularly in the years preceding the Great Famine; traditional trades and crafts; and the changing life of the Irish people at home and at work. You could easily spend 3 hours wandering around here. They also have a thoughtful program of changing exhibitions. As at all the National Museum sites, entry is completely free.

Signposted from N5, Turlough Park, about 8km (5 miles) east of Castlebar, Co. Mayo. www.museum.ie. ✆ **094/903-1755.** Free admission. Tues–Sat 10am–5pm; Sun 2–5pm. Closed Mon.

Westport House and Pirate Adventure Park ★★ HISTORIC HOUSE/AMUSEMENT PARK   This family-friendly attraction requires a deep breath before listing everything there is to do here. It's all centered around an elegant late-18th-century residence—the home of Lord Altamont, the Marquess of Sligo and a descendant, it is said, of Pirate Queen Grace O'Malley (hence the bronze statue of her on the grounds). The work of Richard Cassels and James Wyatt, the house has a graceful staircase of ornate white Sicilian marble, unusual Art Nouveau glass, and carvings, family heirlooms, and silver. The grandeur of the residence is undeniable, but during the summer months a large proportion of visitors come here without even setting foot in the building; just follow the whoops and cheers of a couple thousand excited children and you'll find the sprawling **Pirate Adventure Park.** Here kids can burn off energy on the swinging pirate ship, log ride, go-karts, swan-shaped pedal boats, and giant bouncy castle. When that's over, you can all tour the gardens together in a Toytown-sized express train. Very young children can enjoy some slightly gentler fun at the **Pirate's Den** play area (an extra €3.50–€7 per child, depending on age). Upping the adventurous ante even

A TRIP TO achill island

The rugged, bog-filled, sparsely populated coast of counties Mayo and Sligo makes for scenic drives to secluded outposts. Leading the list is **Achill Island,** a heather-filled slip of land with sandy beaches and spectacular views of waves crashing against rocky cliffs.

Once you've crossed the bridge from the mainland, follow a winding road across the island to the little town of **Keel,** a trip that requires patience but rewards you with a camera full of photos. About 5.7km (3½ miles) west of Keel you'll find the secluded Blue Flag beach of **Keem Bay** (it was once a major fishing ground—basking shark were caught here commercially up until the 1950s—but no more). You can reach the bay along a small cliff-top road, which passes by cliff faces containing rich seams of glittering amethyst. Apparently it's not uncommon to find chunks of the stuff lying loose after heavy rainfall.

Hidden on the slopes of **Mount Slievemore,** Achill's tallest mountain, are the remains of an **abandoned village.** The hundred or so crumbling stone cottages of the nameless ghost town date back to sometime around the 12th century. It was deserted during the Great Famine, although some cottages were occasionally used until the very early years of the 20th century, a traditional practice known as "booleying"—seasonal occupation by farming communities, which continued here long after it had died out in the rest of Ireland. Mount Slievemore is between Keel and Doogort, in the northeastern part of the island.

At Kildavnet, between Derreen and Coughmore, in the southeastern corner of the island, you'll find **Granuaile's Tower,** an impressive 15th-century tower house once owned by Grace O'Malley, the "Pirate Queen" (see p. 223). There's not a great deal to see, but it's a stunning spot to admire. Nearby **Kildavnet Church** is thought by archaeologists to date from the 8th century.

To get to the Achill Island bridge, take N59 heading northwest out of Westport, then join R319, signposted to Achill. The drive from Westport to the crossing is 42km (26 miles) and should take around 40 minutes. Once you're on Achill Island, Keel is about another 14km (8⅔ miles) down the same road.

more, the **Adventure Activity Centre** is the latest addition, piling on bungee jumping, zip wires, tree climbing, archery, and a host of other high-adrenaline amusements. All activities at the Adventure Activity Centre must be paid for separately; prices start at €9 for a child's zip-wire ride and rise to €28 for a couple's "water zorbing," which involves traversing a body of water while trapped inside a giant bubble. You know, for fun!

The Westport Demense, Westport, Co. Mayo. www.westporthouse.ie. ✆ **098/27766. House, Gardens, and Pirate Park:** €22 adults; €20 seniors and students; €17 children; €62–€76 families. **House and Gardens only:** €14 adults; €11 seniors and students; €7 children. **Grounds only** (does not include adventure park): €6 adults; €3 children. **Pirate's Den play area:** €7.50 children 3 and older; €4 children under 3. House and Gardens open June Mon–Fri 10am–4pm, Sat–Sun 10am–6pm; July–Aug daily 10am–6pm; Sept–Oct daily 10am–4pm; Nov–Dec weekends 10am–4pm (daily 10am–4pm the week before Christmas). Pirate Adventure Park open June Wed–Fri 10am–3pm, Sat–Sun noon–6pm; July–Aug daily 11am–6pm. Adventure Activity Centre open June weekends 11am–6pm, July–Aug daily 11am–6pm. Adventure parks closed Sept–May, except school, Easter, and October holidays, and early May bank holiday weekend.

EXPLORING COUNTY SLIGO

County Sligo is known for its extraordinary concentration of ancient burial grounds and pre-Christian sites, most of which are in easy reach of the county capital, **Sligo Town.** Thanks to the impressive energy of the County Sligo tourism offices, however, this bucolic countryside has above all else been labelled "Yeats Country." Although he was born in Dublin, the great Irish poet W. B. Yeats spent so much time in County Sligo that it became a part of him, and he a part of it—literally, as he is buried here.

Top Attractions in County Sligo

Carrowkeel Passage Tomb Cemetery ★★ ANCIENT SITE

Atop a hill overlooking Lough Arrow, this ancient passage tomb cemetery is impressive, isolated, and frequently empty. Its 14 cairns, dolmens, and stone circles date from the Stone Age (ca. 5000 B.C.), and it's easy to feel a mystical connection to that history, standing among the cold, ageless rocks. The tombs face Carrowmore below and are aligned with the summer solstice. The walk uphill from the parking lot takes about 20 minutes, so be ready to get a little exercise. It's worth the effort. This is a simple site—no visitor center, no tea shop, no admission fee—nothing but ancient mystery.

Signposted on N4 between Sligo Town and Boyle, Co. Sligo. No phone. Free admission (open site).

Carrowmore Megalithic Cemetery ★★★ ANCIENT SITE

At the center of the Coolera Peninsula is one of the great sacred landscapes of the ancient world: A massive passage grave that once had a Stonehenge-like stone circle of its own. Encircling that were as many as 200 additional stone circles and passage graves arranged in an intricate and mysterious design. Over the years, some of the stones have been moved; more than 60 circles and passage graves still exist, although the site spreads out so far that many of them are in adjacent farmland. Look for your first dolmen in a paddock next to the road about a mile before you reach the site. The dolmens were the actual graves, once covered in stones and earth. Some of these sites are open to visitors, and you can get a map to them from the visitor center. (Not all are, however; be careful not to trespass on private land.) On the main site, the oldest tomb is thought to date from around 3,700 B.C.—making it one of the oldest pieces of freestanding stone architecture in the world. From Carrowmore, you can see the hilltop cairn grave of **Knocknarea** in the distance. The visitor center has good exhibits and guided tours. Follow signs from Woodville Road heading west out of Sligo Town, or from R292 at Ransboro.

Carrowmore, Co. Sligo. www.heritageireland.ie. © **071/916-1534.** Admission €4 adults; €3 seniors; €2 students and children; €10 families. Late Mar to mid-Oct daily 10am–6pm; last admission 1 hr before closing. Closed mid-Oct to Mar.

Eagles Flying ★★ AVIARY

Some of the biggest birds of prey in the world are displayed at this aviary and educational center near Ballymote. Eagles, vultures, owls, and falcons take part in an hour-long flying show daily

a poetic soul: W. B. YEATS

One of Ireland's greatest and most beloved writers, **William Butler Yeats** (1865–1939) had Sligo in his soul.

The first of Ireland's four Nobel laureates, Yeats (pronounced "Yates") was a poet, playwright, and politician. He was at the forefront of the Celtic Revival, which celebrated and championed native Irish culture and heritage. His work drew heavily on the traditional folklore of Ireland, steeped in myth and imagination.

Yeats grew up amid Sligo's verdant hills and dales, now known (by the tourist board at least) as "Yeats Country." In fact, parts of the county's tourism industry seems to focus on little else. You can cruise Lough Gill while listening to a live recital of Yeats's poetry; follow Yeats trails and buy a hundred items of Yeats memorabilia; and visit dozens of his purported haunts—some reputedly still spooked by his ghost, and some of which have only tenuous connections with the man.

Yeats died in Menton, on the French Riviera, in 1939. Knowing he was ill, he stated, "If I die here, bury me up there on the mountain, and then after a year or so, dig me up and bring me privately to Sligo." True to his wishes, in 1948 his body was moved to Sligo and reinterred at **Drumcliffe Church,** where his great-grandfather had been a rector. Drumcliffe is a village about 10km (6½ miles) north of Sligo Town, on the N15 road. His grave is marked with a dark, modest stone just left of the church, alongside his young wife, Georgie Hyde-Lee (when they married in 1917, he was 52 and she was 23.) His epitaph, "Cast a cold eye on life, on death . . ." comes from his poem "Under Ben Bulben." While you're there, also check out the 11th-century high cross in the churchyard—its faded eastern side shows Christ, Daniel in the lions' den, Adam and Eve, and Cain slaying Abel. There's also a visitor center and cafe on site.

at 11am and 3pm—outside or in a purpose-built arena. Most of the awe-inspiring birds who live at the center can be handled by visitors (under close supervision, of course). For young children who prefer their animals a little less intimidating, there's also a petting zoo.

Ballymote, Co. Sligo. www.eaglesflying.com. © **071/918-9310.** Admission €10 adults; €9 students; €6 children 3–16; children 2 and under free; €30 families. No credit cards. Late Mar–early Nov daily 10:30am–12:30pm, 2:30–4:30pm. Bird shows 11am and 3pm.

Irish National Famine Museum and Strokestown Park ★★ HISTORIC HOUSE/MUSEUM   From 1600 to 1979, Strokestown Park was the seat of the Pakenham-Mahon family, who were granted this vast estate by King Charles II in return for supporting the House of Stewart during the bloody English Civil War. In the 18th century, Thomas Mahon hired Richard Cassells—aka "Richard Castle," the architect behind Powerscourt House (p. 107) to replace the existing house with something more impressive. The result is this stunning 45-room Palladian mansion, a monument to upper-class privilege. In the north wing, note Ireland's last existing galleried kitchen, where the lady of the house could observe the cooking without doing any herself; in the south wing, there's a vaulted stable so magnificent that it has been described as an "equine cathedral." These days, however, Strokestown is also

11 | THE lough gill DRIVE

An essential stop on Yeats Country pilgrimages is this beautiful lake, which figured prominently in the writings of W. B. Yeats. A well-signposted route around the lake's perimeter covers 42km (26 miles) and takes less than an hour.

To start, head 1.6km (1 mile) south of Sligo Town and follow the signs for Lough Gill. Within 3.2km (2 miles), you'll reach the shoreline. Among the sites are **Parke's Castle** (see p. below); **Dooney Rock,** with its own nature trail and lakeside walk (inspiration for the poem "Fiddler of Dooney"); the **Lake Isle of Innisfree,** made famous in poetry and song; and the **Hazelwood Sculpture Trail,** a unique forest walk along the shores of Lough Gill, with 13 wood sculptures.

At the lake's east end, you can branch off to visit **Dromahair,** a delightful village on the River Bonet. The road along Lough Gill's upper shore brings you back to Sligo Town. Continue north on the main road (N15) to see the graceful profile of **Ben Bulben** (519m/1,702 ft.), one of the Dartry Mountains, rising off to your right. One of Yeats's last poems, "Under Ben Bulben," alludes to this majestic rock formation as a silent sentinel looming over Irish history.

If you prefer to see all this beautiful scenery from the water itself, **Lough Gill Cruises** take you around Lough Gill and the Garavogue River aboard the 72-passenger *Wild Rose* waterbus as you listen to the poetry of Yeats. The boat departs from Parke's Castle (see below), daily from Easter to October, at 12:30 and 3:30pm. Tickets are €15 adults, €7.50 children. Trips to Innisfree, sunset cruises, and dinner cruises are also scheduled. Call ✆ **071/916-4266** or visit www.roseofinnisfree.com for further information or booking.

the permanent home of the **Irish National Famine Museum,** one of the country's very best museums devoted to that deadly period in Irish history. It's a fitting pairing, because in the 1840s Major Denis Mahon, Strokestown's owner, exemplified the cruelty and indifference many landowners showed toward their tenants as the Famine spread, evicting starving people because they could no longer pay their rent. (Mahon even chartered ships to send his tenants to Canada.) Among the museum's dramatic exhibits, you'll see pleading letters penned by some of the tenants of Strokestown during the Famine years. In 1847, when Major Mahon was shot to death near Strokestown, two men were hastily convicted, but it was clear many more had motive to kill him.

Dublin-Castlebar Rd. (N5), Strokestown, Co. Sligo. www.strokestownpark.ie. ✆ **071/963-3013.** Admission €14 adults; €12 seniors and students; €6 children; €29 families. House can only be seen on 45-min. guided tours, at noon, 2:30, and 4pm (Oct to mid-Mar 2:30 only). Mid-Mar to Oct daily 10:30am–5:30pm; Nov to mid-Mar 10:30am-4pm.

The Model ★★ MUSEUM/ CULTURAL CENTER One of Ireland's most renowned contemporary art museums, the Model houses an impressive collection of paintings and other visual art. It includes probably the best collection of works by Jack B. Yeats (1871–1957) outside of the National Gallery in Dublin (see p. 73). Brother of William, Jack was one of the foremost Irish painters of the 20th century, painting landscapes and figures in a bold Expressionist style. Other luminaries of the Irish art world who are represented here include Louis le Brocquy (1916–2012), an extraordinary figurative painter, and portraitist Estella Solomons (1882–1968).

The Mall, Sligo, Co. Sligo. www.themodel.ie. ℭ **071/914-1405.** Free admission to exhibitions; tickets to other events free to around €25 (most around €10). Tues–Wed, Fri–Sat 10am–5:30pm; Thurs 10am–8pm; Sun noon–5pm. Closed Mon.

Parke's Castle ★ CASTLE   On the north side of the Lough Gill Drive (see box above), just over the County Leitrim border, Parke's Castle stands out as a lone outpost amid the natural tableau of lake views and woodland scenery. Named after an English family that gained possession of it during the 1620 plantation of Leitrim (when land was confiscated from the Irish and given to favored English families), this castle was originally the stronghold of the O'Rourke clan, rulers of the Kingdom of Breffni. Beautifully restored using Irish oak and traditional craftsmanship, it exemplifies the 17th-century fortified manor house.

On R286, 11.2km (7 miles) east of Sligo Town, Co. Leitrim. www.heritageireland.ie. ℭ **071/916-4149.** Admission €4 adults; €3 seniors; €2 students and children; €10 families. Apr–Sept daily 10am–6pm; last admission 45 min. before closing.

Sligo Abbey ★ HISTORIC SITE   Founded as a Dominican house in 1252 by Maurice Fitzgerald, Earl of Kildare, Sligo Abbey was the center of early Sligo Town. It thrived for centuries and flourished in medieval times when it was the burial place of the chiefs and earls of Sligo. But, as with other affluent religious settlements, the abbey was under constant attack, and it was finally destroyed in 1641. Much restoration work has been done in recent years, and the cloisters contain outstanding examples of stone carving; the 15th-century altar is one of few intact medieval altars in Ireland.

Abbey St., Sligo, Co. Sligo. www.heritageireland.ie. ℭ **071/914-6406.** Admission €4 adults; €3 seniors; €2 students and children; €10 families. Late Mar to mid-Oct daily 10am–6pm; last admission 45 min. before closing.

Sligo County Museum ★ MUSEUM   In the center of Sligo Town, this museum presents a good overview of the county's history, from ancient times to the present day. The most interesting sections cover the region's extraordinary prehistoric heritage, including a couple of ancient artifacts. The other standout sections are devoted to two of Sligo's most famous residents: the poet W. B. Yeats, whose mother was from Sligo and whose love of the county drastically influenced his work; and Constance Markievicz, an aristocrat who grew up in Sligo and became a leading Irish revolutionary.

Stephen St., Sligo Town. ℭ **071/911-1679.** Free admission. May–Sept Tues–Sat 9:30am–12:30pm, 2–4:50pm. Oct–Apr Tues–Sat 9:30am–12:30pm.

NORTHERN IRELAND

12

The vibrant and beautiful six counties of Ireland still under British rule are all the more fascinating for their troubled history. At their epicenter is Belfast, the capital of Northern Ireland—a curious combination of faded grandeur and forward-looking optimism. Belfast boomed in the 19th century as prosperity flowed from its vast textile and shipbuilding industries. The 20th century was not so kind to the city, which spent decades in decline, but it is now forging a new identity, complete with an artsy, edgy underbelly. Out from Belfast you'll find medieval castles, beautiful coastlines, and some truly spectacular natural wonders—all within easy reach of the city.

ESSENTIALS

Arriving

BY PLANE Belfast has two airports: **Belfast International** (www.belfastairport.com; © 028/9448-4848) and **George Best Belfast City Airport** (www.belfastcityairport.com; © 028/9093-9093). From the U.S., United Airlines (www.united.com; © 1800/864-8331) runs one regular, direct flight between Belfast and New York City's Newark International. **Aer Lingus** (www.aerlingus.com; © 01/814-1111), **British Airways** (www.ba.com; © 189/0626-747 in Ireland, or 084/4493-0787 in the U.K.), and **EasyJet** (www.easyjet.com; © 084/3104-1000) operate regular scheduled flights from Britain to Belfast. In the summer, **Virgin Atlantic** (www.virgin-atlantic.com; © 1800/862-8621) and **Thomas Cook** (www.thomascookairlines.com; © 0800/107-3409 from the U.K. only) fly a few direct flights between Belfast and Orlando, Florida. You can fly direct to Belfast from several European cities.

The **City of Derry Airport** (www.cityofderryairport.com; © **028/7181-0784**) is served by Ryanair (www.ryanair.com; © **0818/303030** in Ireland, 0871/246-0000 in the U.K.) from London Stanstead, Birmingham, Liverpool, and Glasgow, plus Alicante and Faro in summer.

VISITING NORTHERN IRELAND: f.a.q.

What is Northern Ireland? It's still part of Ireland, right?
Yes—and no. It's a part of the island of Ireland, but not the Republic of Ireland.

I'm confused. Is it a different country or not?
Bear with us—this is complicated. Northern Ireland is part of the United Kingdom. It has been a separate entity from the rest of Ireland since 1921. If "entity" sounds a little vague, that's because—get this—there isn't even an official term to describe what Northern Ireland is. (Trust us, we checked.) It is referred to, variously, as a country, a nation, a region, and a province. But the easiest way to think of it is like a state of the U.K. (Except the U.K. doesn't actually have states—told you it was complicated!).

What's the border crossing like?
There isn't one. It's basically a line on the map. In fact, it can be hard to tell when you've crossed into Northern Ireland at all. The only immediate difference you are likely to notice is that the road signs change.

Will I need to show my passport?
No. Nor will you need a separate visa. Besides, no border!

Is driving in Northern Ireland the same?
Basically, yes, but with one big difference: road signs show **miles,** not kilometers. Signs near the border usually show both. Don't forget to check that your travel insurance and any car-rental agreements are equally valid in Northern Ireland.

Does Northern Ireland use the euro?
No. The currency in Northern Ireland is the **British pound (sterling).** In practice, euros are accepted in some border areas, major tourist attractions, and hotels; however, you will probably be given change in pounds. ATMs are the easiest and cheapest way to get currency. (Just try using British pounds in the rest of Ireland, though . . .)

What's the exchange rate?
It averages around 1.4 euro to the pound, which sounds pretty steep, but the cost of living is lower in Northern Ireland—so much so, in fact, that people as far south as Dublin have been known to drive to Belfast for their grocery shopping.

What are those letters and numbers at the end of Northern Irish addresses?
They're British-style postal codes. Postcodes are still in the process of being introduced to the Republic, but almost every address in Northern Ireland has one. This is actually a big advantage if you're driving, as it makes GPS navigation much easier.

Any other tips?
Your mobile phone company will treat Northern Ireland as the U.K., so inform them in advance if you think you'll be crossing the border. This might avoid higher international roaming charges. Oh, and one more thing about the money—if you're travelling onward to Britain, be aware that Northern Irish pounds look completely different from standard ones, and many British businesses won't accept them. (They're legally obliged to, but . . . well, *you* try arguing).

BY BUS From Dublin Airport, **AirCoach** (www.aircoach.ie; © **01/844-7118**) runs a regular, non-stop service to Belfast; round-trip tickets are £16 and the trip takes just under 2 hours. **Ulsterbus** (www.translink.co.uk; © **028/9066-6630**) runs buses from Dublin to Belfast and towns across Northern Ireland. The fastest bus between Belfast and Derry, Ulsterbus's no. 212,

Northern Ireland

ATLANTIC OCEAN

Tory I.

Horn Head
Tory Sound
Dunfanaghy
Magheroarty
Creeslough
Gortahork
N56
Lough Beagh
Glenveagh National Park
Derryveagh Mts.
Fintown
L. Finn
Glenties
Ardara
Blue Stack Mts.
N15
L. Eske
Mountcharles
Donegal
Killybegs
Lough Derg
Ballintra
N15
Donegal Bay
Ballyshannon
Belleek
Cliffoney
Bundoran
Dartry Mts.
Lough Melvin
Glencar L.
Manorhamilton
Sligo
Lough Gill
Dromahair
N16
Belcoo
Drumkeeran
Glengavlen
SLIGO
Lough Allen
N4
Lough Arrow
Ballyfarnon
Drumshanbo
Lough Key
Boyle
Carrick-on-Shannon
Drumsna
Lough Gara
N61
Lough Boderg
N4
Dromod
ROSCOMMON
Mohill
L. Gowna
Granard
LONGFORD
Longford

Malin Head
Ballygorman
Ballyliffin
Inishowen
Rosguill
Fanad
Drumfree
L. Swilly
Rathmullan
Buncrana
Carrowkeel
Milford
N56
Ramelton
Eglinton
Kilmacrenan
Gartan Lough
Letterkenny
N13
Derry (Londonderry)
DONEGAL
N13
Foyle
N14
A5
Raphoe
Lifford
Strabane
Stranorlar
N15
Sion Mills
Ballybofey
Newtownstewart
Mourne
Castlederg
Derg
Omagh
A5
Pettigo
Ederny
Dromore
A47
A35
A32
Lower Lough Erne
Tully
FERMANAGH
Fivemiletown
A4
Enniskillen
L. Macnean
Lisbellow
A4
Upper Lough Erne
A32
A34
Lisnaskea
A509
Clones
N87
Newtownbutler
Belturbet
Ballyconnell
N3
Iron Mts.
Lough Oughter
Ballinamore
Butlers Bridge
LEITRIM
Cavan
CAVAN
Arva
Ballinagh
Brosna
N55
Lough Sheelin

NORTHERN IRELAND
Belfast
Dublin
REPUBLIC OF IRELAND

Northern Ireland counties shown are the historic counties. UK counties were reorganized after 1973.

takes just under 2 hours. **Bus Éireann** (www.buseireann.ie; © 091/562000) offers a few buses a day to Belfast and Derry from Dublin, where you can make connections to other cities in the Republic; Derry also has a Bus Éireann connection through Letterkenny, County Donegal.

BY TRAIN   Belfast has two train stations: Great Victoria Street Station and Belfast Central Station on East Bridge Street. Contact **Northern Ireland Railways** (www.translink.co.uk; © 028/9066-6630) for tickets. The journey from Dublin takes about 2½ hours. Trains from Belfast to Londonderry/Derry Station—known by everyone as **Waterside Railway Station** (© 028/7134-2228), on Duke Street, on the east side of the Foyle River—take about 2 hours. A free Linkline bus brings passengers from the train station to the city center.

BY CAR   Driving from Dublin to Belfast is easy; just go north up the M1 motorway. From Dublin airport the journey takes about 90 minutes in good traffic. From Sligo Town take N16 and A4 west; from there it's 124 miles (200km), about 2½ hours.

BELFAST

Belfast's wealthy past has left the city with some handsome industrial remnants. However, it's the more troubled, 20th-century Belfast that many visitors find most intriguing, and a **Black Taxi Tour** ★★★ (see p. 243) is a unique way to explore that history. Meanwhile, a whole new mini-industry has sprung up here with attractions related to the most famous shipwreck in history. Because the SS *Titanic* was built in Belfast—a curious symbol of pride for natives of this city—shipwreck aficionados (aka "Titanoraks") are drawn by the bold new *Titanic* **Belfast** museum (p. 244) and the *Titanic* **Dock and Pump House** (p. 245) in the newly regenerated harbor district.

City Layout

The **City Center** spreads out from around the impressive, domed City Hall building and bustling **Donegall Square.** This is the best place for shopping, particularly along Donegall Place, which extends north from the square onto Royal Avenue. Bedford Street, which runs south from Donegall Square, becomes Dublin Road, which, in turn, leads south to the **University Quarter,** the leafy area around Queen's University. This is where you'll find the Botanic Gardens, art galleries, and museums, as well as a buzzing nightlife scene. Heading north from Donegall Place, it's a short distance to the **Cathedral Quarter,** which surrounds Donegall Street, and holds, as the name implies, Belfast Cathedral, as well as many Victorian warehouses. Finally, there's the **Golden Mile**—the area around Great Victoria Street beyond Bradbury Place. It's considered the city's best address for restaurants and pubs, although it's a bit hyperbolically named. As one local said to us, "It's not a mile and it's not golden. But it's nice enough." Some of the city's biggest attractions are in the new **Titanic Quarter,** a series of commercial developments around Belfast Harbour northeast of the city center.

Visitor Information

The main tourist information center for the city is the **Belfast Welcome Centre** at 9 Donegall Square, BT1 5GJ (www.visit-belfast.com; ⓒ **028/9024-6609**). It's open Monday to Saturday, 9am to 5:30pm, and Sunday, 11am to 4pm. They can help book accommodations in the city, and they also have a bureau de change and left luggage facility. Smaller visitor information points are at **Belfast International Airport** (ⓒ **028/9448-4677**) and **George Best Belfast City Airport** (ⓒ **028/9093-5372**).

[FastFACTS] BELFAST

ATMs/Banks ATMs aren't hard to come by in central Belfast; there are several banks around Donegall Square. In the countryside they can be harder to find, so it's best to get cash before leaving the city.

Dentists For dental emergencies, your hotel should contact a dentist for you. Otherwise, in Belfast, contact **Dublin Road Dental Practice,** 23 Dublin Rd., BT2 7HB (ⓒ **028/9032-5345**) or **Lisburn Road Dental Clinic,** 424 Lisburn Rd., BT9 6GN ((ⓒ **028/9038-2262**).

Doctors For medical emergencies, dial ⓒ **999.** For non-emergencies, your hotel should call you a doctor. Otherwise, there's **Ormeau Health Centre,** 120 Ormeau Rd. (ⓒ **028/9032-6030**) or the **Crumlin Road Health Centre,** 94-100 Crumlin Rd. (ⓒ **028/9504-2610**).

Emergencies For police, fire, or other emergencies, dial ⓒ **999.**

Pharmacies Belfast has branches of **Boots the Chemist** at 35-47 Donegall

Place (ⓒ **028/9024-2332**) and 17-21 Great Northern Mall (ⓒ **028/9031-0530**).

Post Offices Main branches in Belfast include 16-22 Bedford St. and 12-14 Bridge St.

Taxis In Belfast you can catch a taxi at the stand in front of City Hall. Alternatively try phoning **Value Cabs** (ⓒ **028/9080-9080**), **Courtesy Cabs** (ⓒ **028/9032-9988**), or **Aldergrove Taxis** (ⓒ **028/9082-59666**).

Where to Stay in & Around Belfast

Belfast's hotel scene has grown in leaps and bounds during the last few years. A decade ago, expecting to find a top-quality boutique hotel or B&B from £100 per room was a tough task; today, however, you have much more to choose from. Best of all, because Belfast is still developing as a major tourist destination, the prices are still relatively low—although depending on where you're from, that advantage can be quickly wiped out by the exchange rate, which can often be more punishing to pounds than it is to euros.

EXPENSIVE

Europa Hotel ★★ For some time this has been a lodging of choice for big-name politicians, diplomats, and celebrities when visiting Belfast (Hillary Clinton stayed here a couple of years ago). The decor is subtly masculine; the lobby has marble floors with a modern gas fireplace to take the edge off the chill. Large guest rooms are contemporary in style, with comfortable beds and sizeable bathrooms. A little rubber ducky in a top hat is waiting for you as you enter the bathroom (you can take it home if you want). It's a nice touch and indicative of the attention to detail here. Downstairs is a piano bar and the laidback **Causerie** restaurant. Check the website for deals such as a theater package that includes tickets to the Grand Opera House (see p. 248) *and* return train travel from Dublin, for around £100 per couple.

Great Victoria St. Belfast, BT2 7AP. www.hastingshotels.com/europa-belfast. ℂ **028/9027-1066.** 240 units. £117–£198. Free parking. Breakfast not included in lower rates. **Amenities:** Restaurant; 2 bars; room service; gym; Wi-Fi (free).

The Merchant Hotel ★★★ One of Ireland's most luxurious hotels, the Merchant is a real treat. The Victorian building was once a bank, and the conversion is stunning, from the grand dining room (lacquered and gilded Corinthian columns, marble floors, ceiling friezes) to an elegant cocktail lounge (chandeliers and a gently curved, dark wood bar). Guest rooms are thoroughly modern, but ask for one with Art Deco–style decor as opposed to traditional decor—they're larger and better designed. There's an excellent **spa,** complete with hydrotherapy pool and treatment rooms and even a hot tub on the roof with a lovely view over the city. The **Great Room Restaurant** serves top-notch modern Irish cuisine. Afternoon tea is a bit of an event here, so book ahead if you want to indulge. Service is impeccable, and the staff could hardly be friendlier or more helpful.

16 Skipper St., Belfast, BT1 2DZ. www.themerchanthotel.com. ℂ **028/9023-4888.** 62 units. £160–£240. Valet parking. Breakfast not included in lower rates. Dinner, bed and breakfast packages available. **Amenities:** Restaurant, bar, spa, gym; Wi-Fi (free).

MODERATE

Dunnanelly Country House ★★★ This delightful country mansion is just outside Downpatrick, about 18 miles (29km) south of Belfast, but the half-hour or so it takes to drive here from the city is a small price to pay for such an idyllic retreat. The beautiful grounds stretch for miles. The decor inside mixes a feeling of history with a playful edge: traditional Regency-style color schemes and furnishings are offset by pieces of modern art, an interesting sculpture, or (memorably) an antique rocking horse, complete with an oh-so-happy-to-see-you grin. The guest rooms are thoughtfully designed with large, modern bathrooms and have lovely views of the estate, tempting you to take a gentle stroll or invigorating hike. And you may need that exercise to help work off the hearty and delicious breakfasts. Guests have the use of a conservatory, a sitting room, and a separate game room. There's no dinner, but the owners can cheerfully point you in the direction of the best local pubs.

26 Rocks Chapel Rd., Downpatrick, Co. Down, BT30 9BA. www.dunnanellycountry house.com. ℂ **077/1277-9085.** 3 units. £100. Free parking. Breakfast included. No children under 12 unless all 3 rooms booked by same group. **Amenities:** Wi-Fi (free).

Malmaison Belfast ★ This is the only Irish outpost of Malmaison, a British mini-chain that specializes in rescuing unusual historic buildings and turning them into hip boutique hotels. This one used to be a seed warehouse, of all things. It's a gorgeous four-story building, with weathered stone walls and tall, arched windows. Inside, ceilings soar, and they've done beautiful

Belfast

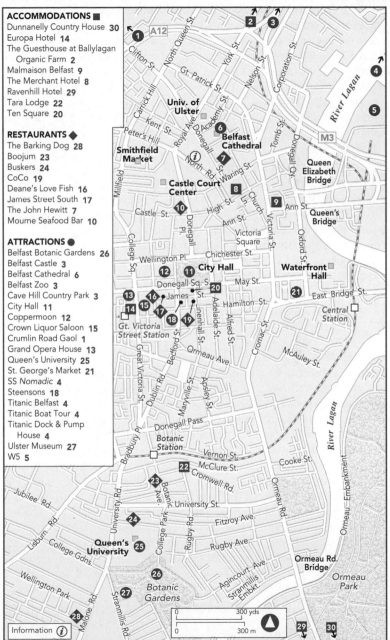

ACCOMMODATIONS ■
Dunnanelly Country House **30**
Europa Hotel **14**
The Guesthouse at Ballylagan
    Organic Farm **2**
Malmaison Belfast **9**
The Merchant Hotel **8**
Ravenhill Hotel **29**
Tara Lodge **22**
Ten Square **20**

RESTAURANTS ◆
The Barking Dog **28**
Boojum **23**
Buskers **24**
CoCo **19**
Deane's Love Fish **16**
James Street South **17**
The John Hewitt **7**
Mourne Seafood Bar **10**

ATTRACTIONS ●
Belfast Botanic Gardens **26**
Belfast Castle **3**
Belfast Cathedral **6**
Belfast Zoo **3**
Cave Hill Country Park **3**
City Hall **11**
Coppermoon **12**
Crown Liquor Saloon **15**
Crumlin Road Gaol **1**
Grand Opera House **13**
Queen's University **25**
St. George's Market **21**
SS *Nomadic* **4**
Steensons **18**
Titanic Belfast **4**
Titanic Boat Tour **4**
Titanic Dock & Pump
    House **4**
Ulster Museum **27**
W5 **5**

Information ⓘ

things with the space, using a chic, playful design that retains some of the original industrial touches. Carpets are dark hued, and walls are painted in deep, matte hues of grey and dark blue, with steel girders left exposed here and there. Bedrooms are large, very quiet, and comfortable, with neutral colors, low lighting, huge beds, and modern bathrooms—most have separate baths and showers. Breakfasts are large and varied. The in-house restaurant serves good, brasserie-style cooking (dinner, bed and breakfast packages are available) and there's a lively bar too.

34-38 Victoria St., Belfast, BT1 3GH. www.malmaison.com/locations/belfast. ✆ **084/4693-0650.** 64 units. £70–£190. Discounted parking at nearby lot (£10 per day). Breakfast not included in lower rates. **Amenities:** Wi-Fi (free), restaurant, bar, room service, gym.

Ten Square ★ This boutique hotel aims to emulate luxurious five-star hotels at a fraction of the cost. The historic Belfast building, minutes from all the sights, recently underwent a large renovation. The decor deliberately contrasts styles—exposed stone and tall arched windows in public areas, while bedrooms are somewhere on the line between chic and kitsch, with polka-dotted carpet and blue velvet fabrics. The king-size beds, draped in pure white linens, are very firm. The overall effect works pretty stylishly. Jospers restaurant specializes in Irish meats, particularly steak, and also serves afternoon tea with all the extras. Check the website for special offers, including a *Titanic*-themed deal.

10 Donegall Sq., Belfast, BT1 5JD. www.tensquare.co.uk. ✆ **028/9024-1001.** 23 units. £95–£145 double. Breakfast included. Street parking only. **Amenities:** Restaurant; bar; Wi-Fi (free).

INEXPENSIVE

The Guesthouse at Ballylagan Organic Farm ★★ Ballylagan is a working, fully certified organic farm (the first in Northern Ireland, no less) and at the center of it all is this welcoming little 1840s farmhouse. The two-story greystone building is covered by lush vines, and looks as if it, too, has grown out of the landscape. Patricia and Tom Gilbert are passionate about what they do, and that ethos shines through, especially in the food. All breakfast ingredients are completely organic (of course), from the fresh baked bread to the bacon and sausages at breakfast; home-cooked dinners can be provided too, if booked in advance. (They can't serve wine, due to licensing restrictions, but you're welcome to bring your own.) The guest rooms are in a separate building from the owners' home, giving everyone a bit of privacy. Bedrooms are painted in soothing colors, with modern prints on the wall. The rooms are large enough to easily fit a sofa and a couple of chairs in addition to the extremely comfortable beds, so you certainly won't feel cramped. There's a guest lounge, where the owners will leave you tea and homemade cakes on your arrival. For an extra £10 you can have the use of a wood-burning stove in your room. A quiet night's sleep is guaranteed. Ballyclare is about 13 miles (21km) north of Belfast.

12 Ballylagan Rd., Straid, Ballyclare, BT39 9NF. www.ballylagan.com. ✆ **028/9332-2129.** 4 units. £95. Free parking. Breakfast included. **Amenities:** Wi-Fi (free).

Ravenhill Hotel ★★   A friendly welcome awaits from hosts Roger and Olive, whose handsome Victorian corner house has been converted into one of the best B&Bs in Belfast. They really know how to make guests feel at home, and nothing seems too much trouble. Bedrooms are simple but neat as a pin, with print fabrics and views of the street. You're in a residential area here, but not far from the action; the city center is about a 10-minute cab or bus ride. Roger cooks delicious breakfasts and guests can expect the full Ulster fry, in addition to a few options such as kippers with parsley butter and scrambled eggs. They also bake their own traditional Irish wheaten bread from scratch, even down to milling their own flour. At certain times of the year you can get a discount for stays of 2 nights or more. You'll be hard pressed to find a better or more hospitable B&B at this price.

690 Ravenhill Rd., Belfast, BT6 0BZ. www.ravenhillhouse.com. ⓒ **028/9020-7444.** 5 units. £85–£95. Free parking. Breakfast included. **Amenities:** Wi-Fi (free).

Tara Lodge ★★   When Tara Lodge opened in the mid-2000s, it was part of a new wave of modern, inexpensive, boutique-style small hotels in Belfast, a city where good budget accommodations were scarce. It has more competition these days, but Tara Lodge still manages to get everything just about right. Guest rooms are simple and contemporary in style, if perhaps a little small, but the beds are large and comfortable. Breakfasts are very good and offer plenty of choice. The **Botanic Gardens** ★★ (p. 242) and **Ulster Museum** ★★★ (p. 245) are about 10 minutes away on foot; you could walk to the city center in 25 minutes, or it's a short cab ride. The hotel doesn't have a full restaurant, but breakfast is served every morning and there are plenty of good eateries within easy reach.

36 Cromwell Rd., Belfast, BT7 1JW. www.taralodge.com. ⓒ **028/9059-0900.** 34 units. £76–£133. Free parking. Breakfast included. **Amenities:** Wi-Fi (free).

Where to Eat in Belfast

A prominent British journalist tells the story of ordering an Ulster fry in Belfast sometime in the 1970s. "No sausage," he asked the waitress. When his food arrived, there were sausages on the plate. He sent it back, asking again for no sausage. But back it came, with sausages still there. "But I said no sausages," he complained. "Chef says sausage is compulsory," came the taciturn reply. Today the Belfast dining scene is, happily, much more cosmopolitan. The number of top restaurants in the city seems to increase every year, from funky little gastropubs to chic fine dining.

EXPENSIVE

CoCo ★★ MODERN EUROPEAN/INTERNATIONAL   Coco's funky dining room is plastered in modern art along with posters and photo-collages that set the tone. The contemporary menu has an international edge, with flavors like roast chicken served with Madeira cream, or monkfish fried in curry-flavored batter. The vegetarian menu is a pleasant surprise; try the linguini made with bell peppers, almonds, and fresh basil. Prices are a little high for the evening service, but the three-course pre-theater menu is just £19. They also do a popular Sunday lunch.

7-11 Linenhall St., Belfast, BT2 8AA. www.cocobelfast.com. © **028/9031-1150.** Main courses £15–£24. Mon–Fri noon–3pm, 5:30–9:30pm; Sat 5:30–9:30pm; Sun noon–9pm.

James Street South ★★ MODERN IRISH   One of Belfast's leading restaurants, James Street South has built a great reputation on interesting modern cuisine with an inventive twist. While the place looks unpretentious, with exposed brick walls and an industrial-chic vibe, the food is outstanding; you could start with some cured salmon with passion fruit, or corned beef with Brussels sprouts, followed by poached Guinea fowl, or a black truffle risotto. A tasting menu is compact and interesting (£40 for four courses, or £60 with paired wines).

21 James St. South, Belfast, BT2 7GA. www.jamesstreetsouth.co.uk. © **028/9043-4310.** Main courses £16–£24. Mon 5:30pm–10:30pm. Tues–Sat 12:30–2:30pm, 5:30–10:30pm.

MODERATE

The Barking Dog ★★ IRISH/INTERNATIONAL   There's something quintessentially Belfast about this place—quirky, artsy, lively, but ultimately no-nonsense. The dining room has a funky pub feel, complete with exposed brick and old candelabras balanced on battered wood tables. If you sit in the front garden, you're separated from the street by a fence with paw prints all over it. The menu is balanced and straightforward—a juicy cheeseburger with fat French fries, for example, or a simple fish pie. Vegetarian choices are more than the usual "mushroom pie" variety—herb gnocchi and green beans, perhaps, or sweet-potato ravioli. The selection of nibbles (a good value at five for £12) puts a nicely Irish-style twist on tapas. There's a good lunch menu, and the Sunday brunch is popular.

33-35 Malone Rd., Belfast, BT9 6RU. www.barkingdogbelfast.com. © **028/9066-1885.** Main courses £11–£24. Mon–Thurs noon–3pm and 5:30–10pm; Fri–Sat noon–3pm and 5:30–11pm; Sun noon–9pm. No children after 9pm.

Buskers ★ INTERNATIONAL   We estimate that you will leave this place feeling an appreciable percentage cooler than when you went in. A favorite hangout of students from nearby Queen's University, Busker's calls itself "musically inclined," which is clear enough from the vintage-style murals of Bowie and Hendrix. The food is best described as a mix of pub and gastropub, although often at distinctly un-gastro prices (lunch specials for just £5, for instance). Choose from generous plates of burgers, steaks, tacos, and seafood, and just say yes if they ask you if you'd like the house specialty sweet-potato fries on the side. The breakfasts here are excellent too, if you're bored of hotel fare—though they're only served on weekends.

44 University Rd., Belfast, BT7 1NJ. www.beatricekennedy.co.uk. © **028/9020-2290.** Main courses £5–£18. Mon–Thurs noon–9pm; Fri noon–10pm; Sat 10am–10pm; Sun 10am–8pm.

Deane's Love Fish ★★ SEAFOOD   Michael Deane is something of a local celebrity chef. **Eipic,** his flagship formal restaurant on Howard Street, is known for very good Irish-French cuisine, but the adjacent **Love Fish** is equally good—and (even better) less expensive. Here you'll find plates such as Dundrum mussels with garlic cream sauce and sourdough bread, or fish pie with a Gruyère cheese topping. After 10pm there's a late-night menu of nibbles and snacks (blue cheese salad; smoked salmon and horseradish; sardines on toast). Also here is the excellent **Meat Locker,** a laid-back grill where you can pick up a three-course pre-theater menu for an incredibly reasonable £18. Michael Deane now has several offshoots across Belfast, each for a slightly different crowd. The **Deli-Bistro** (✆ 028/9024-8800) and **Deli/Vin Café** (✆ 028/9024-8830), a tapas bar, share premises on Bedford Street; while in the University Quarter, next to the Ulster Museum, is the informal bistro, **Deanes at Queens** (✆ 028/9038-2111). The newest addition to the mini-empire is his foray into Italian cooking, **Deane & Decano** (✆ 028/9066-3108), on Lisburn Road. *Tip:* Love Fish has one of Belfast's best lunch deals—main dishes for just £6.50.

36-40 Howard St., Belfast, BT1 6PF. www.michaeldeane.co.uk. ✆ **028/9033-1134.** Main courses £9–£17. Mon–Sat noon–11pm; Sun 1–6pm.

Mourne Seafood Bar ★★★ SEAFOOD   *The* place in Belfast for top-quality seafood. Oysters are a specialty, served traditionally, with Tabasco and lemon, or in more elaborate ways, such as with pickled ginger and soy dressing. Alternatively, you could go for some spicy piri-piri prawns to start, followed by one of the fresh daily specials like seared scallops with pea risotto. The atmosphere is relaxed and convivial, and the prices are thoroughly reasonable for food this good. They don't take reservations at lunchtime, but evening booking is essential.

34-36 Bank St., Belfast, BT1 1HL. www.mourneseafood.com. ✆ **028/9024-8544.** Main courses £6–£15. Mon–Thurs noon–9:30pm; Fri-Sat noon–4pm and 5–10:30pm; Sun 1–9pm.

INEXPENSIVE

Boojum ★★ MEXICAN   Lines have been known to stretch way down the street at busy times for this jaunty, humble-looking emporium. There are no frills, but the food is excellent and fresh as can be. The menu is pretty simple—just choose from burritos, tacos, fajitas or salad, then your main meat or veg ingredients, and one of several kinds of salsa. (Brave souls will want to try the fiery naga; the less masochistic among us may prefer the tasty salsa verde.) Wash it all down with a soda or a nice cold bottle of Mexican beer. They have a few tables, but most people get theirs to go. There's a second branch on Chichester Street (✆ 028/9023-0600). *Note:* Boojum doesn't take credit cards.

Botanic Ave., Belfast, BT1 1JL. www.boojummex.com. ✆ **028/9031-5334.** All items £5–£6. No credit cards. Daily 11:30am–10pm.

The John Hewitt ★ IRISH/INTERNATIONAL   Near the Cathedral, this atmospheric bar is a popular hangout with locals. The gastropub-style lunch menu is a real crowd pleaser—soup of the day with crusty bread, creamy chicken pies, roast cod with chili salsa. From 3:30pm until just before 6, the

the art of conflict: BELFAST'S STREET MURALS

Painted by amateur artists—albeit very talented ones—the huge street murals in West Belfast tell tales of history, strife, anger, or peace. The densest concentration is around the **Falls and Shankill roads**—the epicenter of the conflict during the Troubles, from the late 1960s to the mid-1990s. The Falls Road is staunchly Catholic and Republican (that is, those who want to see Ireland united as a single country). Shankill, just half a mile away, is resolutely Protestant and Loyalist (those who want Northern Ireland to remain part of the United Kingdom).

Although all are deeply political, there is a noticeable divide between the tones of the murals. Those on the Falls Road tend to be about solidarity with the downtrodden (and not just in Ireland—you'll see murals about war and oppression in other parts of the world too). On the corner of Falls Road and Sevastopol Street is the surprisingly small Sinn Féin headquarters. At one end of the building is a mural of the late hunger striker **Bobby Sands** (1954–81), arguably the most famous political mural in Ireland.

By contrast, the Shankill murals are more strident, featuring more violent and threatening imagery, although some of the most offensive were removed a few years ago by the government.

Locals in all districts are very proud of their murals and are fine with visitors taking photos. Still, you should exercise the usual caution you would in any rough city neighborhood. It's advisable to avoid these parts of town on **parade days**—ostensibly celebratory events, these tend toward displays of nationalism, erupting into street violence. The biggest, and most controversial, is the Protestant "Orange Order" parade on July 12th. Any parades likely to cause trouble are well covered by the local media, so it's easy to know when one is coming up.

The best, safest, and certainly the most informative way to see the murals is to take a **Black Taxi Tour ★★★** (see below). The tours are a real Belfast highlight, and could hardly be more convenient—the drivers will pick you up at your hotel and drop you off anywhere you like in the city.

menu shifts to nibbles and sharing bowls. They don't serve food in the evenings or any time on Sundays, but you may still want to drop by—the John Hewitt is one of the best spots in the city for live music, with bands every night from 9:30pm or 5:30pm on Saturday. Admission to gigs is usually free.

51 Donegall St., Belfast, BT1 2FH. www.thejohnhewitt.com. ✆ **028/9023-3768.** Main courses £5–£9. Mon–Fri 11:30am–1am; Sat noon–1am; Sun 5–10pm. (Food served Mon–Sat noon–6pm.)

Exploring Belfast
TOP ATTRACTIONS

Belfast Botanic Gardens & Palm House ★★ GARDENS   Dating from 1828, these gardens were first laid out by the Belfast Botanic and Horticultural Society, but their most important feature came along 10 years later, when noted Belfast architect Charles Lanyon designed the beautiful glass-and-cast-iron conservatory. Now known as the Palm House, this curvilinear Victorian glasshouse contains an excellent variety of tropical plants, including sugar cane, coffee, cinnamon, banana, aloe, ivory nut, rubber, bamboo, guava, and spindly birds of paradise. If the weather's fine, stroll in the outdoor rose gardens, which date back to 1927. The **Ulster Museum ★★★** (p. 245) is also on the grounds.

College Park, Botanic Avenue, Belfast, BT7 1LP. ℰ **028/9031-4762.** Free admission. Palm House and Tropical Ravine Apr–Sept daily 1–5pm; Oct–Mar daily 1–4pm. Gardens daily 7:30am–sunset.

Black Taxi Tour ★★★ TOUR For many years, Belfast was best known for its most conflicted neighborhoods, where in the 1970s and '80s protest and violence occurred daily. Peace has (precariously) held on the Catholic Falls Road and its nearby parallel, the Protestant Shankill Road, for nearly 15 years, so it's finally safe to visit these once-troubled areas. A growing industry supports this new tourism initiative, with the Black Taxi Tour by far the best option. Tours are conducted in London-style cabs that take you through the neighborhoods, past the barbed wire, towering dividing walls, and partisan murals, as guides explain their significance. Drivers, who are all locals, are relaxed, patient, and unbiased, with a talent for explaining this complicated history to outsiders in an easy and engaging way. Tours aren't just limited to politics; the guides will also take you to see the *Titanic* shipyard and other parts of the city if you wish. Just ask when you book. The standard tour lasts about 90 minutes, and guides will pick you up and drop you off anywhere in the city.

www.belfasttours.com. ℰ **028/9064-2264.** £30 for up to 3 passengers, then £10 for each additional passenger, up to 6 people.

Crown Liquor Saloon ★★★ ARCHITECTURAL SITE/PUB Easily the most impressive Victorian pub in the city, and possibly the best building in Belfast, the Crown Liquor Saloon piles on the atmosphere. The old "gin palace" owes its ornate appearance to Italian workers who came to Ireland in the late 19th century to work on churches but ended up building this. Some of the finer features definitely have something ecclesiastical about them, from the stained glass in the windows to the pew-like "snugs," their elaborately carved doors designed to shield the more refined class of Victorians from their fellow drinkers. The floors are intricately tiled, and the ceiling is gorgeous hammered copper. This place was considered so important to the iconography of Belfast that it was actually bought for the nation by the National Trust in the 1970s, ensuring its impeccable upkeep while it continues to run as a working pub.

46 Great Victoria St., Belfast, BT2 7BA. www.nicholsonspubs.co.uk/thecrownliquor saloonbelfast. ℰ **028/9024-3187.** Mon–Wed 11:30am–11:30pm; Thurs–Sat 11:30am–midnight; Sun 12:30–10pm.

Crumlin Road Gaol ★★ HISTORIC SITE From 1846 until its closure 150 years later, Crumlin Road Gaol (known as "The Crum") was one of the most notorious prisons in Northern Ireland. The interior brings to mind the popular image of a Victorian-era prison, with its forbidding, fortress-like exterior, and row upon row of cells. An informative 75-minute tour takes you around the building, filling in some fascinating details of what prison life was like here. It would take a hard person indeed not to shudder as you walk down the claustrophobic underground tunnel connecting to the old courthouse across the street, or stand inside the condemned cell from which prisoners made their final journeys until 1961. Improbable though it sounds, the Crum is now used as a conference center and wedding venue.

53–55 Crumlin Rd., Belfast, BT4 6ST. www.crumlinroadgaol.com. ⓒ **028/9074-1500.** Admission £8.50 adults; £7 seniors and students, £6.50 children 5–15; children under 5 free; £25 families. Daily 10am–4:30pm (last tour).

SS Nomadic ★★ SHIP The last working ship in the White Star Line fleet, the Nomadic was built in Belfast as a tender to the most famous ocean liner in history—the ill-fated SS *Titanic.* ("Tenders" were small steamships that ferried passengers and supplies to and from the ocean-going behemoths.) After seeing action in both World Wars—first pressganged into service by the French Navy, then used by the British to evacuate Cherbourg, where she came under fire from the Nazis—*Nomadic* returned to work as a tender until 1968. She spent the next 35 years in France as a *bateau mouche* floating restaurant, before bailiffs seized the poor ship in 2003. *Nomadic* looked destined for the scrapheap, until the people of Belfast raised enough money to rescue her. After a decade-long restoration, *Nomadic* has been returned to her original 1911 glory. You can tour the whole vessel, from the cramped and claustrophobic crew quarters to the bridge and upper deck. Exhibitions along the way tell the full story behind *Nomadic,* along with profiles of passengers who sailed on her throughout the years. Daily ticket numbers are limited due to space—book in advance if possible.

Hamilton Dock, Queens Rd., Belfast, BT3 9DT. www.nomadicbelfast.com. ⓒ **028/9076-6386.** Admission £7 adults; £5 seniors, students, and children 5–16; children under 5 free; £20 families. June–Aug daily 9am–7pm; Apr–May and Sept daily 9am–6pm; Oct–Mar daily 10am–5pm.

Titanic Belfast ★★★ MUSEUM This ambitious new museum, which opened in 2012 to great fanfare, tells the story of the *Titanic* in revelatory detail. Located next to the site where the doomed vessel was constructed, the enormous angular frontage, clad in 2000 individual sheets of aluminum, juts out in four directions at the height of the ship's actual bow. The innovative design continues across nine well-laid-out galleries, covering everything from the *Titanic*'s construction to her triumphant launch, disastrous sinking, and the lasting cultural phenomenon that rose in her wake. A special ride takes you on a virtual tour of the shipyard to see how *Titanic* and her sister ship, *Olympic,* were built. In a split-level gallery you can even "explore" the wreck yourself, via huge high-definition screens and other interactive gizmos. Finally, the **Ocean Exploration Centre** offers high-tech exhibits on the science of sea exploration, including a live link to an undersea probe. In truth, the content can sometimes feel stretched to fill the space, but it's all impressively done. Needless to say, an extremely well-stocked gift shop is at the end. Crowds can swell at busy times, so it's advisable to book ahead in summer.

1 Olympic Way, Belfast, BT3 9DP. www.titanicbelfast.com. ⓒ **028/9076-6386.** Admission £17 adults; £13 seniors and students (weekdays); £15 seniors and students

(weekends); £7.25 children 5–16; children under 5 free; £42 families. Parking £1.50 per hr. for 1st hr., then £1 per hr. afterward. June–Aug daily 9am–7pm; Apr–May and Sept daily 9am–6pm; Oct–Mar daily 10am–5pm. Last admission 1 hr. 45 min. before closing.

Titanic Boat Tour ★★ TOUR   Many of Belfast's historic shipyard buildings were demolished in the early 2000s to make way for new development—a controversial move, but one that opened up long-obscured views of the harbor from the river. This jaunty and informative boat trip takes you past many of them. There really aren't that many *Titanic*-related sights left, but as an introduction to Belfast's maritime past, it's a pleasant way to spend an hour. With typically dry Belfast wit, the crew t-shirts read, "She was alright when she left here." In summer, the tour goes as far as Musgrave Channel, home to a large breeding colony of seals. The departure point is on Donegall Quay, about 100m (330 ft.) to the left of the big fish sculpture.

The Obel, 66 Donegall Quay, Belfast, BT3 3NG. www.laganboatcompany.com. *©* **028/9024-0124.** Admission £10 adults; £8 seniors, students, and children 6–16; children under 6 free; £30 families. Tours Mar–Oct daily; times vary, but generally 12:30, 2, and 3:30pm (always call to check daily times; fewer tours in summer months).

Titanic Dock and Pump House ★★ MUSEUM   Another of Belfast's ship-related attractions, this fascinating self-guided tour takes you around the dry docks at the old Harland and Wolff shipyard, where *Titanic* and *Olympic* were constructed from 1909–11. Designed to appeal to a general audience, not just enthusiasts, it's a great way to learn what it was really like to work here at the turn of the last century, when Belfast was one of the world's greatest industrial cities. The enormous Edwardian pump house, which could drain a staggering 21 million gallons of water in just over an hour and a half, is worth the price of admission by itself. An audio-visual room includes some rare film footage of the *Titanic* in situ at the dock. The large visitor center has plenty of interesting exhibits, a gift shop, and a cafe.

Queen's Rd., Queen's Island, Belfast, BT3 9DT. www.titanicsdock.com. *©* **028/9073-7813.** Admission £5 adults; £5 children 5–16, children under 5 free; £12 families. Daily 10:30am–4pm; last admission 3:40pm.

Ulster Museum ★★★ MUSEUM   One of Belfast's best museums, the Ulster Museum has a comprehensive collection of everything from dinosaur bones and prehistoric artifacts to art and other treasures from Ireland and around the world. Highlights include 16th- to 18th-century Dutch and Italian paintings; a hoard of priceless 16th-century Spanish jewelry, recovered off the coast near Belfast in the 1960s; clothes, textiles, and ceramics from Asia and Africa; and items relating to the Ascendancy, the period of Protestant rule in Ireland that finally came to a head with the rebellion of 1798. The **Life and Death in Ancient Egypt** exhibit has about 2,000 artifacts from Pharaonic times (including a mummy), as well as items from ancient Mesopotamia, Rome, and Greece. The museum's calendar often has special exhibitions, talks, and even the occasional concert; check the website to see what's on.

At the Botanic Gardens, Belfast, BT9 5AB. www.nmni.com/um. *©* **028/9044-0000.** Free admission. Tues–Sun 10am–5pm. Closed Mon (except public holidays).

JOINING THE national trust

Several of Ulster's best historic sites are managed by the **National Trust,** a not-for-profit organization that preserves thousands of buildings and areas of natural beauty across the U.K. (including Northern Ireland), keeping them accessible to the public. Taking out a yearly membership gives you unlimited free admission to all of them, which can work out cheaper if you plan to visit several. If you also happen to be visiting Britain on your trip, or within a year, it could be a wise investment.

Current membership costs are £56 for individuals, £92 for couples, £26 for children, and £61 to £97 for families. You can sign up for membership at any National Trust property, or join in advance online at www.nationaltrust.org.uk. Alternatively, American visitors can join the U.S. wing of the National Trust, the **Royal Oak Foundation.** Visit www.royal-oak.org or call ✆ **212/480-2889** for more information. Royal Oak members get the same benefits, plus money off lectures, tours, and other special events held in the U.S.

MORE ATTRACTIONS

Belfast Castle ★ CASTLE   Northwest of downtown and 120m (394 ft.) above sea level stands Belfast Castle, its 80-hectare (198-acre) estate spreading down the slopes of what is now **Cave Hill Country Park ★★** (see below). Dating from 1870, this was the family residence of the third marquis of Donegall, and it was built in the style of Britain's Balmoral castle. The outside is more interesting than the inside, which has been sadly modernized over the years and is now a popular wedding venue. The estate, though, is a lovely place to visit, offering sweeping views of Belfast and the lough. Its cellars contain a nifty Victorian arcade, a restaurant (open 11am–5pm Wed–Mon, and 11am–9pm Tues), and a shop selling antiques and crafts. According to legend, a white cat brought the castle residents luck, so look around for carvings featuring this much-loved feline.

Signposted off Antrim Rd., 2½ miles (4km) north of the city center, Belfast, BT15 5GR. www.belfastcastle.co.uk. ✆ **028/9077-6925.** Free admission and parking. Mon–Sat 9am–10pm; Sun 9am–5:30pm.

Belfast Cathedral ★ CATHEDRAL   Although the foundation stone on this monumental cathedral, also known as **St. Anne's,** was laid in 1899, it remained incomplete for more than a century; even now it still awaits a steeple. Crisscrossing architectural genres from Romanesque to Victorian to modern, the huge structure is more attractive inside than out. In the nave, the ceiling soars above black-and-white marble walls and stone floors, and elaborate stained-glass windows flood it with color on a sunny day. Carvings that represent life in Belfast top the 10 pillars. The cathedral's most impressive features are the delicate mosaic ceilings of the tympanum, and a baptistery constructed of thousands of pieces of glass.

Donegall St., Belfast, BT1 2HB. www.belfastcathedral.org. ✆ **028/9032-8332.** Free admission (£2 donation requested). Mon–Sat 9am–5:15pm; Sun 1–3pm.

Belfast Zoo ★ ZOO   In a picturesque mountain park on the slopes of Cave Hill just outside of town, this zoo emphasizes conservation and education. Many rare species are bred here, including Hawaiian geese, lowland gorillas, red lechwe (a kind of antelope), sea bears, Barbary lions, and golden lion tamarins. The Rainforest House is a tropical environment filled with birds and jungle creatures. Special tours and events run all year. Most activity days are quite kid-oriented, although there are some more grown-up events too, such as all-day photography competitions. Check the website for up-to-date listings.

Antrim Rd., Belfast, BT36 7PN. www.belfastzoo.co.uk. © **028/9077-6277.** Admission £8.50 adults; £4.25 seniors, students, and children; £23 families. Apr–Sept Mon–Fri 10am–6pm; Sat–Sun 10am–7pm (last admission 5pm, animal houses close 6pm). Oct–Mar daily 10am–4pm (last admission 2:30pm, animal houses close 3:30pm).

Cave Hill Country Park ★★ PARK   Atop a 360m (1,181-ft.) basalt cliff, this park offers panoramic views, walking trails, and archaeological and historical sights (including **Belfast Castle** ★, above). Its name derives from five small caves thought to have been Neolithic iron mines; several other ancient sites are scattered about the place, often unmarked. These include stone cairns, dolmens, and **McArt's Fort**—the remains of an ancient defensive hill fort in which Wolfe Tone and his fellow United Irishmen planned the 1798 rebellion. It's mostly gone now, but you can explore the ruins, which sit atop the park's most famous viewpoint. The **Cave Hill Visitor Centre,** on the second floor of Belfast Castle, contains a diverting exhibition on the history of the park and the castle. You can also pick up maps of the park here. For a great walk around the entire circuit of the park, check out **www.walkni.com,** a site set up to promote hiking in Northern Ireland. To explore the park's mountain bike trails, hire a bike at **Full Cycle,** 387 Antrim Rd. (www.fullcyclebikeshop.co.uk; © **028/9074-1569**); you'll need to make reservations at least 24 hours in advance, preferably a full week ahead.

Visitor Center: Belfast Castle, off Antrim Rd., 4 miles (6.5km) north of city center, Belfast, BT15 5GR. www.belfastcity.gov.uk/parksandopenspaces. © **028/9077-6925.** Free admission. Park: 7:30am–dusk. Visitor Center: Tues–Sat 9am–10pm; Sun–Mon 9am–5:30pm.

City Hall ★ ARCHITECTURAL SITE   A testament to the city's grand industrial past, this domed building of granite, marble, and stained glass dominates central Belfast. Built in classical Renaissance style in 1906, it has white Portland stone walls and a soft green copper dome. Several statues dot the grounds, including a grim-faced Queen Victoria who stands out front, looking as if she wished she were anywhere else. Bronze figures around her represent the textile and shipbuilding industries that powered Belfast's success. There's also a memorial to the victims of the *Titanic* disaster. Inside the building, the elaborate entry hall is heavy with marble but lightened by stained glass and a rotunda with a painted ceiling. Somehow it all manages not to be tacky. Exhibitions are often displayed inside. Free, hour-long guided tours offer a surprisingly absorbing insight into the building's history.

Donegall Sq. North, Belfast, BT1 5GS. © **028/9027-0456.** Free admission. Guided tours June–Sept Mon–Fri 10 and 11am, 2, 3, and 4pm; Sat–Sun noon, 2, 3, and 4pm. Oct–May Mon–Fri 11am, 2, and 3pm; Sat–Sun noon, 2, and 3pm.

Grand Opera House ★★ PERFORMING ARTS   One of the main landmarks of Belfast's "Golden Mile," the Grand Opera House opened in 1895. The interior is full of late-Victorian detail, including a grand auditorium, complete with an elaborately painted frieze on the high ceiling. Severely damaged twice by IRA bombs, it underwent a full restoration in the mid-2000s that returned the place to its former glory. Today it continues to be a cornerstone of the Belfast live arts scene with a tremendous variety of shows, from touring plays, ballet, and opera to big-ticket musicals, concerts, and stand-up comedy. Ticket prices vary greatly, but expect to pay between £15 and £30 for most shows. Check the website for a detailed event listing.

2-4 Great Victoria St., Belfast, BT2 7HR. www.goh.co.uk. ℘ **028/9024-1919.** Ticket prices vary.

Queen's University ★ UNIVERSITY   Founded in 1845 during the reign of Queen Victoria to provide nondenominational higher education, this is Northern Ireland's most prestigious university. The turreted main building, an imposing example of 19th-century Tudor Revival, may remind you of England's Oxford; its design was based on the Founder's Tower at Magdalen College. But there's much more to this university, which sprawls through 250 buildings and where 17,500 students are studying at any given time. The surrounding neighborhood is a quiet, attractive place to wander, and University Square on the north side of campus is simply beautiful. At one end of the square, Union Theological College, dating from 1853, housed Northern Ireland's Parliament after the partition of Ireland in 1921 until its abolition in 1972. Tours of the campus can be arranged on request; contact the university's welcome center for details. Access to parts of the campus may be restricted during exam times.

Queen's Welcome Centre, Queen's University, University Rd., Belfast, BT7 1NN. www.queenseventus.com/QueensWelcomeCentre. ℘ **028/9097-5252.** Free admission; tours £3.50 per person. Mon–Fri 8am–5pm; also Sat–Sun 11am–4pm during summer vacation.

W5 ★ SCIENCE CENTER   This great, hands-on science play center for kids is part of the Odyssey Complex, a huge modern entertainment center in the Titanic District. Properly known as "Whowhatwhenwherewhy"—you can see why they abbreviate it to W5—this high-tech, interactive learning environment lets kids try out over 250 individual activities, all in the spirit of science-based fun. They can do everything from create animated cartoons to try to beat a lie detector test, and even present the weather on TV. There are also plenty of special events and temporary exhibitions. The Odyssey also contains a cinema, bowling alley, shops, restaurants, and a sports arena.

2 Queen's Quay, BT3 9QQ. www.w5online.co.uk. ℘ **028/9046-7700.** Admission £8.50 adults; £7 seniors and students; £6.50 children; £24–£42 families. Mon–Fri 10am–5pm, Sat 10am–6pm, Sun noon–6pm. Last admission 1 hr. before closing.

Shopping

Coppermoon ★★★   A riotously creative little boutique, Coppermoon sells art and gorgeous little knickknacks. Plenty of local designers are represented, including makers of bags and accessories; funky, steampunk-style jewelry; glass and ceramics; and quirky pieces of homeware, from lampshades made of bottles to wittily embroidered pillows. They also create beautiful, individually designed cards. 3 Wellington St., Belfast, BT1 6HT. www.coppermoon. co.uk. 𝒞 **028/9023-5325.** Mon–Wed and Fri–Sat 9:30am–5:30pm; Thurs 9:30am–8pm.

Steensons ★★★   Behind Belfast City Hall, this long-established showroom sells an outstanding collection of gold and silver jewelry. Most of what's on sale are their own designs, although they sell work by other top Irish designers too. They are also known for their beautiful pieces made for the TV series *Game of Thrones*, which is filmed in Northern Ireland (see box p. 250). Among their most popular lines are some elegant limited edition pieces launched to commemorate the *Titanic*—the owner's grandfather was a crewmember on board. There's a second branch on Toberwine Street in Glenarm, County Antrim (𝒞 **028/2884-1445**). Bedford St., Belfast, BT2 7FD. www.thesteen sons.com. 𝒞 **028/9024-8269.** Mon–Wed, Fri–Sat 10am–5:30pm; Thurs 10am–8pm.

St. George's Market ★   While this iron-and-glass street market dates back to 1896, a market has been held on this spot for much longer. Friday is the **Variety Market,** packed with 250 stalls of fresh produce, antiques, clothing, and bric-a-brac. There's also a lively fish market that supplies many of the local restaurants. On Saturday, the **City Food and Craft Market** specializes in artisan foods with plenty of tempting fresh snacks, plus an assortment of local crafts. The **Sunday Market** is a happy combination of the two, although the balance tends to be in favor of crafts. May St. at Oxford St., Belfast, BT1 3NQ. 𝒞 **028/9043-5704.** Fri 6am–2pm; Sat 9am–3pm; Sun 10am–4pm.

Out from Belfast

Hopefully you've left enough time in your stay to visit the countryside surrounding Belfast, which is rich with attractions. (See map on p. 232.) Where you go depends upon what you're interested in, of course. Medievalists may want to head north to see **Carrickfergus Castle,** while families might gravitate to the **Ulster Folk & Transport Museum.** If ancient sites intrigue you, the **Giant's Ring** and **Leganananny Dolmen,** both south of the city, are must-sees. Active types may want to explore the beautiful countryside at **Castlewellan Forest Park** or **Tollymore Forest Park.** Can't make a choice? You can always combine history, nature, and family fun with a day trip to the **Ards Peninsula** (see box p. 252).

Carrickfergus Castle ★ CASTLE   Built in 1180 by John de Courcy, this massive Norman keep was Ireland's first real castle, designed to loom darkly over the entrance to Belfast Lough. Centuries later, its defensive location would prove prophetic, as William of Orange landed here on June 1690 en route to the Battle of the Boyne. The central part dates to the 12th century, the thick outer walls were completed 100 years later, and the gun ports are a relatively new addition (only 400 years old). The outside is more impressive than the inside, which has been largely designed to trigger kids' interests, with waxwork figures riding horses, threatening to shoot people over the walls, et cetera. Sometimes actors in medieval costume add a touch of hammy fun. The

khaleesi DOES IT

The most popular TV show in the world is filmed in Northern Ireland, and the publicity that HBO's *Game of Thrones* has brought to the region has been a massive boon for tourism. Major filming locations have included **Castle Ward** ★★ (below); **Cushendun** ★ (p. 257) and **Ballintoy** (p. 257) on the Antrim Coast Drive; and the **Tollymore Forest Park** ★★ in County Down (p. 252). **Brit Movie Tours** offers two full-day tours that take in several of the main locations.

The main tour—**Northern Locations With Giant's Causeway**—takes in many of the most scenic places used in the show. It really packs in a lot, in addition to various fan-related hijinks along the way, such as a quiz (dressing up is not unheard of). It includes a 90-minute visit to the Giant's Causeway (p. 258), which hasn't actually appeared in the show, but it would seem silly to pass and not stop.

Tours depart daily at 9am from the main tourism office in Donegall Square, Belfast, and return roughly 9 hours later. (No Mon tour from Oct to Feb). Tickets cost £35 adults and £20 children. Private tours, in a people carrier, can be booked for between £360 to £570, depending on the number of people (maximum six).

The **Southern Locations and Castle Ward** tour takes in some locations to the south of Belfast, including a tour of the castle that stood in for Winterfell on the show. The tour departs from Donegall Square Monday, Friday, and Saturday at 9:30am from March to November; in February and October they run just once a week, on Friday at 9:30am. Tickets cost £40 adults, £30 children under 12.

For details and booking call ℭ **0844/247-1007** in Northern Ireland and Britain (ℭ **44/207-118-1007** in the rest of the world), or visit www.britmovietours.com.

castle has a visitor center and a small museum. In the summer, medieval banquets, a medieval fair, and a crafts market all add a touch of play and pageantry.

Marine Hwy., Carrickfergus, BT38 7BG. ℭ **028/9335-1273.** Admission £5 adults £3 seniors and children. Apr–Sept daily 10am–6pm; Oct–Mar daily 10am–4pm. Last admission 30 min. before closing.

Castlewellan Forest Park ★★ PARK   Surrounding a fine trout lake and watched over by the stately mid-19th-century Castlewellan Castle (sadly closed to the public), this forest park just begs for picnics and outdoor activities. The main draw is the National Arboretum, opened in 1740 and now 10 times its original size; the largest of its three greenhouses features aquatic plants and a collection of free-flying tropical birds. Woodland walks, a formal walled garden, and an interesting lakeside sculpture trail are among the park's other attractions. Anglers can fish for trout (brown and rainbow) in the lake. The **Peace Maze,** planted in 2000, is an enormous hedge maze designed to represent the path to peace in Northern Ireland. The town of Castlewellan, elegantly laid out around two squares, is a short distance away, as is the ancient fort of **Drumena Cashel** (signposted from A25, 2 miles/3km southwest of Castlewellan town).

Forest Office: The Grange, Castlewellan Forest Park, Castlewellan, Co. Down, BT31 9BU. ℭ **028/4377-8664.** Entry and parking: £4.50. Daily 10am–sunset.

Castle Ward ★★ HISTORIC HOME   About 1¼ miles (2km) west of Strangford village, this grand manor house dates from 1760. A hybrid of architectural styles melding Gothic with neoclassical, it sits on a 280-hectare (692-acre) country estate of formal gardens, woodlands, lakelands, and seashore. Inside, kids can dress up in period clothes and play with period toys, while outside, they can roam its vast estate of formal gardens, woodlands, lakes, and seashore, and even ride a tractor-trailer out to see the farm animals. A theater in the stable yard hosts operatic performances in summer. Castle Ward has achieved a degree of latter-day fame as one of the key locations for the HBO series *Game of Thrones*—albeit heavily disguised.

Park Rd., Strangford, Co. Down, BT30 7LS. www.nationaltrust.org.uk/castle-ward. © **028/4488-1204**. £7.50 adults; £3.60 children; £18 families. Grounds: Mar–Dec daily 10am–6pm; Jan–Feb daily 10am–4pm. House: June–Aug daily noon–5pm, Mar–May and Sept–Oct Sat–Sun noon–5pm.

Giant's Ring ★★ ANCIENT SITE   Only a few miles from Belfast, this massive and mysterious prehistoric earthwork, 180m (590 ft.) in diameter, has at its center a megalithic chamber with a single capstone. Ancient burial rings like this were thought to be protected by fairies and were left untouched, but this one is quite an exception. In the 19th century, it was used as a racetrack, and the high embankment around it served as grandstands. Today, its dignity has been restored, and it is a place of wonder for the few tourists who make the journey. It's 3¾ miles (6km) southwest of Belfast center, west off A24.

Near Shaw's Bridge, off Ballynahatty Rd., Ballynahatty, Co. Down, BT8 8LE. Free admission (open site).

Legananny Dolmen ★ ANCIENT SITE   Probably one of the most photographed sights in Ireland, this renowned granite dolmen (Neolithic tomb) is on the southern slope of Slieve Croob mountain. It looks, in the words of archaeologist Peter Harbison, like "a coffin on stilts," but only when you see it up close can you fully appreciate its awesome size, with a massive capstone that seems weightlessly poised on its supporting uprights. The Dolmen is halfway between Dromara and Castlewellan, about 25 miles south of Belfast.

Signposted off Leganny Rd. Leitrim, Co. Down, BT32 3QR. No phone. Free admission (open site).

Mount Stewart House, Garden and Temple of the Winds ★★ HISTORIC HOUSE/GARDENS   Once the home of Lord Castlereagh, this 18th-century house sits on the eastern shore of Strangford Lough. Its lush gardens, a candidate for UNESCO World Heritage status, were named one of the 10 best in the world by Britain's *Daily Telegraph* in 2014. An impressive array of rare and unusual plants flourish here, due to a rare microclimate—the gardens almost never experience bad frosts. Inside the house, the excellent art collection includes the *Hambletonian* by George Stubbs and family portraits by Pompeo Batoni and Anton Raphael Mengs. The Temple of the Winds, a rare 18th-century banqueting house, is also on the estate, but it's only open on

DAY OUT: THE ards peninsula

Southeast of Belfast, the Ards Peninsula curls around the western shore of Strangford Lough, a beautiful bird sanctuary and wildlife reserve. It's Ireland's closest coastline to Great Britain, and it's loaded with historic sites, all of which can easily be seen in a day.

About 10 miles east of Belfast via the A20, the town of **Newtownard**s lies at the north end of Strangford Lough. From there, take Portaferry Road 5 miles (8km) south along the east shore of the lough to the elegant 18th-century manor **Mount Stewart House ★★** (see p. 251) with its world-class gardens.

Only another 2½ miles (4km) down Portaferry Road, the striking Gothic ruins of **Grey Abbey ★** (Main St., Greyabbey, open Mon–Fri) sit amid a beautifully landscaped setting, perfect for a picnic. The abbey was founded in 1193 by Affreca of Cumbria, wife of John de Courcy, builder of Carrickfergus Castle (see p. 249). Amid the ruined choirs, look for a fragmented stone effigy of a knight in armor, thought to be a likeness of de Courcy.

Past Greyabbey, a scenic 12-mile (20km) drive down the shore ends at **Portaferry,** where a car ferry runs to Strangford on the lough's western shore. (Ferries run every half-hour; tickets are £5.80 per car, £1 adult passenger, and 50p child.) From the Strangford ferry

dock, it's about a 10-minute drive to historic **Castle Ward ★★** (see p. 251), which has plenty of family-friendly activities (not to mention the cachet of being a shooting location for *Game of Thrones*).

From Castle Ward, head west on Strangford Road toward Downpatrick. (St. Patrick fans may want to detour to Downpatrick to visit **Down Cathedral** and the **St. Patrick Centre**—visit www. saintpatrickcentre.com for details.) Otherwise, turn north onto the A22, which rolls through lovely countryside 14 miles (23km) to Lisbane; follow signs north to the **Castle Espie Wetland Centre ★** (78 Ballydrain Rd., Comber; www.wwt. org.uk/wetland-centres/castle-espie; ✆ **028/9187-4146**). This marvelous wildlife center, named for a long-gone castle, is home to a virtual United Nations of rare migratory geese, ducks, and swans. In summer, you'll see dozens of newly hatched goslings, ducklings, and cygnets; in early winter, thousands of pale-bellied brents. Guided trails are designed for children and families, and the center sponsors activities year-round. Admission costs £7 adults, £6 seniors and students, £3.70 children 4–16, and £21 families. It's open daily 10am to 5pm (last admission 3:30pm). From here, it's a 40-minute drive back to Belfast via the A23.

Sunday afternoons (and not in winter). Admission to the house is by guided tour only.

Portaferry Rd., Newtownards, Co. Down, BT22 2AD. www.nationaltrust.org.uk/ mount-stewart. ✆ **028/4278-8387.** House and Lakeside Garden: £8 adults; £4 children; £20 families. **House:** Apr–Oct daily 11am–5pm; Nov to mid-Dec weekends noon–3pm. **Gardens:** Mar–Oct daily 10am–5pm; Nov–early Mar daily 10am–4pm. **Temple:** mid-Mar to Oct Sun 2–5pm. Temple closed Nov–Mar. Last admission 1 hr. before closing.

Tollymore Forest Park ★★ PARK   All that's left of the once-glorious Tollymore House is this delightful 480-hectare (1,186-acre) wildlife and forest park. The park offers a number of walks up into the north slopes of the

Mourne Mountains or along the Shimna River (which is known for its exceptionally fine salmon). The Shimna walk has several beguiling little landmarks, including caves and grottos. The park is scattered with follies, such as faux-medieval castle gatehouses and other fanciful fakes. The forest is a nature preserve inhabited by a host of local wildlife like badgers, foxes, otters, and pine martens. And don't miss the trees for the forest—there are some exotic species such as the magnificent Himalayan cedars and a 30-metre (98-ft.) tall sequoia in the arboretum.

Off B180, 2 miles (3.2km) northwest of Newcastle, Tullybrannigan Rd., Newcastle, Co. Down. ✆ **028/4372-2428.** Free admission. Parking £4.50. Daily 10am–dusk.

Ulster Folk & Transport Museum ★★ MUSEUM One of Northern Ireland's best living history museums, it's made up of buildings rescued from demolition and reconstructed, piece by piece. Mostly from the 19th century, they include houses, schools, a chemist's shop, a pub, and even a working farm. The level of detail is impressive—the shops are fully decked out as they would have been in Victorian times, complete with shelves overflowing with authentic bottles, jars, and items of clothing. Costumed guides add to the sense of fun. As you wander about, you may encounter a Victorian housewife engaged in some day-to-day household drudgery or watch a village blacksmith working away in a forge using authentic period methods. There are frequent special events, including craft demonstrations and classes, horse-drawn vehicle days, or wildlife hunts. The Transport Museum contains a wealth of historic vehicles, from old cars and small planes to buses and trams.

Signposted off A2 (Bangor Rd.), Cultra, Hollywood, Co. Down, BT18 0EU. www.nmni. com/uftm. ✆ **028/9042-8428.** Folk or Transport Museum: £9 adults; £7 seniors and students; £5.50 children 5–17; children 4 and under free; £19–£25 families. Both museums: £11 adults, £8.50 seniors and students, £6 children, £29 families. Mar–Sept Tues–Sun 10am–5pm; Oct–Feb Tues–Fri 10am–4pm, Sat–Sun 11am–4pm. Closed Mon (except public holidays).

THE ANTRIM COAST

Although it's just 60 miles long, there is so much to admire along the scenic Antrim Coast drive, you'll want to take a full day or more to do it justice, with plenty of stops along the way. At the end of it all lies the weird and wonderful Giant's Causeway, one of the most striking natural formations in the world.

Most sights are equidistant from Belfast and Derry. It's possible to see them all in 1 day, staying in either city, although if your schedule permits, it's better to stay overnight along on the coast and take your time. See map on p. 232 for locations of the coast's many attractions.

Visitor Information

The principal tourist information centers in North Antrim are at Narrow Gauge Road, Larne (✆ **028/2826-0088**); Sheskburn House, 14 Bayview Rd., Ballycastle (✆ **028/2076-2024**); and the **Giant's Causeway Information Centre,** 44 Causeway Rd., Bushmills (✆ **028/2073-1855**). All offices are open daily, year-round, though the Larne and Ballycastle offices are closed Sundays outside the midsummer season. The Giant's Causeway office stays open until 7pm from April to June, and 9pm in July and August.

Where to Stay on the Antrim Coast

Causeway Smithy ★★★   A short hop from the Giant's Causeway (you can just see it in the distance, across rolling green fields), this warm and friendly B&B is a fantastic find. The guest rooms are simple but stylish, with polished wood floors and contemporary print wallpaper. Big bay windows look out over the verdant countryside, flooding the rooms with light during the day. Each of the three rooms is located in a separate annex, and you have your own key, so you'll have more of a feeling of freedom and privacy than is usual in countryside B&Bs. Tasty breakfasts are served in a guest lounge. There's no restaurant, but owner Denise is full of recommendations about where to go in the evenings.

270 Whitepark Rd., Bushmills, Co. Antrim, BT57 8SN. www.causewaysmithybnb.com. ✆ **075/1506-6975.** 3 units. £100. Free parking. Rates include breakfast. **Amenities:** Wi-Fi (free).

Londonderry Arms Hotel ★   A pleasant Georgian inn, the Londonderry Arms is a well-run, traditional kind of place. The building has its quirks—most of the inn is original, with a well-designed modern extension. A couple of the rooms have views of the nearby sea. Bedrooms are simple but comfortable; executive rooms have a bit more space. Triple and quad rooms are really good value for money. (Check the website for special offers, including excellent weekend packages.) The restaurant is very good, and chef Manus Jamison's delicious menus are full of regional specialties. If you want something a little simpler, a more modest bistro-style menu is available in the cozy bar. An unexpected piece of historical trivia about this place: Winston Churchill was once (briefly) the landlord. He inherited it and sold it soon afterwards, although he is known to have stayed here at least once.

20 Harbour Rd., Carnlough, Co. Antrim, BT44 0EU. www.glensofantrim.com. ✆ **028/2888-5255.** 35 units. £65–£150. Limited free parking (on street). Breakfast not included in lower rates. **Amenities:** Restaurant; bar; room service; Wi-Fi (free).

Lurig View ★   The atmosphere at this sweet little B&B in Glenariff feels akin to a family home. The manager, Rose Ward, and her husband, Chris, are friendly as can be, and happy to help with planning sightseeing trips, making dinner reservations, and so on. Bedrooms are simple but decorated with paintings of flowers chosen to match the accent colors of the room—an inventive touch. Breakfast is served outside if the weather's good. If you really must, the guest lounge has a TV, but a better choice is to get out and explore. Glenariff is a pretty little town and one of the most popular destinations along the Antrim coast. There's a forest park within about 10 minutes' drive, and the beach is a short walk from the front door.

38 Glen Rd., Glenariff, Ballymena, Co. Antrim, BT44 0RF. www.lurigview.co.uk. ✆ **028/2177-1618.** 3 units. £60–£70. Free parking. Breakfast included. **Amenities:** Wi-Fi (free).

The Meadows ★ You can see Scotland on a (very) clear and sunny day from this jovial guesthouse on the main Antrim coast. Bedrooms are basic but cozy, and the bathrooms are modern and well equipped. Most are doubles, but families or groups can make use of a room that sleeps four; another is equipped for those with mobility problems. The hearty, tasty Ulster fry breakfasts are great fuel for a long drive ahead.

79 Coast Rd., Cushendall, Ballymena, Co. Antrim, BT44 0RX. www.themeadowscushendall.com. ⓒ **028/2177-2020.** 6 units. £60–£70. Free parking. Breakfast included. **Amenities:** Wi-Fi (free).

Whitepark House ★★ This fantastic little place, just a couple of miles from the Carrick-a-Rede Rope Bridge (see p. 257), was built in the mid-1700s and still retains a traditional feel. Beds are wrought-iron framed; one is a four-poster, while the others have canopies. Heavy silk fabrics lift the design of the room. Views of the lovely garden are sweet, but ask for a room overlooking the sea if you want a spectacular vista to wake up to. Bob and Siobhan Isles are genuinely warm people; the fact that they've won awards for their hospitality comes as no surprise whatsoever. Breakfasts are delicious—the full Ulster fry is the specialty, of course, but Bob also takes care of his vegetarian guests (he is one himself) with non-meaty options. What a lovely, idyllic find along the Antrim coast road.

150 Whitepark Rd., Ballintoy, Co. Antrim, BT54 6NH. www.whiteparkhouse.com. ⓒ **028/2073-1482.** 3 units. £120. Free parking. Breakfast included. Children allowed, but must have own room (no discount). **Amenities:** Wi-Fi (free).

Where to Eat on the Antrim Coast

Red Door Tea Room ★★ CAFE This sweet little cottage tearoom is cozy and welcoming inside, with a turf-burning stove and the day's menu chalked on blackboards behind the counter. But you'll want to sit outside if the weather allows, because the view from the garden over lush green fields to Ballintoy Harbour is stunning. They serve tempting, fresh cakes and desserts, so dig into the delicious Victoria sponge cake (two layers, separated by jam and cream). They also serve good light lunches—salads, soups, bagels, sandwiches, or plates of tasty fresh fish are all good. It all adds up to a welcome rest stop along the Antrim coast road. Although officially the Red Door closes at 5pm, you may find it open into the evening on busy days in summer.

Ballintoy Harbour, Ballintoy, Co. Antrim, BT54 6NA. ⓒ **028/2076-9048.** Main courses £9–£14. Easter week and June–Sept daily 11am–5pm; week after Easter–May weekends only 11am–5pm. Closed Oct–Easter.

Smuggler's Inn ★ IRISH/INTERNATIONAL A convenient lunch spot right across from the Giant's Causeway, the Smuggler's Inn serves traditional pub lunches. Choose from a few sandwiches and light snack options, or go for the full works like hefty burgers, fish and chips, or Cajun chicken goujons (strips of meat, breaded and deep fried). There's also a separate children's menu. In the evening it's much the same kind of thing, but pushed up a notch

THE GLENS OF antrim

If you can tear yourself away from the coastline views, look inland to see the evocatively named **Glens of Antrim,** nine green valleys stretching north and west from Belfast and curving around the coast toward Donegal. The names of the glens are all based on local legends, and although the meanings are largely lost to the ages, the popular translations are: **Glenarm** (glen of the army), **Glencloy** (glen of the hedges), **Glenariff** (ploughman's glen), **Glenballyeamon** (Edwardstown glen), **Glenaan** (glen of the rush lights), **Glencorp** (glen of the slaughter), **Glendun** (brown glen), **Glenshesk** (sedgy glen), and **Glentaisie** (Taisie's glen).

in terms of choice, when a couple of steaks join the menu, as well as the occasional dish with a bit more ambition, such as roast duck with fruity red cabbage and a sherry reduction. Like several places around here, euros are accepted as well as pounds. The Smuggler's also has rooms available for around £100 per night.

306 Whitepark Rd., Giants Causeway, Bushmills, Co. Antrim, BT57 8SL. www.smug glersinnireland.com. © **028/2073-1577.** Main courses £8–£17. Food served daily noon–2:30pm and 4–9pm.

Thyme & Co. ★ MODERN IRISH   Another nifty little cafe on the Antrim coast drive, Thyme & Co. serves delicious, healthful lunches. The ingredients are locally sourced and the short menu is thoughtfully put together. Dine on fish cakes made from salmon and smoked haddock (something of a house specialty) or a tasty pie or quiche. The dining room is a pleasant kind of space, and the staff is always friendly and cheerful. On Fridays and Saturdays in summer, they stay open into the evenings, when they sometimes serve thincrust pizzas—a popular choice with locals. They do takeout too, which is useful if you're staying nearby and your hotel doesn't provide dinner. *Note:* It's cash only here.

5 Quay Rd., Ballycastle, Co. Antrim, BT54 6BJ. www.thymeandco.co.uk. © **028/2076-9851.** Main courses £5–£11. Pizzas £6–£11. No credit cards. Tues–Sat 8:30am–4:30pm; Sun 10:30am–3:30pm.

Exploring the Antrim Coast

One of the most memorable routes in Ireland, the 60-mile (96km) drive along the Antrim coast offers sweeping views of midnight-blue seas against gray unforgiving cliffs and deep green hillsides. Starting from Carrickfergus, just north of Belfast, it runs to **Portrush,** a few miles beyond from the spectacular **Giant's Causeway.** You could do the whole journey in a couple of hours, but allow much longer if you can—it's the sort of drive you want to savor.

Once you join the coast road (A2), about 16 miles (26km) or so north of Carrickfergus, the first town is **Glenarm,** decked out with castle walls and a barbican gate, followed by **Carnlough ★** (p. 257), a quiet seaside village. Continuing north along the coast, the road passes through the National Trust village of **Cushendun** ★ (see below), known for its teashops and whitewashed cottages. For the most spectacular views, turn off the main A2 coastal road at Cushendun onto the narrow, rugged **Torr Head Scenic Road** ★★ (p. 259).

In the late spring and summer, you can take a ferry from the bustling beach town of **Ballycastle** to **Rathlin Island,** where seals and nesting birds make their homes at the **Kebble National Reserve.** Farther west, the heart-stopping **Carrick-a-Rede Rope Bridge** ★★★ (below) allows the brave to cross the sea on foot over to a small island. Others may prefer to move straight on to the post-card-perfect little town of **Ballintoy,** filled with charming stone cottages and flowery gardens on the edge of Whitepark Bay. On a sunny day, you might find it hard to go farther. But press on, because at the end of the drive lies its most spectacular sight: The bizarre rock stacks of the **Giant's Causeway** ★★★ (see p. 258), one of the world's great natural wonders.

Carnlough ★ VILLAGE The first major stop along the Antrim Coast Drive is this quiet village, known for its glassy harbor bobbing with sailboats. It's a lovely place to wander around, sampling interesting little shops and restaurants. Just outside Carnlough is a peaceful, yet little-known, waterfall called **Cranny Falls.** To get there, look for a marked 1-mile walking trail beginning on the waterfront. After crossing a white stone bridge, the route goes through idyllic countryside, following an abandoned railway bed past a disused quarry until it reaches the falls. Along the way, occasional markers tell you more about the history of the area.

Carnlough, Co. Antrim (no tourism office).

Carrick-a-Rede Rope Bridge ★★★ BRIDGE Each spring, local fisherman put up this rope bridge across a chasm 18m (59 ft.) wide and 24m (79 ft.) deep, swinging over the sea between the mainland and a small island. The bridge has a practical purpose—allowing access to the island's salmon fishery—but visitors can use it for a thrilling walk and the chance to call out to each other, "Don't look down!" (By the way, that is *excellent* advice.) If you are acrophobic, stay clear; if you don't know whether you are, this is not the place to find out. *Note:* The 12-mile (19km) coastal cliff path from the Giant's Causeway to the rope bridge is always open and is worth the exhaustion.

119A Whitepark Rd., Ballintoy, Co. Antrim, BT54 6LS. www.nationaltrust.org.uk/carrick-a-rede. © **028/2076-9839.** Admission £6 adults; £3.20 children; £16 families. June–Sept daily 9:30am–7pm; Mar–May and Sept–Oct daily 9:30am–6pm; Nov–Feb daily 9:30am–3:30pm.

Cushendun ★ VILLAGE Way back in the 1950s, the National Trust bought most of this charming seaside village to preserve it from over-development. Today, the seafront is lined with an elegant sweep of perfect white Cornish-style cottages, and the quaint teashops do a bustling trade. The Glendun River winds through the village, crossed by a lovely old stone bridge, while down on the beach are some atmospheric sea caves. Just north of the village, in a field overlooking the coast, stand the scant remains of **Curra Castle.**

Cushendun, Co. Antrim (no tourism office).

Dunluce Castle ★★ CASTLE   Between the Giant's Causeway and the busy harbor town of Portrush, the coastline is dominated by the hulking skeletal outline of what must have once been a glorious castle. This was the main fort of the Irish MacDonnells, chiefs of Antrim. From the 14th to the 17th century, it was the largest and most sophisticated castle in the North, with a series of fortifications built on rocky outcrops extending into the sea. In 1639, part of the castle fell into the sea, taking some of the servants with it; soon after that, it was allowed to fall into a beautiful ruin. The 17th-century courtyard survives, including a few buildings. The site incorporates two of the original Norman towers dating from 1305. One enticing footnote: A recent archaeological dig here uncovered the remains of a town that was previously thought completely destroyed during a rebellion in 1641. Only a very tiny fraction of what is now thought to exist has so far been excavated.

87 Dunluce Rd., Bushmills, Co. Antrim, BT57 8UY. (C) **028/2073-1938.** Admission £5 adults; £3 seniors and children 4–16; children under 4 free; £13 families. Daily 10am–5pm; last admission 30 min. before closing. Call to confirm times in winter.

Giant's Causeway ★★★ NATURE SITE   A UNESCO World Heritage Site, this natural rock formation is extraordinary. Sitting at the foot of steep cliffs and stretching out into the sea, it is a natural formation of thousands of tightly packed basalt columns. The tops of the columns form flat stepping-stones, all of which are perfectly hexagonal. They measure about 30cm (12 in.) in diameter; some are very short, others are as tall as 12 meters (39 ft.). Scientists believe they were formed 60 or 70 million years ago by volcanic eruptions and cooling lava. The ancients, on the other hand, believed the rock formation to be the work of giants. To reach the causeway, you walk from the parking area down a steep path for nearly 1.6km (1 mile), past amphitheaters of stone columns and formations with fanciful names like Honeycomb, Wishing Well, Giant's Granny, King and His Nobles, and Lover's Leap. If you wish, you can then climb up a wooden staircase to Benbane Head to take in the views, and then walk back along the cliff top. There is a regular shuttle service down from the visitor center for those who can't face the hike. *Note:* The underground visitor center has a cafe, shop, interpretive center, and hugely expensive parking. However, the Causeway is a free, open site, so if you can find safe and legal parking, there's nothing to stop you from just walking straight down.

44 Causeway Rd., Bushmills, Co. Antrim, BT57 8SU. www.nationaltrust.org.uk/giants-causeway. (C) **028/2073-1855.** Visitor center and parking: £9 adults; £4.50 children; £22 families. Visitor center Apr–Sept daily 9am–7pm; Feb–Mar and Oct daily 9am–6pm; Nov–Jan daily 9am–5pm.

The Old Bushmills Distillery ★★ FACTORY TOUR   Licensed to distill spirits in 1608 but with historical references dating as far back as 1276, this ancient distillery is endlessly popular. Visitors can tour the working sections and watch the whiskey-making process, starting with fresh water from the adjacent River Bush and continuing through distillation, fermentation, and bottling. At the end of the tour, you can sample the wares in the Potstill Bar as you learn more about the history of the distillery. Tours last about 25 minutes. The Bushmills coffee shop serves tea, coffee, homemade snacks, and lunch. *Tip:* Try to visit during the week for the full experience. Though tours do take place on weekends, the distillery itself is only in operation Monday through Friday.

Main St., Bushmills, Co. Antrim, BT57 8XH. www.bushmills.com. © **028/2073-3272.** Admission £7.50 adults; £6.50 seniors and students; £4 children 8–17; £21 families. No children under 8 on tour. Apr–Oct tours about every 20 min. Mar–Oct Mon–Sat 9:15am–4:45pm, Sun noon–4:45pm (last tours 4pm). Nov–Feb Mon–Sat 10am–4:45pm, Sun noon–4:45pm (last tours 3:30pm).

Torr Head Scenic Drive ★★★ SCENIC DRIVE This spectacular diversion is not for those with a fear of heights or narrow dirt roads, nor is it a good idea in bad weather. But on a sunny, dry day, the brave can follow signs from Cushendun (see p. 257) up a steep hill at the edge of town onto the **Torr Head Scenic Drive.** After a precipitous climb, the road narrows further and inches its way along the edge of the cliff overlooking the sea. Along the way are places to park and take in the sweeping views. On a clear day, you can see all the way to the Mull of Kintyre in Scotland. Arguably the best views of all are to be had at Murlough Bay (follow the signs).

Torr Rd., heading north out of Cushendun, Co. Antrim.

DERRY

Northern Ireland's second city is a vibrant place, surrounded by 17th-century walls; you can climb the steps to the top and walk the ramparts all the way around the town center. Although they were the focus of attacks and sieges for centuries, the 5-foot-thick fortifications are solid and unbroken to this day. Historians believe the city was modeled on the French Renaissance town of Vitry-Le-Francois, which in turn was based on a Roman military camp, with two main streets forming a central cross and ending in four city gates. It's ideal for walking, combining a medieval center with sprawling Georgian and Victorian neighborhoods.

City Layout

The focal point of the city center is the **Diamond,** a large square with a war memorial in the city center. Four streets radiate out from the Diamond: Bishop, Ferryquay, Shipquay, and Butcher. Each ends at a gateway (Bishop's Gate, Ferryquay Gate, Shipquay Gate, and Butcher's Gate) cut into the thick city walls. West of the walled inner city is the area known as the **Bogside.** The streets near the waterfront are known as **Waterside**, which is where most of the better hotels and many restaurants are located.

While the original walled city was built on the west bank of the River Foyle, Derry has spread across to the east bank as well, with three bridges connecting the two sides: the double-decker **Craigavon Bridge,** the dual-lane **Foyle Bridge** (Ireland's longest bridge), and the sleek, modern **Peace Bridge.**

Visitor Information

The **Derry Tourist Information Centre** can be found at 44 Foyle Street (www.visitderry.com; ℭ 028/7126-7284). From June to August it's open weekdays from 9am to 7pm, Saturday 9am to 6pm, and Sunday 10am to 5pm. From April to May and September to October, it's open weekdays 9am to 5:30pm and weekends 10am to 5pm. The rest of the year (Nov–Mar) it's open weekdays 9:30am to 5pm and weekends 10am to 4pm.

Where to Stay in Derry

Caw Cottage ★★ This charming whitewashed cottage not far from the airport is a great hideaway from the hustle and bustle. It's a taxi ride from the old town, but you make up in beautiful views and peace what you lose in proximity. Owners Dee and Jim are friendly and helpful; they know the city like the backs of their hands and will answer any questions you may have. Rooms are small but charming, with clean white linens, soft comforters, and homey furnishings. One room has an extra bed for families travelling with children. Once you've arrived, you can have tea or coffee in the guest lounge, and generally make yourself at home. Breakfast often features Dee's fresh homemade bread as an extra touch. Rooms have gorgeous views of the River Foyle and Donegal mountains, and you're close enough to the Peace Bridge to visit it on an evening stroll.

1 Caw Park, Derry, BT47 6LZ. www.cawcottage.com. ℭ **028/7131-3915.** 3 units. £60–£80. Free parking. Breakfast included. No credit cards. **Amenities:** Wi-Fi (free).

The Saddler's House and the Merchant's House ★★ Two charming buildings full of character with one pair of owners, these lovely B&Bs are among the best accommodations in Derry. Choose from the elegant Merchant's House, which was built in the mid-19th century (one of relatively few town houses from that period left in Derry), or Saddler's House, a slightly simpler, late Victorian building. (Check-in for both is at the Saddler's House.) Both have been beautifully maintained and renovated with design-magazine interiors and antiques galore. Breakfast is served in whichever house you choose. The same owners also have three self-catering places in Derry, including a small terraced cottage opposite the cathedral; an apartment in the old pump house, within the walled part of the city; and a 1950s-style apartment. *Tip:* The Merchant's House family room sleeps up to five with its own kitchen for just £100 to £135 per night.

36 Great James St., Derry, BT48 7DB. www.thesaddlershouse.com. ℭ **028/7126-9691.** Saddler's House: 7 units. Merchant's House: 8 units. £60–£80. Limited free parking (on street); otherwise, paid street parking nearby. Rates include breakfast. **Amenities:** Wi-Fi (free).

Serendipity House ★ This popular B&B at the top of the hill overlooking Derry has few frills but is a handy, well-priced option. Rooms are small but neat, with modern decor; most have lovely town views. Bathrooms are tiny but clean. Most rooms have en suite facilities, but a few have bathrooms

DERRY OR LONDONDERRY: what's in a name?

The short answer is: quite a lot.

Depending on which side of the border you're on, Northern Ireland's second city is called two different things. Road signs and maps in the Republic say **Derry;** in Northern Ireland they point to **Londonderry.**

This stubborn dispute dates to the Plantation of Ulster in the 1600s, when English settlers were given land in Ireland as an attempt to entrench Protestant rule. A new city was founded by the City of London trade guilds and named Londonderry in their honor. Nationalists have always objected to the term, preferring Derry, an Anglicization of *Daire Calgaich*, the name of the much older settlement that once stood on the same site.

During the Troubles, the dispute was a cause célèbre. Many attempts have been made to change the name, including several unsuccessful court cases. Loyalists fiercely defend the name. But having a city with two names poses a knotty problem for residents and visitors alike—what to call it? The best advice is just to be tactful. If you're drinking in a pub with a big Irish tricolor on the side, it's probably best to use Derry; but if they're flying the Union Jack, opt for Londonderry. Of the two, Derry is probably the more commonly used in town, and certainly throughout the Republic, so we've chosen to call it Derry in this book.

Fed up with effectively being forced to make a political statement whenever they talk about their own city, residents have long since tried to find an acceptable solution to the Derry/Londonderry dilemma. In the '90s, local radio DJ Gerry Anderson suggested the wry compromise "Stroke City." (American readers: Stroke is a slash in the U.K.) Quick-witted locals swiftly nicknamed the DJ "Gerry/Londongerry."

To see more evidence of how far back this titular dispute goes, look no further than a United States road atlas. Near Manchester, New Hampshire, is a small old town called Derry. In the early 19th century there was a dispute over its name, so a group of residents set up a new town just to the south called—you guessed it—Londonderry.

a short distance away; if this matters to you, ask when you book. Breakfasts are of the hearty eggs-and-bacon variety, although sometimes fresh scones and pancakes are on offer. The old city is a pleasant 10-minute walk downhill—which means a pretty steep 10-minute walk uphill when you're coming home later. But taxis are plentiful in Derry if you can't face the climb.

26 Marlborough St., Derry, BT48 9AY. www.serendipityrooms.co.uk/bed-breakfast/serendipity-house. ⓒ **028/7126-4229.** 5 units. £70–£90 double. Free parking. Breakfast included. **Amenities:** Wi-Fi (free).

Troy Hall ★★ A lavish Victorian mansion close to the Derry city center, Troy Hall was built in 1897, complete with the Gothic flourishes that were so popular in the period. Turrets give the red-brick exterior an almost fairytale look, while the sweeping back lawn is a mere remnant of what was once a huge estate. The building suffered terribly over the years until the current owners restored it to its now pristine condition. The spacious guest rooms are individually designed but share a country-house-style chic, furnished with

bogside: THE PEOPLE'S GALLERY

In many ways, the recent history of Derry is embodied in the district known as the Bogside. In the 1960s and 1970s, the neighborhood bore witness to violent scenes that shocked the world. Today, it's known as much for its powerful street art, chronicling those troubled decades of the late 20th century.

Located just outside the walled city center, the Bogside was developed in the 19th and early 20th centuries as a home for Catholic workers. In the late 1960s, civil rights protests became regular events here, and the residents declared their neighborhood as "Free Derry," independent of local and British government. The situation came to a head on January 30th, 1972, later to be known as "Bloody Sunday," when British troops opened fire on a peaceful demonstration, killing 14 civilians. The soldiers said they'd been fired upon first; eventually, in 2010, after an inquiry that lasted 12 years and cost nearly £200 million, the British government finally accepted this was completely untrue and apologized.

Most of the Bogside has been redeveloped, but the Free Derry corner remains, near a house painted with the mural reading: "You Are Now Entering Free Derry." Since the 1990s, local artists known as the **Bogside Artists** have painted more murals around the district, similar to those on the Falls Road in Belfast (see p. 242). Though some are overtly political in nature, many depict simple yet powerful messages of peace. This has effectively turned parts of the Bogside into a free art museum, and together the murals have become known as the **People's Gallery.**

handmade wood or wrought-iron beds and occasional antique pieces. Family rooms sleep up to five. Excellent breakfasts are served in the equally well-restored dining room, also known as the Turret. Central Derry is about 5 minutes by car or cab, and there's a bus stop nearby, too.

9 Troy Park, Culmore Rd., Derry, BT48 7RL. www.troyhall.co.uk. © **078/8436-1669.** 3 units. £85. Free parking. Rates include breakfast. **Amenities:** Wi-Fi (free).

Where to Eat in Derry

Badgers ★ IRISH A friendly, proper local pub, right in the center of Derry, Badgers serves hearty traditional grub—stews, fish and chips, steak-and-Guinness pie, burgers, and the like, plus a few lighter options such as hot sandwiches and wraps. Plates are generous, and of course, you can wash it all down with a pint of the black stuff. The dining room is satisfyingly unreconstructed with plenty of polished wood and low-hanging lamps. No matter what the time of day, there always seem to be a few locals propping up the bar, which helps keep the atmosphere authentic.

16-18 Orchard St., Derry, BT48 6EG. © **028/7136-0763.** Main courses £6–£12. Mon–Sat 11:30am–1am; Sun 11:30am–midnight. (Food about noon–7pm). No children after 9pm.

The Belfray Country Inn Bistro ★ BISTRO This big hotel/restaurant outside of Derry is where the locals go to celebrate. The dining room's plush decor adds a rococo touch to the feel of a country pub. A lot of things are gilded here. For the food, think posh pub fare. The best dishes come from the grill—thick juicy steaks, lamb cutlets, and chicken escalope, with all the trimmings—but there are also several stir-fry options, vegetarian options, and an extensive kids' menu. Sunday roasts are hugely popular. The inn also offers spacious rooms with big beds and neutral decor, but they're a bit pricey (£95–£120) given the location.

171 Glenshane Rd., Derry, BT47 3EN. www.thebelfraycountryinn.co.uk. © **028/7130-1480.** Set menus £12–£24. Daily noon–3:30pm, 5–9:30pm.

Primrose Café ★★ CAFE   This lovely, cheerful cafe is nicely old-fashioned without being at all stuffy. Drop in for a bowl of delicious soup, fresh sandwiches, or a tasty pie (served with a side of excellent chips). Or you could just have a plate of homemade scones and some tea, served the proper way with a teapot and fine china. Service is cheery and prices are reasonable—just what you want for a casual lunch on the go.

15 Carlisle Rd., Derry, BT48 6JJ. © **028/7126-4622.** Lunch £3–£8. Mon–Sat 8am–5pm; Sun 11am–4pm.

The Sooty Olive ★ IRISH   Named after a kind of fishing lure, this trendy eatery in central Derry specializes in locally sourced food, and serves it with class. The decor in the small dining room makes the most of the exposed brick walls, contrasting it with tasteful leather chairs and sofas. Similarly, the cooking makes the most of local seafood in dishes like sea bream with black pudding and new potatoes, and duck breast with potato fondant. There's steak and skinny fries, as well as plenty of vegetarian options. Desserts are to die for.

160-164 Spencer Rd., Derry, BT47 6AH. www.thesootyolive.com. © **028/7134-6040.** Set menus £16–£18. Mon–Thurs noon–2:30pm, 5–9pm. Fri–Sat noon–2:30pm, 5–10pm. Sun 1–9pm.

Exploring Derry

Centre for Contemporary Art ★ ARTS CENTER   Drop in here to see new and touring works by contemporary artists from Ireland and farther afield. Themed seasons include visual art, film screenings, performances, and public debates. Recent seasons have included a retrospective of a pivotal early 20th-century Dublin workers strike; art inspired by people's relationship to the natural world; and creative responses to revolution and unrest in Egypt. Admission to the center and most events is free, but there may be a charge for some events.

10-12 Artillery St., Derry, BT48 6RG. www.cca-derry-londonderry.org. © **028/7137-3538.** Free admission. Tues–Sat noon–6pm. Closed Sun and Mon.

Guildhall ★ ARCHITECTURAL SITE   Just outside the city walls, between Shipquay Gate and the River Foyle, this Tudor Gothic-style building looks much like its counterpart in London. The site's original structure was built in 1890, but it was rebuilt after a fire in 1908 and again after a series of sectarian bombings in 1972. The hall is distinguished by its huge, four-faced clock (designed to resemble Big Ben) and its 23 stained-glass windows, made by Ulster craftsmen, which illustrate almost every episode of note in the city's history.

Shipquay Place, Derry, BT48 6DQ. ✆ **028/7137-7335.** Free admission. Daily 10am–5:30pm. Free guided tours July–Aug; enquire at reception.

Museum of Free Derry ★★ MUSEUM   Thousands of documents and artifacts related to the civil rights movement are housed at this informative museum, while displays tell the story of Bloody Sunday and other key events in the Troubles of the 1960s to '90s. The timeline is clearly laid out and easy to understand; the calm, level tone makes the impact all the more powerful. The Bogside (see p. 262) naturally becomes the focus for much of this history—so afterward, why not take one of the excellent **Free Derry Tours** of the district, which leave from the museum. *Note:* At this writing, the museum was preparing to move to its new location at the southern end of Glenfada Park. This should be complete by the end of 2016, but it has been delayed in the past, so call ahead and check details first.

55 Glenfada Park, Derry, BT48 9DR. www.museumoffreederry.org. ✆ **028/7136-0880.** Admission £3 adults; £2 seniors, students, and children. Joint ticket with Free Derry Tour: £6 adults, £5 seniors and children. Apr–Sept Mon–Fri 9:30am–4:30pm, Sat–Sun 1–4pm (closed Sun Apr–June and Sept). Oct–Mar Mon–Fri 9:30am–4:30pm.

St. Columb's Cathedral ★ CHURCH   Within the city walls, near the Bishop's Gate, this Protestant cathedral was built by the Church of Ireland between 1628 and 1633 as a prime example of the so-called "Planters Gothic" style of architecture. It was the first cathedral built in Europe after the Reformation, although several sections were added afterward, including the impressive spire and stained-glass windows depicting scenes from the siege of 1688 and 1689. The chapter house contains a display of city relics such as the four massive original padlocks for the city gates.

London St., Derry, BT48 6RQ. www.stcolumbscathedral.org. ✆ **028/7126-7313.** Requested donation £2 adults; £1.50 seniors, students, and children. Mon–Sat 9am–5pm; Sun for services only.

St. Eugene's Cathedral ★★ CHURCH   Designed in the Gothic Revival style, Derry's Roman Catholic cathedral is appropriately located in the heart of the Bogside district, just beyond the city walls. The foundation was laid in 1851, but work continued until 1873. The spire was added in 1902. It's built of local sandstone and is known for its stained-glass windows depicting the Crucifixion, designed by famed stained-glass makers Mayer and Company of Munich.

Francis St., Derry, BT48 9AP. www.steugenescathedral.com. ✆ **028/7126-2894.** Free admission. Mon–Sat 7am–9pm; Sun 7am–6:30pm.

The Tower Museum ★★ MUSEUM   This engaging museum chronicles the history of Derry from the earliest times to the 21st century. It's located in **O'Doherty Tower,** a reconstructed medieval fortress originally built in the early 17th century (curiously enough, it was built to pay off a tax debt, rather than for any specific defensive purpose). The **Story of Derry** exhibition

CLIMBING THE walls

One of the best ways to explore Derry is via its 17th-century stone walls, about 1 mile (1.6km) in circumference and more than 16 ft. (5m) thick. Climb the stairs to the top and you can circle the entire walled city in about 30 minutes. Stairways off of the parapets are frequent, so you'll never get stuck up there. If you start at the **Diamond,** as the square in the center of the walled section is called, and walk down Butcher Street, you can climb the steps at **Butcher's Gate,** a security checkpoint between the Bogside and the city during the Troubles. Walk to the right across **Castle Gate,** which was built in 1865, and on to **Magazine Gate,** which was once near a powder magazine. Shortly afterward you'll pass **O'Doherty's Tower,** which houses the worthwhile Tower Museum (see above). From there you can see the brick walls of the Guildhall (see p. 263).

Farther along, you'll pass **Shipquay Gate,** once located very near the port, back when the waters passed closer to the town center. The walls turn uphill from there, past the Millennium Forum concert hall, and up to **Ferryquay Gate.** Here in 1688, local apprentice boys saved the town from attacking Catholic forces by locking the city gates—saving the town from attack, but launching the Great Siege of Derry, which lasted for months. (By the time it ended, nearly a quarter of the town's population had died.)

Next you'll pass **Bishop's Gate,** where a tall brick tower just outside the gate is all that remains of the **Old Gaol.** The rebel Wolfe Tone was imprisoned here after the unsuccessful uprising in 1798. Farther along, the **Double Bastion** holds a military tower with elaborate equipment used to keep an eye on the Bogside—it's usually splashed with paint hurled at it by Republicans. From there you can easily access the serene churchyard of **St. Columb's Cathedral** (see above). From the next stretch of wall, you have a good view over the political murals of the Bogside down the hill.

A bit farther along the wall, an empty plinth stands where once there was a statue of Rev. George Walker, a governor of the city during the siege of 1699. It was blown up by the IRA in 1973. The small chapel nearby is the **Chapel of St. Augustine** (1872), and the building across the street with metal grates over the windows is the **Apprentice Boys' Memorial Hall,** commemorating the boys from the Great Siege of Derry. Walk a short way farther, and you're back to Butcher's Gate.

---

presents a chronology of life in the city from the first monastic settlers through the Plantation era, up to the turbulent 20th century, when the city was a focus of the civil rights movement driven by the Troubles. The main attraction, however, is the large, multi-floor exhibition devoted to a historic shipwreck that happened off the coast of Derry in the 16th century. **An Armada Shipwreck** tells the story of *La Trinidad Valencera,* part of the massive Spanish Armada that attempted to invade England in 1588. The ship was separated from the main fleet and sank during a storm. Four hundred years later the wreck was salvaged, together with an extraordinary hoard of treasure including clothes, shoes, pottery, cannons, goblets, and other items.

Union Hall Place, Derry, BT48 6LU. www.derrycity.gov.uk/museums/tower-museum. ℗ **028/7137-2411.** Admission £4.50 adults; £2.90 seniors, students, and children; £10 families. Daily 10am–5:30pm. Last admission 1 hr. before closing.

PLANNING YOUR TRIP TO IRELAND

13

Chances are you've been looking forward to your trip to Ireland for some time. You've probably set aside a significant amount of hard-earned cash, taken time off from work, school, or other commitments, and now want to make the most of your holiday. To accomplish that, you'll need to plan carefully. The aim of this chapter is to provide you with the information you need, and to answer any questions you might have on lots of topics, including: When to go? How to get there? Should you book a tour or travel independently? And how much will everything cost? Here you'll find plenty of resources to help get the most out of your Irish adventure.

GETTING THERE

By Plane

The Republic of Ireland has three major international airports. They are, in order of size, **Dublin (DUB;** www.dublinairport.com; ✆ **1/814-1111), Cork (ORK;** www.cork-airport.com; ✆ **021/431-3131)**, and **Shannon** (www.shannonairport.com; ✆ **061/712000).** Northern Ireland's main airport is **Belfast International Airport (BFS;** www.belfastairport.com; ✆ **028/9448-4848).**

The Republic of Ireland has seven smaller regional airports, all of which offer service to Dublin and several that receive some (very limited) European traffic. They are Donegal, Kerry, Knock, Sligo, and Waterford. In Northern Ireland, the secondary airports are Belfast City Airport and Derry City Airport. Airline service to these smaller airports changes frequently, so be sure to consult your preferred airline or travel agent as soon as you begin to sketch your itinerary.

To find good deals on airfare, run searches through the regular online agents such as Expedia, as well as metasearch engines like **DoHop.com, Kayak.com, Skyscanner.net**, and **Momondo.com.** For complex journeys, with multiple departures, doing multiple searches (so such affordable intra-European airlines as Ryanair, Flybe, and EasyJet show up on the search) is a good way to find deals; a specialist flight agent such as **RoundtheWorldFlights.com** or **AirTreks.com** may also save you money.

By Ferry

If you're traveling to Ireland from Britain or the Continent, traveling by ferry is a good alternative to flying. Several car and passenger ferries offer reasonably comfortable furnishings, cabin berths (for longer crossings), restaurants, duty-free shopping, and lounges.

Prices fluctuate seasonally and depend on your route, your time of travel, and whether you are on foot or in a car. It's best to check with your travel agent for up-to-date details, but just to give you an idea, the lowest one-way adult fare in high season on the cruise ferry from Holyhead to Dublin starts at around £30. A car usually costs about £80 including one adult passenger, £30 per extra adult, £15 per extra child.

Irish Ferries (www.irishferries.ie; © **0818/300-400** in the Republic of Ireland, or © **353/818-300-400** in Northern Ireland/U.K.) operates from Holyhead, Wales, to Dublin Ferryport, and from Pembroke, Wales, to Rosslare in County Wexford. They also sail from Cherbourg and Rosscoff in France.

P&O Irish Sea Ferries (www.poferries.com; © **01/407-3434** in Ireland © **0871/66-6464** in Britain, or © **352/3420-808-294** in the rest of the world) operates from Liverpool to Dublin and from Cairnryan, Scotland, to Larne, County Antrim, Northern Ireland.

Stena Line (www.stenaline.com; © **01/204-7777**) sails from Fishguard, Wales, to Rosslare; and from Cairnryan, Scotland, and Liverpool, England, to Belfast, Northern Ireland.

TRIPS & TOURS

Package Tours

Package tours are simply a way to buy the airfare, accommodations, and other elements of your trip (such as car rentals, airport transfers, and even activities) at the same time and often at discounted prices.

One good source for package deals of all kinds is the airlines themselves. Most major airlines offer air/land packages, with surprisingly cheap hotel deals. Several big online travel agencies—such as **Expedia** (www.expedia. com), **Travelocity** (www.travelocity.com), **Orbitz** (www.orbitz.com), and **Lastminute** (www.lastminute.com)—also do a brisk business in packages.

Fully escorted tours mean a travel company takes care of absolutely everything, including airfare, hotels, meals, tours, admission costs, and local transportation. Although we hope this book will help you to plan your trip independently and safely, many travelers still prefer the convenience and peace of mind that a fully escorted tour offers. They are particularly good for inexperienced travelers or people with limited mobility. They can also be a great way to make new friends. On the downside, you'll have less opportunity for serendipitous interactions with locals. The tours can be jam-packed with activities, leaving little room for individual sightseeing, whim, or adventure. Plus they often focus on heavily trafficked sites, so you miss out on many lesser-known gems.

Discover Ireland (www.discoverireland.com) can give advice on escorted tours and publishes up-to-the-minute deals on the front page of their website. If you prefer to speak to a person, the website has individual phone numbers for around 50 countries—and every region in the world—on the contact page of the website.

One highly recommended Irish company is **C.I.E. Tours** (www.cietours.com; ℰ **020/8638-0715**). They offer fully escorted tours; help organize self-guided tours; and will even arrange individual, chauffeur-driven tours. Another, **Hidden Ireland Tours** (www.hiddenirelandtours.com; ℰ **087/221-4002**), specializes in more off-the-beaten-path tours of Kerry, Galway, and Donegal.

A good company for travelers from the U.S. and Canada is **Authentic Ireland** (www.authenticireland.com; ℰ **087/221-4002** or 125/1478-7519 outside Ireland). In addition to escorted, self-guided, and private tours, their range also covers themed tours such as castle and golfing vacations.

Those wanting to combine their trip with some serious learning opportunities might be interested in the **International Summer School** program at the National University of Ireland, Galway (University Rd., Galway, Co. Galway; www.nuigalway.ie/international-summer-school), which includes courses on Irish language and history. Contact the course administrator at ℰ **091/495-442** for more information.

Sightseeing Tours

Once you get to Ireland, a limitless array of tour companies offer organized tours, from Ghost Tours of Dublin to trips to the Aran Islands from Galway to horseback rides through the Burren. **Dublin Bus** (www.dublinsightseeing.ie; ℰ **01/703-3028**) runs a good range of tours in Dublin and the southeast. They include a North Coast and Castle Tour, a South Coast and Gardens tour, as well as the extremely popular Ghost Bus. Most tours cost between €20 and €30. **Irish City Tours** (www.irishcitytours.com; ℰ **01/898-0700**) runs several day trips from Dublin to destinations such as **Powerscourt** (p. 107), the **Cliffs of Moher** (p. 186), and the **Giant's Causeway** (p. 258). Prices range from about €30 to €65.

A number of smaller tour companies are run by locals who lead excellent excursions to various regions. **Mary Gibbons Tours** (www.newgrangetours.com; ℰ **01/283-9973**) leads absorbing, in-depth tours from Dublin to Newgrange and the Hill of Tara. And in Belfast, don't miss the extraordinary **Black Taxi Tours** (www.belfasttours.com; ℰ **028/9064-2264**), which take you through the areas where the Troubles had the most impact and explain it all in compassionate, firsthand terms. See p. 243 for details.

Trips & Tours

PLANNING YOUR TRIP TO IRELAND

GETTING AROUND

By Car

Although Ireland has a reasonably extensive network of public transportation, it will only be useful if you don't mind being confined to the major towns and cities, or taking organized tours out to attractions that are farther afield. Trains tend not to go to charming small towns and villages, and great houses and castles are usually miles from any major town. Buses are slow, and service to places off the beaten track can be infrequent. Three or more people traveling together can often get around more cheaply by car than by train, depending on the distances traveled and the size and efficiency of the engine (note that **fuel is very expensive** in Ireland).

Renting a car is not for everyone—particularly if you're not used to driving on small, winding European country roads (and on the *left* side of the road). But if you're intrepid enough to do it, this is by far the best way to get around. It will give you the most freedom and open up more choices to you than any other way of getting around. Put simply: Rent a car and you'll see more of Ireland.

Unless your stay in Ireland extends beyond 6 months, your own valid driver's license (provided you've had it for at least 6 months) is all you need to drive in Ireland. Rules and restrictions for car rental vary slightly and correspond roughly to those in other European nations and the U.S., with two important distinctions: Most rental-car agencies in the Republic won't rent to you (1) if you're under 25 years old or over 74 (there's no upper age limit in the North); or (2) if your license has been valid for less than a year.

DRIVING LAWS, TIPS & WARNINGS

Highway safety has become a critical issue in Ireland during the past several years. The number of highway fatalities is high for such a small nation—Ireland regularly comes out near the bottom of European league tables for accident rates. In an effort to rein in Irish drivers, the Republic now uses a penalty "points" system similar to that in the U.K. and the U.S. While visitors won't have points added to their licenses, they may still be penalized with fines if they speed or commit driving infractions.

All distances and speed limits on road signs in the Republic of Ireland are in **kilometers,** while in Northern Ireland they are in **miles.** Take care if you're driving around the borderlands—the border is unmarked, so you can cross over from one side to the other without knowing it. It's easy to get confused and speed accidentally.

If you're not used to driving in rural areas on the left-hand side of the road, take precautions. Try to avoid driving after dark, and stay off the road when driving conditions are compromised by rain, fog, or heavy traffic. Getting used to left-side driving, left-handed stick shift, narrow roads, and a new landscape all present a challenge, especially if you're driving solo—it's helpful if you can have somebody along to navigate. Some people even use tricks such as sticking a big arrow to the dashboard reminding you that the left is your default lane.

road rules **IN A NUTSHELL**

1. Drive on the left side of the road.
2. Road signs are in kilometers, except in Northern Ireland, where they are in miles.
3. On motorways, the left lane is the traveling lane. The right lane is for passing.
4. Everyone must wear a seat belt by law. Young children must be in age-appropriate child seats.
5. Children 11 and under are not allowed to sit in the front seat.
6. When entering a roundabout (traffic circle), give way to traffic coming from the right.
7. Another roundabout rule: Always go *left* (clockwise) around the circle.
8. The speed limits are 50kmph (31 mph) in urban areas; 80kmph (50 mph) on regional and local roads, sometimes referred to as non-national roads; 100kmph (62 mph) on national roads, including divided highways (called dual carriageways); and 120kmph (75 mph) on freeways (called motorways)

You can also rent a GPS navigation device with your car. These can be invaluable in finding your way around, especially in the remote countryside. Nearly all rental firms offer them.

Roundabouts (what Americans call traffic circles or rotaries) are found on most major roads and take a little getting used to. Remember always to yield to traffic coming from the right as you approach a roundabout and follow the traffic to the left, signaling before you exit the circle.

One signal that could be misleading to U.S. drivers is a flashing amber light at a pedestrian traffic light. This almost always follows a red light, and it means yield to pedestrians but proceed when the crossing is clear.

The Republic has relatively few types of roads. **Motorways (M)** are major highways, the equivalent of Interstates in the U.S. **National (N)** roads link major cities on the island. Though these are the equivalent of highways in North America, they are rarely more than two lanes in each direction (and are sometimes as small as one American-sized lane). Most pass directly through towns, making cross-country trips longer than you'd expect. **Regional (R)** roads have one lane of traffic traveling in each direction and generally link smaller cities and towns. Last are the rural or unclassified roads, often the most scenic back roads. These can be poorly signposted, very narrow, and a bit rough, but they usually travel through beautiful countryside locations. Bear in mind, however, that rural roads are not well-lighted at night. (This is more of an issue in the winter, when it can get dark as early as 4pm.)

Both the Republic and Northern Ireland have severe laws against drunk driving. The legal limit for both is 35 micrograms of alcohol per 100 milliliters of breath. What that equates to varies by person, but even one pint of beer can be enough to put you over the limit. The general rule is: Do not drink and drive.

RENTING A CAR

Major international car-rental firms are represented at airports and cities throughout Ireland and Northern Ireland. Most rental companies offer their best prices to customers who **reserve in advance** from their home country. Note that Ireland is a small country, and in high season it can virtually run out of rental cars—but long before it does, it runs out of affordable rental cars.

In the summer, weekly rental rates on a manual-transmission compact vehicle begin at around €160 and ascend steeply. Rates are much cheaper out of season, and weekly rentals are almost always less expensive than day rentals. Also keep in mind that the vast majority of available rental cars have **manual transmissions** (stick shifts). Automatics are available, but for a premium.

By law, you must be between the ages of 25 and 75 to rent a car in Ireland. The only documentation you should need is your driver's license and photo ID, such as a passport, plus a printout of your reservation if you have one.

When you reserve a car, be sure to ask if the price includes: all taxes including value-added tax (VAT); breakdown assistance; unlimited mileage; personal accident or liability insurance (PAI); collision-damage waiver (CDW); theft waiver; and any other insurance options. If not, ask what these extras cost, because they can make a big dent in your bottom line. The CDW and other insurance might be covered by your credit card if you use the card to pay for the rental; check with your card issuer to be sure that there are no restrictions on that coverage in Ireland. (Not all cards do offer insurance protection for car rentals in Ireland.) Some travelers like to live dangerously and waive optional insurance. But when no CDW is purchased, many rental agencies will make you pay for any damages on the spot when you return the car—making even the smallest dent or scratch a potentially costly experience. To avoid any issues, take cellphone photos of your car with a time stamp, so that you have any dents and dings recorded and won't be charged for it.

By Train

Iarnród Éireann (Irish Rail; www.irishrail.ie; *©* **1850/366222** or 01/836-6222) operates the train services in Ireland. Train travel is generally the fastest way to get around the country. Most lines radiate from Dublin to other principal cities and towns. From Dublin, the journey time to Waterford is about 2¼ hours; to Cork, about 2½ hours; to Killarney, 3¼ hours; to Galway, just under 2½ hours; to Sligo, 3 hours; and to Belfast, just over 2 hours.

In addition to the Irish Rail service between Dublin and Belfast, **Translink** (www.nirailways.co.uk; *©* **028/9066-6630**) operates routes from Belfast that include Coleraine and Derry, in addition to virtually all 21 localities in Northern Ireland.

One useful piece of lingo: when buying any sort of travel tickets—air, ferry, train, or bus—a "single" means one-way, a "return" is round-trip.

By Bus

Bus Éireann (www.buseireann.ie; *©* **01/836-6111**) operates an extensive system of express bus services, as well as local service, to nearly every town in the Irish Republic. The Bus Éireann website provides timetables and fares for bus service throughout the country. Similarly, **Translink** provides detailed information on services within Northern Ireland (www.translink.co.uk; ☎ **028/9066-6630**). Bus travel in both countries is affordable, reliable, and comfortable—but also slow.

By Plane

Ireland is such a small country that there is very little point in flying from one end to the other. In any case, the options for internal flights seem to get more limited every year, partly because of improved roads and faster rail journey times. **Aer Arann** (www.aerarann.com; ☎ **081/836-5000**) runs a couple of flights daily from Dublin to Kerry and Donegal.

WHEN TO GO

A visit to Ireland in the summer is very different from a trip in the winter. Apart from climatic considerations, there are the issues of cost, closures, and crowds. Generally speaking, in summer, airfares, car-rental rates, and hotel prices are highest and crowds at their most intense. But the days are long (6am sunrises and 10pm sunsets), the weather is warm, and every sightseeing attraction and B&B is open. In winter, you can get rock-bottom prices on airfare and hotels. But it will rain and the wind will blow, and many rural sights and a fair proportion of the rural B&Bs and restaurants will be closed.

All things considered, we think the best time to visit is in spring and fall when the weather falls in between seasons, but you get lower-than-high-season prices and the crowds have yet to descend.

Weather

Rain is the one constant in Irish weather, although a bit of sunshine is usually just around the corner. The best of times and the worst of times are often only hours, or even minutes, apart. It can be chilly in Ireland at any time of year, so think *layers* when you pack.

Winters can be brutal, as the wind blows in off the Atlantic with numbing constancy, and strong gales are common. But deep snow is rare and temperatures rarely drop much below freezing. In fact, Ireland is a fairly temperate place: January and February bring frosts but seldom snow, and July and August are very warm but rarely hot. The Irish consider any temperature over 68°F (20°C) to be "roasting" and below 34°F (1°C) as bone-chilling. For a complete online guide to Irish weather, consult **www.ireland.com/weather**.

Average Monthly Temperatures in Dublin

	JAN	FEB	MAR	APR	MAY	JUNE	JULY	AUG	SEPT	OCT	NOV	DEC
TEMP (°F)	36–46	37–48	37–49	38–52	42–57	46–62	51–66	50–65	48–62	44–56	39–49	38–47
TEMP (°C)	2–8	3–9	3–9	3–11	6–14	8–17	11–19	10–18	9–17	7–13	4–9	3–8

Holidays

The Republic observes the following national holidays: New Year's Day (Jan 1); St. Patrick's Day (Mar 17); Easter Monday (variable); May Day (May 1); first Mondays in June and August (summer bank holidays); last Monday in October (autumn bank holiday); Christmas (Dec 25); and St. Stephen's Day (Dec 26). Good Friday (the Friday before Easter) is mostly observed but is not statutory.

In the North, the schedule of holidays is the same as in the Republic, with some exceptions: The North's summer bank holidays fall on the last Monday of May and August; the Battle of the Boyne is celebrated on Orangeman's Day (July 12); and Boxing Day (Dec 26) follows Christmas.

In both Ireland and Northern Ireland, holidays that fall on weekends are celebrated the following Monday.

RESPONSIBLE TRAVEL

Responsible tourism is conscientious travel. It means being careful with the environments you explore and respecting the communities you visit. Two overlapping components of responsible travel are **ecotourism** and **ethical tourism. The International Ecotourism Society (TIES)** defines *ecotourism* as responsible travel to natural areas that conserves the environment and improves the well-being of local people. TIES suggests that ecotourists follow these principles:

- Minimize environmental impact.
- Build environmental and cultural awareness and respect.
- Provide positive experiences for both visitors and hosts.
- Provide direct financial benefits for conservation and for local people.
- Raise sensitivity to host countries' political, environmental, and social climates.
- Support international human rights and labor agreements.

You can find some eco-friendly travel tips and statistics, as well as touring companies and associations—listed by destination under "Travel Choice"—at the **TIES** website, **www.ecotourism.org**).

In the U.K., **Tourism Concern** (www.tourismconcern.org.uk) works to reduce social and environmental problems connected to tourism.

Volunteer travel has become increasingly popular among those who want to venture beyond the standard group-tour experience to learn languages, interact with locals, and make a positive difference while on vacation. Volunteer travel usually doesn't require special skills—just the willingness to work hard—and programs vary in length from a few days to a number of weeks. Some programs provide free housing and food, but many require volunteers to pay for travel expenses, which can add up quickly. For general info on volunteer travel, visit **www.volunteerabroad.org** and **www.idealist.org**.

[FastFACTS] IRELAND

Area Codes Area codes in Ireland range from one number (the Dublin area code is "1") to three. Area codes are included in all listings in this guide. Within Ireland, you dial 0 before the area code. Outside of Ireland, however, you do not dial 0 before the area code, but you add Ireland's country code, 353.

Business Hours Banks are generally open 10am to 4pm Monday to Wednesday and Friday, and 10am to 5pm on Thursday. Post offices (also known as An Post) are generally open from 9am to 5:30pm Monday to Friday and 9am to 1:30pm on Saturday. Some take an hour for lunch from 1 to 2pm, and small or rural branches may close on Saturday. **Museums and sights** are generally open 10am to 5pm Tuesday to Saturday and 2 to 5pm on Sunday. **Shops** generally open 9am to 6pm Monday to Saturday with late opening on Thursday until 7 or 8pm. Most shops in larger towns and cities will also open on Sundays (typically from late morning to late afternoon). Major shops, such as department stores, often stay open much later than other businesses.

Car Rental See "Getting Around: By Car" in this chapter, p. 269. Individual offices are listed under "Fast Facts" in other chapters in this book.

Disabled Travelers
For disabled travelers, Ireland is a mixed bag. Its modern buildings and cities are generally accessible, but many of its buildings are historic, and those often lack wheelchair access. Trains can be accessed by wheelchairs but only with assistance. If you plan to travel by train in Ireland, check out the **Irish Rail** (Iarnród Éireann) website, which lists services for travelers with disabilities under **www.irishrail.ie/travel-information/disabled-access**.

For research prior to your trip, one of the best Irish-based online resources is **www.disability.ie**.

For advice on travel to Northern Ireland, contact **Disability Action** (www.disabilityaction.org; **℡ 028/9029-7880**). The Northern Ireland Tourist Board also publishes a helpful annual *Information Guide to Accessible Accommodation*, available from any of its offices worldwide.

Finding accessible lodging can be tricky in Ireland. Many of the buildings here are hundreds of years old, and older hotels, small guesthouses, and landmark buildings still have steps outside and in. Never assume that a B&B, hotel, or restaurant has accessible facilities; ask about your requirements before booking.

Doctors Healthcare in Ireland is comparable to

that in other European nations. In the Irish system, private doctors and hospitals provide care and patients purchase healthcare insurance. See listings under "Fast Facts" in other chapters of this book.

Drinking Laws The minimum legal age to buy alcohol in Ireland is 18. Children under 18 are allowed in pubs until 9pm, or 10pm from May to September, so long as they're with their parents or guardians. (Pubs serving food often have separate dining areas, which are usually treated like restaurants and so can accommodate children later.) Pubs are allowed to stay open until 11:30pm during the week, and around 12:30am on weekends, though some have licenses that let them stay open later. Many pubs choose to close earlier on Sundays. These times are roughly comparable in Northern Ireland.

Drunk driving laws in Ireland are very strict. Even a single pint of beer could be enough to put you over the limit. If you're arrested for drunk driving, penalties range from a hefty fine to jail time. Rules in Northern Ireland are even more severe. The safest course is simply not to drink and drive.

Electricity The Irish electric system operates on 220 volts, with a large plug bearing three rectangular prongs. The Northern Irish system operates on 250 volts with a similar plug. To use standard American 110-volt appliances, you'll need both a transformer and a plug adapter. Most new laptops have built-in transformers, but some do not, so beware.

Embassies & Consulates   The **American Embassy** is at 42 Elgin Rd., Ballsbridge, Dublin (dublin.usembassy.gov; ✆ **01/668-8777**); the **Canadian Embassy** is at 7-8 Wilton Terrace, Third Floor, Dublin 2 (www.canadainternational.gc.ca/ireland-irlande; ✆ **01/234-4000**); the **British Embassy** is at 29 Merrion Rd., Dublin 2 (www.gov.uk/government/world/organisations/british-embassy-dublin; ✆ **01/205-3700**); and the **Australian Embassy** is at Fitzwilton House, 7th Floor, Wilton Terrace, Dublin 2 (www.ireland.embassy.gov.au; ✆ **01/664-5300**). In addition, there is an **American Consulate** at Danesfort House, 223 Stranmillis Rd., Belfast BT9 5GR (belfast.usconsulate.gov; ✆ **028/9038-6100**).

Emergencies   For the **Garda (police),** fire, ambulance, or other emergencies, dial ✆ **999.**

Internet & Wi-Fi   Wi-Fi is widespread in Irish hotels and B&Bs, even in rural areas. It's not universal, however; in this book we always note in the listings if Wi-Fi is available. Most B&Bs and smaller hotels provide it free, but larger hotels sometimes charge for access.

Language   Ireland has two official languages: English and Gaelic (which is also known as Irish). All native Irish can speak English. Gaelic is growing in popularity, and there is a strong national movement to preserve and expand the language. Areas of the country where Gaelic is protected and promoted are known as the **Gaeltacht** and include Donegal, Galway, and parts of Kerry. In these regions, signs are in Gaelic only, with no English translation. Gaelic is a complex and ancient language that you will not be able to figure out on your own, so don't hesitate to ask for help (in English) if you get lost—despite the government's efforts, everybody in the Gaeltacht regions speaks English.

LGBT Travelers   In 2015, Ireland became the first country in the world to legalize gay marriage by a popular vote, and discrimination on the basis of sexuality is illegal throughout Ireland. However, gay and lesbian visitors should be aware that this is still a conservative country. Cities like Dublin and Galway are quite liberal in their attitudes (particularly among the young), but the same isn't true everywhere, and you should proceed with caution when traveling in rural areas. Recommended websites for gay and lesbian travelers include **Gay Ireland** (www.

gay-ireland.com) and **Outhouse** (www.outhouse.ie).

Lost Property   If your passport is lost or stolen, contact your country's embassy immediately. Be sure to tell all of your credit card companies the minute you discover that your wallet is gone and file a report at the nearest police station.

Mail   In Ireland, mailboxes are painted green with the word POST on top. An airmail letter or postcard to any other country outside Europe, not exceeding 50 grams, costs €1.05. From Northern Ireland to Europe, airmail letters not exceeding 20 grams cost £1.

Money   The Republic of Ireland uses the single European currency known as the **euro** (€). Euro notes come in denominations of €5, €10, €20, €50, €100, €200, and €500. The euro is divided into 100 cents; coins come in denominations of €2, €1, 50¢, 20¢, 10¢, 5¢, 2¢, and 1¢.

As part of the United Kingdom, Northern Ireland uses the British **pound sterling** (£). British currency has notes in denominations of £5, £10, £20, £50, and £100. Coins are issued in £2, £1, 50p, 20p, 10p, 5p, 2p, and 1p denominations.

The British pound is not accepted in the Republic, and the euro is not accepted in the North—if you're traveling in both parts of Ireland you'll need some of both currencies, although shops on the border tend to accept both, as do some of the bigger tourist attractions in the North. For those traveling between Great Britain and Northern Ireland, although the pounds issued in Northern Ireland are legal tender in Great Britain and vice versa, the paper money actually *looks* different, and you may find that cabdrivers and small business owners in the North won't accept bills issued in Great Britain. In that case, you can change the money into locally issued versions at any large central bank, free of charge.

Note that **exchange rates** can fluctuate wildly in the space of just a few weeks, so before departing consult a currency exchange website such as **www. xe.com** to check up-to-the-minute rates. When it comes to obtaining foreign currency, please, **skip the currency exchange kiosks** in airports, train stations, and elsewhere. They give the poorest rates and charge exorbitant fees. Instead, order a small amount of foreign currency from your bank before leaving home, and then figure on using your debit card for the duration of your trip. ATMs (in Ireland also referred to as "cash machines" or "cash points") will give you a favorable rate, and you can withdraw however much cash you need for a day or so, as opposed to carrying around wads of money. The **Cirrus** and **Plus** ATM networks span the globe; look at the back of your bankcard to see which network you're

on. Before you depart, be sure you know your personal identification number (PIN) and daily withdrawal limit. Confirm with your bank that your PIN will work in Europe, and be sure to let them know the dates and destinations to which you're traveling—you don't want to find your card frozen while you're abroad!

Credit cards are accepted just about everywhere, save street markets, small independent retailers, street-food vendors, and occasional small or family-owned businesses. However, North American visitors should note that American Express is accepted far less widely than at home, and Diners Club only at the very highest of highflying establishments. To be sure of your credit line, bring a Visa or MasterCard as well.

Many retailers ask for your 4-digit PIN to be entered into a keypad near the cash register. In restaurants, a server might bring a hand-held device to your table to authorize payment. If you're visiting from a country where Chip and PIN is less prevalent (such as the U.S.), it's possible that some retailers will be reluctant to accept your swipe cards. Be prepared to argue your case: Swipe cards are still valid and the same machines that read the smartcard chips can also read your magnetic strip. However, do carry some cash with you too, just in case.

Passports See "Embassies & Consulates" above for whom to contact if you lose your passport while traveling in Ireland.

Pharmacies Drugstores are called "chemists" and are found in every city, town, and most villages of any size. You'll find listings under "Fast Facts" in other chapters of this book.

Police In the Republic of Ireland, a law enforcement officer is called a **Garda,** a member of the *Garda Síochána* ("Guardian of the Peace"); in the plural, it's **Gardaí** (pronounced *Gar-*dee) or simply "the Guards." Dial ⓒ 999 to reach the Gardaí in an emergency. Except for special detachments, Irish police are unarmed and wear dark blue uniforms. In Northern Ireland you can also reach the police by dialing ⓒ 999.

Safety By U.S. standards, Ireland is very safe, but, particularly in the cities, it's not safe enough to warrant carelessness. Be wary of the usual tourists' plagues: pickpockets, purse snatchers, and car thieves. The standard travel advice applies: Don't leave cars unlocked or cameras and other expensive equipment unattended. Ask at your hotel which areas are safe and which are not. Take a taxi back to your hotel if you're out very late.

In Northern Ireland, safety may be a somewhat greater concern, due to the long-running political tensions between different communities there. Violence is no longer commonplace, and your visit here should be every bit as safe as in the rest of Ireland. However, occasional flare-ups do happen, especially during the Orange marching season in the late summer. Visitors rarely have problems with this, because they are not the targets of unrest. Still, keep abreast of things by reading or watching the news. See chapter 12 for more information.

Senior Travel   In Ireland, seniors are sometimes referred to as "O.A.P.'s" (short for "Old Age Pensioners"). People over the age of 60 often qualify for reduced admission to museums and other attractions. Always ask about an O.A.P. discount if special rates are not posted. **Discover Ireland** (p. 268) can offer advice on how to find the best discounts.

Smoking   Ireland and Northern Ireland both have broad antismoking laws that ban smoking in all public places, including bars, restaurants, and hotel lobbies. However, most restaurants and pubs have covered outdoor smoking areas.

Taxes   As in many European countries, sales tax is VAT (value-added tax) and is often already included in the price quoted to you or shown on price tags. In the Republic, VAT rates vary—for hotels, restaurants, and car rentals, it is 13.5%; for souvenirs and gifts, it is 23%. In Northern Ireland,

the VAT is 20% across the board. VAT charged on services such as hotel stays, meals, car rentals, and entertainment cannot be refunded to visitors, but the VAT on products such as souvenirs is refundable. Save your receipts and present them at the Global Refund Desk when you get to the airport (they're located airside in the main terminals at Shannon and Dublin; at the latter it's now an automated booth located directly after the Starbucks on your way to the gates). They can usually issue you a refund there and then. Some larger stores can issue you with a Global Refund form and refund your VAT themselves, although you'll need to know your passport number, flight number and departure time. In practice, of course, this is usually much more fuss than it's worth.

Telephones   In the Republic, the telephone system is known as Eircom; in Northern Ireland, it's BT (British Telecom). Every effort has been made to ensure that the numbers and information in this guide are accurate at the time of writing. **Overseas calls** from Ireland can be quite costly, whether you use a local phone card or your own calling card.

To call Ireland from home:

1. **Dial the international access code:** 011 from the U.S., 00 from the U.K., 0011 from Australia, or 0170 from New Zealand.

2. **Dial the country code:** 353 for the Republic, 44 for the North.

3. **Dial the local number,** remembering to omit the initial 0, which is for use only within Ireland (for example, to call the County Kerry number 066/12345 from the United States, you'd dial 011-353-66/12345).

To make international calls from Ireland: First dial 00 and then the country code (U.S. or Canada 1, U.K. 44, Australia 61, New Zealand 64). Next you dial the area code and local number. For example, to call the U.S. number 212/000-0000 you'd dial ✆ **00-1-212/000-0000.** The toll-free international access code for AT&T is ✆ **1-800-550-000;** for Sprint, it's ✆ **1-800-552001;** and for MCI, it's ✆ **1-800-551-001.**

To make local calls: To dial a local number within an area code, drop the initial 0. To dial a number within Ireland but in a different area code, use the initial 0.

As in many parts of the world, **phone booths** are slowly disappearing; however, you will still find them. Calls from a phone booth usually require coin payment, but at some you need a calling card (in the Republic) or phone card (in the North). Both are prepaid computerized cards that you insert into the phone instead of coins. They can be purchased in post offices, grocery stores, and shops (such as newsstands).

Time Ireland follows Greenwich Mean Time (1 hr. earlier than Central European Time) from November to March, and British Summer Time (the same as Central European Time) from April to October. Ireland is 5 hours ahead of the eastern United States. Ireland's latitude makes for longer days and shorter nights in the summer and the reverse in the winter. In June, the sun doesn't fully set until around 11pm, but in December, it is dark by 4pm.

Tipping For taxi drivers, hairdressers, and other providers of service, tip an average of 10% to 15%. For restaurants, the policy is usually printed on the menu—either a gratuity of 10% to 15% is automatically added to your bill, or it's left up to you. As a rule, bartenders do not expect a tip, except when table service is provided.

Toilets Public toilets are usually simply called "toilets" or are marked with international symbols. In the Republic of Ireland, some of the older ones carry the Gaelic words FIR (men) and MNA (women). Check out malls and shopping centers for some of the newest and best-kept bathrooms in the country. Free restrooms are usually available to customers at sightseeing attractions, museums, hotels, restaurants, pubs, shops, and theaters. Many of the newer gas stations (called "petrol stations" in Ireland) have public toilets, and a few even have baby-changing facilities.

Visas Citizens of the United States, Canada, Australia, and New Zealand entering the Republic of Ireland or Northern Ireland for a stay of up to 3 months do not need a visa, but a valid **passport** is required.

For citizens of the United Kingdom, when traveling on flights originating in Britain, the same rules apply as they would for travel to any other member state of the European Union (EU).

Water Tap water throughout the island of Ireland is generally safe. However, some areas in the west of Ireland have been battling with out-of-date water-purification systems. Always carry a large bottle of water with you.

Women Travelers

Women should expect few if any problems traveling in Ireland. In fact, the only time you're likely to attract any attention at all is if you eat alone in a restaurant at night—a sight that is still relatively uncommon in Ireland outside of the major cities. Even then, you'll not be hassled.

If you drink in a pub on your own, though, expect all kinds of attention, as a woman drinking alone is still considered to be "on the market"—even if she's reading a book, talking on her cellphone to her fiancé, or doing a crossword puzzle. So be prepared to fend them off. Irish men almost always respond well to polite rejection, though.

In cities, as ever, take a cab home at night and follow all the usual advice of caution you get when you travel anywhere.

Index

INDEX